# Today's Moment of Happiness Despite the News

A Year of Spontaneous Essays by

# Kathie Giorgio

Black Rose Writing | Texas

ISBN: 978-1-68433-129-1
PUBLISHED BY BLACK ROSE WRITING
www.blackrosewriting.com

Printed in the United States of America
Suggested Retail Price (SRP) $23.95

*Today's Moment of Happiness* is printed in Traditional Arabic

To every reader who followed Today's Moment through its incredible year, thank you so much. You lifted me up and gave me the support and encouragement I needed to keep moving ahead.

And to my husband, Michael, and my kids, Olivia, Christopher, Andy and Katie, who lived through it right along with me.
Yes, it all helped. Despite. Anyway.

# Today's Moment of Happiness Despite the News

"I think our moments of happiness
really come from a feeling of unity."
--Gloria Steinem

# Introduction

A couple of days after the 2016 presidential election, my world started to unravel. I was taking my two old beagles for their after-lunch walk. As I rounded the corner toward home, I saw a man walking toward me. He wore a cargo coat, large sunglasses, and a red baseball hat which had gold stitching on it, reading, "Make America Great Again". I tried to move my dogs off the sidewalk so he could pass, but at their age, the dogs moved slowly. To my great surprise, I saw the man draw back his leg and prepare to kick one of my dogs.

I got in between them and he kicked me instead. Then he grabbed me by the shoulders and shoved me off the sidewalk. "It's time to get back into your place now, woman," he said. And he stomped off.

I made sure my dogs were okay, got myself up, and we went home. I didn't recognize that I was in shock. I got myself a drink of water (why is every solution to every problem a drink of water?) and then went upstairs to my computer. I posted what just happened on Facebook, and concerned friends told me to call the police.

The incident ended up on the news. It went crazy on Facebook, shared, the last time I saw, thousands of times. And then the real trauma began. Absolute strangers from all around the country began to send me hate emails and private messages through Facebook and Twitter. I was the topic of a hate-talk radio program. They accused me of lying, saying that since I write fiction, my assault must be made up. They said I wanted to smear the president. And they gave me death threat after death threat after death threat.

It was a very hard time.

With inauguration day, the circus began. Not only did we now have many-times-daily news breaks about what our president was up to (and tweeting), my email inbox was also inundated with information from the resistance. All well-meaning, all things I wanted to know…but there was just so much. Lists of what we had to do. Leaks about this and leaks about that. Pointing fingers, marches, yelling, desperation. From BOTH sides. I was very quickly overwhelmed.

One day, on Facebook, I read a post from one lovely NC poet who said she didn't understand the Women's March, that the women had nothing to protest about. In Virginia, another lovely poet basically began ending all of his posts with "We're all gonna die! We're all gonna die!" These were both people I respected and admired, and their poles couldn't have been planted further apart. They were representative of what I was feeling – strung out between the two factions. And finding it harder and harder to feel hopeful.

I began to realize that I needed to find positives. And not just one or two that would last me a long time, but a positive out of every day. I needed something to hang on to.

Now, I'm a natural skeptic. I don't talk rainbows and unicorns, I'm not a fan of Hallmark cards, I don't watch Lifetime TV movies. For me to say that I needed a positive was almost as hard for me to take as all of the negativity around me. But it felt like what I needed to do. And I also felt very drawn to do it publicly.

Because if I could do it, anyone could.

Where did it come from? I think it came from one of my mentors, years and years ago. Ellen Hunnicutt was a fantastic Wisconsin writer who took me under her wing soon after I graduated from college. She told me I had the voice of a novelist, she told me that what I was writing was literary fiction, and she told me that I was the most dedicated, disciplined, determined writer she knew. I loved her. If I had doubts, Ellen brushed them away. She didn't do so with unicorns. She told me to buck up and keep going.

When I was offered my first teaching job, leading writing classes for our local park and recreation department, I called her in a panic. I had no idea what I was getting into. She told me that no matter what, no matter what manuscripts I read, no matter what I thought, I always needed to lead my critiques, oral or verbal, with a positive. "If you give someone something positive to hang on to," she said, "they'll hold on to it tightly while they listen to the rest of what you have to say. That one positive will get them through."

And now, years later, it was me that was in need of that one positive. One a day.

So I started, on Facebook, posting *Today's Moment of Happiness Despite The News*. The response bowled me over. Facebook suddenly began sending me messages, cheering how many likes and comments I received. Facebook never cared before. I saw responses from people I knew, people I didn't know, people who were well-known, people who I admired from afar. And so…I kept on doing it.

Let me tell you, it was a challenge. Again, I am a skeptic. I tend to look at the world through shades, not rose-tinted glasses. But I managed to come up with something every day (except one) that made me happy. Some things were goofy. Some were funny. Some were poignant. And same came out of nowhere and blew me away.

I didn't write these as The Professional Author. I wrote them as me. Just Kathie. They're personal and they're heartfelt. They are deliberately raw and unedited; I didn't intend to submit them anywhere else. I was asked if one here or there could be used in a publication. I said sure. But that was never the intention.

I vowed to do it every day for a year, and I did. I had no idea when I started how difficult a year this was going to be; one of the hardest years of my life. I believe that is part of the miracle that is *Today's Moment Of Happiness Despite The News*. When I was done with my year, I changed the blog to *This Week's Moment Of Happiness Despite The News*, which continues today (www.kathiegiorgio.org) with a post every Thursday. Readers asked if I would publish the year in a book. I said no. But they kept asking. So I finally talked to my publisher. If he said yes, I decided, I would say yes too.

And so here it is.

No one is more surprised than I am. And my skeptical self is forever grateful.

*Special note: From January 30 to March 9 in 2017, I posted these moments on my Facebook page. When Today's Moment became a blog on March 9, I tried to retrieve all of the earlier moments from Facebook. But some had inexplicably disappeared. So you'll see a couple gaps in the days between 1/30 and 3/9. But the only day I did not post a Today's Moment was 10/4/17.*

# Chapter One

## JANUARY 30, 2017

And so today's moment of happiness despite the news:

I just went out into our unexpected snowstorm to check the exposed three-story straight-up ramp I need to use to get my car into the parking garage. The ramp is, of course, completely snow-covered – there will be no getting Hemi out of the way of our condo's snowplow tonight. I walked back, cursing.

But then I noticed how quiet it was. So quiet, I could hear the snow land on itself.

I stopped to listen, and then saw how snow glitters when it falls into the beam of a streetlight.

Snowlights.

Lightflakes.

And yes, that helps. Despite. Anyway.

## JANUARY 31, 2017

And so today's moment of happiness despite the news:

I told my 16-year old daughter about a magazine that was looking specifically for teenage girl writers, writing poems, stories, memoir featuring strong female lead characters.

Olivia sat right down the next day and wrote one whopper of a poem. Her strong female lead character?

Herself.

And there's our Future.

And yes, that helps. Despite. Anyway.

# Chapter Two

## FEBRUARY 1, 2017

And so today's moment of happiness despite the news.

There was sun.

It's been so gray, both in weather and in mood. But today, the sun broke through. Even though it was cold outside, I had to stand in all of that light. The air was winter and the snow on my deck bit frost-tipped teeth into my feet and ankles. I wrapped myself in my own arms and called myself a fool. It's only February 1.

But then the sun smacked the wind away. It rolled down and wrapped me tight in a "See me!" stream of heat. I raised my face and shut my eyes and I saw yellow.

Bright yellow. Dandelions. Lemonade. Midday sun. Wild mustard.

The sun promised me summer.

And yes, that helps. Despite. Anyway.

## FEBRUARY 2, 2017

And so today's moment of happiness despite the news.

I was reading a student's manuscript, a section from her memoir about owning and running a radio station (wonderful stuff!), when I came to a part where she describes having to send someone up the radio tower to change the light bulbs.

I sat back and looked at my lamp.

Radio tower light bulbs need changing? And someone has to CLIMB those things? Like King Kong, only not like him, because we're little scrawny humans and not a big ape with fingers and toes that grip?

Holy cow.

So why is this my happy moment? Because it was (another) moment when I realized I just don't know everything. Some would see that as a negative, but flip it around. It means I still have so many opportunities to learn something brand new!

I never knew or even imagined that radio towers had light bulbs that needed changing. Just think of the size! Just think of the weight! What happens if one cracks off, leaving the screw-part in the socket?

Holy cow.

I love when I accidentally learn something I didn't know, and I didn't know that I didn't know it! How cool is it to be 56 and still be learning! About everything! Light bulbs. Radio towers. People who climb like gigantic apes. Eyes open. Ears open. Breathe, breathe, breathe. You might graduate, but if you're lucky, you're never out of school.

I'm lucky. My students teach me so much.

And yes, that helps. Despite. Anyway.

### FEBRUARY 3, 2017

And so today's moment of happiness despite the news.

In the mail today, evidence of how I can be seduced by television commercials. I ordered this weird little exercise thing. It looks like a skateboard without wheels, and its ends curve up and have little circular foot-grippy things. On TV, these wheeless skateboards get tossed to just anybody who happens to be romping in a bathing suit on a beach, and these anybodies put their feet on the grippy circles, and then they begin to twist, like the dance, The Twist. Oh, it's so easy! Oh, it's so fun! They whoop! They holler! A woman in her sixties yells, "Look at me! I can do it, and I've never been in better shape in my life!" Hell, the thing was even on Shark Tank.

So my brilliant idea? I'd set a timer, work for an hour, then get up and twist for five minutes, throughout the day. It's so easy! It's so fun! I'd be as fit as the sixty-something year old in no time! (I'm 56.)

I took it out of its box and immediately worried when the instructions said to "hold on to something sturdy when first using your whatever-it's called." No one on the bathing suit beach was holding on. I set it on my kitchen floor, held on to my counter, and climbed on.

And promptly fell off.

Tried again. Managed to stand this time. But as soon as I twisted, I fell off.

It's so easy? It's so fun?

Now granted, I can fall off the ground floor. But really?

So why is this my happy moment?

Because I laughed. I climbed on and fell off at least six more times, getting more hysterical with each trip. This thing will end up at Goodwill, but at least I got a good gasping, crying laugh out of it first.

Sometimes, you just can't take yourself so seriously. Sometimes, you have to just laugh at yourself.

And yes, that helps. Despite. Anyway.

## FEBRUARY 4, 2017

And so today's moment of happiness despite the news.

While storming around Sam's Club, filling my cart with all sorts of munchies and sweets and coffee and hot chocolate and coffee cups and toilet paper and paper towels for my wonderful AllWriters' students, I came to a little table offering samples.

A sample that required an ID card.

Crown Royal Gala Apple Whisky. Mixed with cranberry juice.

I sampled.

Mmmmmmmmmmmmmm...

Do I need to say more?

Suffice it to say my students are NOT going to be included in that little purchase.

And I plan on being very, very happy later tonight.

And yes, that helps (and will help again...). Despite. Anyway.

## FEBRUARY 5, 2017

And so today's moment of happiness despite the news.

Early this evening, my daughter came home from a first date.

Her cheeks were pink.

She giggled.

And she clasped her hands and raised them to her smiling mouth with that special coy, yet innocent look only brand new young women in brand new love have.

Yet I knew that in recent history, this brand new young woman experienced profound heartbreak for the first time. Heartbreak that I thought was going to tarnish the brand new right out of her.

But still. Here she was.

Pink cheeks.

Giggles.

Hands folded with hope. With goofy giddiness. With absolute twitterpation.

Many of us have been dealing with heartbreak lately. With grief.
But I think we can still fold our hands too. Hope. Joy.
And yes, that helped. Despite. Anyway.

## FEBRUARY 6, 2017

And so today's moment of happiness despite the news.

Well, I'll admit it. Today was a day where I thought a moment just wasn't going to happen. It wasn't that it was a day of horrors; it wasn't. It was a day of frustrations, where I felt like I was running in about a dozen directions at top speed and still managed to get absolutely nothing done. The sun was out; I was still snarly. My cats did cute things, the dogs were sleeping, my daughter hugged me, I had great interactions with students; I was still snarly.

One of THOSE days.

And then I had my moment.

Because I know that this day is going to end, I'm going to go to sleep (though I doubt I'll see another meteor before bed), and when I wake up, it'll be tomorrow and hopefully, better.

Which brings me to what seems to be an ongoing theme in many of these posts, which just surprises the hell out of skeptical me. Hope. I'm not finishing the day thinking that tomorrow will bring more of the same. I'm finishing the day thinking that tomorrow will be better.

(Even though I know the first face I see when I turn on my computer will be the asshat. Even though I know the first news item I see will be about what the asshat is doing. Even though I know 3/4 of my email will be about how to protest what the asshat is doing on yet another day, what he did the day before, what he will do tomorrow.)

Hope. I apparently still have it.

And yes, that helps. Despite. Anyway.

## FEBRUARY 7, 2017

And so today's moment of happiness despite the news. And the stomach flu.

Light bouncy yummy red jello.

Just try to eat jello without feeling uplifted. Childlike. Slurp the jiggle and giggle.

Today, red jello is my prime rib. And white soda? My sangria.

Goodnight, everyone. Better tomorrows.

And yes, that helps. Despite. Anyway.

## FEBRUARY 8, 2017

This moment is missing.

## FEBRUARY 9, 2017

And so today's moment of happiness despite the news.

Today was hard. Because I'm sick, I'm not teaching, and so I don't have my interactions with my students and clients, who are my main source of inspiration. My family thinks I have the plague, so I'm being left alone there too. Lots of extra time on my hands, when I'm not sleeping. So I prowled through Facebook more than I usually do.

A lot of what I saw made my jaw drop.

I read an article that said that this new administration is going to force us into formally defining what it is to be Christian. I think a committee should be set up right away to decide what parts of the Bible are to be believed and followed, and what parts are to be ignored, which in the end would be dividing the Bible into "These verses support what we want to enforce" and "These parts do not, so let's chuck'em."

I'm not Christian. Not so sure I'm even a believer. I'm more of a seeker than anything. But I have great admiration for those who have true faith.

For me, my religion is words. And I don't have admiration for those who twist words away from their meanings into what serves their purpose.

But that's neither here nor there, and isn't getting me anywhere on my moment. What the hell is my moment today? I'm seeing my moment overtaken by anger, and I don't want that. That takes away the purpose of this whole exercise.

Hmm.

While walking the beagles today, I heard the geese before I saw them. Raucous! I pulled the dogs to a stop and they actually sat one on either side of me, and like me, they pointed their noses straight up. And there were the geese flying thick in city skies.

So many!

There were V's everywhere. V's that blended into M's and W's and A's. Wings wide out, feet flowing back, and whistles where feathers met air. They were heading toward the river.

Geese heading to the river means spring (though I think the geese are a little too early).

And the river means the Riverwalk, and soon the air will be warm enough again that I can resume walking quietly along the Fox. Finding my peace.

And that made me smile.

And yes, that helps. Despite. Anyway.

## FEBRUARY 10, 2017

And so today's moment of happiness despite the news.

Today, my frustration overflowed. I've been sick all week and had to cancel the trip that was solely for the purpose of getting the final draft of my next novel done. I woke today feeling worse than yesterday, when yesterday, I woke up feeling better. And then, when I settled down to write, on a day when I was supposed to be away and free of such interruptions, I had to:

*argue with an institution we provided services for in November and we STILL haven't been paid;

*send yet another invoice to said institution when they just wouldn't listen;

*walk the dogs, which included wrestling a chicken bone out of Blossom's mouth and dragging Donnie away from someone else's pile of poop which he saw as most delicious (the dog is disgusting);

*act quickly when both dogs chose to poop at the same time on the sidewalk, not the grass, directly in front of three police cars;

*pick the child up from school, which meant waiting and waiting for a train (not to mention I wasn't thinking and I headed toward Starbucks instead of school);

*climb all over my kitchen to try to get to a container of chicken noodle soup which Michael left for me, but didn't bother to put in a place where I could actually reach it (I'm only five foot two and have been for all seventeen years of our marriage);

*lock one cat up in the dog crate so she would quit licking my hands because she looooooooves my body lotion.

*any time I lowered my Word screen to check an email because the business just doesn't ever wait, I came face to face with the Asshat because apparently, there is no other news in this world except for him.

At that point, I cracked and began to cry. I don't cry often. But truly, I'd had it. This has been a week from hell.

And then, at a friend's suggestion that I find a back room to write (hide) in, I realized the AllWriters' classroom was right downstairs, quiet, empty, mine and ready. Ready to take me in, not as the teacher I am in that space, but as the writer I am, first and foremost.

I may be sick, but I ran downstairs.

Where I felt myself uplifted. Where I felt every bit of support and encouragement and love and care and knowledge and experience I've doled, hammered, flung, and cajoled out for the last twelve years come fully back to me. In spades. Nobody was there, but everybody was there, and they said, "For Christ's sake, Kathie, you know you've got this. Leave it all behind. Do what you do best."

So I did.

Final draft. First 113 pages checked, approved, run past this master, and done.

You will all be keeping me plenty of quiet supportive company over the next few days. But I've learned that's what family does. And I know you're there.

And yes, that helps. Despite. Anyway.

## FEBRUARY 11, 2017

And so today's moment of happiness despite the news.

Day two of locking myself in the AllWriters' classroom and working the final draft of the new novel straight through. Straight through.

I have the thermostat set for 80 degrees. I am surrounded by summer and by the warmth of my words.

Partway through today's 100–page run, I realized I was smiling.

Why?

Because the book is doing exactly what I want it to do. It's saying what I want it to say. I'm not even done yet, and...

I DID IT.

You would think with three novels and two short story collections and a poetry chapbook under my belt, I would grow to expect this. But it's a surprise every time. It's magic.

And. I. Love. It.

I am weighing and measuring words, one right after the other, holding each one up, comparing it, considering it, placing it, and moving on. There is no start and stop of earlier drafts. This is a smooth ride forward. And I am seeing the whole. I am seeing the arc.

My gosh. It has a pulse. It has rhythm. Let me roar to the heavens like Dr. Frankenstein: "It's alive!!!!"

I made it to page 213. I still have at least two more days to get through. But I'm doing what I love in a place that I love where I do what I love. Write. AllWriters'. Teach.

Ohmygod. Who can ask for more than that?

And yes, that helps. Despite. Anyway.

## FEBRUARY 12, 2017

And so today's moment of happiness despite the news.

I took a brief break from the book today to run to Goodwill. AllWriters' is participating in a basket raffle to benefit the Waukesha South High School orchestra, and, well, I needed a basket.

So of course, I was paging through the clothes.

You know how you can feel sometimes when someone is looking at you? I did, and when I looked over, there was an itty bitty girl standing in a shopping cart. She couldn't have been more than a year old, only capable of standing when holding on to something. She was dressed all in pink fuzz, from her head to her toes, and she sported a pair of bunny ears. She was a child of another culture, but I'm not going to say what culture, because it doesn't, and shouldn't, matter.

And she was beaming at me.

This was the biggest, brightest, happiest, loveliest, friendliest, hey–I–like–you! smile I've ever seen. Ear to ear doesn't work, because that grin was holding up the chubbiest of cheeks, and her eyes lit up too. She only had two teeth. They sparkled. She didn't make a sound. She just BEAMED.

So what could I do? I beamed back.

That pink little bit and I stood there, and the world held still for a moment, and then her father moved on and so did she.

But I'm still holding that smile.

Today, I saw a headline that said the Asshat is "unhappy with his life in the White House." This pink little bit was gloriously happy in a shopping cart in Goodwill.

And I know there are some who would say to this pink little bit and her father, "Go back where you came from. You don't belong here."

But she does.

And she offers more to our future than the rich white man who isn't happy in the White House.

I'm holding on to that smile tonight.

And yes, that helps. Despite. Anyway.

## FEBRUARY 13, 2017

And so today's moment of happiness despite the news.

I was idling at a red light at one of Waukesha's five-cornered intersections this afternoon when I saw an SUV correctly turn at the green light, but then incorrectly poke its nose the wrong way down a one-way street.

I hit Hemi's horn. The sound was loud and jarring on a sunny Monday afternoon, a day when it was warm enough to have the sun roof open, let the pretend-spring air flow in.

The SUV slammed on its brakes. Then it backed up and turned correctly. It stopped next to me and the driver's window rolled down. A woman, frazzled, her hair sticking out in all directions, her eyes red, looked out at me.

"Thank you for stopping me," she said. "I can't believe I nearly did that. I could have killed someone!"

"But you didn't," I said quickly. "It's okay. We all stop thinking sometimes. We all make mistakes."

She wavered a smile at me and then drove off. I looked up the hill, the direction she came from.

Our hospital is at the top of the hill. I thought of her wild hair and red eyes. Her thoughts, gone, or anyplace but at that intersection.

"It's okay," I'd said.

Amazing, sometimes, how fast forgiveness can come. Understanding too, without an explanation.

And amazing to be glad that you're at a certain place at a certain time. To serve a purpose you didn't expect.

And yes, it helps. Despite. Anyway.

## FEBRUARY 14, 2017

And so today's moment of happiness despite the news.

Some days, an individual moment really stands out. A daughter home from a first date. A beaming little girl in a shopping cart. Stopping a stranger from going the wrong way.

Some days, there's so much crud going on, I have to dig through it to find the happy. Illness. Frustration. Anger.

And some days, like today, provide such an even quiet keel of happy that I can't pluck a moment.

A delivery of pink and white tulips, and a card saying "thank you for walking the journey with me." And saying she nearly sent chocolate-covered strawberries until she saw that I am allergic to all raw fruits so she sent flowers instead (Thank you! Whew!).

Watching 22 of my books (11 Clocks, 11 Lifetime) walk out of here today on their journey to the female inmates at the Waukesha County Jail. The person who picked the books up said that while they only took 22 of the books, ALL the pods want to read them. And I'll be going in to talk about the books with them. I am happy to return to jail.

Finishing the new novel. Oh, finishing the new novel. After experiencing Rise From The River, I didn't think I'd ever write another novel. But look. I did. And you know what? I like it. Well. I kinda love it.

So nothing momentous today. Nothing poignant, stunning, gently mind-blowing. Just a steady thrum of happy, like a river through the frozen countryside. Like the life beneath the snow. Keeps me going. Keeps us all going.

And yes, that helps. Despite. Anyway.

### FEBRUARY 15, 2017

Today's moment of happiness despite the news.

Tonight, I sat in the audience at my daughter's high school orchestra concert. The concert featured a raffle at the intermission, selling tickets to win baskets donated by downtown Waukesha businesses. AllWriters', of course, donated a basket. It held books by ten AllWriters' writers, plus a $30 gift certificate to the studio.

But it held so much more.

I watched as these kids ran around with reams of tickets, encouraging the audience to buy and support the orchestra. Support music in the schools. For $20, they sold tickets "as long as your wingspan!", having the buyer stretch out their arms and the kids unrolled the tickets from fingertip to fingertip. For short buyers, they pulled in tall kids as wingspan substitutes! One innovative boy announced, "For sixty bucks, I will unroll this ticket batch from the top of the auditorium to the bottom, and you can have all the tickets!"

These kids were learning the art of community, the gift of support, as they cheered each other on, and the local businesses cheered them on and the parents cheered them on too (and got out their wallets).

In the AllWriters' basket, the words of my students who have found a home and community at AllWriters'. My own words too, and my husband's, as we supported writers, and then turned and supported our daughter in her music. Supported all the kids there. Supported the school and the arts.

I give back to the community which has given to me.

Every business and every person, adult and child, there tonight was part of a great ring of community. Communities within communities, but the whole supporting us all.

These last months, both pre- and post-election, I've watched and listened as people pointed fingers and yelled. "Your party does this!" "Yeah, well, your party does that!" "Your group believes this!" "Yeah, well, your group believes that!"

Posted memes saying, "Don't support the refugees! Support the homeless!"

More memes saying, "Don't support the homeless. Support the veterans!"

As if we have to choose. There really isn't a choice, you know.

You help whomever needs help.

And when you need help, someone helps you.

"Give me your tired, your poor, your huddled masses yearning to breathe free..."

Words.

I love being at the head of the AllWriters' community. The AllWriters' family. And I love being part of a greater giving community as well. Nights like tonight convince me that despite the Asshat and his Orange Cabinet, we'll be okay. That Cabinet is starting to crumble like the pressed particle board it's made from.

There's still just so much good.

And yes, that helps. Despite. Anyway.


### FEBRUARY 16, 2017

And so today's moment of happiness despite the news.

Oh, it was easy to find today's. It's all about girls.

Early this afternoon, I had to go to school for Olivia's annual IEP meeting (Individualized Education Program, for those of you who don't know). I used to dread these meetings. They seemed to be more about what my daughter couldn't do, than what she could.

But boy, not anymore. This girl SOARS. We talked about her achievements in music, in art, in all of her academic classes. Her work ethic (can't imagine where she gets that), her intelligence (can't imagine where she gets that either!), her determination (yeah, okay). The plan's in place for a four-year college. She wants to be an art therapist. Words like independent, self-motivated, intelligent, determined, were all tossed around that room.

What she has fought through. How she has persevered. How amazing she is.

*Nevertheless, she persisted.*

From the IEP, I went into Milwaukee, to have lunch and coffee with my oldest daughter, Katie. Katie is getting her PhD in math, a male-dominated field. She told me about her dissertation, the research she's doing, how it's in something called "firing squad synchronization". I'm intelligent, but I have no idea what she was talking about. She does though, and so will the math world, and that's what's important. She talked about her support of Hillary, of Planned Parenthood, of girls learning early on that they're capable and equal and amazing. She talked about how she feels about racism and sexism. I sat in admiration of her work ethic (can't imagine where she gets that), her intelligence (can't imagine where she gets that either!), her determination (yeah, okay).

What she has fought through. How she has persevered. How amazing she is.

*Nevertheless, she persisted.*

Then tonight, we had the first class of the new Teen Writers' Workshop at AllWriters'. All girls. Including Olivia. Except for the instructor, Michael.

Quiet girls. Introspective girls. Girls learning to take the words they hear in their heads and throw them down on paper and get them to say what they so want to say.

I remember being that age. I remember writing so hard, my pencil tore through the paper. I remember my brain feeling like it was on fire (still is).

One of the moms emailed me right after the class: "Thank you so much for doing the teen workshop. My daughter loved her first night tonight. She is very excited to continue with your instruction."

And we will continue.

What I've fought through. How I've persevered.

*Nevertheless, she persisted.*

I hear tell there was a ridiculous press conference today. Know what?

I'm not worried. I know of several strong amazing women coming up to take their places.

And yes, that helps. Despite. Anyway.

## FEBRUARY 17, 2017

And so today's moment of happiness despite the news.

Well, really. Is there anything more joyous than a Wisconsin faux spring day in February? Is there anything more likely to bring a smile and a delusion that somehow, winter has ended before the winter months are over?

We get these almost every year, a sudden 60-plus degrees and sunshine, and we rush out with our winter white legs exposed in shorts and capris, our winter white arms bare in t-shirts and tank tops, and we bounce balls and ride bikes and swing kids in the playground as the gray and black streaked snowdrifts melt around us and run down the street to grates. If you stand by the grates, you can hear the enraged whisper as winter rushes away.

Some of us take our convertibles out of storage, lower the roof, and feel the sun and the breeze slap us happy-senseless. Some of us drive down the street and belt out songs from Styx's greatest hits, even when we pull into a drive-through at Starbucks. And some of us are joined at the Starbucks window by Styx-singing baristas who want to share in the spring fever. Some of us. Not naming any names. No-siree-kathie.

Yes, we know it's February. Yes, we know that winter isn't really rushing away, but skulking off to a hidden corner where it's planning its sudden white return.

We don't care.

For today, we aren't just reminded of spring and summer. We're in it, as if we could launch ourselves into a season like a swimming pool. One second, dry, next second, wet. One second, cold, next second, warm and sunny and fresh and oooooooooooh, YES!

(Even when there's a totally maniacal blizzard to end all blizzards raging in the White House.)

And yes, that helps. Despite. Anyway.

## FEBRUARY 18, 2017

And so today's moment of happiness despite the news.

A conversation with my just-turned-four granddaughter, Grandbaby Maya Mae:

"Gamma Kaffee, sometimes my hair falls out."

(The child has hair to her lack-of-hips.) "Why does your hair fall out?"

"My hair falls out when I go outside."

"Oh, Maya Mae. Why would your hair fall out when you go outside?"

<SIGH> "Because that's what hair DOES."

I am, after experiencing four of my own before her, once again immersed in the world of the incomprehensible four-year old.

The Orange Asshat is incomprehensible in his speech too – but I don't find it nearly as charming.

Another conversation with Grandbaby Maya Mae:

<singing a song that ends in an unintelligible word>

"Maya? What is that last word?"

<unintelligible word slowly spoken>

"Oooookay."

<SIGH> "Gamma Kaffee, you just don't get it."

"I'm sorry, Maya Mae."

<SIGH> "Nobody gets it." (said in a very small voice)

Oh, there are so many things I don't get right now.

But what I do get is Maya Mae. Four-year old long-haired brown-eyed wide-smiled pile of flirty grandmother-melting granddaughterliness. Joy.

And yes, that helps. Despite. Anyway.

### FEBRUARY 19, 2017

And so today's moment of happiness despite the news.

This morning, I slept in. Until it was only about a half-hour before it wasn't morning anymore.

When I woke up, I didn't get up right away. I rolled onto my back and sprawled at an angle across the bed – my feet at the lower right corner (on my side of the bed) and my head at the upper left (Michael's side of the bed). Michael was already up, so except for a small gray cat, I was alone.

I studied the ceiling. We have a lovely ceiling, angled, made out of corrugated copper. I don't take enough time to notice it, I don't think.

For about fifteen minutes, I gave myself permission to not be anywhere. To not do anything. Not speak to anyone. Not do anything for anyone. Not hustle to find my list of things that had to get done, not hustle to do anything on the list.

Just lay there and stare at the ceiling.

It was kind of like meditating with my eyes open. I was in a non-space, where, for a bit of time anyway, nothing was expected of me. And I had no expectations of myself either. No ambitions. No desires. No needs.

It was nice.

Of course, then I got up and the day started and it was just one thing after another. The next step. The next to-do. But for right then, I wasn't Any-Of-The-Many-Roles-I-Play. It was just me. In a big bed. By myself. Looking at the ceiling.

I highly recommend it.

And yes, that helps. Despite. Anyway.

### FEBRUARY 20, 2017

*Special note: On this day, my husband suddenly lost his job.*
And so today's moment of happiness despite the news.

Given today's event, I just can't do it. I'm sorry. I tried. I meant this to be a challenge for myself, but not this much.

Well, wait. Okay. I can come up with one.

And that's YOU.

If you look at my status below, you'll see 116 reactions (thus far) to the news that my husband lost his job today, And you'll see a bajillion comments commiserating and trying to make me feel better.

So many came through for me with the assault in November.

And you're coming through again now.

So there's you.

And yes, you help. Despite. Anyway.

### FEBRUARY 21, 2017

And so today's moment of happiness despite the news.

When I first started this, "the news" referred to the daily inundation of reports of the Asshat and his Orange Cabinet, as well as, to be fair, the daily inundation of the well-meaning, but overloading 50 gazillian "we must resist" emails. I was overwhelmed.

I wasn't expecting "the news" to turn into OUR news of Michael's being let go from his job.

You know, God, I knew coming up with something positive every day was going to be a challenge for me. You didn't have to make it even bigger.

Okay. Today's moment of happiness. Are you ready?

Spaghetti.

Tonight, Michael made spaghetti for supper. It's one of my favorite meals. I can eat spaghetti pretty much in any form – I've even been known to eat Spaghetti-O's with those little fake hot dogs (though I add real hot dogs to make it, you know, healthier). But Michael made the real deal, and at my request, he made it with Italian sausage.

The first time I ever had spaghetti with Italian sausage was on our honeymoon in Florida, when we visited Michael's Aunt Dolly. I knew right there and then that I'd married into the right family.

Olivia brought my plate upstairs to me while I was on my computer, in our online classroom with a client.

It looked lovely. Nicely mixed. Sprinkled with parmesan cheese. Steaming. And the aroma...mmmm.

But the best part? The comfort it provided. It was warm. It was (for spaghetti) neat and organized. And it was lovingly created by a husband (who is hurting) for a wife (who is hurting too).

For those spaghetti moments, anxiety fell away. Fear fell away. The ringing of phones, the asking of questions, the why, the what now, the oh please can I just lie down and say I tried and I'm tired and I give up now? all went away. Lost in done-just-right noodles and tomato sauce with chunks of tomato and spices...and Italian sausage.

There was just spaghetti. And it was the best spaghetti ever.

And yes, that helps. Despite. Anyway.


## FEBRUARY 22, 2017

Today's moment of happiness, despite the news.

After leading my wonderful afternoon workshop today, I drove my convertible, top down – in February – in Wisconsin – to my favorite Starbucks. As I followed the line in the drive-through to the window, I lolled my head back and admired the spring-blue sky (in February – in Wisconsin) and let the sun warm my face and bare arms (in February – in Wisconsin).

When it was my turn, the barista leaned out before I could offer her my phone to scan. "For you," she said. "On the house."

My eyes, already sunstruck, were now heartstruck. "For me? Why?" I asked.

"Because you're you. You just make me happy." And she waved me on.

The sun wasn't the only thing keeping me warm as I drove home.

And yes, that helps. Despite. Anyway.

## FEBRUARY 23, 2017

And so today's moment of happiness despite the news.

Well, it sure isn't the sound of freezing rain hitting my windows.

So today, I had a conversation with a friend who is a very kind and gentle man. I often wonder what we look like together, because when I speak, I am very animated. My hands will not hold still. He sits with his hands folded neatly in his lap. I often wonder if people watch us and feel sorry for him - that nice calm man with that hysterical woman.

I told him that I'm really beginning to wonder what I've gotten myself into with this coming up with a moment of happiness every day. "This is HARD," I said, both fists raised. "This is HARD. I am not Hallmark-y. I am not rainbow-y. I am not unicorn-y."

He smiled. He's not any of those things either, though he is sort of Buddha-y. "What's your biggest fear?"

I didn't even need to think. "That I won't be able to come up with something one day. That I'll fail."

"What would it mean if you failed?" His hands didn't even twitch. I decided to stick mine under my thighs so they'd hold still.

"That I couldn't do it. That I couldn't find one thing that made me happy in a 24-hour period."

"Are you doing it?"

"So far."

"There are so many things to notice," he said. And then he just looked at me.

"What?" I said.

"I'm noticing you."

And for the first time ever, I didn't roll my eyes. I wasn't sarcastic. My hands, sat on, were still.

Cripes. I've become Grasshopper. Time to go turn on the Hallmark channel while I address my "I love you just cuz you're you!" cards, decorated with little butterflies. And unicorns. And rainbows.

Which I will grudgingly admit are pretty. Sort of. Sometimes.

And yes, that helps. Despite. Anyway.

## FEBRUARY 24, 2017

Today's moment of happiness despite the news.

Today, as I was walking through Walgreens, I passed a shelf filled with strange rubbery creatures. They were about the size of a softball, and while they were mostly smooth rubber, they had rubbery tentacles sticking and flopping out of odd places. They had eyes and noses, ears and feet. Some had tails. And one was the hottest pink. It smiled.

It immediately put me in mind of Olivia.

As a one-year old, pre-verbal Olivia was introduced to small "rubber guys" by her speech therapist. Livvy abhorred the feel of them – she was extra sensitive to touch. For a little bit each day, the therapist rubbed the rubber guys all over Livvy, and she made the appropriate animal noises. Livvy was soon giggling and plunging her hands into baskets of rubber guys. Then they were all she wanted to play with. The therapist brought all she had. And I went in search of more.

I wiped out the Dollar Store and Wal-Mart, Target and Toys R Us. We had hundreds of rubber guys. The rubber guys made Livvy laugh, and that made us laugh, and then we suddenly had a link to our little girl who would not speak to us.

She speaks and speaks and SPEAKS now. She speaks up. She speaks out. She says what's on her mind and she does so with remarkable clarity, sensitivity and compassion.

In Walgreens, I smiled at this softball-sized rubber guy and I rubbed its ears and I thought of those small hands and fingers that barely touched, then tapped, then stroked, then held whole-heartedly. The rubber guy smiled back. So I bought it.

Because some links have to be celebrated over and over again.

When she came home from school, I gave 16-year old Olivia her new rubber guy.

And she squealed the way she did as that one-year old.

And yes, that helps. Despite. Anyway.

## FEBRUARY 25, 2017

And so today's moment of happiness despite the news.

Actually, today's moment of happiness also led to my largest moment of agitation since this past Monday.

I had to go bow-shopping. Not bows for hair or bow-ties, but bow as in for a violin. I didn't know that bows had to be replaced; I guess I never really thought about it. But it was bow-time.

Olivia and I went to the White House of Music. We were turned over to their "bow-man" and led to a quiet room filled with lovely violins, violas, cellos and basses, just off the sales floor. There was a place for me to sit, a chair on a small carpet atop a gleaming hardwood floor. It was like a teeny recital hall.

Our bow-man told me that bows are priced anywhere from $150 to $700, and I nearly fell out of the chair. If you remember, Michael just lost his job this last Monday.

But I moved ahead.

When he handed her the first bow to try, Olivia quickly went through the scales. Then she began to play. It's a piece she's working on for the solo/ensemble competition coming up. I was watching the bow-man, who was pulling out other bows and lining them up. About five seconds into Olivia's song, I saw his eyebrows go up. He turned and listened to Olivia. And then he sat down.

Outside the little recital area, through the glass doors, I saw the people behind the sales counter stop and turn. I saw customers stop shopping and lift their heads. One woman stood with her eyes closed, hands clasped.

And then I tumbled into the music too. Olivia and that violin – they SING.

This is the girl I was once told would always look at me like I was a wooden log. And this is the girl who, even as I was told this, took a moment every few seconds to touch my shoe, my knee, my arm, to look up into my face.

*Are you there, Mama?*

*I am always here.*

On this day, in this moment of happiness, she stopped the world. She owned it.

When we moved on, when she spoke to the bow-man, discussing how the different bows felt, I doubt he ever once thought she was autistic. He saw her as she is. An incredible young woman. My little girl.

He told me how much the favored bow was. I hesitated. But then I bought it. Despite Monday. Anyway.

Goddammit, I will not cut corners with this child. I will not. I had to with the first three, which I will regret for the rest of my life, and she is my last chance to get this right.

*Are you there, Mama?*

*I am always here.*

Michael will get the job when he interviews on Tuesday. He will. I will not let it go any other way.

I love this girl more than I can ever say.

And yes, this helps. Despite. Anyway.

## FEBRUARY 26, 2017

And so today's moment of happiness despite the news.

Well, you know it has to be about going to my student Lila's book debut this afternoon. As a teacher, watching my students' successes, ALL of their successes, from writing their first story to publishing a book, is the greatest joy.

But today's moment happened as I was on my way there.

As I was driving down the freeway, I had a Moody Blues CD playing. The song "Question" came on, which is one of my favorites.

As I sang along with it, I got to the lines, "I'm looking for someone to change my life. I'm looking for a miracle in my life." And I remembered how I used to absolutely wail those lines with my whole heart, because that's what I wanted. Sometimes, I couldn't get through the verse because my voice would gutter and choke. I used to think, Just please, please, please get me the hell out of this.

While I was singing and thinking about this today, I heard these words, as clearly as I hear opening lines to stories sometimes: "You're living the miracle."

And I realized that I am. I was just washed warm with it.

AllWriters' is a miracle, backwards and forwards. It's a miracle that it's survived, it's thrived, that it's become what it has, that it's done what it's done.

But it's also a miracle in what it's done for me. Its survival, and mine, are linked. Gratitude is a relatively new feeling for me.

But I am just so happy I'm here to feel it. To AllWriters' students, past, present and future, you just have no idea the effect you have on me.

And yes, that helps. Despite. Anyway.

## FEBRUARY 27, 2017

And so today's moment of happiness despite the news.

So I'll admit it. Today was a hard one. I've been staring at my screen for the last ten minutes or so, wondering what to put here. I did let fear take me over today. I did let sadness take me over today. And anxiety was king.

But I'm keeping the faith. He's going to get the job tomorrow. Even though my nerves are rubber bands right now. You know how we used to take rubber bands, wrap the ends around two fingers, then curl it over itself and pull back as far as we could and then we let fly, sending the rubber band across the room, and usually against the back of someone's neck? Well, I'm the rubber band before it flies. I'm either gonna fly or break.

So I sorted through today's events. I looked at the big events, trying to find that jolt of happy. I didn't. Then I looked at the small.

There it was.

At one point today, when I thought the rubber band would snap, I sat down on the couch. I didn't do anything – I didn't cry or yell or shake. I just sat. Had the blank stares.

And then there was Donnie. Little Donnie Dipshit, the beagle from hell. He came over, put his front paws on my thighs, and tucked his head under my armpit.

If dogs could hug, he did.

So I wrapped my arms around him and hugged back. Got warmth and a belch-like beagle grunt.

Happiness is a warm puppy, remember? Even Donnie.

And yes, that helps. Despite. Anyway.

## FEBRUARY 28, 2017

*Special note: On this day, my husband had a job interview at 2:00. When I asked for support on Facebook, hundreds of people chimed in that they were hoping, praying, sending energy. P.S. He did not get the job.*

And so today's moment of happiness despite the news.

This afternoon, at 2:00, I knew I wasn't alone.

And I know I'm not alone now either.

And yes, this helps. Despite. Anyway.

# Chapter Three

## MARCH 1, 2017

And so today's moment of happiness despite the news.

I was walking back home from the parking garage today. It was about four in the afternoon and it was snowing like it was January. A car was coming down the street toward me, and as it drew close, it suddenly slowed down...and stopped. Then the passenger side window went down and a woman peered up at me. I leaned over the railing separating the sidewalk from the street. I figured I was about to be asked directions; people get lost in Waukesha a lot.

Instead, the woman beamed, flung both her hands into the air and cried, "WHERE did you get your HAIR done?"

My hair? We're in a snowstorm and she has her husband pull over on a slippery street to ask about my hair?

"A place called Foxies," I said. "It's on Wisconsin Avenue. Big purple house. My guy's name is John."

She ran her fingers through her hair, a light brown, hanging down in what we used to call a pageboy that curled under her chin. "My hair is thinning," she said, "due to a medical condition. I want to cut it. I want it to look like yours. It's just perfect."

I touched my hair, felt the falling snow that clung to the ends and was likely making me glitter. "I just had it done yesterday."

"It's BEAUTIFUL!" she said. "I'm going there right now! I know exactly where you mean! Thank you!"

And the window went up and she was gone.

So I continued my walk home and considered. It was flattering, of course, to have my hair stop traffic. But I thought of the look on her face, lit with winter light, her hands touching her own hair with the same delicacy that the snowflakes touched mine.

It's amazing, really, the way women identify themselves with their hair. She was scared of losing hers.

I guess my hair brought her hope.

And yes, that helps. Despite. Anyway.

## MARCH 2, 2017

This moment is missing.

## MARCH 3, 2017

And so today's moment of happiness despite the news.

So today's moment will probably seem a little bit "off". But bear with me.

Today is my friend Sam's birthday. He would have been 54. He's not, though, because he chose to end his life almost three years ago. I choose to say chose. I will not say "killed himself". There was so much more to it than that.

Earlier this week, in a workshop, I came down a little heavy on a student. He was presenting a story he wrote some time ago, a story that hasn't sold. I told him then it was because the main character's suicide wasn't earned. It wasn't motivated. He was trying a few different things this time around, but the suicide was still not earned. The student finally flat-out asked me, "Have you ever known anyone whose suicide was earned?"

Just as flat out, I answered yes.

Sam's struggle was profound. Was it insurmountable? For some, probably not. But for Sam, it was. And there was more struggle to come. He wanted peace. He wanted rest. And in the end, he reached for it in the way he felt he was most likely to get it.

I believe Sam found his peace. I believe he earned his rest. And I'm happy he finally found it.

So is it wrong to say my moment of happiness today was when I realized that he's okay now?

I'm sad for me and for all of us left behind, who still feel this loss, almost three years later. But...I'm happy for Sam. I'm happy he's no longer in pain. I'm happy he found his way. I understand the struggle.

I miss Sam.

And...the biggest moment of happiness for me today was when I realized that I'm happy, I'm happy! that when I faced that same decision, more than once, my decisions failed. I didn't find peace. I didn't find rest.

But now I've found that I'm happy I'm still here. Grateful.

And yes, that helps. Despite. Anyway.

# MARCH 4, 2017

And so today's moment of happiness despite the news.

I slipped out of the hotel today to find some lunch. I wasn't paying much attention, and I swung out of the door and came, well, thigh to face with a big honking goose (pun intended). It snaked up its neck, looked me in the eye, opened its pointy mouth and HISSED.

Most of you likely know that I'm afraid of birds. I find them fascinating to watch, hence my love for this hotel, but I always want a good twenty feet between me and them. Or a solid window. Bars.

So I screamed like a five-year old, backed in the way I came out, wound my way to the front of the hotel, came out the main entrance, walked the outside perimeter of the parking lot, and then snuck up to my car. Whew.

As I sat safely behind the wheel, I looked at the goose, still standing by the door, and thought, Man, I have got to get over this fear of birds.

And then I thought, Why?

Years ago, when I confessed my fear of flying to a student (a fear I've since faced and conquered), that student said, "Oh my god. I didn't think you were afraid of anything."

Really?

So I started trying to live up to that belief. Gotta live up to the hype, donchaknow.

But you know what? I'm 56 years old. Being afraid of birds hasn't stopped me in any way. And I've had a pelican fall out of the sky and land two feet in front of me - WHOMP - on the Oregon coast. I've had a bald eagle come so close to beaning me in La Crosse, Wisconsin, that I saw his wing open up in front of my nose. And when Michael's new parakeet got out of her cage in our old house, I spent an unprecedented amount of time with my face pressed into the carpet and my hands covering my head.

But each time, I screamed like a five-year old and then found a way to move on.

So my happy moment today was realizing that being fearless...is STUPID. It's okay to be scared. As long as you keep on going.

Lots to be scared of lately. So scream like five-year olds and then move on. Find a way to walk the far way around your parking lot and get to your destination. Blow your car's mighty horn at the object of your fear and watch him scream like a five-year old too. Laugh when the feathers fly.

Didn't I mention that part?

And yes, that helps. Despite. Anyway.

## MARCH 5, 2017

And so today's moment of happiness despite the news.

The moment today was the result of a previous moment. A few days ago, I posted about the woman in the snowstorm who asked where I get my hair done. Under that post, one of my students commented that I made major progress because I wasn't afraid when I was approached by a slowing car. The comment puzzled me, but I was involved with geese and swans and a lovely lake, so I just didn't pay it much mind.

On the drive home today, though, when I drifted into driving-contemplation, that comment came back with a roar. And I realized what it meant. I was assaulted two days after the election. For a while afterwards, leaving my condo put me in a panic. Strangers, traveling, being alone, unlocked doors, all had me terrified. And yet four months later, on the day of the snowstorm, when the car slowed and then stopped, I stepped right up to the railing and leaned over. I never even thought about being scared. I was ready to help someone with directions. Instead, I helped someone find her identity.

Well. Wow.

The day of the assault, I came home, unleashed the dogs, and gave them their treat. I had a drink of water, the universal balm when someone isn't feeling right. Then I wandered upstairs, sat down at my computer, and posted on Facebook what just happened. I was immediately surrounded by caring people who let me know that I was in shock, that what happened was an assault, and I needed to call the police.

The call to the police and that original post on Facebook led to media involvement, from the newspapers, the television, and one god-awful conservative radio talk show. From there, I was thrown into a horrific shitstorm of hate. My life was threatened. I was buried in Facebook messages, Twitter messages, and more from people who didn't believe me and who wanted me dead. It wasn't the assault that left me afraid; it was this reaction. I began to teach with the classroom door locked. I couldn't be left alone. I was offered the opportunity by two wonderful friends who I've never met to take sanctuary in my favorite spot on the Oregon coast. I made arrangements to go, and then had to cancel because I knew I would never be able to handle being sealed in a plane.

And now...I leaned over a railing and waited to hear what the strangers in a car needed from me.

I'm back.

On the assault day and every day since then, I've been lifted up by the hands of so many. Hands of people I know and the hands of strangers. Hands that voted for Hillary, voted for Asshat, voted for a third party, didn't vote at all. So many.

I believe in the greater good. Not just the common definition of that expression, where you do the most good to help the most people. But that the number of good people is greater than bad. Good > bad. And now I've lived it. I know that, despite everything that's going on, good will still win over bad. And we'll all be okay.

And yes, that helps. Despite. Anyway.

## MARCH 6, 2017

And so today's moment of happiness despite the news.

So tonight, I read at the Milwaukee Public Library. It was a lovely evening.

And it was in a lovely library. The Milwaukee Public Library in downtown Milwaukee impressed me at an early age (my teens) as just being a stunner. From its regal exterior to the breathtaking interior, you are just immersed in history, In mindfulness, in every definition. And the words. Oh, the words. Everywhere.

The last time we visited, Michael took the tour. The guide told the group about how architects liked to put one deliberate mistake into a building. The purpose was to show the world that nothing is perfect....except God. In the library's case, there is an upside down spindle in the ornate staircase climbing to the second floor.

It's interesting that the architects thought to do this. But what makes me happy is that for all the years I've walked through this library, and up those stairs, I never noticed the mistake. Until the guide told this to the group, I never even knew of its existence.

This library to me is beautiful. Period. It never occurred to me to look for or expect imperfections. I knew they were likely there. But they didn't matter.

The mistakes, deliberate or not, were part of the beauty.

So I was a little loathe to have Michael show it to me. But ultimately, curiosity won out, and as he and I left tonight, he pointed it out to me.

Yep, there it was. Upside down spindle. Plain as day.

But you know what? Still beautiful. And I don't think my eye will ever be drawn to the "mistake" again.

Because it doesn't matter. It doesn't affect how I think about this library, or any library, really.

It made me think about how Michael is drawn to me, and I am drawn to him. How I swoon over my children and my grandchild. The people and places I love, the people I don't know, but love anyway because of what they do and how they affect me. The books I've held. The books I write. Words.

The imperfection is perfect.

(And as for God being perfect – well, I think there's a lesson there too. About how perspective works. But let's not get into that tonight.)

What a lovely evening.

And yes, that helps. Despite. Anyway.

## MARCH 7, 2017

And so today's moment of happiness despite the news.

On my way to pick up Olivia from school today, I turned onto College Avenue from Grand. College Avenue, appropriately, runs by Carroll University. Coming toward me, swerving around parked cars and in and out of traffic, were two laughing college-age girls, one on a bike, one on a skateboard. The skateboarder was holding on to the biker's arm and was being pulled along. The biker had on a winter coat, a hat, gloves. The skateboarder had on a short skirt and was completely bare-legged. On pavement, on a skateboard, being pulled by a bike, in traffic.

I slowed the car, watched as they rolled past me, their eyes and mouths wide in exhilaration. I watched them through my rearview mirror until they flew through the stoplight and turned into a parking lot. Mom-like, I shook my head. I muttered that I'd better not ever catch Olivia doing something like that.

And then, for a moment, I wished I was that young and stupid again. That immortal.

I continued down College, turned onto East Avenue, and continued toward Olivia's high school. And my thoughts turned from wistful to where I am now.

The joy I feel at the head of my classrooms. In front of my computer screen, reflecting a new story or book or poem. Reading to readers. Pulling on a favorite sweater and pair of jeans without a thought as to who is going to see me in them. Conscious of living and breathing, instead of flying through my seconds as if the next will always be there, and living and breathing are to be taken for granted. No longer immortal. But mortal and okay with it.

I am very comfortable in my skin, and in the life I've chosen to live.

And you know what? When I do something stupid, it's not usually out of ignorance or a sense of never-ending, but because I just wanna, dammit. I'm old enough to know that there's a difference between doing something even though you might die and doing something because you don't believe you'll ever die.

And I like that.

And yes, that helps. Despite. Anyway.

### MARCH 8, 2017

And so today's moment of happiness despite the news.

One of the very best things about what I do is the wide variety of people I meet. Wednesdays are odd, because I have a double whammy of a duplicated country and a duplicated city. I start my day with a client from Israel, then move to a client from Chicago. Both of these are on Skype. Then I teach a workshop for two hours, It's a workshop just for women where I am surrounded with wonderful women from a variety of backgrounds and representing all ages and philosophies. From there, I meet on the phone with a client from Connecticut. Most Wednesdays, I go from Connecticut to Colorado, but that client was missing this week. Then back to Chicago (phone), and I finish the day with a late-night meeting (from eleven to midnight) back in Israel. That meeting takes place in the AllWriters' online chatroom.

It's a roundtrip day.

Today's moment happened this morning, when I was on Skype with my client from Israel. She's a British journalist and I love her clipped and lyrical accent. We have the best time together, teasing each other about still being in our pajamas. She's one of my newest clients, yet we've already achieved a great level of comfort.

This morning, we began to laugh, she in Israel, me in Waukesha,

Wisconsin. As our voices rose, I was suddenly charmed with the realization that my voice, from Wisconsin, was ringing with laughter that could be heard around the world in a room in Israel. And her laughter, its British lilt, was ringing from Israel to me.

Today was International Women's Day, celebrated since the early 1900's. According to its official site, it is "a global day celebrating the social, economic, cultural and political achievements of women."

Do you know what we were laughing about? Joanna received an ad that day, encouraging her to take advantage of an International Women's Day sale, allowing her to buy a batch of panties for twenty dollars. We were laughing about panties and sales and advertising and how much the world in general still just doesn't get it. (I hear tell the Asshat tweeted and it backfired – oh, there's a surprise.)

But she and I got it, laughing together across time zones and borders and boundaries and life differences. We got it, we enjoyed it, we celebrated it, and we laughed. And we heard each other, a billion miles apart. We connected. We embraced.

And yes, that helps. Despite. Anyway.

## MARCH 9, 2017

And so today's moment of happiness despite the news.

Today, I was a guest in the Waukesha County Jail. Which certainly doesn't sound happy, but it was.

Last summer, I visited the Eastern Oregon Correctional Institute in Pendleton, Oregon, a maximum security prison for men. Inmates there were reading *The Home For Wayward Clocks*. It was a life-changing experience – not in the sense that my life changed, but that I changed. I came out of there that very same day a different person than I went in.

Today's visit, while there were basic differences, echoed that. This was a jail, not a prison. I was visiting women, not men. But they still read *The Home For Wayward Clocks*, and now they're reading *Learning To Tell (A Life)Time*. I spoke with fifteen women. My whole time there, I found myself wondering, just as I did in the prison, how can anyone live like this?

Which I suppose is part of the point of being incarcerated. The rules they live by are strict and strongly enforced. And I know they're forced to follow the rules because of rules they've broken. But I kept wondering how they could possibly be learning how to make choices in a place where there are no choices.

My most striking moment – walking out of the classroom where we met to see the women waiting in line to be patted down before they returned to their cells. Women, who I was just speaking to on a very intelligent, intellectual, but such a connecting manner, were now taking turns to stand spread-eagled, arms wide like a crucifix, while someone padded and poked in places she shouldn't be. All because they'd just been in a classroom where maybe they could have taken something. Where maybe an outsider could have given them something. I felt guilty and horrified at the same time – was it worth it for them to come talk to me?

As I left, I began to question everything. How long since they walked outside (there is no outside rec area at this jail)? How long since they felt a sidewalk under their feet or the cold slap of winter when you're so craving spring? How long since feeling the power of a car under the control of your fingers? The wrap of a coat? A song on your speakers? How long since reading a text from your daughter while you wait in line at the drive-thru at Starbucks?

It left me agitated and uncertain. I don't have any answers for what should be done. But I do know that the two times I've been exposed to this now, it just felt wrong.

But the happy moment.

As we talked about the book, it came up that one of the books (the jail had 11) was missing. And someone said that a woman who was released last week snuck the book out with her. She couldn't stand to leave *Clocks* behind.

Undoubtedly, it's a "wrong" thing to take jail property with you when you go. But I was so glad she did. She took me with her. And now, maybe I can be a way of hope, a way of re-entering, a way of keeping life on a better track. It made me happy to think of her stepping outside, for the first time in however long, with *Clocks* in her pocket, and maybe that night, for the first time in a while in her own bed, she opened up *Clocks* and she read. As if it was something she did every night. As if it was something she would do every night from this point forward. I was happy to be a part of her welcome home.

And yes, that helps. Despite. Anyway.

### MARCH 10, 2017

*Special note: This must have been a really bad day. I have no recollection of it.*

And so today's moment of happiness despite the news.

Today's moment is simply this:

Tomorrow will be here soon.
(some days are like that.)
And yes, this helps. Despite. Anyway.

## MARCH 11, 2017

And so today's moment of happiness despite the news.

In the mall today, shopping for a son's birthday, I ended up in a try-on room with a daughter. Of course. No, I was not trying on things for my son's birthday. I earned "rewards" at this particular store for a previous purchase, and so I ran in to get something for free (uh-huh).

In the try-on room next door, Olivia and I overheard this conversation:

"Oh, this bra is just right for me. See? It makes me all level. My titties are lopsided."

"What? What do you mean?"

"Wait…" Shuffle, shuffle. "Okay, see? This one is up here and that one is down there. And this one sorta perks up toward the ceiling."

"Oh, okay, I see…"

"But a bra like this, now, a bra like this makes'em level. Makes'em happy."

I glanced at Olivia who had both hands over her mouth and was looking at me wide-eyed. I grinned back at her and continued what I was doing.

What a great conversation. And what a wonderful way to show my daughter how to be casual and easy about her body shape and size and proclivities. These women were talking about breasts as everyday as they talked about dinner selections or movie reviews or the day of the week. These women referred to our own specialized body parts with respect, but without any exaggerated sense of secrecy or shame or exhibition or inhibition. There were no titters (sorry, couldn't help myself) or look-both-ways-before-you-speak whispers. They spoke in a regular tone of voice. And the woman with the lopsided breasts was clearly okay with herself. She wasn't complaining, she wasn't berating – she just found what was comfortable, what "made'em happy", and moved on.

She was easy in her own skin. I pulled on the sweater I'd chosen, looked in the mirror, and decided I was too, and that I wanted my daughter to be as well. And then I saw the words on the mirror.

*Go on with your bad self! #ThisBody*

They made me smile further. I got on with my bad self, and so did the women next door.

And yes, that helps. Despite. Anyway.

## MARCH 12, 2017

And so today's moment of happiness despite the news.

Today's was easy. It happened within a half hour of my waking up and floated me the rest of the day.

To me, my studio, AllWriters' Workplace & Workshop, is a miracle. When I think back over its twelve years of steady survival in the rocky world of small business, there are many things that amaze me. But here's one of the biggest – and boy, was it in evidence today.

AllWriters' has never ever received a grant (I've never applied for one – AllWriters' is an LLC, not a nonprofit), nor has it ever received a small business loan (other than right after its incorporation, I never asked for one). Never. AllWriters' survives completely with the enthusiastic support and love of its students. That's one of the reasons why it truly stands out from other similar organizations. They survive with outside help. AllWriters' survives with the heart and soul of the students. Everything flows from the inside out.

This morning, a long-time student reached out to me. He asked how I was feeling. He said, "Are you worried? Scared? Panicked?"

I said yes. And I said that he could add hopeless to the list too. My business was being threatened through no fault of my own. My husband was let go from his job; another business' mistake was causing mine to suffer. My little business is suddenly the sole source of income for my family. It's not ready for that. I'm not ready for that.

My student said, "You've got too much to do. You can't give up. Sorry."

And he said, "I need you."

And then he invested in the studio. And in me.

There was my moment. It took my legs right out from under me.

This isn't the full solution. There is still the overwhelming issue of insurance. We live in a country that doesn't believe that everyone should have access to affordable healthcare. This morning, the front page of the Sunday Milwaukee Journal Sentinel held the headline, "GOP health care plan shifts benefits toward higher income people." Right out there in black and white. No shame. No concern or compassion. We are now without health insurance and will likely remain so until my husband finds a job. The cost of insurance, especially the first months of having to pay for prescriptions until the deductible is met, is prohibitive.

But what this student did for me…priceless.

And so here's the thing. I can tell you that there are times I feel worthless. Like the biggest failure on the planet. Like there are others out there who can do better than me, are doing better than me, will always do better than me, and that ultimately, in the end, nothing I do will ever make a difference. Maybe some of my fear comes from that time I went to a local bank after I incorporated myself and asked for a small business loan, presenting my business plan, presenting who I was and why I could do it, and being told no. Maybe it comes from people around me saying at the time, "Are you crazy? You can't do that. You have no idea what you're doing." Maybe it comes from the memory of my own mother, calling me the night after the grand opening, which wasn't so grand because we had a blizzard that dumped 15 inches of snow, and saying to me, "You failed before you even began. Why did you think you could do this?" Maybe.

But today, I felt like somebody grabbed me under the arms and hauled me up.

"You've got too much to do. You can't give up. I need you."

I felt my worth today. And I felt the miracle that is AllWriters' Workplace & Workshop.

And yes, that helps. Despite. Anyway.

### MARCH 13, 2017

And so today's moment of happiness despite the news.

It snowed! It snowed lots! The roads were covered, we slipped and slid everywhere, stores and schools began to close, the sky was gray, it was cold, it snowed!

Yeah, okay, that's not the happy. I hate snow. I hate cold. I live in Wisconsin why? Because before that was northern Minnesota. At first, Wisconsin was a tropical paradise. Now? Blech.

But…

I had to drive in it today because the school district ran like usual, but then decided to let out early. I couldn't just abandon the child – though tales of how I used to walk home in blizzards did come to mind. But no. Hemi (my Chrysler 300C Hemi) and I braved the elements. We set out to rescue Olivia like Yukon Cornelius going after Hermie and Rudolph.

I swore most of the way. The heat of my language should have melted the snow.

But then I turned onto this side street that leads up to the school. During spring and summer, this becomes one of those idyllic streets where the trees on either side stretch out to grasp each other's limbs and the leaves grow and everything becomes a green living tunnel. Sun dapples through and you drive through glitter so bright, you think you're being rained on with gold. With light. With the newness of spring and the most verdant summer.

Today was winter. Once the leaves fall, those same branches become bony fingers. They don't stretch and grasp. They clutch and snatch and choke. Skeletons.

But not this afternoon.

The snow graced the branches like silk and lace, the bark peeking out of patterns of white that felt fully intentional. Sewed and stitched. There wasn't sun, but snowflakes fell in crystals. And it was so quiet. I opened my window and only heard whispers.

Chandeliers and lace, silk and grace. It was winter, I was warm on a heated seat, and it was beautiful.

For a moment, I loved winter. I could appreciate it, admire it, be moved by it. Even though I knew by the next day, I'd likely be cursing it again. Blue words through a chilly swath.

But not right then. I held the blue inside. Felt warmth in the cold instead.

And yes, that helps. Despite. Anyway.

## MARCH 14, 2017

And so today's moment of happiness despite the news.

I am not a romantic person. I roll my eyes at Lifetime TV movies. I don't bother to read those little candy hearts with the words on them before I pop them in my mouth and pulverize them with my teeth. I don't cry at weddings. I gag in Hallmark stores.

But today, I had a coaching session with an AllWriters' client in the on-site classroom. My husband Michael went down ahead of me to unlock the door, turn on the lights, turn up the heat. When I arrived, he and my client Barb were talking. I got settled, turned to Michael and said, "Get out of here." In my most friendly way, of course.

Barb laughed and called, "Think of your wife while she's gone."

And Michael said, "Then I wouldn't get any work done."

17 years of marriage. Four children, three mine, one ours. Stresses, strains, arguments, frosty silences, worries, fears, aging aching bodies, gray hair (the gray hair is his, not mine).

But every night, when we climb into bed, Michael's arm is wrapped around my waist and he tucks his chin on my shoulder. Every night, he makes me warm. Every night, I relearn the definition of absolute devotion.

It goes both ways.

<melt>

And yes, that helps. Despite. Anyway.

## MARCH 15, 2017

And so today's moment of happiness despite the news.

It came early on today. Two o'clock in the morning, right before I went to bed. Before "today" really even started for me. I meditate before bed and as I finished, a bing from my phone indicated I had a message.

It was from my meditation app, Meditation Timer. It let me know that I'd just hit 365 days in a row of meditating at least once a day (I mostly meditate twice a day now).

365 days. A whole year. A whole year of meditating from someone whose hyperdrive mind makes monkey minds look like sleeping turtles. Who once said she'd never be able to meditate. Actually, I didn't "once" say it. I said it a bazillion times as different people encouraged me to try, and as I tried and thought I failed. I didn't fail. I just didn't know what I was doing.

365 days. One year.

So what have I learned?

First and foremost, I learned that meditation is not about not thinking. That was my mistake. I equated meditation with thoughts grinding to a halt, sitting in silence, and just, well, "being", whatever that is. But you don't stop thinking during meditation. You just become aware of the thoughts and watch them pass. The image that finally worked for me was thoughts as balloons, and I just watched them blow by. Eventually, my meditating mind turned into an aquarium, and thoughts became bubbles that bobbled out of an air hose, in front of my eyes, and away. Blip.

Second, and the most important to me, I learned how to sleep. I'm a lifelong insomniac. But within a couple weeks of starting to meditate, I began to conk out within seconds of my head hitting the pillow. Sleep is now something I look forward to. It's not a struggle, it's not a destination; it's just delicious. And I have years of sleep deprivation to make up for.

Third, I learned that I was not going to turn into a serene, soft-speaking, namaste-chanting, cloth-draped, arms-upraised woman. I am probably the most agitated person I know. I've often referred to myself as a living, breathing roller coaster, and I am still on that ride. But I bend into the curves now. I breathe through the climbs and drops. The upside-down loops still get to me, but I recover faster.

I'm still me.

I'm me, but I'm the me that takes a break during the day to breathe, close my eyes, and sink into bubbles for a bit. I sink as well before bed, and then I sink into dreams.

365 days. A year. Something that I said I would never do. It feels pretty good. I wear a bracelet that says, "She believed she could, so she did." But this was about believing I couldn't, but I did anyway.

So I've decided to do that with this too, with this foray into a daily moment of happiness. I've wondered how long I will keep it up, and now I know. A year. It is definitely something that I question my ability to do. I'm a natural skeptic, and I get into funks where everything looks black and where I even snarl at the sun. But if I can continue to find one good thing every day, and if I can do that for a year...well, maybe. It's a good challenge.

And yes, that helps. Despite. Anyway.

### MARCH 16, 2017

And so today's moment of happiness despite the news.

I suppose, since I'm a writer, it's no surprise that words make me happy. Today, it was one unexpected word in particular that just lit me up like a whiskeyed campfire.

A client this morning said to me, "I feel like I'm growing brazen in my writing."

I immediately grabbed a pen and wrote "Brazen!!!!!" with just that many exclamation points. And I'm not an exclamation point person.

Isn't brazen a great word? It gives the sense of sauciness, of controlled boldness, of strutting, of maybe ripping off all your clothes and writing naked (but put a towel beneath you if you write in a leather chair – skin and leather adhere).

In this particular student's case, it meant she wasn't going to be shy and softspoken anymore about what she's writing. And she's not going to be shy and softspoken anymore about why she's writing it. She's going to get brazen. She's going to say it loud. She's going to OWN it.

As her teacher, that just made my day. And the word choice was a plus. She could have said, "I feel like I'm growing brave in my writing," and I would have cheered just as loudly, but using the word brazen...oh, baby. Fire me up with that sweet, sweet word.

The real definition: *brazen <brayzuhn> bold and without shame*

She's getting so strong, this student.

So then there was news of the Asshat this afternoon. When isn't there news of the Asshat and his latest act of orange abominable asshatiness? He wants to cut endowments that support the arts. Big surprise.

Ready for me to be brazen?

He's an idiot.

My moment of happiness today was a path. From student declaration to brazen word choice to my reaction. I heard he was on an arts elimination tear, I got mad for all of five minutes, and then I scraped him off like dog crap on my shoes and I went on. There's no stopping writers. There's no stopping artists. There's no silencing music or theatre or any of the creative impulses that thrum in our brains and veins. Yes, he can take this support away, though I hope to hell it's blocked. But in the end, he can't stop what makes us run to the blank page, the blank canvas, the blank staff or stage. We will continue creating, and in our creations, we will make the world a better place.

Breaking news for you, Mr. Asshat. That's what you're supposed to be doing. Go to Amazon, please, and purchase *Being The President for Dummies*.

From student to word to response. It made me happy to realize that I'm not feeling hopeless anymore. I'm not feeling powerless or defeated. Because he can't defeat the undefeatable. He can't stop this morning's student. He can't stop tomorrow's. He can't stop any of them.

He can't stop me.

From now on, you can call my studio, AllWriters' Brazen Workplace & Workshop.

And yes, that helps. Despite. Anyway.

## MARCH 17, 2017

And so today's moment of happiness despite the news.

I'm naturally a late-night person. Sleep usually reminds me that it's a necessity around two in the morning. Last night, I fought with it until finally caving in at three.

At eight o'clock, I was dragged out of bed by Olivia's high school with a call from the health room, announcing that my daughter threw up and needed to come home. I don't remember much about how I got into my car or even when I began driving, but I did find myself glancing down at a red light to make sure I'd gotten dressed before I left. I did.

At the school, I pulled up to the front door and waited. I expected to see a washed-out sad-faced child, dragging her backpack behind her suddenly weakened waify body. Instead, Olivia bounced out, threw her backpack into the car, and plunked herself beside me. "Hey!" she said. "Mom, I'm hungry!"

So yeah. That pretty much set my mood for the day.

I vowed right then and there that I was going to take a nap that afternoon. I was going to shut the shutters and check out of this world for a bit. It would happen.

What followed was sessions with two wonderful clients. A trip to the gas station where I realized I forgot my purse and had to run back home to get it, and then a trip to the gas station again. A trip to the bank, where there was a line. A trip to Office Depot, where there was a line, and a clerk who wanted to know all about my purse. Where'd I get it, how much did it cost, and then a trip down memory lane of every purse she'd ever bought in her lifetime, all of which failed to meet her expectations. A trip home where I attempted to install the new cartridges I bought for my printer, but the "tear here" instructions on the packaging didn't work and I ended up clawing my way through. For one, the yellow, the package erupted like a popped potato chip bag and the new cartridge flew across the room and under the bookshelf, where it was determined to never be found. When I finally got it all done, the door hiding the cartridges from view would no longer close and my printer kept yelling at me. "Door OPEN! Door OPEN! I can't function with my door OPEN!" I taped the damn thing shut.

Oh, a nap. I needed a nap. Shut the shutters. Check out.

And so I did. I tucked myself under my favorite blanket, one Michael had made for me, with photographs of my book covers and the studio on it. I turned on my electric fireplace so I could get toasted and roasted. And from the moment I closed my eyes, I was out. I was beyond out. No dreams. No consciousness. Nothing. I shut the shutters. I checked out.

And there was my moment of happiness. For a couple hours, all pressure was gone. Stress and responsibility were gone. Aggravation at daily detritus was gone. I wasn't even aware of myself.

I used writing time for this nap – yes, I should have been writing. Or I should have been working. There were manuscripts to read. There was a child who threw up at school. (She's fine, by the way. One of the common traits of autism is a wonky digestive system. Sometimes, she just backs up, yaks up, and then tra la, we're good.) There were all sorts of shoulds I should have been doing.

But I chose to nap. And it was WONDERFUL.

Sometimes, you gotta put yourself first. I did.

And yes, that helps. Despite. Anyway.

## MARCH 18, 2017

And so today's moment of happiness despite the news.

Today's moment happened because of a nightmare. I haven't had one of those for a while, so it surprised me. I found myself sitting upright in bed, legs already swung out from under the covers, my heart racing, lungs gasping – I was profoundly ready to take flight.

I was dreaming of the house I lived in from 1966 to 1972 in Esko, Minnesota. The doorbell was ringing and ringing and there didn't seem to be anyone else around to answer it, even though I could hear voices coming from behind me. I was young when I lived in Esko, six years old when I moved there, twelve years old when I left. But I didn't have the sense of being young in my dream; I felt like who I am now. Except I was scared, which is more like who I was then.

I went to answer the door and even though the door was solid, I could see who was on the other side. It was a man I recognized, but in that way of dreams, where I knew who he was, but I couldn't have said his name or what he meant to me. He was laughing uproariously — so loud, such banging laughter. His face was turned just barely to my right, so I could see his profile, but I could also see him looking at me full on. I remember sandy brown curls, high cheekbones, a sharp nose and chin, and eyes as blue cold as a Minnesota January. I knew without a doubt that I didn't like him. I felt the pureness of a child's hate, before we're taught that hate is wrong.

While the door was still closed, I was able to reach through it and I tried to shove him away. He kept laughing and smacking at me in those open-palmed slaps that children use. No matter what I did, I couldn't make him go away. And then he grabbed me by the wrists and pulled me through the door. I felt every splinter. And that laugh, oh, that laugh.

And then I woke up on the edge of the bed. On edge.

The moment of happiness? I looked over my shoulder and Michael was there. At the foot of my bed was one of my cats and I patted her head. I went to the bathroom to get that universal balm, the cup of water. And then I wandered the house for a bit. This house, not that one. This house, that I love so much, that we built, and everything in it holds our touch, our passions, our relationships with each other. I stood outside Olivia's door and listened to her sound machine. I patted both dogs and the other cat. I touched things. And I very strongly had the sense of the greater world around me, MY greater world, filled with everyone and everything that I love.

You know, I am one of the lucky ones. When I work, I'm doing what I love with those I love. When I'm at home, I'm surrounded by what I love and with those I love. There is just so much good here. It's all the result of phenomenal hard work, but work I've been overjoyed to do. Work I would do again.

When I returned upstairs, I stood by our window and let the moon fall in. Walgreens is our back yard and when we moved in, we had to do something about how brightly their security lights shine in to our bedroom window. But I couldn't bear to block out the moon. So we put in plantation shutters, just on the lower half of the window. I can see the moon whether I'm standing or laying in bed. I am in thrall of bright moon nights with a sky filled with fast-moving clouds. The silver and gray and black shot through with a light so bright. On this night, the moon shone down on everyone and everything that I love. It illuminated it just for me.

The nightmare, the man on the other side of the door, the banging laughter all fell away.

*MOONGLOW my eyes see the moon but it's my soul that glows bright silver reflection.*

And yes, that helps. Despite. Anyway.

## MARCH 19, 2017

And so today's moment of happiness despite the news.

My car's in the shop. No, that doesn't make me happy. He's been there since Thursday, and the parts he needs won't be there until at least Tuesday. That doesn't make me happy either. However, when I bought him, I was smart enough to buy the extended warranty (which has more than paid for itself with this particular car) which gives me a free rental whenever he's stuck there for than a day.

There was a mix-up at the rental place, which meant that I received my promised car 24 hours after I was supposed to. Because this also didn't make me happy, I refused their offer to come pick me up (they blew it the first time) and I had a friend drop me there instead. The apologetic clerk opened the drawers holding all their vehicle's keys and said, "We are so sorry. Here. Take your pick of whatever vehicle you want."

Most were SUVs. I don't like SUVs. But there was a brand spanking new Dodge Charger. Black. Shiny. Hemi engine, like my own Chrysler 300C Hemi.

Oh, baby.

I've been seduced by cars for a long time. The TR-7 – the shape of things to come – put me in a swoon before I was old enough to drive. The Dodge Neon grabbed my heart because in its ads, it said hi to me. I am well aware that the Dodge Neon is likely not most people's definition of a swoonable car, but he was friendly, he liked me, and so I liked him. That car lived a long life, until my kids killed him by driving him long after his "I need OIL!" light turned on. In a showroom before the Neon, I fell in love with the Chrysler LeBaron convertible and vowed that I would one day own one. I did. A 1994 hunter green model I called LeB (pronounced luh-BEE) and loved til his dying day when I traded him in for a Chrysler Sebring lxi convertible, called SeB (pronounced suh-BEE). Who I loved until his dying day when I traded him in for a Chrysler 200 convertible. That car is called Semi, because my other car is a 300 – 200/300, Semi-Hemi. You can blame Michael for that one. In between SeB and Semi, there was a Nissan Frontier crew cab pick-up that I replaced with the Chrysler 300C Hemi, called Hemi – the car now in the shop.

I loved/love them all.

I never panted for a Dodge Charger. But then I saw that sleek body, those sexy lines, those curves, when I punched his keyless ignition and saw all those cockpit lights zap on, ohmygod. I won't say what I could here, because it would be X-rated. If this car could talk, he would have a voice like Barry White. And he'd say, "Come on, baby. I'm taking you for a ride you'll never forget. Fasten. Your. Seatbelt."

This car's name is Barry. Yes, I even name rentals. If I'm going to ride someone, he's going to have a name.

I put my sunglasses on and I gripped that shift and I hit the gas and I became a different person. If someone was beside me at an idling stoplight, they received a quirked eyebrow and an Elvis sneer.

I'm younger in this car. I'm sleeker. I'm sexier. I'm BADASS. And when I hit the gas, baby, I'm leaving you in the dirt.

God help me if I ever drive a Porsche or a Mercedes.

Don't worry. I'm still me. But until at least Tuesday, I'm Barry's ride. I'm the best ride that he ever had. Oh, yeah.

And yes, that helps. Despite. Anyway.

### MARCH 20, 2017

And so today's moment of happiness despite the news.

So how do I write about a moment of happiness when a 38-year old friend died suddenly and unexpectedly overnight in his sleep?

And how do I write about a moment of happiness when my daughter was unexpectedly and viciously attacked by her two best friends of many years, two girls we considered part of our family?

It's interesting that both of these things involve friendship, I suppose. And endings.

Okla and I were friends for several years. We never met face to face exactly – but we knew each other's faces from Facebook and the backs of our books. We talked frequently. Okla was a fabulous writer, a caring and compassionate teacher, a mentor and an advocate. And he liked to think. To ponder, to ruminate. We ruminated a lot. Our brains would steam.

Okla was never caught up in the herd mentality. He didn't accept anything at face value. If you said something, he checked it out. If he wondered something, he checked it out. Every word Okla spoke or wrote was weighed, measured, flipped over and back, and then carefully set down.

I appreciate that kind of thought and consideration. I appreciate his need to be real, to be thorough, to be painstakingly honest.

On the homefront, my daughter is hurting. After my own muck through adolescence, and watching three older children go through it, I am surprised with this fourth child that I'm surprised. We all want our children to have friends that are safe, supportive, an extension of family. I thought we had that with these two girls. They spent a lot of time in our home, at sleepovers that often extended to two nights or three, and I loved listening to them talk. And giggle. And wonder and explore. All three, Olivia and these two, had outrageous senses of humor and it was like being the audience at an improv theatre.

But all that changed with an online missive directed right at my daughter's heart. So cruel that my daughter wanted me to see it, and my first thought was that the account had been hacked and someone else was speaking for her friend. But no.

Somehow, I missed the red flags. Maybe the red flag was just the onset of adolescence. The second year of high school. Maybe. Either way, I ache right along with my daughter.

I lost my friend today. She lost hers.

So. My moment of happiness. Believe it or not, there are two of them.

The first: I remembered one of my last conversations with Okla. He'd written a review of Oddities & Endings, in which he compared me to Thomas Mann and Ivan Turgenev (whoa!). In private, he said to me, "You're such a weird writer. I can't quite place you. The Mann and Turgenev doesn't do it justice, but close. Bravo."

*You're such a weird writer.*

It made me laugh.

And there's the moment.

He made me laugh.

The second: Olivia, in the midst of her pain, asked me, "Mama, can I do a moment of happiness thing too? Like you do." She asked me in front of the whole Facebook world and everything.

And of course I said yes.

Sometimes, even though you work very hard to help your children, you end up helping them in the most indirect ways. Simply by being. By doing.

She and I will grieve our friends together. And we will witness our moments of happiness.

And yes, that helps. Despite. Anyway.

## MARCH 21, 2017

And so today's moment of happiness despite the news.

Well, today. Today is exactly five weeks after I finished writing the final draft of my seventh book. My fourth novel.

For five weeks, a copy of the book has sat beside me on my desk. On top of it is a little Christmas ornament of a Chatty Cathy doll. The ornament even has a string that you can pull and it has Cathy's authentic voice and phrases. Chatty Cathy figures heavily in this novel. She sat beside me during the writing. Now she waited with me.

And today, a contract landed on my desk, accepting it for publication.

Five weeks.

If you're a writer, you know that an acceptance within five weeks of finishing a book is unheard of.

So my guess is…the book's pretty damn good.

The parallels that show up in my life stagger me sometimes. Last week, I had three different students, all writing books, complain, "This is so HARD! This is so much WORK!" And they all talked about "flow", that ephemeral goal writers are supposed to strive for – hear a deep, dreamy, oval-sounding accent here: "Ooooooh, it just floooooooowed…like my breath onto the page…like my blood through my veins…ooooooh…"

Well, no. It doesn't flow. Chances are if you read something that flows, it originally sounded like a blender eating bricks.

What makes a real writer a real writer? They WORK HARD until it FLOWS.

I've worked hard. I still do. Sometimes, I think we equate "good" with "easy." It's not. I will be egotistical enough here to say flat-out that I'm good. I'm better than good. And it has never come easy. I'm good because I work at it. I'm good because I choose to work hard at it and make whatever it is I'm writing as close to perfect as I can make it.

And that's why there are six books and soon to be a seventh.

This moment of happiness? This one isn't poignant. It's not touching. It's not funny. I tried to shape it that way, I really did, but it just won't let me. You know why? You know what this is?

It's a CROW. I am CROWING. And goddammit, I am going to crow until I'm hoarse. I've earned it.

Seven books. It took me three years to sell my first book. It took me five weeks to sell this one.

Ohmygod. SEVEN.

And yes, that helps. Despite. Anyway.

## MARCH 22, 2017

And so today's moment of happiness despite the news.

This morning, I met via Skype again with my client, Joanna, a British journalist living in Israel. She taught me a phrase in Hebrew. *"Ani afa al ze."* She broke it down for me this way:

*Ani (I) afa (fly) al ze (on it)*

It means, she said, I'm crazy about it, I adore it, I'm wild for it. And in Joanna's own personal translation: I'm flying with it!

Such joy in the words. And I didn't know, in that hour with Joanna, that *ani afa al ze* was my horoscope. I was going to fly with it. My moment of happiness was the entire day.

First, I officially signed the contract for the sale of my seventh book, my fourth novel. I'd made the very difficult decision, with six books under my belt, to find a different publisher with the seventh. It's time for something new, but I was worried about how the search would go. It took me three years to sell my first book. But five weeks from the day I finished the new novel, a contract landed on my desk, offered by a publisher who was excited to have me.

Then, my husband, who lost his job four weeks ago, was offered a fabulous accounting position with a local theatre. He interviewed yesterday. He got the job today. Michael got his start writing radio drama. The idea of working in a theatre…oh, intoxicating.

This week started out in the worst possible way. The death of my young friend, only 38 years old. My daughter, experiencing the mean girl treatment at school. My daughter is going to be traveling soon, visiting Disney World with her high school orchestra. Before he lost his job, my husband and I considered going to Florida as well, staying close by, in case she needed us.

With the loss of the job, we no longer felt we could do this. The onset of the mean girl attack left our daughter vulnerable and we were even more anxious and considered removing her from the trip, even though that would likely feel, to her, like she was being punished.

I felt like I was being pulled apart by practicality and the need to be my daughter's safety net. That's what I am. I didn't want the net to be full of holes. It never has been before, and she needs to know it never ever will be.

Then today: the job. So now Olivia is going to Florida. And so am I. I will be where I need to be. Just in case.

A new book. A new job. The safety net packed and ready to go.

*Ani afa al ze.* I'm flying with it!

But there's still one more moment. In the mail today, there was an envelope, addressed to me with handwriting I didn't recognize. There wasn't a return address. The postmark was smudged. When I opened it, I found a pre-paid credit card. Stuck to it was a post-it note that read:

"Kathie, You have helped so many realize their writing dreams. Please let some of us help a bit now."

Michael turned to me and said, "You've got to know you're loved, dear."

And that's pretty much when I lost it.

I started this daily ritual, this moment of happiness, because of the Asshat in the White House. But you know what? Despite that, despite him and his orange crew, there are still so many good people in this country and in the world. If the Asshat builds a wall, there will be those who will help people climb over it, around it, under it. If he takes away a woman's right to her own body, there will be those who step in and restore respect and compassion. If he keeps insisting that this is going to be an only white, only Christian country, there will be many who raise their faces to the sun and shine who we really are, what we are really made of.

If there's a woman who feels pretty damn close to the brink of despair, there will be many who surround her - her students, her family, her friends, and absolute strangers - to help.

It looks like I have a safety net too.

I have never felt so loved. I'm flying with it!

*Ani afa al ze.*

And yes, that helps. Despite. Anyway.

### MARCH 23, 2017

And so today's moment of happiness despite the news.

I was out driving today when two sandhill cranes crossed in front of me. I took my foot off the gas to let the car coast as I watched the big birds fly across the highway and land in a field. I'm scared of birds, especially big ones, but when they're in flight, they feel like ballet to me. They're not scary in the air. They're powerful and graceful and stunning. For that moment, coasting in the car, I flew with them. I was uplifted. The hemi engine pushing me forward disappeared and there was only air and wingbeat and soar.

Let one land next to me, and it would be a whole different story. But today, all I had to do was admire.

It made me think of a legend someone once told me, that poets are carried to heaven on the backs of sandhill cranes. I've never been able to verify that, which makes me wonder if it was a spur-of-the-moment made-up legend. But still, I like the thought behind it

It does make me wonder what types of birds would carry fiction writers to heaven. Or memoirists to heaven. Or screenwriters or essayists. Why can't sandhill cranes carry all writers to heaven? Did they choose the poets? Did the poets choose them? Was the person who told me this a poet?

It's amazing to me how we constantly divide ourselves into teams, no matter who we are or what we're about. When I was in grad school, there was always a softball game during the summer residency. Poets Vs. Prose. Why? Why were we separated like that, isolated, made into opposing teams? It was a bit confusing for me, a writer who writes it all. Where was I supposed to go? What part of myself was I supposed to ignore?

So I never played.

Boys vs. girls, men vs. women. Academics vs. laypeople. White collar vs. blue collar. Black vs. white vs. Hispanic vs. culture after culture after culture. Upper class vs. middle class vs. lower class. Democrat vs. Republican, liberal vs. conservative.

When you think about it, our gym teachers had it right. We lined up and counted off for teams. One, two, one, two. Sometimes, you tried to count ahead and friends would arrange themselves so that they would be on the same teams, but gym teachers tended to catch that. So you ended up on a team at random. Well, except for those awful gym classes where captains were chosen and you had to wait for your name to be called. I hated that. But the number game? That was all right. You weren't thrown together for any beliefs or qualities or lack of beliefs or lack of qualities. You just were. Next time around, you could be with a whole other group of people.

Remember the experiment every well-meaning teacher did at some point? Divvying up people by the color of their eyes and then making one eye color feel deficient? Like the one-two count-off, that just hasn't seemed to carry over into our adulthoods.

I like being part of a group, when I don't feel that the group is shutting anyone else out. One of my favorite type of human interest stories to read is where one type of animal raises another type, because that's just the right thing to do. Those always make me happy.

I guess wanting to think of everyone as just one big team where members serve different roles at different times for the good of all is idealistic. So then I guess I'll be idealistic and not play when groups want me to choose one over the other.

If the sandhill cranes carrying poets to heaven was a spur-of-the-moment made-up legend, then I'm going to change it. Sandhill cranes now carry everyone to heaven. Birds carry everyone to heaven. Anybody can carry anyone to heaven.

We can all go to heaven, if we so choose. I'll choose, and I'll ask a sandhill crane to carry me. My friend Okla who passed away this week is in heaven. Whoever did so carried him reverently. And I bet he was welcomed.

And yes, that helps. Despite. Anyway.

### MARCH 24, 2017

And so today's moment of happiness despite the news.

Today, I announced yet another student landing a book contract. Successes earned by AllWriters' writers is a major source of joy for me, but this one really raised me up. From an earlier moment this week: *Ani afa al ze*. I'm flying with it!

I've known this particular student for fifteen years. I started working with her before I even had a studio. Before any of my books were published. Way back then, Gwen was smacked down hard by an agent. An ignorant, pretentious, mean agent who had absolutely no idea what she was talking about. But it profoundly affected Gwen. Knocked her off her pins. It took me years to get this amazing writer writing again, and years to get her submitting again. And now her novel is accepted. By the same publisher who is publishing my seventh book. We got accepted on the same day.

Yet instead of seeing a rush of glory from Gwen, I saw fear and self-doubt. She was afraid if she sent back the contract, she'd find out it was sent to her by mistake. An office error. She was afraid if she announced it, she'd jinx it, that it really wasn't true.

Any idea what it does to a teacher's heart when her lovely student emails after an acceptance and says, "I'm scared"?

So I announced it first. And she followed my footsteps.

But in all honestly, this is how it goes with writers. Writers are the most confounding combination of ego and crippling self-doubt that I've ever experienced. Think about it. Not only do we have the audacity to say, "I'm going to write a poem/story/essay/memoir/for God's sake, a BOOK!," but we do so because we think people will want to read it. But I can also tell you that the absolute truth is that while we say we're going to write that poem/story/essay/memoir/for God's sake, a BOOK!, and while we write it, we're thinking, Why am I doing this? Nobody will like this. This is absolute crap. I should quit. I'm wasting my time.

My role as a teacher, pretty much at an equal level with educating, is encouraging. Supporting. Saying yes, it's that good, yes, you're doing it right, yes, this is fabulous, no, you shouldn't quit, no, please don't burn the manuscript. Please don't jump off that cliff.

And as a writer, I say the same damn things to myself, all the time. Because all of those things I wrote two paragraphs ago, those awful things that writers say to themselves, I mutter to myself too. Even after seven books, hundreds of stories and poems and essays.

You know what? This same student who is scared said to me this week during our session, "So I can't figure out where your self-doubt comes from." Well, there's the pot calling the kettle black. But in this case, I'm not sure which of us is the pot and which is the kettle.

I had a happy moment, a giggle moment, earlier this week that I didn't write about. I was at a book festival meeting and my high school creative writing teacher was in attendance. While someone else was trying to describe my role to a new person, my teacher cut in and said, "She does what she does because she has gonads." (The giggle moment? My high school teacher said gonads!) Michael has often said I've got balls as well.

Now yes, I'm offended that a woman who is brave is said to have male parts. But beyond that, I take it as a compliment. Because I'm also that confounding mixture of ego and crippling self-doubt. But I also have balls (or a really strong vagina, as the case may be). And that's what's gotten me where I am, and that's what makes me reach out to others and give them a healthy dose of balls/vagina too, whether or not they naturally have them.

Seeing this student get back on her feet? My happy moment. I am hoping that my next happy moment will be when she tells me it's something she's earned and deserved.

By the way. www.allwritersworkshop.com. My studio makes me happy.

And yes, that helps. Despite. Anyway.

## MARCH 25, 2017

And so today's moment of happiness despite the news.

Today was all about my daughter. And music. And my daughter and music. Olivia was competing/performing in WSMA – the Wisconsin School Music Association – solo and ensemble competition. She played with the Waukesha South Symphony Orchestra, she did a duet with a cellist friend, and she soloed. A pretty intense day for a sixteen-year old musician. Especially one who has difficulty dealing with chaos and with noise.

Can you imagine being pulled toward something that also gives you the willies if it gets too loud, too discordant, too noises-from-everywhere-and-everything? And yet, anyone involved in the arts knows the pushme/pullyou of passion. You love to write, but the blank page makes you want to play solitaire. You love to paint, but that first splotch on the canvas that isn't quite the way you imagined it makes you want to go do your laundry. You sing, you dance, you act, and you love it, love it, love it, HATE IT, love it, love it, love it…

Now multiply that by a billion and you have the autistic artistic child.

Olivia has been drawn to music from day one. She loved musical toys, the radio, commercials with theme music, any children's program with characters who sang. We'd been told she would not speak, yet from her first day, she vocalized, mimicking our intonations and lilts. One middle of the night, this silent-but-not-really child belted out across the baby monitor:

"Bee boy, bee boy, eechagonnaboo? Eechagonnaboo eeday come foh yew."

The theme from Cops. Which Michael watched that day, with her playing on the floor. Listening.

Watching Olivia today, watching her all of her young life, I've been reminded of a priest from Sacred Heart Catholic Church in Cloquet, Minnesota, which I attended as a little girl. This priest bellowed at the congregation one Sunday morning, "Sing! I don't care how you sound! The good Lord gave you voices so you can sing! Raise'em up!" And I did and still do, every chance I get. Singing is a huge joy in my life. And now, music is a joy in Olivia's.

The violin is an extension of her heart. Her voice. It soars. She soars.

I think of all the moments we've had, the hard moments. Being told she'd be nonverbal. Fighting with her to get her to eat because she hated anything in her mouth. I cried over so many meals. Telling her preschool teacher that we fully intended Olivia to live a full life, go to college, be whoever it is she wants to be, and being embraced and told, "Well, we can always dream, can't we."

Oh, we've dreamed. This child is a dream. This isn't a moment of happiness; it's a lifetime. Hers and mine and her father's.

A couple years ago, I combined National Poetry Month and Autism Awareness Month (both in April) and committed to writing a haiku a day. My favorite:

*I look at my girl.*
*I don't see Autism. I see a Miracle.*

Today, I watched that miracle stand in front of a judge, calmly introduce herself and her piece of music by Handel. She talked about what she learned. And then she played. She let it rip. Holy, holy, holy cow. Holy moment.

When she got home, she changed into a shirt. On the front, it says, "I Can And I Will." And on the back, it proclaims, "Watch me."

Oh, I am.

And yes, that helps. Despite. Anyway.

## MARCH 26, 2017

And so today's moment of happiness despite the news.

I look forward to Sunday morning all week long. Sunday morning for me typically starts in the afternoon, because I don't set the alarm and I often don't wake up until noon.

I don't rush to get ready. I don't rush to get dressed, to fire down a breakfast, to get on the computer. Instead, I stagger down the stairs, turn on the fireplace, get a nice hot cup of coffee and two doughnuts. I grab certain sections of the newspaper and I fall into my recliner. Certain articles get read to Michael when I'm ready to talk, which isn't usually until at least half of my cup of coffee is gone. The rest, I hug to myself.

The paper is read in a certain order. Comics first. Then the Tap section, which contains news of the arts and books. Then Fresh, which has recipes and

The Home Of The Week. And finally the Real Estate section, so that I can see what houses and condos have sold in Waukesha and for how much. I have no idea why that interests me, but I've always read it.

It's a routine of comfort and familiarity. And it's the only day of the week that I don't hit the ground running.

This morning, I woke at just before noon to the sound of rain falling. A lot of rain. Again. I lay there for a while and listened. Then I woke Michael. He has an important role on Sundays. He gets downstairs before I do and walks the dogs, picking up the Sunday paper from our stoop on his way back in. Because of this, my Sunday mornings are seamless and flawless...the paper waits for me on the counter. Still lying in bed, I listened to Michael talk to each cat, and each cat talked back. He talked to the dogs through the security gate and they talked back too. Michael is a morning talker. I am not, not until I have that coffee. As a result, he and the animals have entire conversations before I gather the energy to mutter a word. When he went downstairs, I got up and did what I needed to do before my own descent.

But he came back with dire news.

"The paper's soaked!" he called upstairs. "It was thrown into a puddle."

I was aghast. It made my voice croak into action pre-coffee. "Wasn't it wrapped in plastic bags?"

"It was. Soaked through. Every section. I don't think you'll even be able to read it."

Oh, no.

My day ruined, I consoled myself with the fact that everything else was intact: the coffee, the doughnuts, the fireplace, the recliner. I could read a book. I could.

Blech. I love books. But not on Sunday morning. Comics. Tap. Fresh. Real Estate. Dammit.

I went downstairs and got my coffee and my doughnuts and I turned on the fireplace. Then I turned to the counter to retrieve my book. The counter where normally on a Sunday, my paper waited. Something I waited for too, all week long.

My book was there. So was the soaked-through newspaper, a sodden mess of bleeding ink and pages that were impossible to turn. And...another one. Another newspaper! Perfectly dry. Perfectly crisp. All there.

Michael ran next door to Walgreens. He bought me a whole new newspaper, before I even got downstairs.

Hot coffee. Two doughnuts. Fireplace. Recliner. Comics. Tap. Fresh.

Real Estate. A loving husband who knows me better than I know myself. Happy moment.

And yes, that helps. Despite. Anyway.

## MARCH 27, 2017

And so today's moment of happiness despite the news.

Six weeks ago tomorrow, I finished my new novel, *In Grace's Time*. Last week, I celebrated its acceptance for publication, a scant five weeks after completion. Which was wonderful.

But there was something else going on too, that didn't sit with me so well. The day I wrote "The End" on that page was the day I stopped writing. Well, other than these little Moments. I just stopped.

It wasn't writer's block, which I don't believe in. In almost 21 years of teaching, I've learned that when a student says he or she has writer's block, they're actually editing a piece out of existence before it even draws breath. They start to write, mutter, "That's stupid," and hit delete. And again and again. At the end of the day, they say, "I didn't get any writing done. I must have writer's block." No…you just didn't give yourself a chance.

But this was different. I had plenty of ideas. I sat down to write. Sometimes, I put down a sentence or two. But I didn't say, "That's stupid," and hit delete. I said, "I really don't feel like doing this." And I walked away. Sometimes, I didn't write a sentence at all.

I've had times of not writing before. Usually, after finishing a big project like a novel, I give myself a week off. But when that new week comes around, I'm back at it. Sometimes, I've just been flat-out mad, usually at the publishing industry, and I quit. But after smoldering for a couple days, I'm back at it. But that wasn't this.

This time, I really, really just had absolutely no desire.

Writers tend to define themselves by, well, writing. If you're writing, you're a writer. If you're not, you're not. I usually cut myself and my students more slack than that. Writing is a pretty intense thing. You tap into places in your brain that you didn't even know existed. And if you're a fiction writer, you tap into lives that aren't your own, experiences that aren't your own, feelings that aren't your own. No, fiction is not a writer's sneaky way of writing about him or herself. Quite the opposite. At a book festival, I led a panel on writers crossing from a different genre to fiction. A poet writing a first novel said, "All fiction is based on the writer's real life."

Nah. Not even close, baby.

The best thing about being a fiction writer, and also the most exhausting, is that you get to be everyone but yourself. You get to be in life after life after life. You get to learn things you didn't know, understand things you didn't understand, feel things that would never occur within your own lifetime. Oh, amazing.

And I was beginning to wonder there for a while if I was done. Was I tapped out? Wrung out? Was the energy gone, the imagination gone? The need, the desire, the passion? Gone.

Yeah, well.

Today, I wrote. Nine glorious pages of a new novel. A new novel which has to be called something different because the new novel is the one I just finished. And I wrote these nine pages despite:

1) Going to get a copy of the new novel made to mail to a blurber, and having the guy behind the counter at Office Depot have such a case of MondayMorningItis, it took almost an hour.

2) Taking my car to have its emissions tested, it passed, bringing it home, going online to pay the fee and discovering I brought the wrong car in. Get in the right car, rinse, repeat.

3) Interruption here, disruption there.

4) Sat down with an hour before I started meeting with clients. And I wrote.

And yes, that helps. It ALWAYS helps. Despite. Anyway.

### MARCH 28, 2017

And so today's moment of happiness despite the news.

For Christmas last year, I asked for a DNA kit from Ancestry.com. I was curious. I've always been told that I was half German, a quarter French and a quarter Irish. But there are some questionable things in my family tree and so I decided I wanted to know. When that particular present didn't show up under my tree, I went ahead and ordered it on my own. I dutifully spit and drooled into the little test tube – do you have any idea how many times you have to spit to gather approximately a quarter teaspoon of saliva? And then I mailed it off and settled down to wait for my results, some six to eight weeks hence.

While waiting, I've begun paying attention to the commercials for the DNA discovery. The recipients are all thrilled with their results, and they're all super tuned into their "cultures". But I haven't seen one yet where the person found out they were more than twenty-something percent...something. They're all excited, talking about learning everything they can about their "culture", about who they are, trying on costumes and learning languages. Even if they're still three-quarters something else. They all act as if they weren't who they were before this test.

Weren't they?

I want to know what I'm made up of, how gene after gene came together throughout history and settled into me. But I don't feel it really will affect how I see myself, who I am. I don't even know that it should.

Recently, a new friend offered me the opportunity to have the I Ching read. I accepted. The I Ching is an ancient Chinese manual of divination, based on eight symbolic trigrams and sixty-four hexagrams, interpreted in terms of the principles of yin and yang. Some say it is the oldest book in history. I've never had this done before and I've always been interested, just as I like playing around with my astrological forecast and once had my numerology done. I read Tarot cards. And I go a lot by my intuition. So today, Scott and I met on the phone for an hour and he tossed those ancient coins. What came up was the Fellowship of Men hexagram.

Loosely translated, this means success upon crossing the great ocean, or the great water. It means I tend to do things for the greater good, I look beyond myself for how I can help others, I'm transparent and have no hidden agendas, I'm a leader and a role model. Hell, it means I'm just an all around nice person. I'll buy that. I thought of my student just last week saying that what makes me different is that I celebrate my students' successes just as heartily as I do my own. And it made me think of the "great oceans" that I've crossed. What I've survived. Building the studio. Persevering in writing. All in all, there have been a lot of oceans.

Just like there were oceans crossed by my ancestors who slid their genes down the web of time and tangled them all up in me.

But I am who I am, I think, because of my own beliefs, my own actions, my own thoughts, my own oceans. My "culture" is my lifetime. And I embrace it. Who I am today excites me just as much when I look in the mirror as those people on television looking at their reflections while wearing costumes from someone else's country, someone else's lifetime.

I received an email today, saying that there are delays in getting the results back from the DNA test because of high demand from the holidays. But that I should be patient, because I "will know who I am soon."

I already do.

And yes, that helps. Despite. Anyway.

## MARCH 29, 2017

And so today's moment of happiness despite the news.

Early this morning, when I finally finished work, I watched an episode of the Netflix show, *Grace & Frankie*, before going to bed. In this particular episode, one of the gay ex-husbands confesses that he thinks he's going to go to Hell when he dies – that he believes the Bible declares that homosexuality is evil and as such, he's going down instead of up. A friend who happens to be a priest soothes him by telling him his version of Heaven. He says he believes that the deciding factor is how people think of you. He gives the example of Hitler: a man who had great power and success, but who was ultimately hated, and as such, he's in Hell. Then he gives the example of Mother Theresa: a woman who was well-loved. Heaven.

I had the very odd moment of seeing my own emotion reflected on the actor's face. Relief. What a wonderful way to look at the Heaven or Hell question.

And maybe it means that if there's a Heaven and Hell, I'll be going in the right direction too. Which would be, you know, up.

I don't align myself with any organized religion. Nor do I roll my eyes up to the vast sky and sigh that I'm spiritual. I do call myself a Seeker. I don't know what I think, but I am thinking, considering, ruminating, and I'm okay with that.

Later today, after I'd slept like a normal person and then met with a couple clients, taught a class, went to the chiropractor to get crunched and molded into someone three inches taller, I sang along with Hemi's CD player as I drove into Starbucks. The song was Coldplay's "Viva La Vida". I stopped after I sang the lines, "For some reason I can't explain, I know St. Peter won't call my name." It's a line I've always sung with great gusto and sincerity. So there it was again. The Heaven/Hell question.

I thought again of the actor's face on my television screen in the first hour of day when the light is night, but the clock says it's morning. I thought of my own reflection. Relief. I thought of just last week, when an unexpected gift from a class of wonderful students arrived in the mail and my husband said, "You've got to know you're loved, dear." I sought out my own thoughts, even though I couldn't come up with any solid conclusions.

But so many people I know are going to end up in Heaven. Which means that Heaven is right here. Right now.

And yes, that helps. Despite. Anyway.

## MARCH 30, 2017

And so today's moment of happiness despite the news.

I returned today to the women inmates' book club at the Waukesha County Jail. This was my second time there and they were reading *Learning To Tell (A Life)Time*, the sequel to *The Home For Wayward Clocks*. As the women filed in, I saw some faces that I recognized and a few new ones. Especially noticeable to me was a woman who was still new to the jail the last time I saw her. At that first meeting, she looked exhausted and loose-ended. At one point, I heard her say, "I guess I should have brushed my hair today." From where she sat in the front row, her despair and disorientation just came to me in waves. But today, she was bright. She was the first to start talking – not only had she read *Clocks* and *Lifetime*, but she'd read *Oddities And Endings* too. Partway through the meeting, she had to leave to talk to her parole officer and she came back with news of being released on Tuesday. Her happiness waved from her in the same way her despair did just two weeks before.

There was another change too. I'd been given permission – by the women and by the jail administration – to ask the women questions. I had so many, but they were eager to talk about the book and we did. Their insights were down deep and heartfelt.

When the discussion slowed down, my escort told them that I was aware I could ask them questions too and she opened it up to me. I found myself telling the women about my experience at the Eastern Oregon Correctional Institute last summer. How I felt about those men. About the moment when I was surrounded by them and realized I wasn't afraid; I didn't feel like I was with beasts who'd performed violent crimes. I was just sharing my enthusiasm for clocks with men who knew how to make them. And they were happy I was there.

And then I told the women that I felt the same about them. Being there, talking to them, was no different than any book club I've ever been invited to. Not the ones in Waukesha or Brookfield, Shorewood or Sussex. The state of Oregon or in Minnesota. In libraries or private homes or coffee houses or restaurants. Or even, I predicted, when I skype into a book club in Israel in

May. They're doing *Lifetime* too.

I looked at these women and I said, "I see you. I don't see what you've done. I see you."

And suddenly, I had an entire group of crying women, including the escort. Tissues had to be passed. One woman, the only one in blue scrubs and not orange, said, "Thank you for giving us back our personhood."

Well, holy cow.

When the women left, they were duly reminded to dispose of their tissues – they could not take anything except the books with them back to their cells. I watched them go. I wished I could leave them with something – even though I think I already did.

As I waited for my escort in a different room, I noticed the clock on the wall. It was encased in a heavy wire barrier. Even the clocks were in cages.

When we treat humans like humans, that's who we get. But when we treat them like animals...

Oh, those women. They are often referred to as ladies or girls or females in that place, but I refuse. Those Women. On this gray and rainy day, they lit up my life. Under the fluorescent lights, the only light they receive, they were summer sunshine.

And yes, that helps. Despite. Anyway.

## MARCH 31, 2017

And so today's moment of happiness despite the news.

I posted on Facebook today: "That moment where you find out your daughter has to have a pair of khaki pants or capris for her trip to Disney World with the orchestra, and you were just at the mall last weekend to buy a swimsuit for same trip, but you know, no one could tell you about it then. That old 'By the way, I need two dozen yellow frosted cupcakes for school tomorrow' thing just keeps finding new ways of manifesting."

A friend commented that I should cherish these moments because they're gone too soon. So I tried, really, I tried hard to cherish a moment where I'm told I need to have something I didn't know about done yesterday. I pictured those faces, my sweet daughter's, my husband's (he attended the mandatory meeting two weeks ago where this need was brought up, and the only thing I heard about was that the meeting was totally boring). And I tried to cherish.

And I failed.

As I drove to the mall to find said khakis, drove during the time I usually reserve for writing, a time that was completely taken up this whole week by other things, I considered this. My thoughts rested on my older kids. They are 33, 31, and 30-in-a-little-over-a-week. Which means my big kids will all be in their thirties.

And I realized something.

I take great joy in my adult children. It's not that I don't look back on their young'un years with wistfulness from time to time. Remember having child-arms wrapped around my neck and child-legs around my waist, back when I had a waist. Sticky kisses. Whimsical mispronunciations. A time when firsts were in more abundance than lasts or agains. Times when only their mommy would do.

But I love talking to them now. Interacting with them on an adult level. Laughing with them just as I did when they were little, admiring them just as I did when they were little, and loving them just as hard if not harder. And thinking the whole while, man, I had a part in growing those!

These grown kids will always be my little boy, my little boy, my little girl. But now they are also and always my son, my son, my daughter.

There are still full-body hugs, sticky kisses, mispronunciations and firsts. From my granddaughter. I get my fix.

As for the child who sent me to the mall today…I'm head over heels for her too. But I look forward to the interactions with her that I have with my big kids now. She wants to be an art therapist. I imagine meeting her for coffee when she has a break between clients. I will have my grande cinnamon dolce latte, extra hot, and she will have her grande cinnamon dolce frappuccino. She'll tell me of her life and ask about mine. And when I watch her walk away, it will be with the knowledge that she's off to help someone, or to play her violin or paint a new painting. Or maybe even to work on her novel. As with the first three, I will think, I had a part in growing that!

I can pretty much guarantee that I won't look wistfully back to the day I had to run to the mall to buy khakis I should have known about two weeks ago.

But it's my enduring love for all four of them that gives me my moment of happiness today. That, and knowing there are still times when only their mother will do.

And yes, that helps. Despite. Anyway

# Chapter Four

## APRIL 1, 2017

And so today's moment of happiness despite the news.

Today's is a rough one to write, as it exposes a moment where I feel ashamed. But as this moment is what keeps playing in my head, I will follow through. It's a happy moment that springs from a low moment.

I've written about the issues my youngest daughter is facing at school. She's been abandoned by her social group and by friends she's had for years. Two girls at the core sent out the trumpet call to dump, and the effects just keep spreading. From her current friends at school to old friends she doesn't even see anymore, my daughter is getting messages on social media saying that she's no longer worthy of their friendship.

Call Mark Waters. It's time for a new *Mean Girls* movie.

For me, one image is stark. My girl, a sophomore in a large high school, is eating at a table all by herself in the lunchroom.

Her grades are amazing. Her talent in playing the violin, writing, and drawing incredible. But she's alone.

Today, Olivia read an earlier Moment from this week, the one I wrote on Heaven and Hell. When she was done, she asked me quietly, "Mom, will I go to Hell? If there is one?"

I was horrified. "Of course not! Why would you think that?"

She was quieter. "Because of all the people turning their backs on me."

That image, the lunchroom image, hit me hard right then. Every hackle went up. And I spoke out of pure anger. "No! You won't go to Hell. They will, if there is one. THEY will."

She gasped. "Mom!"

It was her turn to be horrified. By me. That I would think that, say that, about her "friends."

Which brought me to my moment. Through her reaction, I realized:

*I am raising a very kind daughter.

*I am raising a very compassionate daughter.

*I am raising a forgiving daughter.

*I am raising a girl who sees the good in all people, even when they are displaying their worst.

Which put all together, means this.

My daughter is now, and always will be, a better person than I am.

I understand that I was responding out of MamaBearness. My child is being hurt and there's not a damn thing I can do.

But Olivia, at the center of all this misdirected meanness, from her friends, and now from her mother, is still herself. It hasn't changed her.

She's going to be one hell of a woman. She's going to change the world.

And yes, that helps. Despite. Anyway.

## APRIL 2, 2017

And so today's moment of happiness despite the news.

My earliest memories involve dreaming. Dreaming of where I wanted to go, what I wanted to do, who I wanted to be. I've dreamed my whole life, even as I've lived it. And I've spent a lot of those years thinking that my dreams would always be dreams and I would always want to be somewhere else, want to do something else, want to be someone else. My dreams were impossible. Everyone told me that. But I dreamed them anyway.

All of my dreams, all of them, had something to do with writing. From the very beginning. Writing and dreaming felt synonymous to me. Words and the way they sound, the way they impact, the way they twist the mind around and create new paths, had me in thrall.

The dreams have definitely evolved. I wanted to be a children's writer when I was a child. I wanted to write fantasy when I was a teenager. I shifted to mainstream fiction when I was a young adult. And then, somewhere around the age of twenty-seven, the dream opened to literary fiction. It's pretty much stayed there, though I write other things too. When the dream calls for it.

Teaching dreams started in 1996. I was thirty-six. But the dreams still centered around writing. I was going to teach writing. And so I did.

From there, the dreams expanded to forming a writing community, rich in encouragement and support and realistic, concrete education.

I kept dreaming.

Today, I introduced a student at the debut of her first published novel. As I did, I looked out into the audience and saw several other students who had books already out, books soon to come out, books underway. I saw students who write poetry, nonfiction, and fiction, short and long, in every genre. I saw students from this class hug students from that class, onliners hug on-siters, and coaching clients hug workshoppers. And they all hugged me.

Then Michael and I went to the professional theatre where he's working now. We watched a phenomenal one-woman play and I was in thrall again. Every word that came out of that actress's mouth was written by a writer. A writer who was able to figure out how to keep an entire audience in thrall with just one actress, one setting, one continuous dialogue, no intermissions. Every word packed with meaning. Every word so well chosen.

In thrall. Amazing.

On the drive home, I realized that while I'm still dreaming, I'm also living the dream. Living the dreams, plural. I'm going where I want to go, I'm doing what I want to do, I am who I want to be.

I am who I want to be.

There is so much thrall in that.

And yes, that helps. Despite. Anyway.


### APRIL 3, 2017

And today's moment of happiness despite the news.

This morning, before my life broke loose in its usual way, things were quiet. My husband was at work. Olivia was at school. When I climbed out of bed, the only sound was my feet padding on the floor. I went downstairs and poured myself a cup of coffee and retrieved some breakfast. The dogs lifted their heads from the couch, but didn't say anything. The cats didn't say anything. There were no sirens passing outside, no buses either. No geese, no shouts from passersby, no muffled loudspeaker from the bus depot across the street.

No sound. No sound, no interactions, nothing, nothing at all, as I drank that first lovely cup of coffee.

I love my family. I love my life. But at heart, at my core, I'm as introverted as they come. Because of what I do, I've had to push myself, transform myself into extroversion. I am now comfortable speaking in front of large groups. I teach one on one, I teach workshops, I teach it all. I speak to readers, to book clubs, to audiences. And I'm okay with that. Within the family, Michael and Olivia are morning chatterers (and afternoon, evening, middle of the night, in their sleep...) – they start talking before they even throw the covers back. I don't say a word in response and I'm often tempted to throw my hands over my ears.

But this morning…the silence. Oh, that deep and simple silence.

Some people say, Oh, I can finally hear myself think. But in that silence before the day launches, I don't. Even the voices in my head stay mute. It's not like meditation. This is different. It's just suspended motion. Not of the body, I have to chug down the stairs to the coffeepot and back up. But the mind is just…still. Quiet. Thoughtful without words. There is only me and the air around me and the expectation of the day to come, but no rush to get there.

Silence.

Mother Theresa said, "We need silence to be able to touch souls." Lau Tzu said, "Silence is a source of great strength."

I do gather strength in the silence of the first moments of morning. And the soul I touch is my own.

And yes, that helps. Despite. Anyway.

## APRIL 4, 2017

And so today's moment of happiness despite the news.

When I finished teaching tonight, I was straightening up my classroom when my escort from my jail visits showed up. She brought me an envelope. In it were thank you notes, written by the women I visited last week, for the book club at the Waukesha County Jail.

My escort also picked up more books. The women want me back. We're doing *Enlarged Hearts* this time.

The women want me back. And I am so eager to go.

After my escort left, I sat down and looked through the cards right away. I didn't wait until I finished cleaning up or went to my office. I just looked.

They were all brightly colored with markers. Nobody wrote in black. There was purple and hot pink and red and blue and yellow and orange. All of these rainbow words just fell across my table. It was pitch dark outside, but my room sparked.

There was a card by the entire group and cards that were made individually. In the group card, one woman said, "You acknowledged things people over-see. We're just us people too." This same woman, in her individual card, talked about *Learning To Tell (A Life) Time*, and said, "So when you said, 'Can you love someone who hurt you so badly?', it hit me. I know how Cooley felt, maybe not to a T but very, very close."

I touched someone.

Oh my god. I have never ever wanted anything else.

But there was something else too. The colors on these cards. The colors in their words.

I know from a student who experienced prison that there are no colors there. Color is taken away. Everything is plain and drab. I know from these women that in the jail, there is also no natural light. No windows, no outdoor space. There is only fluorescent lighting. The women are only allowed access to colored markers under certain circumstances (like in a class) and under surveillance.

Having the opportunity to write thank you notes to me gave them access to color. Color to see, color to touch, color to create. Color to speak.

Imagine a world where colors are taken away. Imagine a world where there is no sun. Yes, the women are there because of something they did. I haven't forgotten that. But I also see their faces. And now I see their words. Bright. Sparked. They're just us people too.

For a certain time, under certain circumstances, under surveillance, I indirectly provided the women with color.

And yes, that helps. Despite. Anyway.

### APRIL 5, 2017

And so today's moment of happiness despite the news.

So it hit me today that it's April. Granted, it's April 5th, it's been April for five whole days now, so I should have already been aware of this. And I was, on a surface level. But today, April became real.

I can already hear my first daughter/third child saying, "Well, of course April is special to her. That's when I was born." And yes, she was, on the 8th. I've often said that Katie is my favorite because the child was born after only five hours of labor and before I even switched to heavy hee-hee-hee-hoo LaMaz breathing. The other three kids were 18 hours, 12 hours, and 19 hours, respectively. To be fair, I didn't need to do hee-hee-hee-hoo breathing with Olivia – I had that modern amazing invention, the epidural, with her. I slept. But she still took her own damn time getting here. Katie – easy peasy. I love that child. (As, of course, I love them all.)

But that's not why April hit me.

This April, the one in 2017, means that I've now been teaching for 21 years. 21 years! And it's become one of those weird sort of things – I feel like I've been doing it forever, but I just started yesterday.

21 years ago, I was 35 years old when I stepped reluctantly into my first

classroom. At the end of those two hours, I learned that I had a whole lot to learn. And I learned that I couldn't wait to learn more. And I learned that there actually was something else in this world that I could love almost as much as I love writing. I love teaching writers.

I mean, how many jobs do you know come complete with comments like these?

"I googled it and found out the word slut wasn't around yet. So I had to go back and throw in a whole bunch of whores. And I sprinkled some harlots in too."

"I really don't see anything wrong with a monkey eating a bowl of chili. I mean, they don't live on bananas."

"I can't wait to kill off this character. I modeled him after my fifth grade math teacher. And he's going to diiiiiiiiiiiiiieeeeeeeeeee! Horribly. Horrible, horrible. Oh, this will be fun."

April 1996 was the year I learned that a job can be a passion. It doesn't have to be something that you get up for in the morning, immediately count how many hours there are until you can return home, grumble through the day, then come home and try not to count how many hours before you have to go back. My day usually begins with my sitting on the side of my bed and listing in my head who all I get to see that day, who I get to talk to, who I get to work with, and what words they wrote. My day usually begins with looking forward.

Well, usually. I admit, I've dealt with a few clunkers. But that's not what I'm writing about.

I'm writing about April. And 21 solid years of teaching. 12 of them at the helm of AllWriters'.

I love what I do.

And yes, that helps. Despite. Anyway.

## APRIL 6, 2017

And so today's moment of happiness despite the news.

I don't think there is anything more frazzling than the day before a traveling vacation. And in our case, it's two people going to the same state, but different areas, and on different venues.

Olivia is going to Disney World with her high school orchestra, and another high school orchestra, and another high school band, and another high school chorus. They're taking buses. Many buses. 30 hours on a bus. 30 hours back too, if you're counting. We are drowning in instructions. What goes in the backpack on the bus, what goes in the suitcase under the bus, how to pack the instrument, what to do with drugs, even over the counter, what can they do on the bus, what can they do off the bus, what can't they do anywhere, what meals are covered with a meal ticket, what meals have to paid for individually, what app has to be downloaded, ohmygod, it's crazy.

While I figure this out, Olivia's freaking over her wardrobe.

I'm going to Madeira Beach in Florida, to the same hotel where Michael and I honeymooned, but I'm going without Michael. The original plan included the both of us, but then there was the job loss and then the job found, and you just don't say to a new boss, "Hey, thanks for hiring me, but can I take a week off?" So I'm traveling alone. While I get Olivia ready, I am also preparing myself. Boarding pass, check-in, upgraded the seats to the comfort zone, wondering if I really should have eaten those enchiladas the night before a flight.

And for me, there's something more.

This will be the first time I've really traveled since my assault two days after the election. I've not been able to travel, which has been more than frustrating as the assault did not take place while I was traveling. But the fear has generalized itself and I've been unable to talk myself onto a plane. Or to a place I've never been (or not been recently). Originally, I had the comfort of knowing Michael would accompany me.

But now I'm traveling alone.

It's important that I do this. I have possible appearances coming up that would require me to travel. I want to be able to do those.

It's important that I be in the same state as my daughter, who will be a two-hour drive away, just in case she needs me. It's important that I learn to let her go in little careful steps. Not for her. For me.

But it's most important that I get myself back. I need to be who I was before Thursday, November 10.

A student in my Wednesday Afternoon Women Writers' Workshop said this week that she loves reading the Today's Moments because she's enjoying watching my "transformation". I wasn't aware of transforming. Why do I immediately hear the Transformers' theme song: Transformers! More than meets the eye!

There's definitely more going on here than meets the eye. I'm opening mine wide. In fear, for sure. But also anticipation.

I look forward to meeting myself again. I look forward to whatever it is that's new.

And yes, that helps. Despite. Anyway.

## APRIL 7, 2017

And so today's moment of happiness despite the news.

It's weird, really, the way today's moment comes because yesterday's moment fell through. But it's okay that it did. And I'm figuring there's probably a lesson there. Happiness bends.

Yesterday, I was thinking that by this time today, I would be looking at an ocean and my daughter would be on a bus somewhere between home and Disney World. My anxiety was ramped, but I thought we pretty much had it all under control. Earlier, in the late afternoon, I'd told a friend that my gut level feeling was telling me I shouldn't go. And that my daughter shouldn't go. Something was off.

Then, late last night, my daughter finally admitted she didn't want to go on the trip. She didn't feel up to it. There were so many unknowns, and to the mind enhanced with autism, those unknowns can grow pretty big and powerful. Olivia was surrounded with those telling her that this was a marvelous opportunity, it would be fun, it would be exciting, it would be great…and all along, her gut was telling her that maybe this wasn't right for her, right now. So she did the bravest thing I've ever seen her do. She said no. She said I'm not ready. She put herself first.

We've always told her she knows herself better than anybody. And last night, she proved it.

And she taught me a lesson too. I also know myself better than anybody.

It's been a long hard winter for me, starting with the assault in November. For the most part, my life has gone back to normal. I walk the dogs around the block without thinking twice about it. I no longer lock the classroom door when I'm teaching. I don't look over my shoulder wherever I go. Every sudden noise is no longer ominous.

But getting on a plane? Still a bugger. And an illogical one, given that the assault had nothing to do with a plane. But it's still there.

This trip was quickly pushing me over the edge of overwhelm. Looking at it now, in the relief that comes from finding myself still in my home, I can't help but wonder what I was thinking. Taking on the fear by traveling completely by myself to a place I haven't been to in almost 18 years, a place I only visited once so it's hardly familiar, at a time when I was also anxious about my daughter…Not exactly the place to start, was it.

Healing takes time. I will return to travel. I've no doubt of that. But not right now. There is still more settling to do first.

So I planned this trip in order to be able to rescue my daughter, should she need to escape the external chaos of Disney. Instead, she rescued me from my internal chaos.

The friend I spoke to yesterday about my gut emailed me this morning, He said, "We talk about following our "gut instincts." In fact, the only other organ in the body with more neurons than the gut is the brain. It knows."

I knew. Olivia knew. How do we teach our children to listen to themselves? By listening to them. By listening to ourselves.

We're not staying home, by the way. On Monday, Olivia and I will drive up to the Mall of America for some retail therapy. It's a familiar drive, a familiar place, a great favorite for both of us. If we're lucky, it will be warm and we can take the convertible, Semi, and drive with the top down. We'll get a little bit of that hoped-for Florida tan.

Learning to listen. Internally. Externally. I'm taking the hard way, maybe, but I'm still learning.

And yes, that helps. Despite. Anyway.

### APRIL 8, 2017

And so today's moment of happiness despite the news.

My first daughter/third child turned thirty years old today. This means that three out of four of my children are in their thirties.

My fourth child is sixteen. So I can still say I'm the mother of a teenager.

Three out of four of my children are older than I was when I had them. By nine years, five years, and three years, respectively.

Olivia won't be older than I was when I had her until she's forty-one.

Which is way more math than I wanted to think about on a Saturday night.

But what this all adds up to is that I'm getting old(er).

Earlier this week, Michael and I were talking about someone he used to work for. He showed me this man's photo, and I said, "He's older than I thought he was."

"He's about sixty," Michael said.

"About my age then," I said. And instantly wanted to smack both hands over my mouth. (I'm 56.)

Over the last week, when I picked Olivia up from school, she had to move a plate from the passenger seat several times. I didn't have time to sit down and have lunch at home, so I made it, plated it, and brought it with me as I ran. Today, I not only sat down to eat, I read a book while doing so (I'm on a week-long break from the studio). I said to Michael, "I can't wait to retire." And then I wanted to smack both hands over my mouth again. (Still 56 – but I'll be 57 in July.)

Coming full circle, when Olivia and I went scrounging in Goodwill today, she found some crazy-looking capris and I found a shirt to go with them. She squealed, "It's so retro!" The capris look like they're from the 80s. The 80s are when I was having my first three children. Who are now in their thirties and older than I was when I had them. I'm used to having the decade I was a teenager be retro, but now my young adulthood has gone retro too?

Oh, dear.

But I realized something as I laughed with Olivia in the fitting room. I'm pretty okay with it. This getting older thing – it does come with lots of creaks and groans and pops in the morning (and the afternoon, and the evening and the middle of the night), more health concerns, brain blanks that drive me absolutely nuts (for example, I just forgot how I've been ending these Moments and had to go look at yesterday's to get it right), seeing my life go retro, but…it's all right. I'm comfortable with it. What many have said before me is starting to make a whole lot of sense now.

"It's better than the alternative."

I'm happy to be here. I'm happy to be alive. That isn't something I could have always said. But I can say it now.

And yes, that helps. Despite. Anyway.

## APRIL 9, 2017

And so today's moment of happiness despite the news.

Tonight, we returned to the professional theatre where Michael works to watch *The Glass Menagerie*. One of the perks of Michael's new job is we get free tickets! I love his new job.

At the end of the play, the character/narrator Tom, addressing the audience, talks about how in his travels, he found himself on the street late one night, looking into a shop where there are tiny glass bottles of perfume. This reminds him of his sister, and he turns from the audience to speak to her memory. Overall, it's a pretty sad ending. Nobody in the play seems to find happiness.

When the lights went up and we stood to go, Olivia said, "So…Laura ended up in a city, running a perfume shop?"

At first, we laughed and attempted to explain what the ending meant. But the more I thought about it, as we drove back toward Waukesha, I liked Olivia's interpretation better. In Olivia's mind, Laura, the fragile girl who loved her glass menagerie more than anything else in the world, ends up in a store where she is surrounded with glass. With reflections and refractions. With stories she could tell herself about each perfume bottle, bolstered by the exotic scents within. She could duck in a back room when she needs to, and interact with the world when it was within her ability and her desires. She would be surrounded by what she loves.

I like that ending.

We stopped on the way home at Denny's for a very late supper. As we ate, I noticed a young woman sitting all by herself. She was the only person alone in the restaurant. She was very pretty, with long blonde hair and high cheekbones, a careful nose, a gentle mouth. I wondered at her aloneness in a Denny's late on a Sunday night. I pictured sad things. Running away from a family. An inability to speak or communicate keeping her isolated. A new divorce, or suddenly dead parents. You know, things that someone like me tends to think of and imagine. Conclusions I leap to.

But as she waited for her meal, the young woman suddenly picked up her phone. Whatever she saw there made her burst into the prettiest smile. It was genuine and delighted. For the next several minutes, she texted furiously, and someone texted back, and at one point, she laughed out loud, there all by herself in the Denny's.

But she wasn't alone, was she.

So I decided she runs a perfume shop, surrounded by the delicacy of glass and aroma. She was on her way to a perfume conference, and she left behind a husband and young child, who were already missing her. The child was texting goodnight, the husband telling her what went on with their day without her. And she was laughing. I pictured her settling into her hotel room, smiling, knowing she was being thought of. Knowing she was loved. Even when she wasn't there.

My daughter can find optimism in a Tennessee Williams play. And with her help, I might be able to find it in myself.

And yes, that helps. Despite. Anyway.

And so today's moment of happiness despite the news.

I drove from Waukesha, Wisconsin to Bloomington, Minnesota today. I'm now in my hotel overlooking the Mall of America, that queen of American consumerism. But also a great vantage point for viewing our country's population. I know when we go there tomorrow, I will hear at least three languages, likely more. I will see all ages, all skin colors, all genders. There will be times when the noise and the crowd gets overwhelming and I'll have to find a quiet corner and breathe for a bit. But I'll be agog, mostly.

I traveled the whole way with a sixteen-year old in my front seat. I've traveled this way with another teenage girl too, and a teenage girl and teenage boys and a toddler Olivia, and with sons, daughters, and daughter-in-law. Oh, and don't forget husbands. Two different ones. And it's always been pleasant! Today, I gave Olivia the option of playing her own music in the car. She played one disc – Three Days Grace – and then demurred when I asked her to choose another. She likes my music choices. We listened to the Moody Blues, Linkin Park and Coldplay.

Even as I grew antsy with the long drive, irritated by the rain, one of those spitfalls that keeps you from seeing out the windshield, but if you put your wipers on, it just smears, I also felt my shoulders drop in relief and release. I am on a break. There was no screen in front of me. No radio, so we didn't hear any news. I have no idea what happened in the greater world today.

I know from glancing at Facebook that somebody got dragged off a plane. And that there was a school shooting that was apparently a murder-suicide. And a governor in Alabama resigned after being threatened with impeachment. When Olivia and I stopped at a McDonald's for supper, their television screens were showing this governor resigning. We chose a place to sit that was well away from the sound and the sight.

And so my shoulders stayed down. In relief. In release.

I remember many times coming here as a break, as an escape. From work, from my everyday life. But today, I turned my back on the news. And that's where the relief and release comes from.

From now until Friday, I plan to shop at the big mall with my daughter. To come back to the hotel at night and soak in the hot tub. To work on my new-new book (as opposed to the new book, which will be released in September). I'm going to pretend that I don't know who is president, who is vice-president. I'm going to pretend I don't know what's going on in the world. I'm going to pretend to be ignorant and uncaring.

I'm going to breathe deep.

I won't actually stop caring, you know. And I won't be ignorant. But I've heard that ignorance is bliss, and there hasn't been any bliss, really, since November. So I'm going to be blissful. For now. And I'm going to remind myself that despite what's going on in that greater world, and despite its direct or indirect effect on me and mine, I have a lot to be blissful about.

And yes, that helps. Despite. Anyway.

## APRIL 11, 2017

And so today's moment of happiness despite the news.

I picked up a couple bottles of water today at Cinnabon in the Mall of America. Yes, I only bought water at Cinnabon. The woman behind the counter admired my purse, which looks like a clock. A friend saw it and told me about it, saying that I had to have it. And I did.

The Cinnabon woman said a friend of hers collected clocks. I said I do too. She said her friend had about eighteen. I said I have over sixty in my living room and kitchen alone. She looked dumbfounded – most people do. I told her my first novel was set in a clock museum.

"You're a writer?" she said.

I agreed with that and we got into a discussion about books. All over the purchase of two bottles of water. She loves to read, she said, which just did my heart all sorts of good. She said she wants to read The Home For Wayward Clocks and give it to her friend who collects clocks. I gave her my card.

And then I said, "My seventh book will be released on September seventh."

It wasn't the first time I've said that. It won't be the last. But for some reason, saying it right then and there just knocked me over with joy. Those characters, housed between what will be two covers, are going to see the light of day. They're going to live outside of my head. They're going to live inside of other people's minds and imaginations.

And for heaven's sake…it's my seventh book. My seventh!

My first book was accepted the year I turned fifty and was released the year I turned fifty-one. Clocks happened the year I was prepared to give it all up. I mean, if something hasn't happened by the time you're fifty…

But then it did.

There is so much emphasis on youth in our world. In every industry, in every advertisement, in every, well, everything. Even in publishing – I see magazines all the time touting Twenty Under Twenty or Thirty Under Thirty. I think I saw Forty Under Forty once. After I was forty. But fifty? We see long-time established authors at fifty and beyond. We see memorials to them and tributes to them.

I really was well underway by fifty. Stories everywhere. But the book? Oh, the book wasn't looking too certain. I'd been through four agents, two of them top-notch New Yorkers. But nothing. And no, I was not going to self-publish. If it was going to happen, it would happen the way I dreamed it would. Dreamed it since my first publication at fifteen. Kinda fun, isn't it, that my first publication ever was when I was 1–5, and my first book was when I was 5–1.

But that's how it happened. When I was ready to give up.

And now…my seventh book will be released on September seventh.

Just imagine what can happen at sixty. Or at seventy.

I do.

And yes, that helps. Despite. Anyway.

## APRIL 12, 2017

And so today's moment of happiness despite the news.

Today was day 2 of a spring break trip to the Mall of America with my daughter, Olivia. Every time I've visited the big mall before, I've glanced at the ads and the entrance to the aquarium. But we've never gone. What kind of aquarium could be in a mall? In Minnesota? I pictured something small, something limited.

Wrong.

Olivia and I ventured down the escalators to the bowels of the Mall of America. And there it was. Tunnels led everywhere. Overhead, sharks and stingrays and strange, strange creatures swam. On the other end of the spectrum, there were teeny seahorses and surreal jellyfish.

Honestly, it was way more than I expected. We took a back-scenes tour and got to see everything from above all the tanks. Very cool.

But by far, our favorite spot was the large stingray pool. To say they move like birds in the sky is cliché, but that is what they do. Blue of the sky, blue of the water, fins, feathers, they're so much alike. They even both have beaks, the birds and the stingrays. And they're graceful. Joyful. Determined.

And then there was this one. The stingrays were gray and silver. This one, this different one, was brown.

All of the stingrays were going in one direction, a delighted flapping freeway underwater. Zipping, zooming, passing each other. But this one? The big brown one? He insisted on going the other way. Against the flow.

There were no collisions. He just skimmed over the others and they kept on going. If they could have laughed and shrieked, they would have. Maybe they were.

Every time Big Brown went by, I called, "You're going the wrong way!" and my daughter laughed.

I've gone the opposite way plenty of times. And not necessarily with this brown guy's grace and gentle cooperation. And not with the acceptance that these stingrays showed for their big brown rebel.

The last time we saw him, and I called to him, Olivia laughed, but then said, "He's okay. He's going his own way. There's nothing wrong with being different."

Got that right, little girl. And I am so glad that at sixteen, she still feels that way. This age when everyone wants to be the same. This age that seems to stay with us.

I like being a big brown stingray. Doing what I do, I'm surrounded by other big brown stingrays going in every which direction. But we have that gentle cooperation. I encourage it. I teach it. And in Olivia, I raise her up.

"There's nothing wrong with being different."

And yes, that helps. Despite. Anyway.

### APRIL 13, 2017

And so today's moment of happiness despite the news.

This week, I've worked hard to be ignorant by choice – a five-day rebellion in which I turn my back on the news and just focus on having fun with my daughter at the Mall of America. But there was no way I could avoid the headlines this morning. There they were, when I signed on to the internet.

Trump drops the Mother Of All Bombs on Afghanistan.

At first, I wondered about the colloquialism, and about the use of the capital letters. But then, as I reluctantly read the article, I found that this particular bomb is called exactly that – the Mother Of All Bombs. MOAB.

It was hard to turn an ignorant-by-choice back on this one. But I tried.

After two solid days of shopping, I was aching and the thought of any more extended periods of walking made me ache more. So we decided to go to the Mall of America's amusement park instead, housed in the middle of the mall, with the four floors of shopping and entertainment rising around it. We bought an all-day pass for Olivia and then wandered from ride to ride which Olivia rode and rode and I watched from a bench. Thoughts of the MOAB and flashes of photographs from the events I learned about in history classes throughout my schooling came to me at odd times throughout the day. Those photographs. The ones we all know. The mushroom cloud, of course. The Napalm girl in Vietnam. The raising of the flag in Iwo Jima. Even Kent State. And in those times when those photographs crossed my mind, I had to push aside fear. I had to focus instead on what was in front of me.

People having fun. Families having fun. Children who just couldn't walk, but had to skip, jump, gallop beside their parents. A mom whose child wandered away being reunited, and Mom hugging the child even as she scolded. "I was so scared when I couldn't find you!" Middle schoolers getting just so far in a line for a ride, but then backing out. "It's too scary!" My own daughter, whimsically reunited with her favorite carousel animal, the chicken, which she rode and rode during a family visit to the mall when she was only a toddler. All five of us, Mama Daddy, big brothers, big sister, had to take turns with her on it, as she couldn't ride alone. Her feet didn't even reach the chicken's stirrups then. Now, she could touch the floor with her toes and she didn't need me to stand next to her, one hand around her waist, as she spun. There was no fear. Not on the chicken, anyway.

I don't want there ever to be fear. For her.

But the other rides. Over and over, I watched her scare herself on roller coasters, log rides, weird flying and twirling contraptions that spun and whipped her body around.

Over and over, I watched families scare themselves and then walk away hand in hand. Skipping. Jumping. Galloping.

Over and over, I watched my daughter scare herself, and then laugh in exhilaration.

Over and over, that made the pictures in my own head seem not so scary.

And yes, that helps. Despite. Anyway.


### APRIL 14, 2017

And so today's moment of happiness despite the news.

I was driving home today from the Mall of America. I had a powerful car under me and around me and I had my daughter next to me in the front seat.

We were both singing to Coldplay and she was patting her new plushie dog because there's still a little girl inside of her, despite all the growing up she's been forced into this year. We were singing, together. She was playing. The car was humming. And it wasn't raining.

So things were already great when I crested a hill and plunged headfirst and hood-first into one of those moments, THOSE moments, where the whole world opens up and your mind opens up and before you is the fresh glory of this great earth the greening of spring winter's golden brown patches the blue of the sky streaked with oncoming summer stubborn fall leaves still gripping branches and there it was the whole year your whole life laid out in the downfall of a hill and the purr of an engine your child singing beside you and you just know then, in that moment, in that very moment, that all those other moments those OTHER moments that ripped out your ribs tore your thighs broke your fingers broke your heart despite those OTHER moments it's all worth it it's all worth it You sing.

You sing.

One moment. Supreme. Epic. Down the slide of a hill in Wisconsin.

And yes, that helps. Despite. Anyway.

### APRIL 15, 2017

And so today's moment of happiness despite the news.

Even though today was a Saturday, it was still my first day back from a break and it was filled to the brim. Because that's how I roll. I went from haircut and hair color (have a photo shoot on Tuesday) to teaching a class for three hours to running out to buy a new rug for my office which necessitated rearranging my office (kinda like how buying a new shirt means you have to buy new pants, shoes, jewelry…), to getting the third floor deck set up for spring and summer. It was a glorious day, weather-wise. Temps in the middle seventies. Sunshine. Maybe, maybe, maybe winter is over.

While I was outside on the deck, shoving the bar table here, the stools there, the rocking chairs here, the angel statue there, my Lady Big Butt fountain here, I suddenly heard something. I stopped to listen, then moved to the railing and leaned on it.

Across the street, in the Metro Station, a young man was playing the piccolo. From three stories up, I could see him, walking loosely around a bench, playing, waiting for his bus. The sound of the piccolo rose larger than life in the acoustics of the bus garage. The echo reverberated from the mechanics of music, but also from emotion, and the song was sweet and gentle. It blended with the city birds and the traffic and distant sirens.

I bowed my head. I listened.

Michael joined me after the young man finished his song. I thought he left, that his bus came and took him and his blessed instrument away. Michael helped me finish the deck and when we were done, we sat in the rocking chairs. The breeze was steady and cool and it was quiet. As quiet as the city gets, anyway.

We rocked for a few minutes. And then Michael said, "I love it here."

From the bus garage, piccolo notes, and a young man's heartfelt song, rose again.

Me too.

And yes, that helps, Despite. Anyway.

## APRIL 16, 2017

And so today's moment of happiness despite the news.

There was so much I wanted/needed to get done today. Manuscripts needed to get read and critiqued. Rides needed to be given. Laundry had to get done. Errands weren't going to run themselves. I wanted to watch the new episode of the only television show I watch. And I wanted to meditate. And I wanted to go for a walk on the Fox Riverwalk. I hadn't been on the Riverwalk since winter set in, and it was warm today, and I really wanted to get out.

All of which led to one colossal case of the grumps.

Eventually, I decided to sacrifice the television show for the walk. It was better for me, I reasoned. Fibromyalgia is a conundrum; moving hurts, but moving also helps to decrease the pain. So – I needed to move.

As I pulled into the parking lot, a bubble appeared out of nowhere and floated over the hood of my convertible, Semi. I instantly smiled, but the case of the grumps continued. I kept playing in my mind the list of things I should be doing. It extended to all the things I need to get done in the week ahead, and the grumps began to include a dose of overwhelm. The bubble floated away and it took my smile with it.

I parked the car and began to walk. Within a few steps, I met up with a woman who was plugged into her earbuds and talking to someone on her phone. We were going different directions, but we nodded at each other as we passed.

Then I turned my attention to the whispering water, to the trees and the ducks, the geese, the robins and the red-winged blackbirds, all the things that I so love about this place (even though I'm terrified of birds). I thought of the things I'd heard about moving meditations and so I tried to lower myself into a meditative state, thus accomplishing two things on my to-do list simultaneously. As thoughts bubbled up, that's just what I did to them, encased them in a bubble like the one that crossed my hood, and I floated them across the river.

And I felt myself relax. I listened to the birdcalls, the water-ripple of conversation, the leaves in the trees. I created bubbled and floated them and felt lighter with their flight.

On the opposite side of the river, I was approached again by the earbud-wearing woman. I could hear her voice, still talking on the phone. But when we got close, she suddenly reached up and tugged her earbuds out.

"You," she said, "are definitely an angel."

I was startled. I thought maybe she was still talking to someone on her phone, but her earbuds were out and she was looking right at me. Then I realized she was referring to my shirt. I wore a t-shirt, black, and in bold white letters, it said, "#ImNoAngel". I laughed and said, "Oh! Thank you!"

She laughed back and shook her finger at me. "You glow!" she said. "You glow!"

And then we went our separate ways. My grumps and overwhelm? Gone. My stolen smile returned. It stayed with me all the way back to my car.

Oh, stranger-woman on the Riverwalk, you have no idea how you made my day.

I glow!

And yes, that helps. Despite. Anyway.


### APRIL 17, 2017

And so today's moment of happiness despite the news.

This morning, there was a surprise in my email box – an invitation to be the guest reader at a local university's launch of the annual issue of their literary magazine. Last year, I was a visiting author in a couple of the creative writing classrooms, and I really enjoyed meeting and working with the students. Now, they wanted me there at the launch of their magazine.

Then in my snailmail box, another surprise – an invitation to attend the recognition ceremony at the Waukesha County Jail, which includes several of the women inmates I've met through the book club. Some of the women have earned their GEDs. Others have completed self-improvement workshops or learned English as a second language, or completed classes helping them to become employable. Now, they wanted me there to witness their achievement.

In both cases, a graduation of sorts. In both cases, a connection through words and literature. And in both cases…vastly different situations.

I am supremely happy to be there.

Celebrations of learning, celebrations of changing, celebrations of moving forward – celebrations of hope and determination. The students and the inmates prove that it's possible to do the impossible. Write a story, a poem, a memoir, that others want to read and that a magazine wants to publish. Break an addiction. Right a wrong. Learn to control anger, to raise a child properly, to step away from an abusive relationship, to reach out for help when help is exactly what's needed.

To connect through words. Through writing, in one group. Through reading, in the other. Learning took place in both.

And in me.

In an afternoon email, I found out that a story of mine was accepted for publication. It's a story I wrote about a woman with a hamster mind who wants to learn how to meditate, yet fights it at every step. In the end, she falls into the sky and learns what she intuitively knew how to do all along. She learns to trust herself and her own interpretations.

It's one of the few stories I've ever written based on my own experience. It's a story about how I learned.

I will attend these two celebrations within a couple days of each other. I will immerse myself in others' immersion in learning. I will shake hands, grasp shoulders, hug, pump my fists in the air. Celebrate!

Where there's openness to learning, there's growth. And where there's growth, there's hope.

And yes, that helps. Despite. Anyway.

## APRIL 18, 2017

And so today's moment of happiness despite the news.

Last week, during our trip to the Mall of America, a song came across the speakers in Ragstock that I hadn't heard in years. As the gently jiving rhythm insinuated into my memory and my veins and my bones, my body also slid into what it was in 1987. My head began the side to side sway, the hips rocked, and I was twenty-seven years old. Pregnant with my third child in four years. Fertile. Sensual. Woman of all five senses and an additional sense, a sea sense, a connected to the earth sense.

Olivia's response: "What the hell is that?"

"That's Heart and Soul," I said. "By T'Pau. Ohmygod, I love this song."

And I loved who I was then. My belly full of baby, rocking with me, two other little ones holding on to my thighs and swaying by my side. My arms wrapped around that unborn child and we danced around the living room and my boys danced with me. Free. Unafraid.

I was All Woman. Populating the world.

"Yuk," Olivia said.

When we returned home, I ordered the CD. It came today. I only play CDs in the cars these days, so I waited until it was time to pick Olivia up from school. The CD went in. I played the song three times on my way to school. Three times on my way back, despite the curled lip and wrinkled nose of the girl next to me. I dropped her off and continued on my way to Starbucks. Two more times until I turned it off when I got to the speaker.

"Your usual, Kathie?" my favorite barista called out.

"Yes, please." I was fourth in line. There were at least two other cars behind me. I was in the convertible. The CD went back on. Volume up.

And I was twenty-seven again.

The line moved slowly. I didn't care. My body jived in my heated leather seat. Then I noticed the head in the car in front of me, bobbing. In sync. I looked in my rearview mirror. More bobbing. Windows slid down.

We were all twenty-seven again. I felt it, felt the music, felt all those around me, felt the young and unabashedly sexual woman I used to be. Felt the promise of the future.

When the song was over, the woman in the car behind me poked her head out the window. "Hit replay!" she said.

From the speaker now behind me: "Yes, please." My favorite barista is only in his early twenties. I knew there was a reason he was my favorite.

When I swayed my way to the window, he handed me my iced grande cinnamon dolce latte. He jerked his head backwards. "You did this, you know."

I looked. The other baristas swayed from counter to grinder to customer.

"On the house," he said.

I jived all the way home. Two more times. I'm fifty-six again tonight. But tomorrow...I will be twenty-seven.

And yes, that helps. Despite. Anyway.

## APRIL 19, 2017

And so today's moment of happiness despite the news.

Today's moment is about happiness, and empowerment, and relief.

My daughter Olivia has been experiencing school bullying through social media sites over the last several weeks. This was a devastating experience. Awful, hateful posts kept appearing on a variety of the sites that she and others her age frequent. I felt helpless; how do you fight the internet?

That helplessness came from an orientation five years ago, when Olivia was in sixth grade. The principal of the middle school told us that if we allowed our children on social media and bullying occurred, there was nothing the school could do about it. I took him at his word. I took this as the truth. When this bullying started and I spoke with Olivia's caseworker and a teacher about it, the teacher turned to the caseworker and said, "And the school won't...?" and the caseworker just shook her head. And again, I took her at her word. I was helpless.

But things kept getting worse and worse.

So I finally decided to try my voice. To raise my truth. I sent the school a screenshot of one of the hate posts. I explained that this was what Olivia was being subjected to, and that while it was on social media, it was being posted with school property – the school-issued iPad. That made it a school issue, as far as I was concerned. I asked for help – I didn't demand and I didn't rant or blame – but I also said that if help wasn't forthcoming, we would be looking for a lawyer.

That was 48 hours ago. Today, all the girls involved have been spoken to and given disciplinary action (I don't know what that action is – I'm not allowed to know because of privacy issues). One of the girls offered up a flimsy excuse, trying to blame Olivia, but the school investigated and found absolutely no truth to her statement. I was told the girls are "very contrite." The posts have been taken down. And that since the whole thing is now part of school record, along with the screen shots, there will be "extreme discipline" if it reoccurs.

"Kathie," the assistant principal said, "it's stopped. It's not going to happen anymore. Please let me know if you or Olivia ever need anything else."

And at that point, my voice dissolved into tears.

Don't ever assume that you can't use your voice, even when you're told it won't do any good. Raise it anyway. Speak the truth. Not necessarily with loudness, but with firmness and with the power and knowledge of what's right.

Mama Bear didn't use her claws. She used her voice. She spoke the truth.

And yes, that helps. Despite. Anyway.

### APRIL 20, 2017

And so today's moment of happiness despite the news.

I personally hate the phrase, "When one door closes, another opens", or as some say, "When a door closes, a window opens". It's usually said with the best of intentions, but it's trite and sometimes, it makes me angry. I want to say, "Sometimes, when a door closes, it slams. It's nailed shut. And there's no other open door anywhere," or "When a door closes, a window opens so you can throw yourself out of it."

Despite writing these moments of happiness every day, I'd still call myself a natural cynic. The actual phrase comes from Alexander Graham Bell, and he said, "When one door closes, another opens; but we often look so long and so regretfully upon the closed door that we do not see the one which has opened for us." So maybe that's my issue. Maybe I just don't always see the newly opened door. But it does seem to me that sometimes, a closed door is a closed door. Bam. Logically, I can't imagine that some doors aren't forever.

But today felt like a newly opened door. It felt like open windows. It felt like June at five o'clock in the new evening. It felt glorious.

The day after a crisis ends, and ends favorably, every door and window opens. When I woke up this morning, my first thought was of my daughter. But it wasn't about worry and fear. It was relief.

She smiled yesterday. She laughed.

And I slept better than I have in a few weeks.

When the morning spooled away and I finished with my clients, I stood in front of my deck doors and looked outside. There was a storm last night and everything is everywhere on the deck. The chairs and table are knocked over. The umbrella is on the opposite side of where it should be. It was still cloudy and there wasn't any warmth today. There was a chill and damp in the air. The planters are still empty.

But I realized I'd gotten through the morning without glancing at the clock and wondering how my daughter was doing.

When I looked out the deck door again, the sky was blue despite the overcast. It was sunny despite the shade. And I saw us all sitting there, in June, with a picnic dinner, with corn on the cob, with hamburgers fresh from the grill, with a still-warm pie bought from a bakery waiting for dessert (I'm not going too Waltons on you – I don't cook. I buy pies, I don't bake them, except at Thanksgiving when I make a pumpkin and a pecan, and a pecan again for my son's birthday in March).

And my daughter was smiling again. Talking, talking, talking. Giggling over boys and dates and what-do-I-wears.

I smiled at the overcast day. I noticed the newly open door. I no longer wanted to throw myself out the open window.

Even a skeptic can be hopeful on the day after a crisis has ended.

And yes, that helps. Despite. Anyway.

## APRIL 21, 2017

And so today's moment of happiness despite the news.

Sometimes, good can come out of a bad back.

On Christmas Eve 2004, I ruptured a disk in my lower back when I bent down to lift my chihuahua, Cocoa, into my bed. That was bad enough, but a week later, on New Year's Eve, it exploded into sciatica involving the fifth sciatic nerve. Pain roiled from the base of my back, over my left hip, and all the way down my leg to my toes. I lost feeling in those toes for six months – I was told they might never recover. But they did, and so did I, and I have only suffered a few real relapses. Twinges, yes. Full-blown sciatica, only twice.

Today made the third.

I also deal with fibromyalgia. Consequently, the pain that hinted over my back and hip over the last week, which I blamed on fibro, was likely the warning signs of what was going to hit this morning.

I woke up with that pain, THAT pain, that makes the word pain not nearly enough. I couldn't walk, mostly hopping on my right foot and putting my left foot down only enough to keep from teetering over. Hello, sciatica. Walking and standing, impossible. Sitting, uncomfortable. Laying down, preferable. So I reintroduced myself to the medicine cabinet and muscle relaxers and even broke down to take Tramadol, which I never take because narcotics make me paranoid. Then I settled into bed with an ice pack and disturbing dreams.

Midafternoon, when the Tramadol gave me my brain back, but still kept the pain in a haze that seemed to float beside me, but not in me, I got up. I made it to my deck door and then decided it would be better if I took a break on the deck rather than making the long trek back to bed. So I sat down in a rocker and, not for the first time, wished I hadn't gotten rid of the hammock that used to be there.

But then I saw the sky.

The overcast disappeared today and the sun returned. The sky was a deep blue, that particular blue that is only for skies and not for oceans or lakes, though we assigned that blue to those when we still used crayons. It's the RIGHT blue. The BEST blue. The blue that SHOULD be called blue. And there were white clouds which I normally would call cliché, but on this day could only be called beautiful.

In the story that was accepted for publication this week, Sitting, I have this description (yes, I am about to quote myself):

*Oh, the blue. The vibrant and cascading soft blues of the sky. Wide. Flat. Lit somehow from within. Abigail opened her eyes wide into the blue and the blank and the entire world fell into her gaze. She leaned into the sky, slack-jawed, open-eyed, and fell thoughtless into the blue and the blue and the blue. For untold minutes.*

And that's what I did today, though I didn't lean into the sky. It leaned into me. And for untold minutes, I was pain-free.

I didn't have Tramadol for the rest of the day. I thought of the sky instead.

Oh, the blue.

And yes, that helps. Despite Anyway.

## APRIL 22, 2017

And so today's moment of happiness despite the news.

Today, as I was driving out of a parking lot, I was thinking about what I would write for today's moment. And it made me realize that my thinking has changed.

I'm looking for happiness now. I'm keeping an eye out. For heaven's sake, I'm expecting it.

As I've said before, I'm a skeptic, and I call myself a natural skeptic, though I honestly don't know if it's natural or not. I don't know if I was born this way or if the skeptical attitude came over time and experience. But I'm not usually surprised when bad news happens. I'm known as an edgy writer, a controversial writer, a disturbing writer. I'm okay with most of the descriptions given to who I am as a writer, but I've never liked being called disturbing.

Though at the same time, a student said to me yesterday, "No, you're not Little Mary Sunshine, but you're the most positive person I know."

Well, I liked that. That would have been a good moment for yesterday. But I chose another.

There was another!

And now, for about three months, I've been doing these Today's Moments as a response to the election of the Orange Asshat and his slimy arrival in the White House. I found myself so bogged down after the election, swamped with constant photographs of him and reports of the next outrageous thing he did and requests and demands for what needed to be done to stop him and lists and figures and ohmygod, it was hard to breathe. It felt like the darkest of times and I had to do something to keep that darkness from taking me over. So I began to look for just one bright light in my day.

I started this to help me deal with Orange Asshat Fallout. But the effects have pond-rippled so much further. I didn't realize how dark my vision had become until I started trying to find light.

As I drove out of the driveway today and down the street, I realized I've been finding it. I'm smiling more. I feel better. And at the same time, I'm still me. I haven't spouted a unicorn horn, I don't wear rainbows, my writing isn't worthy of Hallmark cards. Yes, I still get angry, I still get sad, I still (sometimes) wonder how I'm going to get out of bed in the morning. But there's this search I'm on now, an everyday search for one, just one, bright moment. And so far, it's always been there. Sometimes there's two. Sometimes there's more.

Well, okay, once it was sorta questionable. But even then, I said that the moment of happiness was that tomorrow was coming. I still found a way of looking ahead. That's new too; I didn't used to look forward to tomorrow. It always seemed just like something to get through.

But now I'm looking ahead. I'm looking for happiness. And I'm finding it. And yes, that helps. Despite. Anyway.

## APRIL 23, 2017

And so today's moment of happiness despite the news.

This afternoon, I went to see a medium do a group reading. I've known Mollie for almost ten years now. The day I met her, I was - big surprise! - skeptical. I didn't believe in an afterlife. I didn't believe someone could talk to the dead. But a friend invited me to see Mollie and it gave me the opportunity to post my favorite Facebook status of all time:

"*I'm going with my friend Nancy Drew (really!) to see Mollie Morningstar (really!) talk to the dead (really!). Oh, and Nancy is wearing a Grateful Dead t-shirt (really!).*"

As statuses go, it doesn't get better than that.

But Mollie knocked me off my feet. When she began talking about a man who died from something to his chest, likely heart, a man who had a thing about orange juice, I sat up. My father loved his orange juice. He had to have a specific brand, a specific pulp, at specific times of day in his specific glass. In order to give evidence that this was my father and that he was aware of what was going on in my life, Mollie asked me if I had a dog that was having potty problems – I'd just bought diapers for the first time for my beagle Penny that day. She also mentioned a pair of pants I'd bought the day before. And she talked about seeing a book floating down a river – my first novel had just been accepted.

I was sold. And I was delighted to hear from my father. Especially when he told me he was proud of me. Something he never said while he was alive.

As I sat in the crowded room today and watched Mollie up on the stage, I also watched the faces in the audience as people received messages. Even though I didn't receive a message today, I realized that Mollie has given me a great gift.

A belief that there's something afterwards. Not a great and vast void. But something.

I don't know what that is, exactly. Heaven? Maybe. A parallel universe? Maybe. But there's definitely a feeling of ongoing-ness. And there's a familiarity there too. People that I've known. People that I've loved. Well, I suppose people I haven't been too crazy about either – but then maybe there's a second chance.

Second chances and hope seem to go hand in hand.

It's interesting how all of this works, really. Often, when I meditate, I use a guided meditation recording. One of my favorites has a moment in it that talks about letting a thought pass if one comes up, that all thoughts pass, "just like everything will pass." I listen to that one on my most stressed-out days when it's such a relief to hear that everything will pass.

And yet, with Mollie, I find great comfort in the idea that things will go on. Differently, but on.

Finding great comfort. Knowing things will pass, but also seeing that there will be the familiar in the unknown. Second chances. Hope.

And yes, that helps. Despite. Anyway.

## APRIL 24, 2017

And so today's moment of happiness despite the news.

Yesterday, my daughter had a date with a new boy. He expressed interest in her, they met over sandwiches at Subway, he gave her his sweatshirt. Sweatshirt and hoodie-giving is apparently the new class ring swap. Instead of wearing a boy's love on a chain around her neck, bearing a thickly yarn-wrapped ring, she wears it tugged over her head, draped past her hands, down to her knees.

An hour after coming home, she came upstairs in tears and said the boy texted and said he decided he wasn't ready for a relationship – he was better off single.

Today, when I picked her up from school, she came out beaming and told me in the car that he changed his mind. Now they are officially boyfriend/girlfriend. They are, in their lingo, "shipped."

Hooboy.

Driving her home, after I heard her announcement, my left thumb tucked over my palm and gently touched the underside of my wedding ring.

My first marriage lasted for seventeen years and one month.

My second marriage, the current one, is also at the seventeen-year mark. Seventeen years, six months, and approximately 15 days (approximately because some months have 30 days, some 31, and then there's February).

In my first marriage, after seventeen years, I looked at that husband and said, "I am better off single." After I left him and had been gone for a few months, I said to that not yet ex-husband, "I've changed my mind. I want to come back." He said, "I've changed my mind too. I don't want you."

And now, in my second marriage, here we are. Seventeen years. At times, he makes me crazy. At times, I make him crazy.

But we are still crazy about each other.

In that manner of long marriages, we are as familiar with each other as we can be. There's not much we don't know. But we still like each other. And even though I live the curves and loops of a living, breathing roller coaster, we are as steady as can be.

Steady. In our lingo, we are going steady. We are beyond steady. We are "shipped" on level waters.

Our daughter is caught up in young love with this boy. And devastation.

And young love with that boy. And devastation. And young love with this boy. She is twitterpated, agog, Hallmarky, schmaltzy, ooey-gooey-eyed in love. And in love. And in love.

I'm glad it's her and not me.

I am so glad to be fifty-six. I am so glad to be married for seventeen years, six months, and approximately fifteen days. I am so glad to be made crazy by him, and to be crazy about him.

I am so glad.

And yes, that helps. Despite. Anyway.

### APRIL 25, 2017

And so today's moment of happiness despite the news.

A few years ago, there was a commercial on television – I believe it was for Merry Maids. A business woman comes home from work. She opens her front door and steps inside and looks around. All the surfaces are sparkling. Nothing is out of place. She stands in the middle of the room, in front of the large island that separates her living room from her kitchen and this smile spreads across her face, so slowly and utterly full of glee. After drawing her fists under her chin in a little girl's expression of delight, she thrusts both arms in the air and yells, "Yes! Yes! Yes!" From behind the island, two Merry Maids pop out, startled. The business woman blushes, giggles, and whispers, "Good job!"

I don't have Merry Maids. I hate the name and I prefer to support small businesses – like me. I do have a cleaning service, a luxury I allow myself, in the form of a spitfire named Tracy who shows up every other week armed to the teeth with mops and vacuum cleaners (one that she wears on her back, making her look like she's a ghostbuster) and rags and cleansers…and treats for the dogs. Normally, I'm here when Tracy is here, as I live in a live-where-you-work condo. AllWriters' is the first floor and I live on the second and third floors with my family and beasts. But today, I had a meeting at school and a meeting with my publicist, and so I ran out before Tracy arrived. I got home as she was coming out the door. We high-fived and off she went with her battalion.

And I had the television commercial moment.

I went up to the second floor and opened the door and walked into my kitchen. And I inhaled. It smelled soooooo good! It was spotless! It was shiny! Everything around me sparkled and was its correct color, not hidden beneath a veil of orangey-brown beagle and cat hair. The counters were clear. The pillows were on the couch. It was clean! It was clean! It was clean!

And it was warm outside today too, so my windows and deck doors were open. There was Spring in my house.

I didn't yell and pump my fists. I just don't do that sort of thing. But I did smile and climb up to the third floor to get to work in my (clean) office. It was lovely.

Except for the puddle. Blossom the beagle had to ground me in reality. This is no television commercial. But I suppose nothing in this life can be perfect. It can still make you happy.

And yes, that helps. Despite. Anyway.

### APRIL 26, 2017

And so today's moment(s) of happiness despite the news.

I'll be honest here. I've dealt with a lot of idiots lately. People who made me incredibly angry, angry to the shaking-hands level, the curl-fingers-into-fists level. People who made me wonder at the collective IQ of our country. People who made me glance at the latest passing photo of the Orange Asshat and think, Oh, so that's how you got into the White House.

People, in general, who made me want to damn all of mankind and decide that this world is an awful place and really, for god's sake, what am I still doing here?

You know. That kind of idiot.

But today, as I always do on Wednesday afternoons from one to three, I found myself immersed to the heart with the nicest group of women. Variety of ages, variety of backgrounds. But united in compassion and intelligence and just hearty GOODNESS. There's not a one I don't love to pieces. This is my AllWriters' Wednesday Afternoon Women Writers' Workshop. They are my students. This is my job.

But they are so much more.

Every now and then in this life, you find yourself immersed with a batch of people that just makes you happy. Warm. And that today, helped me remember that the brand of idiocy I've been dealing with lately is not the norm. It's not the whole world. They've helped me remember that before too.

In the middle of the workshop, we discussed if a student's 16-year old male character would really be as nice and empathetic and compassionate as he's made out to be. And we talked about kids we've seen on the news, kids who have collected amazing funds for the needy or collected teddy bears for sick children or knitted hats for the homeless. Kids who care. Kids who look beyond themselves and embrace the world and grace the world and restore your faith in humanity.

Like this group of women does for me, time and time again.

And like a young woman did on my daughter's Facebook page recently. Olivia's been going through a lot. And this young woman, part of a group that has gone out of their way to make sure that Olivia does not sit all alone in the lunchroom, posted, "I'm always there for you, if you need someone to talk to."

I'd like to find this young woman and tell her that someday, she's going to sit in a lovely room with a bunch of lovely women and she's going to uplift them all.

So. We have me having this amazing moment with my students, realizing that not everyone in this life is awful, and we talk about how often it is that kids aren't awful, and realize again that it's more common than the idiocy league, and then I go on Facebook and I see a meme that says:

*"Life is only a reflection of what we allow ourselves to see."*

Typically, memes make me hurl, but this one walloped me upside the head. And then it led me to an old song, The Wall, by Kansas, and the lyrics:

*"The moment is a masterpiece, The weight of indecision's in the air, Standing there, The symbol and the sum of all that's me, It's just a travesty, Towering, blocking out the light and blinding me. I want to see!"*

So do I. I've been blinding myself. And today, one masterpiece moment led to the next and I can see again.

And yes, that helps. Despite. Anyway.

## APRIL 27, 2017

And so today's moment of happiness despite the news.

So lately, I've not been sleeping well. I'm sleeping – which is a huge change in my insomniac life – but it's not a happy sleep. For weeks now, I've been having a recurring dream. It's not a nightmare. I don't wake up shaken and scared. But I do wake up disturbed.

It takes place in a house I lived in from 1966 to 1972, when I was six years old to twelve. It's in Esko, Minnesota, a teeny community way the heck up between Duluth and Cloquet. This house has been prevalent in many of my dreams for the last several months, and, in fact, was the scene of my last nightmare. But now it's decided to stick itself firmly as setting into a dream that happens again and again.

I'm in the house and I'm looking for a man named Mr. Hughes. That's all I know. He's in there somewhere and I am going from room to room to room and up and down from the basement, looking for him. I'm all sorts of ages, depending on the night. I'm the age I was when I lived there, I'm older, I'm who I am now. The rooms, for the most part, are true to the layout of the house as I remember it, though from time to time, another room arrives from another house that I lived in. My parents are there in that way of dreams, somewhere behind me, a presence. I don't see them and I don't hear them. Yet I know they're in the house.

But I'm looking for Mr. Hughes. Over and over and over. Room after room after room.

I'm getting really tired of looking for him. I don't even know who he is. I can't remember ever knowing a Mr. Hughes.

I didn't find him again last night. Which led to my moment of happiness today. Around six o'clock, after a long day of running around, doing a ton and accomplishing nothing, I sat down to meditate. According to the app I use, Insight Timer, I've now been meditating 408 days in a row. It was cold today, and I was cold today, so I pulled out my heated throw, turned it on high, and climbed under it. I was joined by a cat, of course. And then I plugged my head into the headphones and tuned into one of my favorite guided meditations, Create Inner Peace, by Glenn Harrold.

I've already written that my original idea of meditation was that you have to stop thinking. That's truly not the purpose or even the goal at all. But every now and then…it happens. At least for me. It's not a sleep. I'm just gone. There's no sound, no light, no dreams, no thoughts, no people, no problems, no to-do lists, no expectations, just nothing, nothing, nothing. If you're doing a guided meditation, as I do, you don't even hear that. Gone. A state of happy, happy goneness. And that's where I went today.

Ohmygod, what a relief. Even Mr. Hughes wasn't there. Well, he's never there, that's the freaking problem. But even the search for him wasn't there.

Twenty-five minutes later, I was suddenly conscious of Glenn Harrold saying, in his delicious British accent, "Open your eyes! Open your eyes!" Obedient me, I did. And I was back. Rested. Brain calm. Body relaxed.

Happy.

The search may continue tonight. It might continue until I finally, in my dreams or awake, find Mr. Hughes. But at least right now, I've had some deep, deep rest.

And yes, that helps. Despite. Anyway.

## APRIL 28, 2017

And so today's moment of happiness despite the news.

Today, we drove up to Green Bay, Wisconsin, where Michael and I are participating in a book festival. Over the next three days, I'm doing a reading/signing/Q & A, and three different workshops on a variety of subjects. Michael is joining me for one of them.

I was stressed by the time we arrived, after dealing with delays that had me leaving home over an hour late, and then construction that slowed me down further. My first event, my reading/signing, started at five. We got in to the hotel room at 4:15. Clothes flew everywhere as I tried to transform instantly from Driving Kathie to Performing Kathie.

Green Bay is a scary place for me. Since 2011, when my first novel, *The Home For Wayward Clocks*, came out, I've been asked to do countless readings. A reading at a Green Bay bookstore stands out for me as it is the one time no one showed up. And I mean no one. No one even came into the store while I was there. It was me and the bookstore owner and her two cats. It was like someone put up a billboard at all the major entryways to Green Bay: *Don't Go To The Bookstore Tonight! Kathie Giorgio Is There!*

Ohmygod. Awful.

Back in my hotel room that night, I started a poem which I never finished. It was called Doubts:

*Sometimes, when you stand in a room full of chairs, you wonder if you should have ever said anything at all.*

Yep, I felt pretty smashed. And now I faced Green Bay again.

I was part of a trio of events tonight, and one, concurrent with mine, was with one of Wisconsin's sweethearts. I'd already pretty much figured my reappearance would be an echo of my first. I arrived disheartened and stressed and prepared to fail. Hello, Green Bay. Did you recycle that billboard?

When I glanced at the festival's schedule, I saw that the organizers described my event as "a command performance."

I was surely not feeling very command-y.

Fifteen minutes before the start of my reading, no one was there. Fourteen minutes before, the first person arrived – the volunteer doing the introductions. And then…and then…there they were. There they were!

They came!

Not a standing room only audience, but an audience. A good-sized, almost-filled-room, wonderful, appreciative audience.

And let me tell you…the performance I gave? Command, baby, with a capital C. Two walloping poems and my Pushcart-nominated short story.

They got ME.

And oh, did it feel good.

And yes, that helps. Despite. Anyway.

## APRIL 29, 2017

And so today's moment of happiness despite the news.

I've been sitting here for a while, trying to think of a moment to write about. Part of me considered waiting and putting this up later than usual, just in case a moment was still going to occur. But that seems silly to me. That would be like going out into the parking lot, flinging my arms wide and yelling at the sun (although it's a sunless day), "Hey! Hit me with some happiness please! I have to write about it!"

Silly.

Today was busy. I taught an avid, rapid, hungry group of people. Extra chairs had to be brought in and lined the periphery so that everyone could attend. Some hung around outside the door. We had fabulous discussions and deep laughs and moments of insight so bright, I had to blink. Afterward, one woman came up to me, took my card, and said, "I learned more from you than I have in any of the other sessions." Another woman found me later, in a different location, and she said, "You told me exactly what I needed to hear. Thank you." I ran out of business cards. I almost ran out of books.

Oh, what that second woman said. She didn't say, "You told me what I wanted to hear." She said, "You told me what I needed to hear." That's my goal, when I teach. If I wasn't glowing, I'd be amazed.

There was literariness everywhere. People talking books, people talking writing, people being intense, people smiling, people drinking coffee, coffee, coffee. Arguing, laughing, whispering, dancing their hands when their words couldn't keep up. And one person, of course, who started our conversation by telling me she doesn't write, but she "works with the extra-terrestrials."

My kind of world.

Afterward, Michael and I went off-site for a while, for a very quiet late lunch at Perkins. And then, of course, we passed a Goodwill and had to stop in. Oh, do I have some nice things in my trunk... After coming back to the hotel, I meditated and Michael fell asleep. He's snoring right now, filling this room with the sound of familiarity and home. And I'm sitting here, pondering how to choose one moment of happiness.

How can I pick one moment? There wasn't one moment. It was a DAY.

It happens sometimes.

And yes, that helps. Despite. Anyway.

## APRIL 30, 2017

And so today's moment of happiness despite the news.

Most people take time in their childhoods to admire superheroes. Super-power comic book or cartoon characters, sports figures, movie or television stars – whoever embodies what they want to be when they grow up.

My superheroes were writers.

Well, and Secretariat. I can't forget Secretariat.

But writers. Marguerite Henry. Beverly Cleary. Louisa May Alcott. Walter Farley. Mary Stewart. Victoria Holt. And on and on as I grew up with literature and with writers who surrounded me with family, both with their characters and with themselves. With what they did, how they did it, and the lovely way their minds mated words and imagination.

I've never stopped having superheroes.

Tonight, I was able to see two of them. The capstone event at the book festival featured appearances by Sherman Alexie and Margaret Atwood. I fussed and fumed over whether I would stay. Practicality said I should go home. It was late, I'd get home later, Monday morning came early, I don't have my reading done, and my list went on and on.

But Sherman Alexie and Margaret Atwood. Superheroes.

I stayed. And oh, what I would have missed if I'd left.

At 3:20, I finished my last appearance. I pulled off my name badge, went to the conference center, and became a part of the audience, rather than standing in front of it. And every inch of exhausted me was enthralled.

Sherman Alexie, superhero, whose book, *The Lone Ranger And Tonto Fistfight In Heaven*, grabbed me so hard with his lyrical language and storytelling that I ended up reading most of it out loud to Michael – and he listened.

Margaret Atwood, superhero, who has everyone talking about the Hulu adaptation of her novel *The Handmaid's Tale*, but I fell in love with her *Cat's Eye* years ago and hold it to me as one of the finest books I've ever read.

And then they were there, right in front of me.

Alexie, saying he was the warm-up act for Nostradamus.

Atwood, putting on a puppet show.

Alexie, saying (I'm paraphrasing), "Us brown people didn't vote for him. It's you white women and white men. This is where you learned that putting that Black Lives Matter sign in your window didn't do a damn bit of good."

Atwood, on the same topic, saying, "You might want to try voting next time, people."

Alexie's irreverent stage presence and humor, followed by an uppercut of poignant emotion, Atwood's intelligence and wisdom, mixed with a Canadian sex joke and the puppet show.

I'm going to pay for staying. It's 11:15 and I'm only just now getting down to work that has to be finished. But I'm so glad I stayed. Sometimes, you just have to throw away practicality in order to experience brilliance.

And yes, that helps. Despite. Anyway.

# Chapter Five

## MAY 1, 2017

And so today's moment of happiness despite the news.

For many, today is known as May Day. The first of May. Celebrated by children skipping around maypoles in a lovely little braiding dance. More children creating baskets and hanging them from doorknobs to surprise the people within. Sunshine, blue skies, hello, Spring, goodbye, Winter, it's time for warm!

Well, except in Waukesha today, you would have gotten soaked if you danced around a maypole or delivered a basket. You would have needed a good jacket too.

But inside our condo? We're dancing and throwing flowers everywhere. Today in the mail, we received our health insurance identification cards.

Hello, Spring! Goodbye, Winter! It's time for warm!

This past February 20, Michael was let go from his job. He was given one week's severance. And insurance until the end of the month. February is a short month.

Eight days of insurance. Then no more. All gone.

From March 1 until May 1, we went without health insurance. Even though nothing catastrophic or even mildly crisis-y happened, it was plenty hair-raising. I'm fifty-six years old, and while I deal with asthma and fibromyalgia, my health is pretty great. But still – fifty-six? We all know that can change in a heartbeat. One afternoon, I was heading down the stairs and my heel slid on the step halfway down. As I started to fall, I clearly remember myself thinking, You may not fall. There is no ER. There is no doctor. You must stop. I swear I froze myself in midair and set myself down. Intact. Freaked out, but unhurt.

Hair-raising.

I've heard arguments on both sides of the healthcare issue. And I'll say this. We could not afford Obamacare. The monthly fee was barely within our reach, but the deductible made it impossible. The cost of medications for my husband prior to reaching that ridiculous deductible would have put us under. We couldn't afford COBRA either. Now please consider that. We are not poor. We're not rich either, but we're okay. But we couldn't afford it.

I know there are some who say that those who want healthcare should go out and get a job and work for it. I work a minimum of 85 hours a week and have for twelve solid years now. Michael, before he was let go, worked a full-time job and he also teaches for me. We work for it. We work for it in spades.

Everyone deserves good quality healthcare. Michael, Olivia and I deserve good quality healthcare.

For the last two months, everything became about possible illness or injury. I drove freakishly carefully. I looked left, right, left, right, left, right, left at every intersection. I got honked at for driving slowly. I don't get honked at. I don't drive slowly. Every sniffle, every cough, every twinge, every pain became a worry. Was this something? What would we do if it was?

But now, Michael is employed again, and has been employed long enough to have the health benefits kick in. Today, May Day arrived in our mail. Sunshine. Blue skies.

Health insurance.

I never knew a little plastic card could make me so happy.

And yes, that helps. Despite. Anyway.

## MAY 2, 2017

And so today's moment of happiness despite the news.

I've been active on the internet now for...well, for a really long time. Spam email is a part of my day, just as it is in anybody's day. Most get deleted without a second glance. Sometimes the headers make me laugh. Sometimes they make me disgusted. And a few make me truly perplexed.

Today, I was sitting in Hemi at a stoplight. Yes, it was red – I do not email or text while driving. But I was stopped and so I checked my email. My phone treats email differently than my computer. Besides telling me who sent the email and what the header is, it also gives me the first few words. I appreciate this, as I often have strangers emailing me out of the blue who turn out to be readers or potential students.

At this red light, the glimpse of this email definitely caught my attention.

"*It shall be well with you...*"

It wasn't from anyone I knew, and the header was the annoying (no subject). So I clicked on it.

"*It shall be well with you Amen*"

And then a stream of Hebrew.

The light turned green and I tossed my phone to the passenger seat and hit the gas. I found myself feeling peeved and I said to the windshield, "How do YOU know?"

Then I saw the bumper sticker on the pickup truck in front of me. The sticker was bright blue with white lettering and it said:

"*Just for today.*"

I was on my way to Starbucks and then to a meeting and I muddled over this as I clenched my steering wheel. *It shall be well with you Amen. Just for today.*

Serendipity? I wondered if I was going to have a good day today, on just this day, and then all hell was going to break loose. I wondered if this was a new and cosmic way to say, Have a nice day! which made me laugh (I crack myself up).

And then I thought, Okay. Just for today, I will try to behave and feel as if someone is watching over me. Someone is telling me it will be okay. I will not worry. I will not fret. I will not obsess or even roll my eyes or assume something isn't going to turn out the way I want it to. Just for today, it will be well with me. I am being watched over.

It took some really conscious effort. This was about one o'clock and a lot of the day was still before me. But I worked at it. If I felt anxiety ramping up, I said, *It shall be well with you.* If I felt annoyance or anger or negativity, I said the same thing. And I made myself, not shove it away, but give it away. Someone was watching over me. *Just for today.*

I will admit, it felt nice. I didn't perseverate over who or what that someone was. Higher power or human, animal, vegetable or mineral, it didn't matter. I will also admit that quite often I caught myself in a smirk and in the thought, Who are you trying to kid? Really?

I didn't see any burning bushes. I didn't see the Fox River parting so I could get across. There were no voices. There was not the touch of an angel's wing on my cheek.

Mostly, it just felt nice. And my day was just fine.

Hmm.

And yes, that helps. Despite. Anyway.

### MAY 3, 2017

And so today's moment of happiness despite the news.

My moment today could be seen as cheating, I guess. The impetus for the moment actually happened on Monday. But I still found myself smiling over it today.

Wednesday is a day that I don't write, but I do tend to feel myself most fully as a writer. I teach from ten in the morning until midnight. I talk writing, talk writing, talk talk talk writing. I am surrounded by writers all day long, whether in person, on the phone, or on the internet.

On Monday, I posted on Facebook about my being the guest reader at the debut of the new issue of the Windy Hill Review, the literary magazine of the University of Wisconsin – Waukesha. My son noticed the post and remembered that a co-worker told him her story was accepted by the magazine. So he texted her and mentioned that his mother was the guest reader at the debut earlier that day.

Her response:

*KATHIE GIORGIO IS YOUR MOTHER !?!?!?!?!?!?!?!?!?!?!?!?!!!*

When he agreed, she said, *Oh. My. God. No way.*

That response just tickled me to no end. Even now. I would like to print it, put it on posterboard, and mount it someplace in my son's apartment where he will see it every day.

Why? Because when I get on my literary high horse (I like my literary high horse, thank you), this boy has (for years) pranced around the house, singing in an awful falsetto, "I am a writer! Doot-doot-doot-de-doot."

Now really. Such disrespect. Such irreverence. Such low horsiness. What a donkey.

After the reading on Monday, I headed for the doors, following at a little distance behind someone who was at the debut, someone who knows me and has worked with me on the book festival. She went around a corner into her office, and before I came around the corner too, I heard her say to her assistant, "My god, is there anything that woman can't do?"

As I walked to my car, I began to count what I can't do. Math. Name all fifty states. A cartwheel. Understand why the bass clef has notes that look exactly like notes on the treble clef, but aren't called the same thing. Understand why the Orange Asshat is in the White House.

Yes, there are things I can't do.

But today, in the middle of the day, in the middle of Crazy-Busy Wednesday, I was just suddenly filled with literary oats. (Lord, the horse references – well, I am a writer, you know. Doot-doot-doot-de-doot.)

But it was more than oats. It was brought on by that young woman texting my son, and by Is-there-anything-she-can't-do. Especially since I once believed I couldn't do a damn thing. Because that's what I was told. But now, every now and then, I am just overwhelmed with feeling like I'm in the right skin. I'm where I'm supposed to be. I'm doing what I'm supposed to do. I am, well, who I am.

Oh, hell. I suddenly wanted to pound my chest and bellow, in reference and agreement to that young woman's textspeak:

*I AM KATHIE GIORGIO!!!!!!!!!!!!!!!!!!!!!!*

And then I immediately heard my son's voice. Doot-doot-doot-de-doot. And it made me laugh.

I can't do everything. But I know what I can do. I know what I do beyond well. And I know who I am.

I am Kathie Giorgio.

And yes, that helps. Despite. Anyway.

## MAY 4, 2017

And so today's moment of happiness despite the news.

No, I will not be writing about what happened at the White House today where the Asshat cavorted around the White House lawn with a bunch of morally depraved, elitist privileged people and gloried over sticking it to those less fortunate. Again.

That's not what this little blog is supposed to be about. It's about forcefully reminding myself (and anyone who reads this) that the entire world was not cavorting on the White House lawn, this afternoon or at any time. I wrote on my Facebook page today, "You know, it's getting harder to believe this 'good will always win over evil' thing." So here, with this Moment, is where I prove to myself that I can still believe in the good.

Today, I found a bare spot on a wall and I hung a new clock. A new old clock. A new old clock that looks like a copper frying pan and that has only one hand. And then I stepped back and admired it. Loved it. Ran my fingers over its black numbers and wondered how many other people have done the exact same thing.

I hung it next to my microwave, a bright red modern number which glowed the time with neon green digital numbers. These two, the clock shaped like a copper frying pan and the microwave, immediately seemed to like each other. They both shone in the afternoon sun. They both told me what time it was – well, sort of. The clock with the one hand told me the hour, but not the minutes. It's not the first clock in my house to not tell me the time. But the microwave filled in.

For a minute, I shone with them.

I don't understand my own attraction to clocks. I've collected them for well over twenty years. There are over sixty clocks in my living room and kitchen alone. I have no idea how many are in the rest of the house. And of course, my first novel, The Home For Wayward Clocks, was set in a clock museum. I carry a purse that looks like a clock. One of the things I love most about Chryslers is that they have a regular numbered clock with hands in their cars.

It's about the history, mostly. These clocks have seen way more than I have or ever will. It's about the timelessness in a timepiece. I look at them and see eternity. I feel the clock within me too. That's not so eternal, I guess.

This copper frying pan clock showed up in the mail yesterday. A friend from Facebook saw it in an antique store and thought I would like it. She was right.

So first off, I'm kinda happy to be the type of person who would fall in love with a clock shaped like a copper frying pan, sporting only one hand. I'm happy that I can still see its worth, despite the fact it only has one hand. And it looks like a frying pan. And I am more than happy to give an orphan a loving home.

But I'm also happy that in a world where a sick president could cavort on the White House lawn with his sick cohorts, mostly white, mostly men, and exult over robbing the less fortunate of their health and longevity, there is someone who can see an odd thing in an antique store, and she can pick it up and admire it, buy it, package it, and send it to someone she barely knows, just because she thinks it will make that person happy.

It did. Thank you.

And yes, that helps. Despite. Anyway.

## MAY 5, 2017

And so today's moment of happiness despite the news.

The universe or fate or what-have-you certainly does seem to be conspiring to make this a challenge for me lately.

Yesterday, I walked away from a cause I worked hard for over the last six years. I truly believed in it – well, I truly believed in what I thought was a shared vision for its purpose – and it was a difficult decision to make. But I also saw this cause taking advantage of and disrespecting those I hold in the highest esteem. And I just couldn't take that anymore. I realized I was only still there to try to change the situation to what was my original vision, and I also had the hard realization that I just can't fix everything. So I walked out.

I also found out that the health insurance that we so hoped for, and that we thought would come with my husband's new job, also comes with something else – a ten thousand dollar deductible. Which means that we're still in the same situation we were in when we were uninsured – trying to figure out how to pay for impossibly expensive prescriptions.

It's been a rough forty-eight hours. For that matter, it's been a rough five months. Today was one of those days when I expect to look in the mirror and see bruises.

But…I'm not looking for bruises. I'm looking for the moment of happiness now.

It was a sunny day. It was the first fully sunny day that we've had in a while. It actually was warm enough to drive the topless car. At the end of way too many errands that had to be performed during my usual writing time, I found myself in line at the drive-thru at Starbucks.

Yes, I've noticed that several of my Moments have happened in the drive-thru at Starbucks.

The line wasn't moving very fast and I had a few minutes where I didn't have to do anything but wait to move forward. Everything for those minutes was out of my control. If someone wanted me or needed me, I couldn't do a damn thing – the barrier between the drive-thru and the parking lot was too high to drive over. And for those minutes, nobody wanted me or needed me anyway. My phone was mercifully silent. My computer was far away.

There was one thing I could do. I could lay my head back on the headrest, close my eyes, and let the sun soak me. So I did.

I had sunglasses on, and the light behind my eyelids glowed rosypink. The sun was a blanket I could breathe through, on my face, my shoulders, arms, torso…so warm. I had my heated seat on, and for those minutes, the heat provided by the blessed sun and by the mechanics of a smooth-running car were indistinguishable. There was warmth. There was light. There was an embrace that I so needed.

And when the line moved forward, there was a grande iced cinnamon dolce latte, handed to me by a barista who knows my name, knows who I am, and who asked me sincerely how my day was.

And I said, "Just fine."

And yes, that helps. Despite. Anyway.

# MAY 6, 2017

And so today's moment of happiness despite the news.

Today was the Kentucky Derby. The Derby always throws me backwards into memory, into thoughts of the only athlete I ever loved and held up as a role model.

Secretariat.

I was thirteen years old when Secretariat won the Triple Crown. I was a horse nut, surrounding myself with Breyer's models, reading everything by Walter Farley and Marguerite Henry, and avidly following horse racing. I had a great uncle who was one of Man O'War's handlers, and when that great uncle visited, I sat at his feet and listened to his tales. I made friends with girls who lived on farms with horses, and I rode whenever I could, which wasn't often enough.

But Secretariat. Oh, he was my hero. I had scrapbook after scrapbook filled with articles and photographs of him. I think I still have them packed away somewhere. But I didn't love Secretariat because he was a winner. I loved him long before that.

He was described as an ugly horse. He didn't have the usual delicate features of a thoroughbred. He was stocky, muscular, and some said he was a plow horse. I thought he was beautiful. He was magical when he ran. He didn't run because he was told to. He clearly ran because he loved it. His jockey, Ron Turcotte, said that he never lifted his whip. He just got up there and held on for dear life. At the Belmont Stakes, he gave Secretariat his head when it was clear he was going to win…and he won by 31 lengths.

He was called ugly. It was said he couldn't win. He did. Out of pure joy.

I met Secretariat when I was twenty-three years old. My first husband and I took a vacation to Kentucky, ostensibly to see the Derby – but I was bound for Claiborne Farms, to meet Secretariat. Of the Derby, I only remember that Sunny's Halo won. But of Secretariat, I remember everything.

I saw Riva Ridge and Foolish Pleasure first. I saw the grave of Bold Ruler. And then I rounded a corner and saw Secretariat. The handler with me told me I wasn't allowed to touch. I stood about a foot away from the fenced-in pasture where Secretariat was grazing. The handler whistled and that massive head went up and then Secretariat came to the fence and pressed his chest against it. I stepped forward until I was inches away. I talked to him and I thanked him and my hands were clasped so tightly, I couldn't wipe at my tears.

The handler looked around. Then he gave me an apple. "Go ahead," he said. "No one is watching."

So I gave Secretariat an apple. I felt his muzzle. And then he took his broad long face and pushed it against my chest and I rubbed his ears and neck and I thought I went straight to Heaven. And I said thank you again. Several times. For being different. For succeeding anyway.

Every Kentucky Derby day, I remember that moment. And every time, I get goosebumps.

And yes, that helps. Despite. Anyway.

## MAY 7, 2017

And so today's moment of happiness despite the news.

Sometimes disconnected things come together.

Yesterday, I asked a question on Facebook: *Define "woman of an age" or "woman of a certain age". What age is a woman when she becomes a woman of an age or certain age?* I was doing a general survey for the current NIP (novel in progress). I didn't want an academic answer or an answer based on literary references. I just wanted to know what people think that phrase means.

The answers were as varied as there are people. Some saw it as youth, some saw it as age, some saw it as sexual, some intellectual, some the age of fertility, others post-menopausal, some an individual distinction, some societal. Some saw it as an example of sexism and some as a sign of a special season women hold unto themselves. And some were just plain goofy.

I got what I needed to know, but I also received so much more – an example of the incredible diversity of humans, all the way down to the way they think and the way they perceive words. Even in definitions, we are individuals.

Then today, I had the honor of Skyping in to a book club in Israel. This lively and lovely group of women read *Learning To Tell (A Life) Time*. I laughed as I watched them all crouch together, trying to fit into my screen. They told me I sounded midwestern. They sounded like the world.

It was interesting that among the women, not one was a natural-born Israeli. There were Americans from the midwest and the east coast, Brits, an Australian, a Russian, a Scot. Accents beat rhythms. They spoke of immigration and home and life in Israel. They spoke of my book too. One thing that struck me was their discussion on repetition. I used some phrases repeatedly and deliberately in *Lifetime*, a refrain of sorts, a thrumming in the character's mind. One woman found it annoying, another found it lyrical and poetic, and another didn't notice it at all.

In this room of diversity, unified by their home, they brought different meanings to the same words. The incredible distinction of the individual. In these adults, the boldness to be different.

Later this afternoon, I visited a different Starbucks than my usual. This one has a fireplace and I sat in the easy chair in front of it and toasted myself as I read student manuscripts. Four adults and a child came in, the adults clearly parents and grandparents, the child, about seven. The adults sat at a high table, after the mother plunked the little girl in the easy chair across from me. She gave her a Starbucks cup and warned her it was hot. The little girl had a book. Her legs stretched out in front of her, sneakered feet bobbing. She pulled the green stopper from her cup, licked every inch of it, and then dove into her book.

I figured the drink was likely hot chocolate, but I pictured it as coffee. I started drinking coffee in early elementary school, drawn to it as most children are to milk. I read at an early age and was reading adult novels by the time I was in second grade. Books were my toys. Writing was my game of pretend. And this little girl in Starbucks read with an intensity I recognized.

Other children would have run around the café. They would have pestered their parents to go, interrupted conversations, climbed on the furniture. This one drank her hot drink and didn't take her eyes away from her book. Not until her mother told her it was time to go, at which point she sighed, closed the book, clasped it to her chest, and followed the adults out. I knew without a doubt that when she was buckled into her seat, the book would be opened again. In that walk from café to car, she wasn't watching the world. She was watching the story.

I wanted to lean forward and tell her, "It's all going to be okay."

As the French say, " *Vive la différence.*"

And yes, that helps. Despite. Anyway.


### MAY 8, 2017

And so today's moment of happiness despite the news.

Today, I had an afternoon coffee break with the creative writing teacher I had in high school.

I am fifty-six years old, soon to be fifty-seven. But I was back in high school, in a classroom that looked amazingly like Starbucks. Listening to my teacher. And he was listening to me. Just like in 1977.

So weird. So wonderful.

When I was a second semester junior, my family moved to Waukesha, Wisconsin, and I started school at Waukesha North High School. I'd registered to take the journalism class, but the morning I showed up, I was told the class was filled and I was to take creative writing instead. I wasn't thrilled. I didn't want to write poetry.

But it ended up being the best schedule shift I ever experienced.

By the end of the second week, this teacher was throwing book after book at me. Books that were not on the school reading list. *Dinky Hocker Shoots Smack. Wanda Hickey's Night Of Golden Memories. Say You Love Me, Junie Moon. Howl. The Pill Versus The Spring Hill Mind Disaster. The Dharma Bums.* Along with the books, he threw extra writing assignments, challenges that got my ire up, raised my hackles, raised my blood pressure, and had me scribbling until the early morning hours. What I wrote, he praised to the rooftops, but he also ripped into, telling me to dig deeper, deeper, deeper.

And I did.

And then he told me I had a gift, which felt to me like a miracle, which felt like a gift he was giving me, because he said it to me and he meant it. He meant it! But with that gift, he said, came responsibility. The gift was worthless unless I used it. And I had to use it. I couldn't let myself stop. He said there would be times I would be miserable, but it would be all right. I had to be responsible. I had to live up to what I could do.

Teachers change lives. Mine was changed by this man.

This teacher came back into my life in 2011, when my first novel was published. He showed up to its debut and bought a copy for himself and a copy to donate to the school where he taught. Since then, he's shown up at every debut. He introduced me at the last one, the tandem debuts of *Oddities & Endings; The Collected Stories of Kathie Giorgio* and *True Light Falls In Many Forms*, a chapbook of the poetry I didn't want to write. He surprised me by showing up to the celebration of my 20th year of teaching, and he introduced me there too.

He said, "I can still see where you sat in my classroom. You liked to sit on the floor, behind the desks, your back against a corner. You hid. But you never hid in your words. You still don't. You never will."

Not only can teachers change lives, they can save them.

Today, when I sat down with Duane, we talked like two adults. He used swear words, and I didn't gasp at the teacher who dared. I used swear words, and he didn't tell me not to.

He has never told me not to use my words. No matter what I had to say.

Then he asked me, "Are you writing? Tell me what you're writing."

And I did. He listened to me just like I was sixteen again.

I was heard.

And yes, that helps. Despite. Anyway.

### MAY 9, 2017

And so today's moment of happiness despite the news.

This morning, I was clicking through saved files on my computer, looking for something for a student. As I scrolled down, I saw one I'd titled "Gilbert Horses At Midnight Without A Moon". I had no memory of what it was or why I'd saved it, so after I took care of my student, I returned to this file. It held this excerpt from the Jack Gilbert poem:

*Our heart wanders lost in the dark woods.*
*Our dream wrestles in the castle of doubt.*
*But there's music in us. Hope is pushed down but the angel flies up again taking us with her.*
*The summer mornings begin inch by inch while we sleep, and walk with us later as long-legged beauty through the dirty streets. It is no surprise that danger and suffering surround us.*
*What astonishes is the singing.*

I originally saved this on December 3, 2014. I have no idea why. Did I use it in a lecture? Did I intend to use it as a lift-off point for a story? Did I just like the words?

I don't know. But I'm glad I did.

When I came to the final line today, *What astonishes is the singing,* I felt a resonance I've never felt before. When I read it back then, in 2014, I probably read it as, *What astonishes me is the singing that they all can still do, despite the danger and the suffering. What astonishes me is the hope. How can they feel that?*

I would have understood and admired the poem, but it would have been an outside observation, me watching others.

But today, I am astonished at my own singing. My own hope. Writing these little moments every day is my version of being taken up by that angel.

Last night, when I went to bed, I meditated. I used a new guided meditation, and one of the themes was "You can relax now. You are free from today." I'm new to that kind of freedom. And I'm new to a sense of hope when I climb into bed at night and when I climb out in the morning.

New at 56.

When I finished meditating, my app told me that I'd now meditated 420 days in a row. I slept well. And when I started my day and found this poem, which I'd saved for some forgotten reason, I found that I connected to it in a way I likely hadn't before. From the inside, not the outside.

Hope.

And yes, that helps. Despite. Anyway.

## MAY 10, 2017

And so today's moment of happiness despite the news.

I was in a hurry today as I stepped out of the condo. I'd just finished teaching my Wednesday afternoon workshop and it was 3:20. I had exactly an hour and ten minutes to drive to my chiropractor, get electrocuted and crunched, drive through Starbucks and get my fix, and get home for my 4:30 client. It was a tight squeeze and it was going to be even tighter as this week is Starbucks Frappuccino Happy Hour, where your second frap is half price. I hate Frappuccino Happy Hour week. I don't drink the darn things – I drink grande cinnamon dolce lattes. But people come from out of nowhere to take advantage of the special and the line typically extends out onto the street. Normally, I fight this by going to Starbucks at a different time, but my Wednesday schedule prohibited that.

So I was in a hurry.

But my garage door opened and I stepped outside and there it was. I can't say I was hit or slapped – too violent. This was gentle. This was welcome.

I was insinuated with the scent of Spring.

It was raining, which is nothing new lately. It's been raining since February, I think. But this was different. It wasn't pounding, it wasn't a deluge. It was a whisper. It made me believe in the rhyme about flowers, even though it's no longer April. And it smelled like Spring.

You know the one. Lighter than the scent of cucumber, but filled with the promise of that exact vegetable, sliced green from the garden. The scent of sunshine, of breeze and light on sheets that have hung on a line. The scent of sitting on your deck with your book flattened on your chest and your eyes closed and your face upraised and the sun's fingers tracing your skin and it's okay, you're not tanning, you're just rejoicing.

So in my hurry, I stopped. And I breathed Spring in. I even felt the tangy promise of Summer.

Then I resumed letting the hands of the clock shove me forward.

And yes, that helps. Despite. Anyway.

## MAY 11, 2017

And so today's moment of happiness despite the news.

I'm asked quite often when I find the time to write. It is a challenge – 85 hours a week teaching and running a business, raising my daughter, being a wife, doing some community volunteer work, yes, I'm a bit busy. I meet with clients in the morning, write in the afternoon, meet with clients in the early evening, and then continue through the evening or lead a class, and then read for the next day. I have a steadfast work ethic that some would call workaholicism. My day doesn't usually end until two or three in the morning. And then it begins again at ten.

But my afternoons are supposed to be writing time. They're sacred, or they have been. Over the last year, I've let interruptions in, and it shows, I think, in my mood and level of life quality. I'm trying to change that, and return to my protectiveness around that writing time.

I typically write in my office. But from time to time, I shake it up and head out to a coffee house. That's always a different perspective. I become very aware of the world around me in coffee shops, and it's like I sense the reader looking over my shoulder. I feel witnessed. Coffee house writing is a great place to edit, for me anyway, to bring that outside eye in. I don't want to think about the reader until subsequent drafts. First and foremost, I only want to think about the characters. I take myself on retreat once or so a year too, and in those times, my writing day extends to all waking hours. I become fully immersed, and in order not to lose myself into someone else's life, I head out once a day, again to a coffee house, usually Starbucks, for human interaction and familiarity.

But today, it was warm. Finally. And so I wrote outside.

I don't know how to write this, exactly. But when your words are lit by natural light, and not indoor light, electric light, artificial light, they look different. I become much more aware of the shape of a sentence, the shape of words, the way paragraphs look on the page, the artistry of the whole, not just the individual letters. In natural light, my vision changes and so does the feel of writing.

I usually sit in front of a space heater when I write – I love and crave heat. Outside, the sun is my space heater and my skin is warmed the way it's supposed to be. Not electric heat, but natural heat drapes me. My joints feel more fluid.

And there's the air – not air-conditioned, not heated and trotted through the ducts of the condo. I don't know that I'd say totally natural, as I live in the city and the bus garage is right across the street, so I do have exhaust. But in between buses – the light and the heat combine in the air and lay the lightest of welcome pressure on me.

This afternoon, I didn't let anything interrupt me. I let what is sacred to me become sacred again. I ignored phones (home, studio, cell), I ignored email, I ignored social media. What is natural to me, the act and art of writing, was performed out in the natural. In a genuine Wisconsin spring.

It just felt so good.

And yes, that helps. Despite. Anyway.

### MAY 12, 2018

And so today's moment of happiness despite the news.

I'm from a generation that still looks forward to getting the snail mail. For those younger than me, email has taken over that anticipation, hearing that computer voice say, "You've got mail!" (or in my case, hearing Barry White say, "Hey, baby, you've got mail!"), clicking on the mailbox icon, seeing who is there and what was said. I like email too, but every day, I go downstairs, eagerly flip up my mailbox lid, and stand on my tiptoes to peek inside. It's like opening a metal present.

Most days, I end up wasting my excitement on bills or ads. But sometimes, there's cool stuff in there.

Today was one of those days. There was a big padded envelope. I wasn't expecting anything, so I skipped right over the "Maybe this is the {insert item here} that I ordered!" heartrate increase. Instead, there was a surprise. I deliberately did not look at the return address to see who it was from. I hugged it and the rest of the mail as I went back up the stairs.

Wanting to draw the moment out, I placed the envelope face down on my counter and looked painstakingly at the rest of the mail first. I opened it, sorted it, threw away what was junk. Then I stood in front of the package, felt it all over, determined that it felt like a book, and turned the envelope over.

It was from a friend.

Giving in to abandon, I ripped the envelope open and pulled out a slender volume of poetry.

Just yesterday, I was talking with someone I will call a colleague. He told me he'd read an article about how poetry changes the brain. "I didn't send it to you," he said, "because you don't like poetry."

"Um…" I said. "I write poetry. I have a poetry book. I just spent the entire month of April writing a haiku a day on my daughter for National Poetry Month and Autism Awareness Month."

"Oh," he said. "I once mentioned Yeats to you and you said you didn't like him."

I don't. But that doesn't lead to a dislike of all poetry.

But this friend of mine sent me an envelope of poetry via the US mail. He wrote an inscription, just for me, on the title page, making this book no one else's but mine. I'm sure all of the poems in the collection are lovely, but it was the surprise, the thinking-of-you moment that didn't stop at the thought, but grew into a gesture, and then the words just for me that made my day.

Sometimes, that's all we need, isn't it. To know that we're thought of. And to know that we're known.

And yes, that helps. Despite. Anyway.

## MAY 13, 2017

And so today's moment of happiness despite the news.

My daughter Olivia is on an overnight field trip with the orchestra. I decided to take advantage of her absence and strip her bed, wash the sheets, blankets and bedspread, and in general, neaten up the chaotic room of a sixteen-year old.

At first, as I worked, I flashed forward, to two years from now when she will be off to college and I will stand in her room and not know where she is or what she's doing. But my mind didn't dwell there long. Instead, I moved backwards.

As I smoothed the sheets onto her bed, I was the mother who brushed her hair every morning, marveling at the waves, tugging them into a simple ponytail or a set of braids.

As I neatened her desk, putting scribbled papers into a pile, I was the mother who was mortified and filled with laughter when her daughter clearly said her first word – "Dumbass!" – to a complete stranger in the men's department of Sears.

As I found a place to store her stacks of sheet music, I was the mother whose mouth dropped open when her fifth grader came home from school, stood with her hands on her hips, and declared, "I want to play the violin!" I was the mother who brought her daughter to a poetry reading that weekend, because it was preceded by a violin quartet, and I watched as my daughter, the wiggly one, sat perfectly still on the edge of her seat and listened. She wiggled through the poetry, including mine. And I was the mother who a month later, watched her daughter open the violin that was hidden under the Christmas tree, tuck it under her chin, play her first squeaky notes, and laugh for joy, for found language, for communication. She'd found her voice in the sleek curves of a violin and the round notes of music.

As I replaced her stuffed animal bins with new bins, I was the mother who watched her daughter's imaginary family grow through a variety of obsessions. There was the Care Bear phase, that lasted forever, the turkey phase, the chicken phase. And then I found a little stuffed rhino, purple, created after the artwork of John Lennon. Michael and I bought this for our baby, newly discovered, newly confirmed, still tucked away deeply inside me. We named the rhino Lennon and put it in the crib that our child would sleep in, long before we knew our child was Olivia.

But I think we always knew our child, Olivia Grace.

As I found and marveled at her artwork, I was the mother of a preschooler taking a class in an art studio, a preschooler who refused to follow the teacher's orders and instead of being faithful to Van Gogh's blues, painted her Starry Night in pink. Her dog in pink. Her trees and grass and sky in pink. I celebrated my girl's insistence on a pink world, and today, I hung the painting of a delicate flower she had tucked away in her closet. I celebrate her still.

I hope my daughter doesn't mind that I straightened her room today. At sixteen, privacy is important. But when you're the mother of a daughter who is that sixteen, it's also important from time to time to remember that child you used to hold, to ease into sleep, to comfort after a night terror, to tell stories to, and sometimes, just to hold. Because of the sheer joy of her life in yours.

Today, I held on tight.

And yes, that helps. Despite. Anyway.

# MAY 14, 2017

And so today's moment of happiness despite the news.

Well, of course, Mother's Day. That's the positive side. And on the negative, there was the news break that told me that North Korea has announced its missile testing shows that it can reach US targets with nuclear warheads. Oh. Good. I'm sure the Orange Asshat will soon be thumping his chest and saying, "You just try it! I'll sue you!"

But enough of that.

I needed to meditate today, and I wanted to take a walk on the Riverwalk, and I didn't have time to do both. Sundays are always full of preparing for the week ahead and I was already behind for Monday before the sun went down on Sunday. I didn't want to throw both goals away so I decided to give walking meditation a try.

I drove to my usual starting point on Waukesha's Fox Riverwalk. Then I plunked on my headphones, searched my Insight Timer app for walking meditations and found two that lasted an hour. I started the first and headed off.

I lasted about five minutes before pitching that one into internet ether. The woman on the tape wanted me to walk so slowly – to not move my left leg before my right came to a complete standstill. Not only was that uncomfortable, I didn't even know if it was possible. Maybe meditation can be about teaching patience, but I didn't have any. Not today.

The second tape was all music and so I hit play and began to walk again. This one lasted longer – but not with expected results. Instead of allowing my mind to slow, to open, to quiet, the music began to lead me down thought pathways I didn't want explore. The notes were ominous, even creepy, but I stuck with it for fifteen minutes, waiting for redemption. It didn't come. I turned it off. I took the headphones off. I turned my phone off. I tried to shut me off. And I just began to walk. I figured meditation was a wash for today.

I was on the side of the river away from the playgrounds and the park. This was the quiet side. And it wasn't long before my breathing and steps evened out and then my mind evened out too. I discovered there is meditation in the river. In the trees. In the steady sound of my shoes against the bricks, the whisper of my sleeves against my sides, in the sound of a distant train to my right, the distant traffic on my left. Birdsong. The splash as ducks landed, the flicker of their wings as they took off again. It was all a simple rhythm, strong, steady, my heartbeat, my breath, my footfalls, the blinks of my eyes, the riverflow, the leaf flutters, the birds, the train, the cars, the squeals of children, the squeak of the chains on the swings. Even as I kept moving, kept pressing forward, I felt my shoulders release and drop, and my thoughts, while they still occurred, just hovered for a second, then floated away.

I've been walking on the Riverwalk for years now. Turns out my walks were about meditation before I even knew how to meditate. I just didn't realize it.

Relief. Release. Rhythm.

And yes, that helps. Despite. Anyway.

## MAY 15, 2017

And so today's moment of happiness despite the news.

The internet is an amazing thing.

I suppose for the younger generation (and I can't believe I'm old enough to say that), it's a given. Something that's always been there. But I still marvel at it, even on days when I swear at it because it's not doing what I told it to do. Which I did a lot today. But I'm still marveling anyway.

Today, I sat down to meditate for a half-hour at 4:30 in the afternoon, central time. I stroked on my app, reclined my chair (no walking meditation today), put on the headphones, and disappeared.

But when I came back, I found that while I disappeared, I was not invisible. Others who also disappeared sat quietly by my side. When I tapped a button to log my time, I found a variety of "thank you for meditating with me" messages from:

Cape Town, South Africa
Jakarta, Indonesia
Shorewood , Wisconsin
Sun Prairie, Wisconsin
Stamford, Connecticut
Birmingham, United Kingdom
Bay Area, California
The Philippines
Exeter, United Kingdom
Grayslake, Illinois
New York, New York
Greenville, Mississippi
India
Rio de Janeiro, Brasil

And that's only those who messaged me. All in all, there were 3604 people sitting and meditating at the same time I was.

So I was all alone in my headspace, but I wasn't. I was surrounded by like-headspaced people. Some who have "friended" me. Some who just wanted to reach out. And at the same time, were willing to offer their company in a silent, nonintrusive, noninvasive way.

Unlike a certain cat who insisted on climbing on my lap and kneading my thighs with her pinpointy claws. I very peacefully, very Namaste-y pitched her to the floor.

How nice to know you're not alone even when you're alone. That you can choose to be alone, but have fine company.

I like that.

And yes, that helps. Despite. Anyway.

### MAY 16, 2017

And so today's moment of happiness despite the news.

This one's a rollercoaster. Ride with me, please. There is a steep loop-de-loop.

Every day, I receive a goofy little email that contains a digital fortune cookie. I click a button, the cookie cracks open, and I get a fortune. Today's was, "*You will soon witness a miracle.*"

I smiled. I mean, haven't I already witnessed miracles? A business that should never have survived is thriving. A writing career that almost matches my dreams (where the hell are you, Oprah?). A child who was nonverbal is now so verbal, she doesn't use periods when she talks. I'm sleeping, for heaven's sake. Yes, there's been a few miracles. But I acknowledged I'd be okay with more.

Then a book read at lunch set off a series of chain reactions. Dominoes going down. I'm reading Marjorie Maddox's story collection, *What She Was Saying*. In the story, "Learning To Yell", I first read:

*In such silence, she wrote a life, tried on the words that fit, and erased the others.*

And I instantly felt a deep strike. Then I read, on the next page:

*"This is how you do it," she read in the kit she ordered over eBay. "Open your lungs and lips. Let the past pour out." But in the midst of those bruises on 5th and Park, she had been too scared to practice. Something got caught*

*behind her teeth. She thinks it was her soul.*

And I felt more than a strike. I felt run over. Plowed into.

A few days ago, on Sunday, I walked by the river and tried to listen to a walking meditation tape. It was filled with ominous music and I found I just couldn't listen. There were few vocals, but the line I heard before I ripped off the headphones was:

I can't say what my eyes want to say.

And now I was reading a story called "Learning To Yell". And I thought of all the years I've been silent. With that, those years took me over, and the sound that came out of me wasn't silent at all.

In that moment, I realized why these last months since November have been so hard. So hard that they made me, me! a skeptic who writes dark, try to find some light by writing a moment of happiness every day.

In November, we elected a bully to the White House.

Two days after that, I was assaulted by a bully who threw me off the sidewalk after he attempted to kick my dog. He told me it was time to "put you back in your place, woman."

And since then, I've been watching my daughter get bullied, by a now ex-boyfriend, by now ex-friends. I've watched what she's going through. I've watched the school being ineffective, despite posters about bullying, programs about bullying, books about bullying. The school subscribes to policies put into place to protect itself, not those being bullied. And I've felt like an ineffective parent, despite fighting it with everything that I have.

I was born quiet. Introverted. Shy. I was also born with strabismus, or crossed eyes. The quiet and the crossed eyes and the sensitivity of a soon-to-be writer made me a perfect target. From day one of school, when I was dubbed Clarence, after Clarence the cross-eyed lion on the *Dakatari* television series, until I graduated, I was bullied. I was teased, tripped, thrown into lockers, my face slammed into water fountains, I was pantsed, my clothes ripped, gum in my hair, hands on my body, whispers in my ear, shouts in my face, and excluded, excluded, excluded.

A line I read in this same book last week, from the short story "Weeds":

*We hoped we were singled out, not left out.*

I was left out, except when I was singled out by all of the above.

I was told, at home and at school, that I had to fight back. I had to stand up for myself. It was my responsibility. It was my problem, my fault, if I was pushed around.

I was a quiet girl.

So I stayed quiet, and quiet turned into silence. I couldn't say what my eyes wanted to say. My soul got caught in my teeth.

And since November, and then December, I've been silently screaming as I've relived it all over again, but watched the new bruises form not on me, but on the tender skin, the tender heart of my daughter. My girl. My quiet girl, with the sensitivity of a soon-to-be writer, a violinist, an artist.

I was born in 1960. My daughter, in 2000.

We haven't changed a bit. We even put a bully in the White House.

And so today, the primal sound as my soul finally broke through my teeth. And the realization as to why this has been the worst winter of my entire goddamned life.

So why is this my moment of happiness? Loop-de-loop.

Because. When you let out something that has been so heavy in your heart and your mind and your memory, when you at last acknowledge what it is you refuse to speak about, refuse to write about, what you refuse to draw attention to or pay attention to, there is an instant new lightness of being. And even when it leaves you weak-kneed, you are stronger.

I'm learning how to yell. I'm letting the past pour out and I'm acknowledging it and I'm letting it go. This is my miracle.

I am also making sure that my daughter knows she doesn't have to be silent. She doesn't have to yell back, she doesn't have to fight those that torture her, it's not her fault, it's not her responsibility, and most of all, she doesn't have to be who she isn't. She can come home. She can talk to her parents who know exactly who she is, how amazing she is, and how amazing she's going to be.

There's no silence for her. There are only open arms. And a soul, no longer trapped behind teeth, who understands.

And yes, that helps. Despite. Anyway.

## MAY 17, 2017

And so today's moment of happiness despite the news.

As sometimes happens, the moment of happiness came in three parts today (not nearly as dramatic as yesterday, I'm afraid, but…still a moment of happiness).

Yesterday morning, I had an email from a student. He received a contract for his novel and he wasn't sure it was real.

It was.

Today, he signed it. His novel, a dream, is going to be published.

This morning, before I heard that my student signed his contract, I had an email from another student. A publisher is calling her tomorrow about her novel. I've dealt with this publisher before. His acceptances come with a phone call.

Her hope is through the roof. So is mine.

This afternoon, I went through the drive-thru at Dunkin Donuts. Not Starbucks, but don't worry, I haven't gone crazy. I wanted chicken salad, and DD makes a great chicken salad croissant sandwich. And during the summer, they have iced butter pecan lattes. As the person behind the counter handed me my order, she recognized me. She said, "I have a friend who took class with you once. She wants to be a writer." She told me a name that I recognized – someone I had years ago in creative writing camp, when she was just a little bitty young'un. Now she's a college age young'un. My DD person said, "She said she learned so much from you. And she is going to be a writer. You taught her she could be."

I drove off with way more than a chicken salad croissant sandwich and an iced butter pecan latte.

Three. Not three strikes. Three...what? I don't like baseball. Three...oh, just THREE! Three dreams made, and when their dreams are made, so is mine.

I had a student a few weeks ago tell me that I was different because I honestly want my students' successes, I honestly feel them, they are as exciting to me as my own. Well, yeah. Of course! I can't imagine it any other way.

I guess today, the three, bing bing bing, added up to this. I'm happy to be myself, and I'm happy that brings success to others.

And yes, that helps. Despite. Anyway.

## MAY 18, 2017

And so today's moment of happiness despite the news.

I returned today for the third time to the Waukesha County Jail and the book club for female inmates. This time, they were to have read my story collection, *Enlarged Hearts*.

But here's the thing with a book club housed in a jail. The members tend to move on. Either they're released back into their lives, or they move to a prison. There'd been a large turnover recently, and the majority of the women

I'd met before were off on their paths. Just a handful were still there that I knew, and there were many new attendees. This meant that most had just gotten the book and hadn't read it yet; those that read it moved on before I got there.

So I looked at a bunch of new faces today. New stories. New lives behind the stories.

This was the final day of their "semester." I watched as they exclaimed like children over "treats" – two small pieces of candy, a juice box, a bag of chips. And I wondered how treating women like children helped them to learn to never be in such a place again.

It's hard to talk for two hours about a book that hasn't been read, so we moved on to other subjects. They talked to me mostly about my life and about writing. I was asked to describe all my books, and so I did. When I got to *Rise From The River*, my novel about a young single mother who becomes pregnant as the result of a rape, one of the women suddenly shot out of her seat. She ran to the door, lifted the receiver of the phone beside it and slammed it down – this alerts the guard that someone needs to be let out to use the restroom. Yes, we are locked in a room while I'm there. I kept talking while this woman shook and the tears flowed without sound, but she kept her back to me, so I didn't address her directly. After several phone slams, the guard came and this woman took off.

I wondered if it was me that made this woman cry. I felt horrible.

Several of the women asked if they should go check on her when she didn't come back right away. They said a sensitive spot had been touched. But they aren't allowed out more than one at a time. I couldn't leave them, and my escort couldn't leave me.

Helpless.

Eventually, she came back. Several of the women whispered to her, asking if she was okay. She nodded. I wondered if I should apologize, but I wasn't sure what I'd done, so I just kept on going.

When the conversation slowed, I asked if anyone else had any questions. And the same woman turned and leveled me with her eyes. There was no place else in that room I could look. "Have you ever," she said slowly, "gotten to the point where you wanted to give up? I mean…just give up?" She took a breath, and then amended, "Writing, I mean."

But every part of me knew that this wasn't about writing. Her intensity spread over me like paste. Paste doesn't like platitudes. I knew I had to answer honestly.

"Yes," I said. And then I told her the story about the sand dollar.

After the release of *Rise From The River*, I went into a slump like I'd never sunk into before. I no longer believed I had a purpose. I believed I wasted my entire life. People wanted *50 Shades Of Gray*. They didn't care about literature. They didn't care about fine writing. They didn't care about words.

They didn't care about the treatment of women. Even women didn't care about the treatment of women. Reading or watching a movie about the abuse of a woman was entertainment. Couples night at the theatre.

I retreated – literally – to the state of Oregon. The day I arrived, I stood in the Pacific and I yelled, at God, at the Universe, at the ocean, to show me if I was on the right path. To show me there was a reason for my life. When I wasn't surprised by a bolt of lightning or the sudden ability to walk on water, I went specific. "If I am on the right path, let me find a whole sand dollar while I'm here. A WHOLE sand dollar."

And a week went by.

One night, it was foggy, and the fog on the Pacific is like nowhere else. It sparkles. My daughter and I walked in stars and stardust and glitter. In the distance, an older man came toward us, and no matter where I stepped, he moved himself so he was directly in my path. We stopped when we were practically nose to nose. I noticed I wasn't afraid.

He looked right at me. He didn't say hello or how are you. He said, "Have you found a whole sand dollar?"

I could have dissolved right there. "No," I said. "I've been looking, but –"

"Choose one," he said, and he pulled three out of his pocket.

I did. Then he told Olivia to choose one too. And he walked on his way.

When I finished telling this story, the locked-up room in the jail was silent. One of the women I'd met before whispered, "I have goosebumps."

I looked at the woman who asked me the question. Have you ever gotten to the point where you wanted to give up? I locked her in the same gaze that she gave me. I hope she felt my paste. I didn't know what to say, but I did.

"Don't you do it," I said. "Don't you do it. I know it hurts like hell now. But it's worth it. You keep walking."

Well, you know. Dissolve. Tears.

I went into writing to make a difference. Today, I made a difference through writing with a woman who hasn't even read me yet. I hope she does. I bet I know which book. And I hope my paste sticks.

And yes, that helps. Despite. Anyway.

## MAY 19, 2017

And so today's moment of happiness despite the news.

This week, my moments of happiness have included thoughts on bullying and a soul-stirring moment while leading a book club for female inmates in jail. Today, I was lucky to experience something even more profound.

Rainbow sherbet.

We've had some lovely weather this week. It seemed like spring and summer finally arrived, in tandem, holding hands. Temperatures in the low 80's. Abundant sunshine. Winter clothes were thrown aside, capris, sandals and sleeveless shirts came out from hiding in my cedar chest. When I walked, I was accompanied by the gentle smack-smack-smack of sandals, leaving the sidewalk to meet my heels and turn them into the drumbeat of summer. We had thunderstorms too, but you've gotta take the bad with the good. I'll take thunderstorms over a blizzard any day.

Then today. Temperatures in the forties. Sneakers, pants, long-sleeved shirt, jacket. Gray skies. Cold rain.

This afternoon, I meditated under my heated throw and I fell into a half-hour hibernation, the sleep of winter. At this very moment, I am sitting in front of my turned-on-high spaceheater. My daughter is soaking in the Jacuzzi tub. I'm contemplating the furnace.

But right before that, there was dinner. As if Michael knew the cold was coming, he threw a pot roast into the crockpot this morning. Complete with cooked-all-day tender carrots, potatoes, little onions and gravy, it was a meal that filled the condo with a scent of winter that warmed, but was still welcome on this cold spring day. Then I went looking for a little dessert.

In the freezer, I found three small containers. Rainbow. Watermelon. Three Citrus.

SHERBET!

I chose Rainbow. Oh, summer. There you are. The bright colors of a passing storm sky, the taste of sweetened fruit plucked from no tree in reality, but a tree of the imagination, a tree with fruit the color of crayons, the perfect dessert to a day spent on the beach, in the sun, in the heat, after a meal of hamburgers on the grill, corn on the cob, potato salad…

Or a perfect cold day dessert melting summer on my tongue, dreaming of June, July, August…

And yes, that helps. Despite. Anyway.

## MAY 20, 2017

And so today's moment of happiness despite the news.

Fear is not a fun thing. And an irrational fear is worse. Your mind tells you to stop being ridiculous, but your entire body gets caught up in a raceway. Run! Run! Run!

Today's moment of happiness occurred after I had to run through one of those fears and I came out the other side mercifully intact. But I know I will face this fear again and again, and I know I have to do something about it.

A little history.

From 1966 to 1972, when I was six years old to twelve, I lived in a tiny community in northern Minnesota, tucked between Duluth and Cloquet. I didn't lose my first tooth until I was six, and then I lost four at once, at the hands of a dentist who didn't have much going for him but an ether mask. Baby teeth are supposed to fall out when the roots dissolve, but mine never did. It was time to lose a tooth when the permanent tooth began coming up behind. Each one. Except for a few, every one of my baby teeth was pulled by a dentist. And for every one, I was knocked out with ether.

What is ether like? The mask was black rubber and it fit snugly over my nose and mouth, tucking up under my eyes. The smell was like gasoline, but a little bit off. It threw me into a wild black cyclone, swirling round and round, sucking me down. Flashes of light accompanied a bizarre sound, like a cross between maniacal laughter and a whoop-whoop-whoop siren. Sometimes voices broke through. Sometimes the crunch of a tooth being removed broke through. Always, my screams broke through. When I came to, I was nauseated and dizzy for the rest of the day. My mother always complained of being embarrassed in the waiting room, knowing it was her daughter who was screaming. My mother had no clue what I was going through.

I was ethered for the first three of five eye surgeries as well. To this day, I have ether nightmares.

When I was twelve, we moved to Stoughton, Wisconsin, and the dentist there introduced me to novocaine. Which had no effect on me. The dentist would give me five or six shots, then declare me a baby and go ahead and either fill the tooth or pull it out. More screaming. It wasn't until I had my first child at twenty-four that I realized my immunity. My doctor was stitching up my episiotomy and I felt every stitch. He stopped and asked me if I had issues with dental procedures. He then told me I had an immunity and that for future children, he would order ahead a special anesthetic.

But by then, even armed with the immunity information, my terror of dentists ran through my veins and psyche. I couldn't even watch it on television. Tim Conway's dentist comedy skits had me either leaving the room or covering my eyes. Taking my kids to their dental visits was excruciating.

So on Friday morning, when I brushed my teeth and my tongue discovered a crack in a filling, my reaction was immediate. Cold sweat. Legs turned to noodles. Tears. But I reached for the phone and made an appointment.

For years now, I've only seen a dentist when I've absolutely had to. They've been kind. They haven't hurt me. They've used special anesthetic. But it's been no match for the fear.

This morning, early (yuk), I went in. Michael, bless him, came with me. I cried all the way there. The staff was wonderful. The dentist was kind. He told me immediately that the fix was easy, releasing me from visions of drills and needles and pain. For the entire visit, Michael sat at my feet, one hand on my ankle. For comfort, for sure, but probably also to keep me there. At one point, while the dentist touched all my teeth and talked in code to the hygienist, tears ran freely down my cheeks. He kept his voice soft. She put her hand on my shoulder, a gentle touch. And then he fixed me. He took what he called dental spackle and filled the crack. No drills, no needles, no pain. He told me to come in for a cleaning and then he would fix the tooth more permanently with a new filling. He said that would take no more than fifteen minutes and wouldn't require an anesthetic.

This is the part in a dental visit where I typically smile and nod and then say I'll check my calendar and call in for an appointment and then I get the hell out of there and plan to never visit that clinic again. But today, I took a deep breath and felt something shift. I made the appointment. June 6.

Now we'll see if I keep it. We'll see if I can face this thing.

I think I can. Maybe, at almost fifty-seven years old, I can leave that screaming little girl behind.

And yes, that helps. Despite. Anyway.

## MAY 21, 2017

And so today's moment of happiness despite the news.

Years ago, when my big kids, now 33, 31, and 30, were getting ready to make the choice of whether or not to participate in their school's music program, I had one rule. No violin. Absolutely no violin. I couldn't stand the sound of a new player, smacking a bow to the strings, squeaking, squawking, scratching. For me, it was akin to the sound of fingernails on a blackboard – something that never bothered me, but made the greater population cringe.

No violin.

My oldest played the trumpet. My middle played the drums. My youngest (then) played the flute. They had their share of rude noises too, but I was always relieved that it wasn't the violin.

Then came my fourth child. My baby, when I was forty years old and the three big kids were 16, 14, and 13. She let me know very quickly what she thought of my rules and expectations. I thought I'd seen it all by the time I had her; in reality, I hadn't seen anything yet.

In fifth grade, she came home from school, put her hands on her hips and declared, "I want to play the violin."

Oh, no, no, no, no, I thought. Come on, really?

But there is one word that describes Olivia best. Determined. Whatever she chooses to do, she does. If she wanted to play the violin, she wasn't going to let it go. There would be no substitute.

And so she went on to prove me wrong. The squeaky, squawky, scratchy phase was over so fast, I don't even have any memory of it. I only have memories of that little girl, tucking her first instrument under her chin, drawing the bow across the strings, and smiling.

That smile.

Today, I watched her perform in a recital. She stepped up to the stand, placed her bow reverently on the strings the way she did so long ago, smiled, then leveled the smile as her whole body became involved with the music and with concentration. She played a slow movement, rich in emotion. And then she flew into a fast movement, so fast that I thought her violin was going to burst into flames from the friction.

I am so happy that she insisted on breaking one of my rules. And I am so happy to have been a part of the squeaking, squawking and scratching. What I hear coming from her now is music at its purest. And what I see is better than any vision.

Her smile.

And yes, that helps. Despite. Anyway.

## MAY 22, 2017

And so today's moment of happiness despite the news.

I am a hyper-organized person. When people ask me how I manage to get so much done, the answer is in one word: organization. Things are in their place, and their place is set in cement. My desk calendar is meticulous. I don't use an online scheduler, either via my phone or my computer, because there's too much chance for a screw-up. I know where I'm supposed to be when, and what I'm supposed to do when I get there, and I'm prepared. Things. Get. Done. I was that person everyone hated in college – my papers were always done at least two weeks in advance of the due date. I don't write papers anymore, but I do have deadlines, and they're met well in advance.

Until today. From now on, I have to add "almost always" to my sense of organization. I have to add "usually". I have to add "typically" and "probably".

I knew I was in trouble this weekend. I organize the work for the week ahead around a Saturday night outing. But this weekend, everything went crazy. There was the sudden interruption of a dentist appointment early Saturday morning, followed by my once-a-month three-hour workshop. Followed by my having to take my daughter into Urgent Care because she couldn't stop coughing. Followed by my falling asleep (as the result of no sleep the night before because of nerves for the upcoming dentist appointment) during meditation, which led to an unplanned nap, which led to dinner out, which meant I didn't even sit down to do any work until almost ten o'clock Saturday night. This led to Sunday, which had two extra activities: my daughter's violin recital and going to see the play Jane Eyre at the Milwaukee Repertory Theatre, where my husband works. I brought folders with me to the play and I read during the twenty-minute intermission.

But ohmygod. Organization plans all awry.

Then came today. I deliberately got up early, so I would be showered, dressed, and fed before my morning phone clients. That way, I could hang up the phone and get right into my own writing and still get my own creative work done while trying to catch up with my teaching work. Instead, my coughing daughter was still coughing. So I had to take her to the doctor. At 12:45, the only time available. And he was running late and didn't even get into the exam room until 1:30. I only got an hour and fifteen minutes of writing in, and then I decided to sacrifice the rest to meditation, to try and calm myself down. After meditation, I was in the process of signing on to Skype for my 5:00 client when I realized I couldn't remember what my client wrote this week and what I said about it. And a chill went flying up my spine.

BECAUSE I NEVER READ HER WORK.

I read the two clients before her and the client after her and the class after her. I checked her off as completed on my calendar. But I completely leaped right over her.

I had to show up a few minutes late to our appointment so I had time to wipe away tears of absolute frustration and failure. When you're as organized as I am, perfectionism is, of course, right there in bed with you. It's a threesome: Me, Organization, and Perfectionism. We don't have room for a fourth: Failure. But it felt like Failure was all over me. It was Armageddon.

But I got on Skype and I told my client what happened. She was gracious, kind and forgiving.

And you know what? My world didn't end. I am back in my chair, trying to get my ducks all lined up in a row again, my cats all herded. And I know they will be. I also know now that if one wanders off, if one of my things isn't in the place it's supposed to be, if I drop a ball…I'll be okay. The world won't suddenly hate me.

Tomorrow will be a better day.

And yes, that helps. Despite. Anyway.

### MAY 23, 2017

And so today's moment of happiness despite the news.

It's a hard news day.

Manchester. A concert for tweens and teens.

Little girls.

And a suicide bomber.

In an international conversation with a coaching client today, she said, "How do you do that sometimes after the news, like out of Manchester, I don't know."

I answered, "That's why it's called Today's Moment Of Happiness Despite The News."

She said, "My happy moment was seeing my daughter happy yesterday, despite the news."

Later, she said, "God almighty, just makes you hug your children tighter."

Today, the day after the news in Manchester, I gave my teen daughter a guitar. Pink, because this girl's world is pink and always has been. A guitar, because while she's an amazing violinist, she's had a hankering to try the guitar. A surprise gift, because the school year has been rough socially, but she's toughed it out. She finds joy and solace in music. So I wanted to give her more music.

I want her world to always be pink.

She beamed. That smile.

I hugged her tight. Tighter.

My happy moment was seeing my daughter happy, despite the news.

Tomorrow, I will hold her tighter. Again.

And yes, that helps. Despite. Anyway.

## MAY 24, 2017

And so today's moment of happiness despite the news.

Six times now, I've written down a small idea that grew into a book manuscript. And six times, I've watched a publisher turn that book manuscript into a real book, a book-book, one that perfect strangers can hold in their hands and read. Six times now, I've had a day where my book suddenly develops a face.

A cover.

Receiving the electronic galley of your book and its cover is like holding an ultrasound photo of your baby. With the cover, with the face, your book suddenly has a personality, an identity. It becomes real. It becomes Someone – at least, I think of my books as Someones.

Today, it happened for the seventh time.

When I received the file, I opened the cover photo first. And then I just sat and gazed at it. There it was. And then I opened the galley file and looked at the words, the words now no longer looking like Times New Roman 12 Point Font, double-spaced, on a screen, but...like a book. A book-book. Real.

I can remember back to when I decided my name was going to be a household word by the time I reached twenty years old. As each of my decades reached its ninth year, 29, 39, 49, I changed when that household word would be reached. 30. 40. 50. With some decades, not only did the numbers slip by, but my name changed too. Kathleen M. Thomas. Kathie Lokken. Kathie Lokken-Giorgio. Kathie Giorgio.

That last name felt like I finally fit in my own skin.

My first book came out when I was fifty years old. This year, I will turn fifty-seven, and this is my seventh book. It will be released on September 7, 2017.

I'm not a household word. I know that. But I know I'm in a lot of households. I know my books have been held in many hands, some belonging to people I know, some belonging to perfect strangers. This one will be too.

I do not have a goal to be a household word by the time I'm sixty. I'm letting that go. I'm learning to accept that not all lifelong dreams are realized. But that doesn't mean a life hasn't been lived.

I set out at an early age to achieve some pretty lofty goals. Last year, when books five and six came out, I decided I could now say I had a body of work. This year, with book #7, and hundreds of short stories, and essays and poems too, I feel like I can say I've produced a lifetime of work.

And I'm not done yet. Book #8 is underway.

There's a lot that I haven't accomplished, and at times, that's left me feeling like a failure. I focused more on what I didn't than what I did. But I'm learning to tilt my head the other way and seeing instead what I have done, and not all the empty space in between. Don't look at the empty. Look at the full.

It was a somewhat melancholy moment of happiness today. A bright happy, but with the slight blue tone of regret.

But I feel full. Book #7. *In Grace's Time.*

In my time.

And yes, that helps. Despite. Anyway.

### MAY 25, 2017

And so today's moment of happiness despite the news.

Despite being a night person, I don't like the night. The dark brings with it dark things. Dark things that were once real. Dark things that are memory now. I think sometimes my tendency to be a workaholic – okay, I do my best to be honest in these things, so let me change that. I think sometimes my absolutely being a workaholic who works into the early morning hours is a way to combat the dark and also to fight away the deepest dark of all – sleep, where nightmares dwell.

And so I sit at night with the lights on and I work. What is that quote about a single light in the dark?

*It's better to light a candle than curse the darkness.*

So I sit in light. And I work the darkness away.

Tonight, just a little while ago, I was at my computer when evening began to fall in earnest. I hadn't yet turned the lights on. I am the only one in the house right now – Michael is downstairs in the AllWriters' classroom, leading the Teen Writers' Workshop, and Olivia is a teen in the workshop. This is probably the quietest moment I've had all day. I started to get up to turn on the lights, to ward off the creeping dark, but then I noticed a light blue tone to the graying of nightfall. And so I made myself, just this once, sit and watch.

I've watched sunsets. I know their beauty. But this was the first time I watched evening, and evening turn to night.

Other words for evening: twilight dusk eventide vespers nightfall witching hour

Everything turned the quietest of blues. It wasn't a sky blue or an ocean blue, but a blue like a featherbed. There were no birdcalls, no birdsong. It was as if silence became something I could dip my hands into. Let run through my fingers.

Another phrase for night: the dead of night. Well, that's the fear, isn't it. What all dark things lead to.

But I didn't feel fear. I only felt admiration. And the sense that, metaphorically, evening can be okay. Just like autumn can be okay. November can be okay.

Dark can be okay. Memory can be okay. What used to be dark can lead to light. That's what I'm doing with these Moments, isn't it.

And yes, that helps. Despite. Anyway.

## MAY 26, 2017

And so today's moment of happiness despite the news.

Yesterday, I received a rejection for one of my short stories. Normally, this would not be a reason for a moment of happiness. Normally, it would be a reason for me to kick, scream, pout, cry, hold my breath until I turned blue, and take the editor's name in vain. But not this time.

This time, it was a personal note from an editor I greatly respect, from a magazine I greatly love. It was addressed to me, by name. It told me how much the editor liked my story, and it told me where I lost him, and it told me that if I chose to rewrite the story, he'd love to see it again.

And here's the thing. Typically, letters like this are about making a story shorter. This was about making a story LONGER.

Ohmygod.

The story was its length because I was trying to be a good little writer and stay within the Rule for appropriate short story word count. I deliberately sacrificed content and style for the Rule. It's still a good story and I was very happy with it. But there was this little part of me, usually on my inside right elbow, that itched for more. Tingles in my fingers that said, Hey, you're not done pounding the keys yet. And the hamster in my brain kept insisting the wheel needed to turn and turn and c'mon, let's go.

But the Rule. Break the Rule?

Now, here was this editor, who I respect, telling me to let loose. Telling me to stretch. Telling me to let go of the reins of control and let my horse run.

He gave me permission to break the Rule. Well, you don't have to tell me twice.

So today, I set aside the NIP (novel-in-progress) and I returned to this story. I spent most of the afternoon with this character, who is a repeater in my stories and books, but usually, as a dead person. As a memory. This is only the second story I've written of her alive. And I love her. And I turned her loose. I STRETCHED. The wheel turned and turned and turned.

I busted right through that Rule. Shattered it to smithereens. And man, did it feel good. I wrote with such a sense of freedom and abandon, I swear my hair was whipping in the wind I imagined.

Years ago, I took part in a class at an art studio that encouraged you to go back to kindergarten. The walls were made out of whiteboard and we stuck our sheets of canvas paper to the walls with masking tape. The paints and brushes were in a huge trough down the center of the room and we were encouraged to just paint at will. Not think ahead. Mix colors. Go off the paper. Use our fingers. Use our bodies.

Break the Rules.

There were days I came back covered in paint. On my clothes, face, under my fingernails, in the lines of my palms. I came home exhausted. I came home happy.

Today, I wrote until I was exhausted. I wrote happy. I just freaking wrote. I returned to the organic, the very basic dirt floor, of who I am and what I do.

And I think this editor is going to love it.

And yes, that helps. Despite. Anyway.


## MAY 27, 2017

And so today's moment of happiness despite the news.

Know what happens when the sun comes out and the temperatures go up?

1) My daughter asked – ASKED – if she could clean out her closet. (I know – I'm still stunned.)

2) When I drove out in the convertible to get our lunch, there was a man

sitting on a ledge at the intersection where I had to stop for traffic. When I looked over, he was beaming. I beamed back. We seat-danced to the music I was playing. And he called, "You have a wonderful day!" when I pulled out.

3) Two teenage boys held a door open for me. When I said, "Thank you," they smiled and said, "You are very welcome."

4) At another intersection, which I hate because there's no light and there's tons of traffic, always ill-timed, I had to wait forever. And I didn't care.

5) When I went for a walk on the Riverwalk, my daughter came with me. Even though she snap-chatted all the way around, she was at least with me and out of her closed-door room.

6) On the Riverwalk, everyone was smiling.

It was a beautiful day.

And yes, that helps. Despite. Anyway.

## MAY 28, 2017

And so today's moment of happiness despite the news.

For two days in a row, we've had glorious weather. Sunshine. Blue skies. Rain at night when it doesn't bother anyone except my storm-phobic batshit beagle. And so, for the second day in a row, I ventured out to Waukesha's Fox Riverwalk for a three-mile walk.

Walking two days in a row is a big deal for me. I live with fibromyalgia. I've been told and I've read that movement decreases fibro pain. I've yet to see that in action. I woke up in pain this morning. The hips, the shoulders. And, in true bizarre fibro-fashion, the collarbone. I was stunned when I first learned that collarbone pain is a hallmark of fibro – I'd had that and thought I was nuts.

For the first quarter of my walk, I moved to the left foot-right foot mantra of this hurts this hurts this hurts. Eventually, though, the perfect sky and soft river eased me into a walking meditation, where I could leave pain behind, at least until I stopped moving.

I wore a favorite t-shirt today. It's black, and in bold white letters, it says, #Plus Is Equal. On the back, it says, It's time to represent. The #PlusIsEqual movement was started in 2015, by Lane Bryant. Their statement: 67% of US women are size 14 to 34. But they're underrepresented on billboards, magazines, TV...everywhere. We believe all women should be seen and celebrated equally. As a well-rounded woman, I fully agree and I wear the shirt with great pride and joy.

On my walk today, many women called out to me, "I like your shirt!" I smiled and said thank you and kept on going. Men, I noticed, didn't say anything. They glanced at my shirt and then away.

I was about halfway around when a woman caught up to me and fell in step. "Can I walk with you for a bit?" she asked.

I was surprised, but agreed. She wore headphones like a necklace. Clearly, she planned on walking alone, but now she matched me, foot for foot. We walked in silence for a bit.

"I like your shirt," she said finally.

"Thanks," I said. And yes, this woman fit in with the 67%.

"I always feel funny when I walk here," she said.

I asked her why.

"You know. People zip by me. They're running or they're power-walking or they're rollerblading or they're biking. And I always feel like they look at me as if I don't belong here. Like you're only supposed to be doing this –" she waved her arms, "—if you're skinny. In shape. You know. The body beautiful."

"Doing what?" I waved my arms like hers. "Enjoying the day? Listening to the river? Admiring the sky?" I turned to look at her and scanned my eyes up and down, in a way I knew would make most people uncomfortable. But I had a point. "Your body is beautiful." Left foot, right foot. This didn't hurt so much anymore. "Know what else? So is mine."

She looked ahead at our path and she smiled. We walked along, down the brick walkway, up the small hill, over the bridge, stopping for a moment to lean on the railing and watch the water. Then past the park and the squeals of children. Under weeping willow trees. Through the calls of red-winged blackbirds and robins. And yes, we were passed by those who were running. By those who were biking. By those who looked like they'd been doing that sort of thing for a while.

As we reached the parking lot where Semi was waiting for me, the woman said, "You made me feel better. Thank you."

I felt better too.

And yes, that helps, Despite. Anyway.

## MAY 29, 2017

And so today's moment of happiness despite the news.

My holiday weekend has been anything but a holiday. I've spent most of it hunkered over my computer, working. I did take the time yesterday and the day before to get outside and walk the 3-mile loop of the Riverwalk. But today, I couldn't even do that. I was aching. And there was just too much to get done before tomorrow. There still is – I'm not done.

But this afternoon, I shoved it all aside. I stayed on my computer, but the words that came up on the screen, the words I worked on, rearranged, read aloud, took apart, put back together, and ultimately loved, were my own.

I wrote.

A Moment last week was about a much-respected editor of a magazine I love telling me to make a story longer and then to re-submit it. I started that process a few days ago. When I did, when I cracked that story back open, there was so much more to it that rushed out. My first time through it, I added 1279 words. When I looked through it again, those 1279 words looked like they belonged there all along. They shook their fingers at me for not noticing them before. I laughed, grabbed them by their wagging fingertips, and they pulled me back in for more.

Today, the real finessing began. The polishing, the trimming, the not-this-word-but-that-one, the sinking into a character so hard, my edges disappeared and became hers. And those words became mine, my playthings, my balls to juggle, my clay to shape. There are times I wish I could write with the old plastic magnet letters from my childhood, the ones that presented to me the alphabet and that A means apple and C means cat, and every letter can join with another letter and make a word and words can make sentences and sentences can make stories with meaning. With lives. Peopled with people who aren't real, but are. I know them better sometimes than I know myself.

And then I had it. The moment I teach about. The moment I tell all students to look for, when they ask me how I know when a story is done. The *Damn, I'm good!* moment. I looked at that story in its new wholeness and I thought, No one else could have written this but me. And I was warm with the accomplishment. And grateful to the editor who told me to stretch.

Oh, that stretch felt good.

And it's not done yet. I will stroke this story through several more drafts yet before I declare it finished. When it occurs to me to write the words The End, I will send it off and I will celebrate.

This is why I write. This joy. This loss of self and this experience of others. This wordplay. I can feel those plastic magnet letters in my hands and I can feel the weight they promised me then and they deliver to me now.

This is why I write.

And yes, that helps. Despite. Anyway.

## MAY 30, 2017

And so today's moment of happiness despite the news.

I've started working with a new massage therapist. His focus on me is split – relaxation and convincing my hips to loosen up and let go of the pain. This means that I spend half the massage wondering why I have to battle my own body, and the other half in total bliss.

Today, the massage therapist also sprung a floodgate.

At the very beginning, as he worked on the back of my head and I faced the ceiling, he said, "How was your holiday weekend?"

My holiday weekend was missing the word holiday. I closed my eyes tightly.

Then later, when I was on my stomach, he pressed down on a spot between my shoulderblades where I tend to carry stress. And the next thing I knew, I was soaking the little doughnut face pillow with tears. Frustration, stress, sadness, self-anger – you name it, it was there.

I took on a project this weekend that I never should have. It was a project that would normally take me, sandwiched into my usual schedule, at least a month to accomplish. I edited a client's 400-and-change page novel in two days. There was no holiday. And now, my regularly scheduled program is so far behind, I swear I can see the underside of last April.

Why did I do this?

Because I'd seen this project right from its start and I wanted to see it through to the end. Because I love this client and all my clients and students. They're family. Because I wanted to make damn sure it was done right. Because I have played the part of Superwoman now for at least 21 years, keeping incredible work hours, raising a family, writing my own stories and books (and having them published and doing the required promoting), raising a business, and growing very used to people saying, "I don't know how you do everything you do," and wanting to keep that bar up high. Because I had years and years of some influential people in my life telling me I was lazy and I never was, but I harbor a very deep fear that maybe they were right. I have to keep proving them wrong. And…because I have a terrible inability to say No.

So again…why did I do this?

Because I love my students and my clients. Because I want them to love me. Because I love my family. Because I want them to love me. Because I love my readers. Because I want them to love me.

Because I want to be loved by the whole freakin' world.

And so I picked myself up off the massage table. Apologized for the leakfest. And I went home.

Trying to ease up my schedule some this week, I emailed two students, asking if they could each switch their meeting times. Doing so meant that I wouldn't be facing reading and critiquing five coaching clients' work (100 pages total) and critiquing a class' work (varies each week), starting at 10:00 tonight because that's how late it is by the time I finish teaching and land at my desk. The first student said yes, of course!, the second told me she couldn't switch to when I needed her to, but we would figure it out, I wasn't to worry. When I said I would try to get her done at the usual time, she said she wished I wouldn't. She said, "I don't want you to overdo more than you already overdo."

And I realized something.

My students and clients do love me. My family loves me. My readers love me. I don't know about the whole world, that might have to be relegated to the lofty dream category, but really, it's enough to love and be loved back. And I realized that, along with learning to say No, I also have to learn that love isn't taken away so easily, so thoughtlessly. I am surrounded by really thoughtful people.

So my happy moment today? I learned I can say No and it will be all right. And now...I've got to get some work done.

And yes, that helps. Despite. Anyway.

## MAY 31, 2017

And so today's moment of happiness despite the news.

I was back in the Starbucks drive-thru lane today. It was grande iced cinnamon dolce latte time. There were two cars ahead of me and more behind me. I had the top down and the music off, because I'd had a busy day already, with more to come, and I needed a few minutes of quiet.

It's one of the things I like about the Starbucks drive-thru. It's quiet. All you have to do is wait. And follow the line.

The young woman in the car behind me called out her order for a tall caramel macchiato. That was my second love at Starbucks – the first was a mocha malt frappaccino. I remembered on year when I was teaching at an elementary school creative writing camp at Carroll College's Project Create. I'd asked a young barista to be my aide – she was in school to become an

English teacher. Every morning, she brought me a grande caramel macchiato, with extra caramel, just the way I liked it. It was a sweet week. I smiled at the memory.

The first car in the row drove off and we all moved up. And then the car behind me erupted. In my rearview mirror, I saw a flurry of arms and hands and flying hair. I also heard a stream of curse words and "I can't believe it!" and "Oh, no!" and "Not today!" The young caramel macchiato woman scrounged in the seat next to her, papers flying, she looked in her visor and tossed down CDs, I think she looked in her glove box, I thought I saw her car's manual, all accompanied by wild eyes and rounded mouth and words, words, words. She threw the car in park and stood in her seat to lean over into the back. Then I assume she was looking on the floor and under the front seats...all I saw was her blue–jeaned butt wagging frantically in the air.

Anyone who has been in a drive–thru multiple times knows this predicament. She didn't realize she didn't have any cash on her, or any way to pay. She may have forgotten her purse or her wallet. And in this particular drive–thru, there is no way to pull out and leave. There's a high curb. And there was a long line of cars behind her. There was just no escape.

I've done that.

I thought of my young barista aide, bringing me my caramel macchiato with extra caramel every morning. She made them a gift every day, she said because I was giving her the gift of watching me teach. I wondered where she was now. I wondered who she was teaching.

Eventually, the young caramel macchiato woman behind me rested her forehead on her steering wheel. There was no more cursing. There was no more flailing. But slowly, her head began to bounce against the wheel. Once. Twice. Thrice. I winced each time.

I pulled up to the window and paid for my drink, and one for my daughter. Then I asked if I could pay for the young caramel macchiato woman behind me too. "Please," I said. "Tell her it's okay. Tell her everyone makes mistakes. Tell her to breathe. And tell her to take care of someone else when she has a chance."

And then I drove off. I smiled the whole way home.

I hope the rest of the young caramel macchiato woman's day was truly stellar.

And yes, that helps. Despite. Anyway.

# Chapter Six

## JUNE 1, 2017

And so today's moment of happiness despite the news.

What do you do on a day where the "leader" of your country declares to the world that he doesn't care about the world? He doesn't care about the people that are standing on the world. And he doesn't care about the world that we stand upon. Truly, he grinds the Earth under his heels.

It's very hard to turn away from the news on a day like today.

But I did. I turned to the Earth.

The sun was glorious today. In between an appointment and a meeting, I stopped at a park. By then, I'd read the news break. And I felt a need to sit quietly and admire. I don't know that the Earth has ears, that it listens. But I felt the need to let the world know that not all of us are without respect. That not all of us are one big ridiculous package of orange ignorance.

So I went to the river and I found a picnic bench and I sat down. I looked and listened to the current, which was gentle today. Gentle, not tentative. I took off my shoes and socks and I burrowed my toes into the cool blades of grass.

There were ducks. Male ducks chasing females. Females raising featherfuzz families. Rejected bachelors or confirmed bachelors snoozing in the sun. I am scared of birds, but I listened to them anyway. Robinsong. The red-winged blackbirds' calls made me flinch and duck, as they always do. But I acknowledged that they did not hurt me. And I don't intend to hurt them.

Heady lilacs. Their blooms were weighty and lowered the branches and I breathed them deep.

And the water. Despite the news, despite the outcries, despite the cheers of encouragement, the river just kept on moving. I admired its steadfastness and its determination. I wished for the same.

When I was at my appointment today, the person I was with spoke reverently of backpacking next week in the wilds of the Pacific Northwest. At the meeting, a woman spoke of gardening, of lilies of the valley, almost bursting peony buds, trillium, bridal wreath, and the soon-to-be red stalks of rhubarb. A client tonight spoke of hummingbirds.

And I thought of Earl Hamner, creator of *The Waltons*, my favorite television show. Hamner was a lover of nature, and he made me love words such as trailing arbutus and rhododendron. For one show, Hamner's character, John-Boy Walton, wrote,

*At night across the mountain, when the darkness falls and the winds sweep down out of the hollows, the wild things with their shiny eyes come to the edge of the clearing. At such an hour, the house seems safe and warm, an island of light and love in a sea of darkness. At such an hour, the word home must have come into being, dreamed up by some creature that never knew a home.*

We had a different sort of hour of darkness today, Earl. It occurred in the middle of a weekday afternoon, in blatant and brilliant sun. At such an hour, the word home had a deep-thrummed resonance among creatures such as us who know this planet as our home. This Earth. This World.

To the river, to the lilacs, to the grass and the ducks, and even to the red-winged blackbirds, I whispered, "I'm so sorry."

When I returned to my car and my phone, I saw the new news that dozens of US mayors immediately declared that they were going to continue to uphold the Paris Agreement. While our "leader" is intent on destroying anything his little orange hands can touch, there are many who simply will not follow.

The breaking news email header on my screen said, "*The world shudders as Trump pulls US out of Paris Agreement.*"

Oh, no. Not at all. The World is throwing back its shoulders.

And so are we.

And yes, that helps. Despite. Anyway.

## JUNE 2, 2017

And so today's moment of happiness despite the news.

After picking up my daughter, whom I love to distraction, after school today, I idled the car by my garage and told her to go on in, I'd be home shortly. Time for a Starbucks run, I said.

"Can I have one too?" she asked, her voice high and sweet and suddenly six years old again, despite the sixteen-year old body sitting next to me. "Pleeaaaaassssseee?" She dropped her head on my shoulder, twisted to look up at me with wide and love-filled eyes and, of course, that glorious smile on her face.

I reminded her that she gets a frappuccino when I have a free drink, a reward from Starbucks whenever I earn a certain number of points as a valued and faithful customer. I had a free drink available this past Wednesday – my daughter, whom I love to the stars and back, benefited.

"Pleeaaaaaaassssseee?" she said again, her eyes wider than possible, her smile beyond glowing, her voice a reflection of every day, every moment with her since October 17, 2000. After nineteen hours of labor. And many more hours of labor since.

No, I said, and reminded this girl, whom I love more than life itself, that I'm not made of money.

"Sure you are," she said, sitting up. "Your name is Mommy and that means Money. It has the same first letter and it even sounds the same. MommyMoney."

I watched her, this daughter of mine, whom I love more than the hills and valleys, the trees and lakes, the rivers and oceans, the moon, the sun, the stars, and all the space in between, I watched her walk into the home I provide for her.

I drove to Starbucks, Coldplay on my CD player, and I sang the whole way. When I arrived at the drive-thru window, the barista said to me, "Do you want your usual grande iced cinnamon dolce latte today, Kathie?"

I said yes.

He said, "And will there be anything else?"

I said no.

And then I drove home, singing and sipping.

I love this child, and all of my children, more than I ever thought possible. But Mommy ain't no sucker.

And yes, that helps. Despite. Anyway.

## JUNE 3, 2017

And so today's moment of happiness despite the news.

It wasn't the best of days, and it came after a week that was difficult. I added a few extra things to an already over-full schedule and it showed. I met with clients, but forgot to do the work. I did the work, but then forgot to show up. I switched appointments to try to make the work I had to do more balanced out over the days, and then didn't write those changed appointments down and totally forgot I changed them. On top of it all, I have pneumonia, gifted to me by my lovely daughter. Everything culminated yesterday when I woke up and found myself just unable to get out of bed. I ended up canceling an appointment with a client (who understood) and canceling an event I was supposed to be a part of at an area high school. I apologized profusely, but as I've not heard from the organizer, I'm not so sure I'm forgiven. It wasn't a great moment for me.

But I thought, when I got up this morning, that that was all behind me. My schedule was back to normal. I could fit back into the groove. But...not quite. Things still interfered. A ticket saying that I hadn't moved Olivia's car in 72 hours – I had. Olivia's car failing the emissions testing to get its plate renewed because its monitors haven't reset since its last repair – you have to drive a car about 100 miles to reset the monitors if the battery has been pulled. And the plates expire on Monday. Trying to figure out how I was going to have time to drive the Beetle 100 miles and get the emissions retested and passed by said Monday (I still haven't figured that out). Trying to figure out how I'm ever going to be able to take my daughter out driving enough for her to past her test. Trying, trying, trying.

On edge? I wasn't on the edge. I WAS the edge.

I nearly canceled our plans to go to the Waukesha Civic Theatre tonight. They're doing Neil Simon's *Barefoot In The Park*, which is one of my favorites. But we went. I put on a new summer dress. We went and we laughed with a great crowd of people. Then we went to a late dinner at Denny's.

While we were waiting for our meals, the waitresses pulled together several tables. And then...the square dancers arrived. Still in full stiff-petticoated skirts and natty vests. They sat down boy-girl-boy-girl-boy-girl on one side, and boy-girl-boy-girl-boy-girl on the other. And every single skirt went PHOOM when they sat, blooming in crinoline fullness to the sides and resting on the lap of every man, and causing a massive tucking in the front, getting the skirts to fit and behave under the table.

And I discovered a most important universal truth: It is impossible to be grumpy or sad when you're seated next to square dancers.

They were raucous. And I laughed all through my scrambled eggs.

I discovered something else too. If this had happened before I started doing the Today's Moments – and trust me, days like this happen all the time – I would have canceled going to the play. I would have snarled up in my office and eventually I would have snarled my way to bed and I would have awakened the next morning still snarling.

But now...I went looking.

And I found it. My Moment. Square dancers with PHOOMing skirts and natty vests at Denny's.

And yes, that helps. Despite. Anyway.

## JUNE 4, 2017

And so today's moment of happiness despite the news.

Yesterday, I complained when my daughter Olivia's car, a VW Beetle named Starlight Lashes, flunked her emissions test. A pass is required to renew her license plates. The man at the testing site told me that since she had her battery pulled during a repair, she needs to be driven approximately 100 miles to reset her monitors.

100 miles.

I asked my sons if they could take the car for a drive. They couldn't. My daughter isn't driving yet – this is the car she's learning with. I couldn't just plunk her in the driver's seat and tell her to drive by herself for 100 miles. And my husband doesn't drive. I looked at my own schedule and despaired.

Today, I took the Beetle by her Buggy horns. I decided not to meditate – a half hour – and not to walk – an hour. Instead, I would get in Starlight Lashes, aka Bane Of My Existence, drive her to Milwaukee, cruise down Downer Avenue, wave at Boswell's Books, curve up to the bluff overlooking the great lake, sit on a bench and ponder, and then drive home. If I wasn't going to meditate or walk, I was going to at least say hello to the lake. My daughter decided to tag along.

No, I didn't plunk her in the driver's seat to give her practice. The stretch of freeway we were going to be on is undergoing hair-raising construction for the next millennia or so. Olivia somehow got through behind-the-wheel class without being taken on the freeway. I wasn't going to teach her this way...and I was determined to visit the lake.

It's hot today and Starlight Bane doesn't have working a/c. So our windows were lowered. I tried to put on my favorite radio station, because she only has a cassette player. But for some reason, the only stations she would pick up were Christian. So we drove down the freeway, hot wind whipping through our hair and Starlight's hot pink lashes, and Olivia looked up every now and then from Snapchat while we talked.

About stuff. The way moms and daughters talk about stuff when they're stuck in a car with no tunes and no a/c, and with frequent breaks for Snapchat. It was fun.

When we got to Milwaukee and I worked my way up toward Downer, I made an unfortunate discovery. EVERYONE goes to the lakefront on Sunday night to have dinner in the cooler air when it gets hot out. The traffic was beyond bumper to bumper. People swore and yelled. We barely moved. And that's when Starlight Christian Bane chose to overheat.

The Beetle has no temperature gauge. A blue thermometer lights up when she's cold. And a red flashing siren of a thermometer shows up when she's hot-hot-hot. No in between. No warning.

Luckily, we were by a quadplex. I swung around traffic and pulled her lengthwise into the lot and shut her down, popping the lid. One of the residents came out and talked nicely to us as he headed out to buy milk. Another came out and talked not so nicely to us. Starlight cooled down quickly. In 20 minutes, I started her back up, we zipped into traffic, I turned at the light that was just about twenty feet away, and we got out of there.

I made my way down my favorite curvy hill, we drove by the lakefront and the art museum, and then I came to the cluster of confounding signs for the freeways. And of course, I chose the wrong one. Instead of heading west toward Waukesha, Starlight, Olivia and I went up and over the Hohn Bridge. I love the Hohn Bridge; the view is tremendous. On the way over, Lake Michigan was on my side of the car and I waved and Starlight batted her left eyelashes. When we turned around and came back, it was on Olivia's side and she waved and Starlight batted her right eyelashes.

And then…we went home. Starlight remained cool. Olivia and I talked the whole way. The air was warm and we laughed.

It was fun. It wasn't meditating or walking and it was two hours out of my day, but it was fun. With my daughter.

And yes, that helps. Despite. Anyway.

## JUNE 5, 2017

And so today's moment of happiness despite the news.

Well, my goodness. Let's see. It is just after eight o'clock at night and:

*I have one more client. So far, all clients have shown up, we've had a wonderful time, and I had all of their work done. On time. I didn't forget anybody or anything.

*I had time to write this afternoon. Not much…I didn't get through an entire scene. But I wrote.

*My daughter's car, which flunked her emissions test on Saturday, passed today. Her registration expires tomorrow. I'm not late. She has a shiny new sticker on her license plate that says 18 (for 2018).

*There were no surprise phone calls.

*No children asked for money.

*Nothing broke down.

*There wasn't a long line at Starbucks.

*It didn't rain.

*Leaks from pets were at a new minimum. Not absent, but not many.

*I had time to meditate. I didn't get walking in, but I meditated. And wrote.

*I still have work to do for tomorrow, but that's pretty typical. I'm on schedule.

*This was a Monday and it didn't suck.

*My dentist appointment is tomorrow. Not today.

So…wait. Everything went right today? There wasn't a huge OHMYGOD LIFEISGREAT! Moment, but there weren't any Moments In The Abyss either.

Huh. How about that?

Some days, all it takes to have a Moment Of Happiness is to have the day go as planned. Really.

I'm grateful.

And yes, that helps. Despite. Anyway.

### JUNE 6, 2017

And so today's moment of happiness despite the news.

To tell you the truth, I don't even know what the news was today. I spent most of the morning and early afternoon in a sweat, waiting for a dentist appointment, the middle of the afternoon in a sweat at the dentist appointment, and the rest of the day reveling that I lived.

Yes, lived. Phobias are awful things. So are stark raving terror-filled memories from your childhood and adolescence.

I'm scared of things, just like anyone else. Thunderstorms make me nervous. Flying still scares me some. Doing new things makes me uncertain.

The dentist…makes me convinced I'm going to die.

When I cracked a filling a few weeks ago, there was no avoiding the dentist. I only go (until today) when I absolutely have to. When something happens, I call a dentist, go in for an emergency procedure, make an appointment for a cleaning, and then call in the next couple days and cancel it. When the next emergency comes along, I go to a different dentist. Why? Because of horrible experiences as a child that leave me literally frightened of death, not to death, but of death, if I go today.

It's ridiculous. It's irrational. It's embarrassing. But berating myself just would not make the fear go away.

I was determined to do it differently this time. The tooth was temporarily fixed and I was told to make an appointment for a cleaning before the permanent filling is put in. I did. Then I sat home and waited to cancel it. I didn't. Part of my talking about it on Facebook and here was to hold myself accountable – did I really want to admit to the world that I failed again?

So I drove to the dentist. I sat in the parking lot. I announced I was going to die. When I finally went in, I was in tears. The nicest hygienist named Heather came out and took me back to the gallows, her arm around my shoulders. I told her I was worried she would clean my teeth and they would fall out. She showed me on the x-ray that my roots and bones are in great condition and my teeth have absolutely no movement. I told her I was worried she would clean my teeth and they would crack and break. She promised that wouldn't happen. When she told me she was going to use pressurized water and not the old picks and pokes, I asked her if I was going to drown.

Okay, then we both laughed.

We got started and she began to talk. Once she knew who I was, she told me she was an avid reader and that her favorite author was Wally Lamb. She said she was so sad because he passed away.

"No, he didn't," I said. "We went to the same grad school. He's fine."

I made her day. She made mine by not hurting me once. And by trying to keep me distracted. It's hard to be distracted from someone poking around in your mouth and from the possibility of pain and imminent death though. Even though it was ridiculous, even though it was irrational, even though it was embarrassing, I kept my eyes peeled for an ether mask.

It never came. And tonight…I have the weirdest-feeling teeth. But they're supposed to feel this way. I never knew that.

Is there any better feeling than being alive when you thought you were going to die?

I can't say I'm cured. I still have to go back to have the filling fixed permanently – and I have already made the appointment. It's a few weeks from now, to give me time to recover. And now I have an armory of yeah-buts.

Yeah, it used to hurt, but it doesn't now. Yeah, you're scared, but you made it through.

And I've got this mouthful of teeth. How about that?

And yes, that helps. Despite. Anyway.

## JUNE 7, 2017

And so today's moment of happiness despite the news.

My moment of happiness happened today when today was barely born. In the wee morning hours, when I was still awake, getting work done for the class and clients that lay ahead, my daughter messaged me on Facebook. "Look at Carla's page," she said. "She's doing a moment of happiness now too."

Carla is a friend of my daughter's, and through the magic of Facebook, she's one of my friends too. She's one of the bravest young women I know. Though faced with lifelong health challenges, she into every day, determined to experience everything. I watch her from a distance and marvel. I want her to write a book.

So I went to her Facebook page. I read on her status, "A friend of mine has posted a 'moment of happiness despite the news' every day since the election, I think, and it has really inspired me. I love reading them. And now I'm starting my own. Mine is a daily 'moment of happiness besides that I'm still breathing.'"

And then she listed her first one.

One of my primary motivations as a writer has been to effect change. It's a hard motivation, a difficult goal, because I don't always see the results. I know they're there, and there have been many times a reader has contacted me to let me know just what a book or a story means to him or her. But many times, I'm left wondering if I've accomplished anything at all.

With The Moments, I didn't set out to effect change in anyone but myself. With the new orange regime (and yes, I intended to use that word) in place, I found myself becoming increasingly negative-minded. My outlook for the future was negative; my present was negative; my presence was negative. I have never in my life been a Pollyanna, so it's not like negativity was new to me, but I'd hit such a new low that Eeyore looked like a unicorn. So I began, in a public way, and in an act of desperation, really, to try to come up with just one, only one, moment of happiness each day. It kept me, as John Irving would say, walking past the open windows.

I don't approach these as a professional writer; I just write them raw, with minimal editing. My motivation as a writer was not in place here. My motivation to lift myself up was.

And somehow, I've effected change not only in myself, but in others. I've received many emails and private messages, saying that people are writing their own daily Moments of Happiness. And when they can't find one, they look at mine. The moments are being shared and sent on and they're multiplying. Turns out I wasn't the only one out there that needed a lift, that needed to look out open windows for the loveliness of the view, and not for an escape.

And now Carla.

As long as we've brought up Pollyanna, Eeyore and unicorns, not to mention John Irving, let's bring up Dr. Seuss too. Like the Grinch, my heart grew three sizes today.

And yes, that helps. Despite. Anyway.

## JUNE 8, 2017

And so today's moment of happiness despite the news.

I am surrounded right now with hubbub over the new novel, *In Grace's Time*, being released on September 7. Every day, my email box is full of messages from the publisher himself and different people in different roles at the publisher's and from the publicist, and I have decisions to make and things to think about. Do I want to do this? Do I want that? Here, there, and up, up and away. Which is wonderful. I am exhilarated.

But you know, what a writer does is write, and in the middle of all this, preparing for book #7 to come out, I am working on book #8. It's like being a cheerleader, and I'm waving my pompoms and I'm yelling, Go, Team!, and kicking high at the winning team, at the star quarterback, but at the same time, my eyes are trying desperately to look at the cute boy behind me in the bleachers.

Well, maybe it's like that. I've never been a cheerleader.

But there is the struggle, between the books already out, the book coming out, and the book underway. Every day this week, I've tried to sit down long enough to finish just one scene. And every day, I had to leave it for the next time because I just didn't get there.

Today, I did. I sat down and I finished the scene. I read it over a couple times.

And then I wanted to pound my head through a wall. I HATED IT. Not only did I hate the scene, I hated the whole damn book. All almost–90 pages of it so far. I hated the title. I hated the characters. I hated the premise. I hated the freaking words, they were all the wrong words. Blech! Yuk! I went through the whole litany. *What is this book about anyway? What were you thinking when you started to write it? This thing sucks! It's the worst thing I've ever written! I should just delete it and put it out of its misery.*

Yeah. One of THOSE days.

So why in the world is this my moment of happiness?

Because I sat back and let it roll over me. I heard all the charges and insults. I felt all the despair and disgust and self-hatred and intellectual self-mutilation.

And then I leaned forward and started on the next scene. Actually, the next chapter.

Why? Because I know better now. It took years, but I know this is all perfectly normal. Writing is a love-hate relationship with your own work. And the most important thing to learn is to ride through the hate and know that the love is just circling around to the other side. Like a square dance. Do-si-do. It'll come back. It always does. And then you'll promenade home.

(Cheerleading and square-dancing. Good lord.)

And I also knew I would profoundly regret it if I deleted it. I am doing my absolute best not to deal in regrets anymore.

So. Six books out. Seventh on the way. And eighth lovingly and hatefully bouncing around inside my head, inside my heart, and coming out of my fingers.

Perfect. Wouldn't have it any other way. Go, Team! Promenade home!

And yes, that helps. Despite. Anyway.

## JUNE 9, 2017

And so today's moment of happiness despite the news.

Tonight, I had to go to Target to buy new filters for our heating/cooling units. Yes, I know – I lead an exotic life.

Because it's lovely out, I decided to take Semi, my Chrysler 200 convertible. As he and I drove carefully around downtown Waukesha, stunningly alive with Friday Night Live revelers, a young man at an intersection looked at us, raised his eyebrows and pumped his fists in the air. "Nice ride!" he called.

I said thank you. As I drove off, I thought about those two words. Nice ride. I was, in fact, in a lovely car, and to be fair, I love both of my cars, Semi and Hemi. Hemi is a Chrysler 300C Hemi. And yes, I have a thing for

Chryslers. My first car was a 1969 Chrysler Newport 4-door sedan, which I bought for a buck from my father in 1980. And if forced to admit it, yes, I have a passing affection for my daughter's whackadoodle VW Beetle, who sports hot pink eyelashes and will soon strut in hot pink decals and hot pink seat covers. I have a thing for cars.

But "nice ride" means so much more than that.

When my novel, *Rise From The River*, came out in 2014, it was with this dedication:

*It's been such a wild ride. In continued gratitude for everyone for your steadfast love and encouragement. Thank you for hanging on tight.*

When *In Grace's Time* comes out in September (and by the way, that book features a 1969 Chrysler Newport 4-door sedan), anyone who cracks its covers will see a similar dedication. The ride continues.

My nice ride, I decided tonight as I tooled toward Target, includes being surrounded by an amazing number of amazing people. People who prove to me, over and over again, that there is more good in this world than bad. A woman who shares a photo of her granddaughter dipping her baby toes in a fountain. A man who is brash until he says to me in a quiet voice, "Do you really think this is publishable?" and then lights up brighter than high beams when I tell him yes. A husband who texts me while I'm still sleeping so that I wake to a message on the day I have a dentist appointment and I'm terrified: I love you, Punkin. And he sends a bracketed hug. A daughter who rolls her eyes when I brush her hair before a date and who thinks she hides her smile from me when I tell her she's beautiful. A son who, when I decide not to fly first class because I don't want to spend the money, finds a way to pay me back some of what he owes and tells me to get that first class seat. I've never flown first class before. I will soon. Readers. Students. Family. Friends. So intertwined that I really don't put any divisive lines in those human genres. They're all family.

And yes, a couple of really nice cars. One that gave me an open-air ride tonight with a full view of a sherbet sunset. That gave me the ability to fully breathe unrestricted even as I had to run to Target to buy a filter.

On the way home, I had to wait out a light behind a Porsche SUV (frankly, I don't know why anyone who would spend the money on a Porsche would get an SUV. Drive topless, for God's sake.). And I stopped singing long enough to nod and mouth, Nice ride, in the man's rearview mirror. He waved.

But I'm happy with mine.

Nice ride.

And yes, that helps. Despite. Anyway.

## JUNE 10, 2017

And so today's moment of happiness despite the news.

This afternoon, after I spent the morning teaching my New Year's Resolution Write-A-Book Workshop students, and then taking a rousing nap, the family and I went to the mall. I had a gift card from Mother's Day burning a hole in my pocket, along with rewards cash from a couple of my favorite stores.

Olivia ventured off on her own, bought a few things, and then came to join me. I was poking around in a bin of underwear. Out of the blue, Olivia said, "Mom, how did you get to have such a good body image? I sure don't."

The question took me aback. I hadn't really thought about if my body image was good, bad or in between.

Not many people know that before I began to teach creative writing classes, I was a weight loss instructor. I worked for three different companies over the course of about ten years. I never lost weight with any of those companies; I'd lost over eighty pounds with Weight Watchers, but they weren't hiring when I reached goal. So I went elsewhere.

During those years that I taught, I got down to a size 4. I worked out at the gym every morning, went to work after lunch, stayed til close at 9:00 at night, and I worked six days a week. At the gym, I did advanced stepaerobics three times a week, regular stepaerobics twice a week, and lifted weights every day, alternating upper and lower body. I considered going into the amateur body-building circuit. And yes, I will be the first to admit that I looked amazing.

I will also be the first to tell you that I was absolutely and profoundly miserable.

My whole day was consumed with what I was putting in my mouth, how I was working my body, and how much I weighed. I weighed myself at least 25 times a day: before and after showers, before and after getting dressed, before and after meals and snacks, before and after going to the bathroom. I even weighed myself before and after haircuts. I never saw my kids; I was either at the gym or at work. My writing life went downhill; At work, during my meal break, I wouldn't eat, but would go out to my minivan with a spiral notebook and a pen, sit in the backseat and try to write. Half the time, I fell asleep. I was so exhausted. And my mind and body both were depleted.

Did I look good? Oh, yes. But I did not feel good. Physically or emotionally. My body ached. My mind rotated, counting calories consumed and energy burned. Eventually, I broke.

And I quit.

Sure, the weight came back on. But so did the self-respect, the self-satisfaction, the joy in what I do and think. Who I am.

So I turned to my daughter today and answered, "I guess when I became happy with my whole self, my body image just came along for the ride."

And she became thoughtful.

I don't know what conclusions she'll draw. But I'm glad she asked.

And yes, that helps. Despite. Anyway.

## JUNE 11, 2017

And so today's moment of happiness.

One day a year, I pretend I like flowers and plants. It's not as bad as when we lived in our house – there was a lot more space there and I felt required to fill it up with flowers and green things so that it would look at least a little bit similar to the other houses in the neighborhood.

Here at the condo, we don't have a yard. I put a basket of flowers on the small deck off the second floor, facing the parking lot. I've always called this Olivia's deck, even though the door out to it is in Michael's office. On the third floor deck, off of my office, I have two big ceramic pots, and I put flowers in those too. A basket of flowers goes by our front door, next to our Little Free Library and Little Literary, our concrete lion. It gives Little Literary the vague idea that he's in a jungle. And there's a teeny strip of dirt in between the studio's windows and the sidewalk where I have hostas and lilies. I have to weed there. I don't like it.

I have never liked digging in the dirt. I have never liked getting my hands dirty. I like looking at flowers; one of my favorite places in the world is a labyrinth at Regnar Park in West Bend, Wisconsin. The swirls of the labyrinth are outlined by flowering plant after flowering plant, lovingly administered by a garden society, and I am full of admiration and gratitude for them. But actually do and maintain the planting? Ick.

I tried really hard when I lived with my first husband at our house where he lives still. There was a great patch of lilies of the valley in the back yard.

One afternoon, I was out there weeding and my hand hit what I thought was a rock. I pulled it out and discovered I was holding a dead bird, maggots and all. Even though it was dead, it still flew. And that pretty much ended my gardening days.

But once a year…I bought my flowers today.

Pushing my cart, I wandered the colorful outdoor aisles of Home Depot and I tried hard to look like I knew what I was doing. I was surrounded by growing things, green things, orange, purple, red, yellow things. Some were downright startling. I decided to pretend I was at the labyrinth and the aisles were the swirls and all I had to do was enjoy the flowers.

And I did.

And then I picked out what I thought were the prettiest and I brought them home. The flowers rode next to me in the front seat of the convertible and they looked like they enjoyed the ride. At home, the only place I really had to dig in the dirt was in the pots on the third floor deck. I had to pull out the remains of last year's flowers and tuck in the new ones. But I think I might have gotten smart this year – I put in the same lilies that line the studio's windows and they come back every year. So I might not ever have to dig in the dirt again.

When I was finished, I looked at my dirty hands and shuddered even as I felt satisfied. Somehow, accomplishing something you want to do but don't enjoy doing is twice as satisfying as accomplishing something you want to do and enjoy doing.

All I had to do was wash my hands and the distastefulness went away. The lasting memory of a flying dead bird and maggots went away. I was left with some really pretty color around my house and business. That I put there.

I brought summer home today.

And yes, that helps. Despite. Anyway.

## JUNE 12, 2017

And so today's moment of happiness despite the news.

Well, I'm not in Wisconsin anymore. I am in Boulder, Colorado. I've never been here before.

I came here to surprise a student whose first book, a memoir, has just been published. The launch is Thursday. Julie has been with me since 2009. I've watched this book grow, I've watched her grow, and I've been astonished by both. I needed to be here. Adding in the surprise just made it that much better.

Julie works in a sandwich shop and she was on a delivery when I arrived this afternoon. So I ordered lunch, sat down, and waited. I saw her pull up on a bicycle, lock it, and then come flying in.

Only to come to a dead halt when she saw me.

She went from speechlessness to talking a bajillion miles a minute to tears over the course of the next half hour. I don't know that I've ever been so happy to surprise someone.

So much joy.

But there's more to this than that.

Ever since I was assaulted last November by a man in a Make America Great Again red baseball cap, I've been unable to really travel. I was offered the opportunity to go to my favorite place in the world on the Oregon coast and I ended up turning it down. I was supposed to go to Florida in April, but I didn't. I couldn't make myself get on a plane or leave home for any length of time. It drove me nuts that my fear seemed so irrational; I was attacked on the street, so why was I having such a hard time getting on a plane? I just kept thinking about the moment that big door would close and seal, and I'd be sealed too, with no way out.

It took until about a month ago for me to make that connection. I was terrified of having no escape.

Knowing it, understanding it didn't make it any easier. I began to think I would never be able to travel again. I love to travel.

But then there was Julie. And her memoir, Two Trees. I've watched her struggle and I've watched her pull herself back up, and now...well, I had to be there to celebrate her success. I needed to be there. So I had to struggle and pull myself back up too.

I could do it for a student. Beyond a student, as all my students are. A member of my family. The AllWriters' community.

Until I actually set foot on the plane this morning, I didn't know if I was going to be able to do it. Not only was I flying, I was going someplace I'd never been, a place I couldn't picture and grasp onto the security of familiarity. When I did get on the plane, I was in the front row and I kept my eyes on that open door until the big thing swung up and clunked with the finality of a coffin. I was gripping my own shirt so tightly, you can see the scrunches where my fingers twisted the fabric.

But once we were airborne...it was okay. It was like other flights I'd taken. The familiarity soothed. I even slept a little.

And then...I surprised Julie.

I did it. I traveled. Tomorrow morning, when I wake up, I will be in an unfamiliar place. And I think I'm okay with that.

I'm hoping that's all behind me now. The Make America Great Again hat man snarled at me as he threw me off the sidewalk, "It's time to get back in your place now, woman."

I am. I am in my place. There is no going back. I've pulled myself up.

And yes, that helps. Despite. Anyway.

## JUNE 13, 2017

And so today's moment of happiness despite the news.

I had a lovely day today. Sometimes, it's hard traveling to a place you've never been. While you love the new sights and sounds and colors and world, you miss having something familiar.

At least, that's how it is for me. That's why I typically scout out a Starbucks wherever I go. I've yet to find a Starbucks that doesn't feel like home as soon as I walk into it.

But today was all about how the new can be the familiar. I have two students who live in Boulder, and one of them came today to take me out to coffee. We went to the Trident, on the Pearl Street Mall. I'd read about it and wanted to (I know this is going to sound weird – deal with it) feel it. It sounded like an amazing place.

And it was. Funky. Filled with familiar-looking people that you would see in a coffeeshop anywhere. My kind of people. And it's connected to a used bookstore. Heaven.

My student and I got our drinks and went out back to a covered patio. We sat and talked like we'd known each other for years – but she is a new student. I haven't even read her work yet. But this is one example of the new familiar. She is new to me, but she isn't. We were comfortable.

At the other end of our long table, a young girl stared at her laptop screen. I noticed she didn't do much typing. Her face at times turned toward ours, but she didn't say anything. Every now and then, she wrote something down in a notebook.

Familiar. I know the signs of an eavesdropping writer. I often am one.

Before we went into the bookstore, my student ran upstairs to the restroom. While she was gone, this young girl turned to me. "So you're a wordperson?" she said.

How cool. Yes. I am.

I talked with her for about five minutes. She was, she said, experiencing a block. I don't believe in blocks. And when I left, she was tapping away wildly on her laptop. The only eavesdropping she was doing was listening to her own characters' conversations and inner thoughts.

The new familiar. Someone I don't know and will likely never see again. I didn't think to give her my card. But...I was teaching. I helped. There is no better feeling.

I think I might rename myself the writer-whisperer...

And now? I was rescued from my very, very divey, rundown, worn-out, cigarette-smelling hotel room by Julie, the student whose book debut we're celebrating. I'm writing this in a private little room on the basement level of a beautiful house. There's a window and a door that opens to the outside. Trees. Rocks. Wide open sky. And a creek. The sound of singing water is everywhere.

I am at my happiest around water.

Happiest.

And yes, that helps. Despite. Anyway.

## JUNE 14, 2017

And so today's moment of happiness despite the news.

I thought I knew ahead of time what my moment of happiness was going to be. Whenever I travel, I try to find a labyrinth to walk. I've been successful and I've found some really beautiful spaces. So with Colorado, I researched before I came and I found a church, located in downtown Boulder, that has a lovely labyrinth and weeping wall that was built and painted into their church structure in 2001. On Wednesday nights, they do a candlelit walk.

I've never walked a labyrinth with others, and I've never done a candlelit walk. Most of the labyrinths I've walked have been outdoors. So I eagerly planned to attend and thought it would be a great experience.

This morning, I called the church and made sure that the walk was indeed taking place. It was. I asked if the church had its own parking lot or if I would have to find street parking. Street parking in downtown Boulder is a nightmare. I was assured the church had a parking lot. So this evening, I set out.

I found the church. I never found the parking lot. If there is one, it's so well-hidden that maybe only Christian eyes can see it. My eyes did not.

The walk began at 6:30. I arrived at 6:25. I began driving the blocks around the church in ever-widening squares, trying to find an empty parking space. There were none. Finally, at 7:05, I gave up.

And I admit, as I drove back toward the house I'm staying in, I thought out loud, "Well, NOW where am I going to find my moment of happiness?" And I also admit I may have used the word "stupid" before moment. I was a little pissed off. Labyrinth walks don't usually leave me pissed off.

I snarled my way to the closest grocery store. I bought two pieces of fried chicken and some deviled egg potato salad. Comfort food. I thought about buying some ice cream, but I didn't, because I had a package of fudge stripe cookies at home. With a cup of coffee, that would do.

I snarled my way into the house. Well, first, I was met by a huge St. Bernard named Montana, who has one hell of a sense of rhythm with his panting. I can tap my foot to it. I patted his head and he woofed, which made me lose some of the snarl and begin to smile. I then semi-stomped into the house.

Where I was met by Frannie, the black lab. The black lab who used to come to class in Waukesha when her owner lived there. The black lab I love.

Her face was in a potato chip bag. MY potato chip bag.

"Oh, NO!" I said, and her face popped out and she slunk away. I grabbed the bag and then saw the remains of my package of fudge stripe cookies. Gone. Gone, gone, gone.

"Oh, Frannie," I said. "Oh, Frannie. What did you do? Your mother is going to kill you." I sat down.

And that dog came up, put her big head on my knee, and gave me the look of angels.

And I laughed.

At a candlelit labyrinth walk, I may very well have been among angels. But here, in this house, I had a big-eyed angel dog with her horse head in my lap.

I've just texted her mother, requesting ice cream. I will fill her in on Frannie's misbehavior when she gets home. Until then, I'm petting the angel. And Montana too. Tapping my foot to his breath.

And yes, that helps. Despite. Anyway.

## JUNE 15, 2017

And so today's moment of happiness despite the news.

I'm late tonight because I was at a student's first book debut. And because of that, this will be short and sweet.

Watching a student, ANY student:
*write when she says she's not good;
*write when he says he can't;
*finish a poem, a story, or a book when words have only been a dream;
*submit for publication when she doesn't believe she's good enough;
*receive rejections and believe them, but still submit again anyway;
*receive an acceptance, an ACCEPTANCE!, the acceptance;
*achieve the dream of a lifetime;
*not believe that it's happening;
*hold her book in her hands for the first time;
*stand in front of me and the whole world and read from it;
*hear the world's reaction;
*know that she can. Know that he can. Know that he's good enough. Know that she's good enough;
*get the chance to say to a student, "I told you so."

THAT is the happiest moment ever. It is the best feeling ever.
Well, except for my own books and stories, of course. I am only human.
Ohmygod. So happy. And proud.
And yes, that helps. Despite. Anyway.

### JUNE 16, 2017

And so today's moment of happiness despite the news.

So I go home tomorrow. And I'm ready to. As of yet, anyway, I'm not nervous about the plane. I'm just looking forward to getting there.

There are times, well, lots of times, that I thoroughly question what I'm doing. Starting a small business is such a risk. Starting a small business like a creative writing studio is even riskier. Then add to that the fact that I didn't have any experience in business at all...What I decided to do was downright dangerous. Some would say crazy. Some did say that. Some called it stupid.

I was talking with one of my students late at night a couple nights ago. I said to her, as I've said to a few others, that my hard lesson is learning to have faith in myself, faith in what I've done, faith in what I can do, and faith in the studio. I've often said that I have to have faith in AllWriters', and people have told me over and over again that I AM AllWriters'. But it's only been recently that I realized that having faith in the studio means having faith in me.

That's a tall order.

I worry all the time. A client finishes their project and I worry that there will be no one to take that person's place. I worry that a class won't fill. I worry that I won't be able to pay this bill or that bill, that something will go wrong, that a catastrophe will happen, and that all my hard work will be for nothing.

I have to start looking at just the hard work and stop that sentence right there. I have to start looking at what I've done.

I traveled from Wisconsin to Colorado to celebrate a student's success. But at her event last night, I was in the same room with four students. Four. All with me in a place that I'd never been before. And I talked with several more who will likely become students.

Every place I go, I have students.

I've learned that it's hard for me to see what I've accomplished unless I see it reflected in my students' eyes, in their words, and in their happiness.

I have to start seeing it reflected in my own.

I have faith in the studio.

And I have to have faith in me.

I was sitting in a parking lot today, outside of a (of course) Starbucks, not my Starbucks, but a Starbucks, and I was getting ready to start the car. I'd spent the morning, here in Colorado, reading student manuscripts. I'd worked on the next scene of my own book (I'm two pages away from page 100 of the first draft!). And I was thinking ahead to what is going to be an incredibly busy week, as the studio's annual retreat begins on Thursday.

And suddenly, I just teared up. Not from overwhelm, not from anxiety.

From pure and absolute pride. Pride always makes me feel ashamed for some reason. But this time, I took the shame, throttled it and threw it out the window.

And I said, out loud in this little Ford Focus that I'm not too crazy about, I said out loud to my rearview mirror, "Would you look at what you've done? Would you just look at what you've built?"

I've spoken a lot about helping students reach their dreams.

But I've reached my own, haven't I. What an incredible thing.

I'm still going to worry. But look at what I've done. Just look.

And yes, that helps. Despite. Anyway.

## JUNE 17, 2017

And so today's moment of happiness despite the news.

This morning, I had breakfast with a St. Bernard.

Montana is an older dog, and an old soul. While he's big and fuzzy and huggable, he's also dignified. He walks in a stately old man way. And his eyes are just amazing.

During the week I was in Colorado, he and I had quite a few conversations. When I was home for breakfast or lunch, I ate at the kitchen table and he would come to stand next to me. I told him what I was reading, whether it was a book for my own enjoyment, or students' pages. We talked about what I liked or didn't like and discussed literature. I told him what I was working on and he seemed to think it was an interesting idea.

Thank goodness, since I'm almost 100 pages into it.

But this morning, I told Montana I was going home. I know it's very likely I won't see him again because of his age and because Colorado isn't a typical destination for me. He looked a little sad and I felt a little sad. Yes, I have dogs at home, but the beagles don't quite have the intelligent, thoughtful stature of this St. Bernard. They'll maybe develop it in time, but for now, their conversations usually concern food or having to go to the bathroom. Montana was different. There was a person in there somewhere.

I told Montana I was a little nervous about traveling home. About working my way through the Denver International Airport, which makes O'Hare look like a bus stop. About getting on another plane and letting that door shut.

Montana just listened. When I scratched him on the ears, he bonked that broad head into me. I'm pretty sure he said, "You'll be fine."

When I made my way through that airport (which wasn't easy – that place is so confusing), I saw a man waiting in one of the seats with a dog by his side. This was a really big dog – an Irish Wolfhound. The dog had on the jacket that identified him as a service dog. So I didn't attempt to say anything to him or pet him. But I did smile at him as I passed. I noticed along the side of his jacket was stitched, "Service Dog. Emotional Support."

I've seen plenty of service dogs, but I never saw it spelled out like that.

I decided I need to find a jacket like that for Montana. I had breakfast with a champion this morning.

And yes, that helps. Despite. Anyway.

### JUNE 18, 2017

And so today's moment of happiness despite the news.

In the middle of an ordinary busy day, an ordinary moment becomes extraordinary.

Today was all about running from store to store, buying supplies for the AllWriters' Annual Retreat, running this Thursday to Sunday. We'd made it through Sam's Club and I dropped Michael off at Woodman's while I ran to Starbucks. I knew there was still Target to go.

On the way back to Woodman's, I was sipping my latte and humming to the Moody Blues when I crested the top of the Moreland Boulevard hill. My convertible soared over it like Thelma and Louise with a safer landing and the world opened up and my mind did too. Just like that. There was the sky, an inverted bowl of blue with impossible clouds in gray gone to white and the trees were in full green. The river was a lazy ribbon and there was a train and I didn't care. It was all good. It was all summer. It was warm and alive and there was music and possibility and the clouds were dreams I could see. Nothing was in my way.

It was everything church should be. My spirits rose and my voice rose and I sang to the music and the world.

It was a moment of beyond okay. It was a moment of right. It was a moment where hope was now and hope was the future and hope was already fulfilled. I was uplifted. Held well. Held strong.

And then I went on with my day. But I see those clouds still.

And yes, that helps. Despite. Anyway.

## JUNE 19, 2017

And so today's moment of happiness despite the news.

I had a great surprise when I was in Colorado last week and happened to wander into a used bookstore. I was looking for myself (of course – it's what you do when you're a writer and you go into a bookstore of any type) and instead of finding me, I found my favorite woman author, Ellen Gilchrist. She apparently had a new book released way back in 2014, and somehow, I didn't know about it! I was horrified that I'd missed it, and then a breath later, thrilled that I found it.

For any reader, this is like rounding a corner and coming face to face with the best friend you once thought you couldn't live without, and when you are face to face again, you realize you haven't lived without and would never live without, because that person is just too damn important. When you're a writer and this happens, it's like running into that best friend, but also a best friend who understands truly and deeply what it is you do because that person does it too. That person gets *it*.

In other words, it's wonderful.

On my flight home on Saturday, I dove into that book and I relished the words and the voice and the stories and I didn't look up until the plane touched down. Since then, back in real life, I've thrown myself back in whenever the opportunity presents itself. Ellen Gilchrist, you'd probably blush at the unmentionable places I've read you – but then, you would know how wonderful it is to be totally in love with a book. You would get *it*.

I was in my mid to late twenties when I first read Ellen. I was stunned by her courage, by her willingness to go against convention and tradition, and by her absolute way of just saying things the way she wanted to say them, no matter the taboo or the moral or the rule. I was stunned, I was impressed, I was enthralled…and boy, did I want to do that.

So I did.

It's amazing how much your life can be changed by a best friend you've never met. By a voice you've never heard.

Today, at lunch, I dove in again. And at the end of the story, "High Water", I read this:

*The human race. You have to love it and wish it well and not preach or think you have any reason to think you are better than anyone else. Amen. Good-bye. Peace…*

With Ellen, and with her character, I said, "Amen."

And I am caught afire again with the "boy, do I want to do that." That resonance. That impact. That solid sense of understanding. Getting it. Helping other people to get it.

Last night, I turned to Michael and said, "You know what I want for my birthday?" My birthday is July 29.

He rolled his eyes and said, "What?"

I said, "I want Ellen Gilchrist to read one of my books."

An eyeroll again as he said, "I'll get right on that."

Yeah, well. A girl can dream. Dreaming makes me happy. And this woman can dream about one of her books in the hands of the best friend she never met.

And yes, that helps. Despite. Anyway.

## JUNE 20, 2017

And so today's moment of happiness despite the news.

Well, this is going to be a hard one.

How do I come up with a moment of happiness on a day where mammogram results go the wrong way?

I went in today for a routine mammogram. I expected to be in and out. Instead, the radiologist saw something in my right breast on the pictures and he asked for an ultrasound. Then he saw something there too. On Monday, there will be a needle biopsy. On Tuesday, I will know what I'm facing or if I'm facing nothing at all.

And to think I was scared of the dentist.

New fear now. New what-ifs.

But a friend said today, "Don't get your head too far out over your skis now." So I got off the skis entirely. And I will wait the long wait until Tuesday.

So what's the moment of happiness?

Just this. I know if I'm facing something, I won't be facing it alone. And I know if I'm not facing anything at all, there will be many celebrating with me.

Not skiing, but standing.

And not alone.

I'm grateful.

And yes, this helps. Despite. Anyway.

## JUNE 21, 2017

And so today's moment of happiness despite the news.

Being told you could possibly have breast cancer is not a good thing. That's sort of stating the obvious, isn't it. Yet today, that led to a series of good things that added up to just one big warm mushy mess of happiness.

First and foremost, I have received so many messages of encouragement, support and hope. Face to face messages, emailed messages, instant electronic messages, posts on my Facebook page and on Twitter. Offers for prayer, offers for good energy, offers of love. One student put out a call for prayer on her

Facebook page, looking for at least one prayer from every possible religion. Holy cow (maybe literally). If there is a God, there's no way he can avoid not hearing this.

In my AllWriters' Wednesday Afternoon Women Writers' Workshop, I received the best hugs. The hugs released tears I've been holding back, and they also allowed the fear to surface and for me to voice that fear – which brought relief.

I said yesterday that I knew I wouldn't be alone. Not only am I not alone, I am SURROUNDED. I feel a solid circle of support and protection.

Then came late this afternoon. I was in between my two final clients of the day. I decided to meditate. When I do guided meditations, my favorite artist to listen to is Glenn Harold. Since hearing the news yesterday as I worked my way through mammogram, ultrasound, and scheduling the needle biopsy, I've been feeling the pull to listen to Harold's guided meditation for spiritual healing. I wasn't looking for spiritual healing, I was looking for physical-healing-if-it's-necessary, but I still felt pulled toward it. It's a 41 minute meditation. I got out my heated throw, crawled under it in my recliner, stuck my head in my headphones and listened.

Harold's voice is an amazing thing. In my own mind, every time he said "spiritual", my voice followed his and added, "and physical". Partway through, I found my own hands resting on the – well, geez, I nearly said offending. Not offending. It's the possible victim. So I found my own hands resting on the possibly afflicted breast. My hands were warmer than the heated throw.

I felt myself sink. I stopped listening. And essentially, I disappeared. It might have been sleep. But it was a relaxation so complete, I stopped hearing, I didn't dream, I had no sense of time. The only thing I felt was the warmth from my own hands.

When I reopened my eyes, it was with the most incredible sense of well-being. I hadn't heard the end of the recording. I hadn't heard the chime I'd set up to wake me if I fell asleep. But I was instantly alert, and I also just...felt fine. I moved my hands to my face and felt the warmth dissipate.

I believe I'm fine.

Am I in a state of denial? Maybe. If I am, I can accept that. The mind can do wondrous things in stressful situations. But I don't think so.

I believe I'm fine.

And yes, that helps. Despite. Anyway.

## JUNE 22, 2017

And so today's moment of happiness despite the news.

Today marked the start of the 12th AllWriters' Annual Retreat. AllWriters' Workplace & Workshop, my studio, is going to be 13 years old in January. And today…oh, the retreat.

20 writers from 10 different states. 22 writers if you count Michael and me, which of course, I do. All under one roof, all for four days, all to write and to celebrate writing.

Kid in a candy store? Oh, that's me, during these four days.

I love writers. I love writing. I love teaching. And these four days always create a concrete embodiment of what I do. I get to see the faces of writers who I typically only hear as voices over the phone or streamed discussion in a chatroom. And I get to see the writers I work with face to face for more than an hour at a time.

I get to be with family.

It's difficult for me to tell you, to describe, what this means to me. And how it means even more now, since I know that on Monday, I will be having the needle biopsy.

All I know is this:

I am at my happiest when I am immersed in writers, in writing, in teaching, in the love of the written word, in the shared passion, in my very greatest joy.

There are so many words I could use. I am fulfilled. I am satisfied. I am ecstatic. I am empowered. I am proud.

But it all comes down, I suppose, to one thought:

I am so happy to be here. "Here" in every different level and depth you want to give it. Here, at the retreat. Here, alive. Here, despite everything. Here.

Alive.

Happy.

And yes, that helps. Despite. Anyway.

## JUNE 23, 2017

And so today's moment of happiness despite the news.

I am at my happiest when I am teaching at the AllWriters' Annual Retreat. This is the weekend, a solid four days, when my life passions completely collide and blend together. I am both writer and teacher here. I see my dreams and aspirations coming true here. And I see the AllWriters' community, something that I have built, in a way that is concrete and metaphor, all at the same time.

This year, it's a little surreal. I am astonishingly happy here. And, with the mammogram gone south last week, I am also at my most terrified.

In the language of the test results, the radiologist wrote that this is to be considered cancer until proven otherwise. And I've been told by one of my students that this is language used when they're pretty damn sure it's cancer.

I feel like I've been declared guilty in a court of law without ever being brought to trial.

So bit by bit, I am seeing my hope for an "it's nothing!" outcome on Tuesday shrink and fall away.

There have been many moments during this weekend thus far, when I am immersed in writing and immersed in teaching and thinking, ohmygod, I love this, that the thought, the wonder, the worry that I might not be here next year to do this sneaks in. The worry that I might look different. The worry that I might become someone different.

But I am here now. I am seeing students light up. I am seeing them come together. I see the passion that burns in me burning in them. And I am so happy to be here.

To say I am scared out of my mind is an understatement. To say that I'm happy out of my mind is an understatement.

What a weird place to be in.

My moment of happiness today? All of it. Spending time with each student individually in private consultations. Sharing meals. Leading a workshop that is as fun as it is informative and affirming.

I know Monday is coming. I know Tuesday is coming.

But I am here now.

And yes, that helps. Despite. Anyway.

## JUNE 24, 2017

And so today's moment of happiness despite the news.

I don't know how many times this weekend I've been called a strong woman. A brave woman. A "tough bitch who doesn't take shit from anything or anybody."

Well, jiminey.

I don't always feel so strong or tough.

And I've been told you can't be brave without being scared.

In which case, I'm pretty damn brave.

I know that we're taught that our sense of ourselves have to come directly from ourselves, from our own beliefs, from our own feelings. But I've always listened hard to those around me. And I've always tried hard to be who they believe me to be. To live up to their expectations.

I had a student tell me today, "I just never want to disappoint you."

Oh, trust me. The feeling is very, very mutual.

I had another student email me from the other side of the world, telling me that, in all capitals, I WILL BE FINE BECAUSE THERE ISN'T ANY OTHER OPTION.

Well, okay then.

I am trying to find the vein of happiness here. There's a vein of fear running parallel.

I just never want to disappoint.

I'm working so hard on the attitude here. Really.

And it means so much to be buoyed by the beliefs of others. The faith of others. The love from others.

There's another vein too. It's filled with gratitude.

And there's the happy.

And yes, that helps. Despite. Anyway.

## JUNE 25, 2017

And so today's moment of happiness despite the news.

On the way home today from the AllWriters' Annual Retreat, my sixteen-year old daughter texted me. Don't worry – my husband fielded the texts for me since I was driving. I do not text and drive. And the irony of the resulting interchange did not go under my radar.

Olivia texted, asking if she could go out to a park or something as she was in the house ALL weekend and it was so LOOOOOOOOONG and she was STUUUUUUUCK and BOOOOOOORED. I said sure, but to make sure she locked up and let us know where she was going.

A short while later, she texted the following:

*"At I am at the cool new park by Frame"*

*"*ate"*

*"St"*

*"Ay"*

This little incoherent exchange puzzled and alarmed me. Did she start to text me when she was dragged away by someone? Was she hurt? I knew the park she was referring to and it had a lot of bizarre new age playground equipment. In true mother fashion, and especially in true–mother–fashion–when–said–mother–is–totally–exhausted–from–teaching–at–a–retreat–for–the–last–four–days–not–to–mention–worrying–about–breast–cancer, I freaked out and yelled for Michael to CALL THE CHILD RIGHT NOW AND MAKE SURE SHE'S OKAY!!!!

And then the next text came in:

*"Note to self don't text while swinging lol"*

Well then. Therein lies an important lesson for us all.

And yes, that helps. Despite. Anyway.

## JUNE 26, 2017

And so today's moment of happiness despite the news.

I went in for the needle biopsy today, a result of a mammogram gone south last week. I was scared going in; the image of "needle biopsy" that flared in my head involved a syringe that probably would have been more appropriate for drilling into concrete. But the procedure was painless, thank goodness. I was worried about the numbing agent, since I'm immune to novocaine. But what they use, while it's similar to what dentists use, is a shade different, and that shade made the difference. I didn't feel a thing.

It's a very strange thing, having a numb breast.

The sound of the needle collecting samples was exactly like the sound of an ear–piercing gun. That surprised me too, and while I lay there, staring at a ceiling that was supposed to look like the Milky Way, my arm over my head, I idly wondered about that. Was it a sign? Should I have pierced my nipples years ago, instead of piercing my ears three times in one, four times in the other? Then none of this would be happening?

I also caught the irony of staring at the Milky Way in a room that is for breasts. God help me, I giggled on the table.

Writers are like that. We think in metaphor, simile, symbol. So we look for things. It keeps us busy.

When I got home, I found a card in the mail from one of my students. In it, it said, "So here you are on this journey of facing fears – all these opportunities to dump fears and increase resilience."

So I sat with that for a while. It's true, I have had to face a lot of fears lately.

*fear of pretty much everything for a while – a result of last November's assault;

*fear of standing up for myself and for who I am by leaving my original publisher – would I ever be published again? (new novel is coming out September 7);

*fear of the dentist;

*fear of being in a plane – not of flying, but of being sealed inside without an escape;

*fear of losing everything when my husband suddenly lost his job;

*fear that my daughter would be forever changed when she went through a life-changing experience;

*and now this. A fear of cancer.

And then, while I was thinking about this, I began to laugh. Because I have one more. Not a fear, but a sign or a symbol. Are you ready for this?

Among all the students I have writing novels, I have one I've been working with in coaching who just finished his book. His title is – really truly – "*Face Your Fears*".

OH, FOR CRIPES' SAKE!

I get the message.

And I have no intention of piercing my nipples.

And yes, that helps. Despite. Anyway.

## JUNE 27, 2017

And so today's moment of happiness despite the news.

One week ago today, I started my Moment with this sentence: "*How do I come up with a moment of happiness on a day where mammogram results go the wrong way?*"

And today, I'm starting it with this:

How do I come up with a moment of happiness on a day when I'm given a diagnosis of breast cancer?

It's amazing how everything can change in the course of a week. A day. A moment. One minute, I was in the shower, taking care around the incision from yesterday's biopsy, and picturing how I would announce "benign!" on

Facebook, and the next, I was standing naked in the bathroom, dripping on the floor, phone in my hand, with my doctor's voice saying to me, "The biopsy came out positive."

For a moment, I let myself think that positive meant good news. You know, positive. But only for a moment.

And so the world spun away for a bit.

Never in my life have I considered that I would be a container for cancer. The closest I thought I would come to cancer is my brother's astrological sign (he's a Cancer). I spoke with him today, and as far as we know, only one person in our family, covering both sides, has had breast cancer.

Well, now I'm number two.

I am suddenly more aware of my breasts than I ever have been – with the possible exception of when they "sprouted" and I was in thrall, watching them pop out of my little girl chest like rising loaves of bread. Mostly, they've just been something that's there, that's a part of me, like my arms or legs. But in the last week, I've been very conscious of how they sit on my chest, where they are at which times when I'm in different positions, their weight, their shape, their history and personality.

I've even been talking to them. The left has been a bit smug. The right, apologetic and sad. I've told her I don't blame her – this isn't something she's doing to me. She's under attack, and because we're attached, so am I. I guess I didn't defend her very well, protect her very well.

It's been a surreal week. This is what happens when writers get breast cancer. The breasts become characters. But baby, it's not surreal anymore. This shit just got real.

So back to my original question: How do I come up with a moment of happiness on a day when I'm given a diagnosis of breast cancer?

Well, since I posted the diagnosis on Facebook and also called/texted some specific people, my landline and cell phone have been raucous. My cell phone chimes every time someone reacts or comments on my Facebook page, and for a while, I had to silence it because the chime was continuous and cathedral-worthy. I was also inundated with texts and Facebook private messages. My landline erupted with phone calls. It was a little overwhelming, but also wonderful. Because of the support and encouragement and love, of course. But also because…

NEVER BEFORE IN MY ENTIRE LIFE HAVE SO MANY PEOPLE BEEN DISCUSSING MY BREASTS!

And they've been worthy of that discussion, lemme tell you, since they were little tiny bread loaves.

And yes, that helps. Despite. Anyway.

## JUNE 28, 2017

And so today's moment of happiness despite the news.

It was sort of a family day today.

I have this week and half of next off, as I always give myself a break after teaching at the AllWriters' Retreat. I wasn't expecting to spend my time off learning about breast cancer. I wasn't expecting to spend my time off trying to add the word cancer to my daily schedule, my life, my self-definition. I was expecting my time off to be easy, relaxing and fun.

Yeah, well. Best laid plans, you know.

Today, my older daughter Katie suggested I come down to the University of Wisconsin – Milwaukee, where she is earning her PhD in math, and we'd go out to Starbucks. By the time I left home, I'd added my younger daughter Olivia to the car and my younger son, Andy.

We sat and talked in Starbucks for a couple hours. I was told I once yelled at them for using words such as "dumb butt" and "fart". I insisted, they said, that they use "bottom" and "passing gas".

I have absolutely no recall of this. As my fourth child's first word was "dumbass," I think my older children are hallucinating.

Or…it could be that I'm just a completely different person now.

I am.

Later, my oldest boy dropped off my granddaughter on his way to work. Unfortunately, I was on the phone when he arrived, so all I experienced of him was a "Hi, Mom!" and "Love you!" and then he was gone. But Grandbaby Maya Mae was here, all four years and long-haired big-eyed adorableness of her.

At one point, Maya ran up to me and said, "Gamma Kaffee, wisten."

So I wistened. And she sang. She sang the way all four-year olds sing. Gobbledy-gook and nonexistent melody, incomprehensible words and open-faced expression. Full heart. Full passion.

Absolutely beautiful.

"See it?" she asked at the end. "Gamma Kaffee, did you see the song?"

I looked around my living room and kitchen. At my boy cooking spaghetti, my girl, using one hand to hug a stuffed pony and the other to tap secret messages to her boyfriend. At my grandgirl, eyes that put saucers to shame, wide abeam and arms flung wide in "See it?" I thought of my older boy, on his way steadfastly to work. Of my older girl, working on her dissertation of something called firing squad synchronicity, something I will never understand, but I'm oh so proud that she knows.

"I see it," I said to Maya Mae. "I wisten."

Beam.

And yes, that helps. Despite. Anyway.

## JUNE 29, 2017

And so today's moment of happiness despite the news.

Riches! I can't choose which one to write about (there are four), so I'm going to write about all of them. One drenched me with hope and warmth; the other three made me laugh.

So the laughing ones first.

Around two this morning, before we went to bed, Michael called up the stairs to me, "What do you get if you cross an insomniac, an agnostic and a dyslexic?"

"What?" I called back.

"Someone who stays up all night, wondering if there's a dog."

I love jokes like that.

This afternoon, Grandbaby Maya Mae was over again for a visit and she filled me in on fashion. We were watching Frozen (ick) and she said, "Gamma Kaffee, Elsa doesn't wear pants. Her doesn't wear pants because her's frozen. You can't wear pants if you're frozen."

Good to know.

And then at dinner tonight, Olivia suddenly announced, "I think I'm gonna be a cool old lady. I want to be a hippie old lady. I want to wear hippie clothes and have blue hair."

When she is old, she shall wear purple.

And then the hope.

I sat and talked with a friend this afternoon. There were tears. He told me that while I am a strong woman, while I am a brave woman, I don't have to be right now. I can be sad. I can feel weak. I can be terrified out of my mind.

I am all of those things.

And then he told me about the hiking trip he took recently, just a couple weeks ago, along the coast of Washington state. One night, as the tide was coming in, he watched it pushing all of this stuff with it. Broken shells. Rocks. And bits of sand dollars. He thought of me, and of my story of the sand dollar and how I could never find a whole one (refer back to May 18). As he thought about me and about this, he looked down. And there was a whole sand dollar.

He brought it home to me.

A reminder that I'm on the right path.

And a reminder that just because I'm on the right path doesn't mean that it will be easy or that there won't be bumps.

I treasure this.

And yes, that helps. Despite. Anyway.

## JUNE 30, 2017

And so today's moment of happiness despite the news.

I saw the surgeon today and if it's possible to have good news about cancer, I had it. I'm only at Stage 1, Grade 1. I will have a lumpectomy on July 25 and a sentinel lymph node biopsy. It will be day surgery. Then four weeks later, I will start four weeks of radiation, Monday through Friday, ten minutes a day. The cancer is estrogen/progesterone sensitive, so I will be taking antihormone medication for the next five to ten years.

This is manageable. This isn't overwhelming. I can DO this.

I was asked today, for the second time, why I've been so public with this. For that matter, why I'm so public with everything. One person even told me flat-out that I needed to quit "collecting sympathy." I'm not collecting sympathy. But there is a reason I'm so public.

First and foremost, I'm already public. Between the writing and the teaching, I'm well-known. I live a public life. Rather than fighting it, I embrace it. I automatically assume that everything I do is being witnessed. It probably keeps me out of trouble, for the most part. I'm always aware of the greater world.

But it's more than that. With the breast cancer in particular, I was looking for knowledge. I was looking for information. And I was looking for hope. I got it all, in spades. I've learned more about breast cancer in the last couple weeks than I ever could have by scouring the internet. I was actually told to avoid sites like Web MD, and I did. I needed to hear from real people. I particularly listened to those who experienced breast cancer themselves. Hearing those success stories helped me more than I can ever repay.

But I do try to repay it, which again, is why I'm so public. Already, as the result of my talking about this in the blog, I know of at least five women who have gone out and had their mammograms, and two who either made an appointment for a biopsy or had one, after holding off doing so because they were scared. My experience motivated them to get'er done. One has found that she's just fine. We're still waiting on the other.

Knowledge. Information. Hope. Experience. There is such richness around us, that we can tap into so easily without having to look into an impersonal screen. Yes, I am still looking at a screen, but it's personal. People have been talking to me. Encouraging me. Soothing me. And getting me to the point that when I walked into that surgeon's office today, I felt prepared. I knew what to ask, I knew what to do, and I understood what she told me, because people shared with me. They didn't hide away. They reached out from every corner of the earth. Some know me personally. Some know me professionally. Some know me from a distance, as a writer they've read. Some don't know me at all. But they all reached out.

I think if we did that with each other more often, it would really help.

You know what my moment of happiness is, besides the obvious? It's this. When I started this blog, back in January, it was because the world went crazy around me. I thought we'd all lost it, we'd all lost our humanity, our compassion, our sense of decency, our love and respect for all people. I thought we were all whacked – it was the only way I could explain the Asshat in the White House.

But what happened today on my Facebook page and in other social media, and what's happened over the last couple weeks, and even what's happened over the last five months has shown me that the world can still be a pretty wonderful place. We can still lean over the newfangled white picket fence of the internet and talk to each other. We can still connect. We can still help.

Yes, there is plenty of whackiness out there. But ohmygod, there is so much good. I needed to see that. And that's exactly what I am witnessing.

And yes, that helps. Despite. Anyway.

# Chapter Seven

## JULY 1, 2017

And so today's moment of happiness despite the news.

The day didn't start out so well. Yesterday, upon receiving my very positive prognosis and plan of action, I felt pretty good. Stage 1, Grade 1. Lumpectomy – day surgery. Four weeks radiation. Antihormone pill for five to ten years. All lined up and clear. Beginning, middle, end. Conflict, resolution. Just like a story.

I see everything as a story. It gave me a sense of familiar. I could do this. I could write this. It was just a different genre.

But this morning, I still woke up scared. I didn't think I would, but I did.

I told myself those steps again. Day surgery. Four weeks radiation. Antihormone pill. Beginning, middle, end. Conflict, resolution. But the more I reminded myself, the more I realized something.

I have a diagnosis and a prognosis. I don't want them. I have these steps to follow. I don't want to. I don't want any of this. I am not a cancer container. I'm NOT.

But…now I am. At least until July 25, when hopefully, it will all be removed.

Then the mail came. In it, addressed to me, was a card from the people at the breast care clinic, where I had my mammogram, my ultrasound, my biopsy. They thanked me for my trust. And they thanked me for choosing them, for giving them the opportunity to serve me.

I did not choose them. I did not choose any of this. I don't want to be served. I don't want to be thanked. Thanked for what? Having breast cancer?

This was a tough day. This is a hard moment of happiness.

But I carried on. I spoke to a few people. A close friend. My new mentor, found through ABCD (After Breast Care Diagnosis), a wonderful organization that matches women up with other women who are their same age, same lifestyle, and had the same form of breast cancer and survived. Talking with Lana helped. She told me I could call her anytime, text anytime. I get the feeling I might be doing a lot of that.

Then Michael, Olivia and I got in the car. It was a really nice summer day and so I drove Semi, my Chrysler 200 convertible, top down, music up. I wanted to walk my favorite labyrinth, located in Regner Park in West Bend, Wisconsin. It's a gorgeous place – a labyrinth that is lovingly attended by a garden society. I've found peace there before; I thought I would again. I also wanted to drive from there to Port Washington, to spend a little time with Lake Michigan.

I get strength from walking a labyrinth. And clarity. I get strength and comfort from being by water.

But the moment of happiness came before I got to either of those places. We have a new interchange near Milwaukee, where you can move from I-94 east to US-45 north. It used to be a godawful left exit, a sharp turn that slowed you down and then dumped you into fast-flying traffic with little time to merge.

But now...oh, now. It was my first time driving it and it was a total surprise. I rose up. I rose up in a topless car. The single lane transition rose higher and higher and I could see all around and it was smooth and the air was warm and there was sun and blue sky and white clouds. I was in a beautiful car that moved at my every beck and call and my husband was beside me and my daughter directly behind me, yelling, "Whoa!"

And for that moment, rising up, I was invincible. I was immortal. I could do anything.

Even beat this. But more than that. I could be free of it. I didn't have to have it. For that moment, I was just me again. Just me. Who I was just four days ago.

Just me.

When we came back down and merged into traffic, my husband looked over. "Why are you smiling?" he asked.

I shrugged and said, "Just driving."

But it was so much more than that.

And yes, that helps. Despite. Anyway.

## JULY 2, 2017

And so today's moment of happiness despite the news.

One of my least favorite chores is the switching of seasonal clothes. My closet isn't large enough to hold both winter and summer wardrobes. So the current season resides in my closet and the off-season sleeps in my hope chest at the foot of our bed. Switching involves taking down all the clothes in the closet, removing the hangers, folding the clothes, and placing them in stacks on my bed. Then the clothes come out of the hope chest, onto the hangers, and into the closet. Final move: taking the stacks on the bed and settling them in the hope chest. It's tedious, back-breaking, and for someone with fibromyalgia, the repetitive motion causes aches to erupt pretty much everywhere.

It's just turned into July and with my schedule lately, I've not had time to do the switch, which means every morning, I was throwing pillows and blankets off the hope chest, scrounging around through the piles for what I of course could never find, swearing a lot, and finally settling for wearing either light winter clothes from my closet or taking whatever was on top in the hope chest.

Yes, I know. First world problem. But annoying nonetheless.

This was the week I was going to get it done, because I've been off of teaching, on full recover after the intensive AllWriters' retreat. However, with the biopsy early in the supposed week off for relaxation, things have been thrown out of whack. My emotions were elsewhere. And physically, I wasn't supposed to be lifting or doing repetitive motion while I healed from the biopsy. Lemme tell ya, my breast has never been the colors she is right now. I can't imagine what surgery is going to do.

So today, Michael stepped in to help me.

This is a day-long chore, and so I had the television on. The show *Reba* was playing episode after episode, so I settled there. I never watched it when it was on in real time, but I did get hooked on it in reruns on Hulu, to the point that when Hulu didn't have the final season, I purchased it so I could find out what happened. Today, it made for a nice backdrop. Over and over, the theme song came on, and over and over, I hummed and sang with it.

*My roots are planted in the past and though my life is changing fast, who I am is who I want to be.*

And of course, the refrain line and the title of the actual song: I'm A Survivor.

It took a while for all the words to sink in, these words that I was singing and hearing simultaneously. Over and over. While I did again the chore I did last fall. That I will do again next fall. That I will do again next year. And the year after that.

Because I am a survivor. Always have been. Always will be.

And you know what? I am exactly who I want to be. That didn't happen overnight. It happened by following a path that was pretty harrowing at times. But I always knew who I wanted to be.

And I am.

I don't give up easily. Actually… I don't give up.

Thank you, Reba, for reminding me of that.

And yes, that helps. Despite. Anyway.

## JULY 3, 2017

And so today's moment of happiness despite the news.

Today was the first day I found myself all alone for a short time since the possibility and then the realization of breast cancer cropped up. I've been consistently surrounded by students, by friends, by family. Which has been a wonder and a comfort. At moments of weakness and substantial fear, I've had someone there to distract me, to hug me, to tell me I'm going to be fine.

Which is good. But I am also always aware that I am not alone in all of this. It's affecting my kids, my husband, my extended family and the community I've grown and dwell constantly in – AllWriters' Workplace & Workshop. This awareness has kept me in check, I think – I watch my behavior and my words, so I don't upset anyone.

I'm used to being the caretaker. I don't need the comfort – I offer it. I don't cause the problems – I solve them.

I am so not used to worrying about myself, or being a worry to others.

So then this afternoon. Because of the 4th of July, I tacked on an extra three days off to my usual break after the AllWriters' retreat. I don't return to teaching until Thursday. I dropped Michael off to do the grocery shopping and Olivia was on a date with the boyfriend. I came home, expecting to actually spend some time writing (this was supposed to be the focus of my week and a half off – I haven't written a word), but instead found myself in a very quiet house. The dogs and cats were sleeping. The television was off. No one was here.

Just me.

Well, just me, and this new gremlin in my right breast. I picture it sort of R2D2-shaped, with dashes for eyes and a jagged mouth. Maybe with a tendency toward Space Invaders. And it's blue. No clue why. And it's male. And I really don't like it.

I'm told it's at the ten o'clock position. My breast, mine, the clock person's, the clock writer's, was described as a clock, and the nasty evil gremlin was at ten.

I remember having to shut my eyes for a few seconds when I was told this. And thinking, For god's sake, don't use a clock. I cannot think of cancer as a clock.

This afternoon, all by myself with the gremlin, I completely and totally lost it. I went batshit. I raved, I ranted, I cried, I screamed. I went through the it's-not-fairs and why-mes and how-could-yous and if-you-exists. I very uncharitably asked why not someone else. I tore at my hair, I pounded my fists. If I could have torn open my breast and ripped out the gremlin with my bare hands, I think I likely would have.

I'm pretty sure I was certifiable there, for about ten minutes.

And yes, this is my moment of happiness.

Why? Because ohmygod, did it ever feel GOOD to let all of that out. To react without having to worry about who I was affecting. I now know that the violent act of explosion is an amazing thing, a wonderful thing, a release, a relief, and whew.

And the gremlin in my right breast? He's scared to death. He's going down. He's not at ten o'clock. He's at X-marks-the-spot. For destruction. For annihilation.

I feel much better now.

And yes, that helps. Despite. Anyway.

## JULY 4, 2017

And so today's moment of happiness despite the news.

Well, for starters today, I looked in the mirror and saw that my right breast no longer looks like she substituted for Muhammad Ali's punching bag. She almost looks like herself again, and that helps my attitude. Though I have to admit, if a needle biopsy caused that kind of bruising, I can't imagine what I'm going to look like after the lumpectomy. I admit that I keep envisioning my breast as a pie with one slice missing. This does not help my attitude and so I try not to picture it.

Then, this afternoon, for the second day in a row, I actually managed to sit down and work on the new Novel-In-Progress. And I watched it surge past page 100. I started it last March.

When you write a book, whether it's a novel or a book-length memoir, there is something magical about the number 100. The book suddenly becomes more than a possibility – it becomes real. It has weight and heft. I miss the days when we worked on typewriters and a steady pile of paper grew on our desk as we completed page after page. We had a visual every day of what we'd done, what we accomplished, and how it was growing. Now, we go by little numbers on the lower corner of our screens. That 1-0-0 should come with the clanging of a typewriter bell. It's a milestone.

And for me, especially now, it feels like the future. There is a book to finish. I never leave anything incomplete.

Writing is magic in so many ways. Today, and yesterday, I was able to sink into story for a while, into another person's life (her name is Audrey), another person's issues (his name is Frank), and leave my own behind. When you write fiction, you have to, of absolute necessity, disappear. Sink. Body-snatch. I've always found great relief there, and it is a relief I very much need now.

This afternoon, a lovely student texted me:

*'Do what you do best. WRITE.' Quote from Kathie Giorgio, author and writing teacher par excellence.*

Healer, heal thyself.

When I do author visits in schools, particularly in elementary schools, I come equipped with baggies of small folded sheets of paper. In one baggie, each piece of paper contains a letter. In the other, there are words. First, I have kids select a piece of paper and write the letter they unfold anywhere at random on the board. When all the letters are up there, scattered, nonsensical, we talk about how they don't say anything, they don't do anything. But then...Magic! I put the letters in a certain order and we have a word. Treehouse. Dinosaur. Wizard. Horse. Magic! Then I have the kids do the same thing with the second baggie. Random words everywhere all over the board! Chaos! Nonsense! And then...Magic! I put the words together into a sentence.

The magic isn't just on the board. It isn't just in the sentence. It's in the light on those kids' faces when they see the sentence come together and then they start writing the next one. And the next. And the next. And before you know it, from a random group of letters, then words, on a board, we have thirty different stories growing from that same first sentence.

Magic!

The light on their faces. I imagine it was the same light on mine, as I sat down this afternoon and watched that page number roll past 100.

Healer, heal thyself.

Tonight, I went to the fireworks display in Waukesha. My oldest son was three when I moved back here, and he is thirty-three as he sat at my feet today. Next to him was his daughter. My granddaughter. I watched her face light with the fireworks and with a light of her own as she shouted, "Beau-ful! Pink!" She laughed her chipmunk laugh and I laughed with her.

I so look forward to showing her the magic of letters to words to sentences. To seeing her write the second sentence, the third, and the next. I so look forward to seeing that light on her face. Magic!

I so look forward. Bruised breast, possible pie-slice breast, and all.

And yes, that helps. Despite. Anyway.

## JULY 5, 2017

And so today's moment of happiness despite the news.

*Can I sail through the changing ocean tides?*
*Can I handle the seasons of my life?*
*I don't know.*
-   *Stevie Nicks, "Landslide"*

When I write a novel, I always assign a song to it, which I then listen to every day before beginning to write. I often do a finger labyrinth as I listen to the song as well. Both of these routines help me to unwind from my life and wind in to the life of my characters. The song acts like the bell listened to by Pavlov's dogs – they heard the chime and drooled, I hear the song and write.

Working on book number 8, the Novel-In-Progress, I assigned it the song "Landslide", performed by Stevie Nicks. I prefer the live version, where she dedicates the song to her father. *This is for you, Daddy.* I've loved this song for a long time, and I'm delighted to be writing a book that benefits from it.

So today, I sat down, called up the song, began to listen and trailed my finger through the wooden labyrinth. But instead of losing myself, I got to the above lines and lost my composure. I had to set my head down on my finger labyrinth and let tears flood the grooves until the end of the song. I still have the grooves in my forehead to prove it.

Why? Because I don't know if I can sail these ocean tides either, if I can handle this new season. I don't know.

Since starting meditation practice a little over a year ago, I've heard time and again that I need to learn to stay in the present. That I am not my past, that I am not the worst thing I've ever done, and I'm not the worst thing that's ever been done to me. Stay in the here and now. Right now. Focus, focus, focus.

But my present is now all about breast cancer.

So does that mean that's what I am?

In the last few weeks, my life has been turned completely upside down. Going to doctor's appointments, scheduling surgery-prep and surgery appointments, learning new words, having a needle biopsy, discovering that positive can be negative, talking to mentors, talking to strangers. One of my newest goals is to get through one day without tears. Another is to get through one day without a new message in MyChart.com.

So is this who I am now? And can I handle it?

It's a new season. A new present.

I don't know.

When the song ended and my tears evaporated, I sat up and draped both of my wrists over the top of my laptop lid. It's a common pose for me, used to rest, used to allow the blank thoughts in, the chaotic thoughts out, or sometimes to focus down hard on something. This time, I had the blank stares. Until my eyes focused.

In front of me was my bookshelf where I keep spare copies of my books that I bring to sell when I present in venues without a bookseller. They were all there, including number 7, which won't be released until September 7. With a white spine, it glowed. To the left, on my reading chair, is a bag that looks like a cow's hide. Inside, I know it's lined with the brightest gold fabric. And it carries a big plastic binder with information on breast cancer, with handy dandy sleeves to help me keep my cancer organized into questions, appointments, medications, resources. There's also a pink notebook and a pink pen.

The first day I received this gift at my surgeon's office, a gift given by Kohls Cares, I looked inside and pulled out a magazine. On the cover was a smiling woman in a bright pink headwrap. On the lower left corner, a woman sporting something called the "Olivia Wig". I shoved the magazine back in, brought the cow bag home, parked it on my chair, and haven't looked at it since.

Maybe I will, later tonight.

But you know, I looked up and there it was. Those books...are ME. Me here in the present, me in the past, and me in the future. The cow bag is something I brought home to be a part of my life for now, but it's not on a shelf, it's not even unpacked. It's transitory.

For now, I am a writer who has breast cancer. Breast cancer is temporarily something I have.

A writer is who I am.

ME.

So then I played the song again. I trailed my finger through the labyrinth. I wound in. And then I wrote.

And yes, that helps. Despite. Anyway.

## JULY 6, 2017

And so today's moment of happiness despite the news.

So. A week and a half "break", which was supposed to be filled with lots of time to write, reading for pleasure, and closing my eyes in the sun, turned into chaos with a breast cancer diagnosis.

Today, I returned to teaching.

No. I didn't return to teaching. I RAN to teaching.

The moment that first student's voice hit my ear, that moment when we began to talk about her pages, about story, about her characters and language and clarity and conflict and resolution, and always, always, beginning, middle, end, well, my life snapped back into place with the solidity of my spine at the chiropractor's yesterday.

My backbone's back.

From there, I moved on to a second client. And then to my own writing. And then to a client. And then to another. And then to reading/critiquing more clients' work. Tomorrow, there will be six clients. I will be overjoyed to speak to each one.

On Monday, my old world and the new will collide. The day will start with a breast MRI. Then two clients. Then writing. Then client, client, class, client. Then reading/critiquing.

But today, it was almost all old world. My world. The world in which I do what I love and I love what I do.

Almost all old world. When I was done with the clients this morning and before I wrote, I was on the phone with a breast cancer mentor, given to me by ABCD (After Breast Cancer Diagnosis). She was supposed to tell me what radiation was like, and she was also to talk about how it affected her fibromyalgia, because that's what I have, and I needed to know.

She did.

I told her how relieved I was when I found out that I'd be able to keep working through all of this.

She said, "Oh, but make sure you take care of yourself. Make sure you take time for yourself."

And I said, "You don't understand. Working is how I take care of myself."

Some people relax by relaxing.

I work.

And today, that's exactly what I did. And it felt GREAT!

Someone else told me today, in an echo of yesterday's blog, "You are not breast cancer. Breast cancer is just something you have."

Yes. I am a writer, a teacher, an editor, an advocate, a small business owner with immeasurable passion and dedication…who happens to have breast cancer. One of those things is temporary. Guess which one.

And yes, that helps. Despite. Anyway.

### JULY 7, 2017

And so today's moment of happiness despite the news.

Today, I brought Olivia to her first guitar lesson. When we walked in to Outpost Music in downtown Waukesha, she carried a pink guitar. When she walked out, she had a gig bag, picks, a strap (pink), and a clampy thing (pink) that goes on the guitar's neck (see how I know the technical terms?).

And she walked out with music. MORE music.

She's already an avid violinist. And an avid listener, with CDs ranging from Trans-Siberian Orchestra to Coldplay to Evanescence to Linkin Park to Skillet. And now, the guitar.

Both of her instruments were self-motivated. We didn't decide for her. She demanded them.

One of my favorite times of the day is listening to her practice the violin. I've yet to tell her to practice – she does it on her own. And now, I can start listening to the steady strumming and plucking of the guitar. I might even hear her raise her own voice in song. Raise her voice.

I want my daughter to raise her voice.

Amazing.

And now, every time I pass a piano, I stop and look at it. That's the instrument I always wanted to play. But beyond lunchtime renditions of Heart and Soul in the chorus room in high school, it never happened.

But I always thought it could. I thought I could do it.

I think I might want a piano for my birthday. I think I might want to learn. And even if I couldn't, I could play Heart and Soul. Over and over. With heart. With soul. I could teach Olivia and we could play it together.

I could maybe find a player piano and I could sit in the dark late at night and listen to it play for me. And I could imagine that it was my fingers on the keys. I've always imagined that, when I've listened to someone not-me playing the piano.

Or I could learn to play it myself.

My birthday is four days after my lumpectomy.

I gave my daughter music today.

Maybe it's time I gave it to me too.

There's still time.

And yes, that helps. Despite. Anyway.

## JULY 8, 2017

And so today's moment of happiness despite the news.

A friend and a student just messaged me on Facebook. She's getting ready to move across country and she said she has a clock that she and her husband don't want to move. According to Bonnie, "It's heavy. It's antique, but it doesn't have a key to wind it, so it doesn't work. If you are at all interested, it is yours."

SCORE!

Back in 2011, when my first book, *The Home For Wayward Clocks*, came out, I was invited to a book club in Indiana. They'd read the book and wanted me to come talk about it. The club met in a lovely restaurant (that is no longer there, unfortunately). They were my third book club and the first outside of Wisconsin and I wasn't very experienced in this sort of thing yet, so I showed up, feeling a bit nervous and shy. I told the restaurant's host, "I'm here for a book club."

"Oh," he said. "Are you with that large group in the back?"

Large?

He took me back to a private room and when he opened the door, there was a long table with over twenty women sitting around it. I poked my head in and said, "Are you looking for me?"

They gave me a standing ovation. So I guess they were.

They presented me with a bottle of wine...and a broken clock. I know I ordered my lunch and a glass of sangria, but I don't remember imbibing. We were too busy talking about the book. MY book. And they LOVED it.

That night, I waited until Chicago rush hour traffic died out before going home. I sat at a Starbucks and worked on book 2, *Enlarged Hearts*. When I did drive home, it was around nine o'clock on a weeknight, temperatures in the upper eighties, and I flew through Chicago in my Chrysler Sebring lxi convertible, top down, music up, and my spirits soaring beyond the fabulous Chicago skyline.

And a broken clock on the passenger seat. It sits now on a bookshelf in my classroom.

Yes, I collect clocks, like the main character, James, in that first book. Yes, I love them broken, working, ugly, beautiful, with missing parts or whole. Like James, all my clocks are key-wound or weight-driven. No batteries here. If I want to know what time it is, I look at my cell phone, my computer, my microwave or my stove.

When I need a sense of soul, of beauty, of history, of timelessness, I look at a clock. I lay my hands on them, I talk to them, I get them repaired if at all possible, I keep them even if it's not.

I think I'm the Statue of Liberty for clocks.

*Give me your tired, your poor, Your huddled masses yearning to breathe free, The wretched refuse of your teeming shore. Send these, the homeless, tempest-tost to me, I lift my lamp beside the golden door!*

I lift my lamp. I've got to paint my door golden.

Today, the fact that my friend thought of me when it came to her clock makes me happy. Tomorrow, I welcome a new one to the fold. And even though a friend is moving, I get to keep a piece of her.

Thank you, Bonnie.

And yes, that helps. Despite. Anyway.

## JULY 9, 2017

And so today's moment of happiness despite the news.

Before the gift of the clock yesterday, I had a whole other moment I was going to write about. Then the clock happened, and I wrote about that instead. I felt a little bad for the first moment, but as it turns out, a connecting moment happened today, and so now I can write about it anyway.

Yesterday, Michael and I went to the White House of Music in Waukesha. We had to get new music for our daughter and her violin. We got there just before closing time and so we hustled. The ever-adept folks there quickly found exactly what we needed and we headed toward the door, which was being held for us by an employee. We would be the last customers out that day.

The employee stepped outside with us as he told us to have a great day. He saw my convertible, Semi.

"Whoa!" he said. "You've got yourself the right car there!" He was talking to my husband. I've noticed that when Michael and I are together, men instantly assume that he is the owner of the cars, and that he is the driver. Michael doesn't drive. This assumption irks me. The cars are mine. Chosen by me. Driven by me. Maintained by me. Mine.

A woman.

So I jumped in fast and said, "Yes, I (hear the very strong emphasis on I here) certainly do."

"Oh," he said.

Michael and I walked away. Then, from the White House door, the man called, "You got yourself the right girlfriend there!"

I laughed. (And I was tempted to say that Michael's girlfriend is actually pretty trashy, but his wife is perfect.)

So today, I was driving Semi again when I went to meet my friend and pick up yesterday's Today's Moment clock. On my way home, I was on Ann Street, the street that is a non-street running between Walgreens and my home. An older woman, I'd say early 80's, was walking toward me, pushing her walker. I carefully steered next to her, then stopped at the stop sign.

"Hi," I said as I looked left, right, then left again.

"Hi," she said back. "Niiiiiiiiiiice car."

I beamed. "It's the right one, yep," I said, remembering the man from yesterday.

"Well, what're you waiting for? GUN IT!" she said, raising one hand off the walker, curling her fingers into a fist and pumping the air. "FLY!"

Hell, I respect my elders. So I did.

She made me laugh too. And now I know who I want to be when I'm in my 80s.

Gun it! Fly!

And yes, that helps. Despite. Anyway.

## JULY 10, 2017

And so today's moment of happiness despite the news.

Tonight, the moon was orange.

It was orange as I drove through the ten o'clock dark to pick up my daughter and her boyfriend from the movies.

I followed the moon and I remembered when summer meant the movies on a weeknight, with the promise of not much to do the next day.

I remembered when summer meant a new boyfriend and humid nights, the air moist and warm, but not as hot as our skin, the fireflies little orange moons above the grass.

I remembered when going to the movies meant not remembering one bit of the plot, but remembering every bit of the story I lived.

I smiled at tonight's orange moon.

Last week, I walked with my daughter as we toured her new high school. The same high school I used to go to. The same one I loved. She's starting there as a junior and so did I. I watched her walk through those same halls I walked through and I remembered trailing my hand along them as I did, as if my fingertips would remember the new ways and keep me from getting lost. In the silence of last week, I remembered the noise between bells, the strangers who became friends, this strange land that became home.

A home that influences me still, thirty-nine years later. Even now, there is a teacher I still listen to. And there will be teachers she listens to. And friends who used to be strangers.

I looked at the orange moon tonight as if it was for the first time. And I remembered first times. I remembered summers and how the sun even now makes me close my eyes and lift my face and turn glory into a verb. I remember learning and how my mind and my heart fell open like a blank page and a page and a page and I know I am learning even now. I remembered feeling like I was going to live forever.

And I still look ahead.

Tonight, the moon was orange and I looked at it as if it was for the first time.

And yes, that helps. Despite. Anyway.

## JULY 11, 2017

And so today's moment of happiness despite the news.

I know that many people believe, thanks to Charles Schulz, that happiness is a warm puppy. I do love puppies. But happiness to me today, and pretty much any day, is a hot hairdryer.

I honestly don't remember how old I was the first time I sat under a salon hairdryer. Comfortable chair. Big bucket over my head. Hot air blasting out of it onto my hair, down my neck, onto my shoulders. White noise that blocked out everything else in the room. I do know that I fell in love that day.

It probably helps to know that I was a child who sat on heat registers too, with my shirt belled over it, so that the heat surrounded me. I drive my convertible with the heated seats on. In my currently air-conditioned house, I use a space heater on my desk, and I often sit under a heated throw.

I kinda like heat.

Today, in the middle of all that's been messy lately, I went for my standing hair appointment at a salon in Waukesha. I started going there when Olivia was in kindergarten – she's going to be a junior in high school now. So it's been a while. John, my hair guy, is the person responsible for the red spiky hair that I'm recognized for now. At first, when I had my hair cut short and kept it brown, he would spike it for fun before I left the salon. I'd smile, then go home and wash the gel out, and return me to my flat-haired, brown-haired existence.

But something happened when Olivia was five and I was forty-five. Not only did I let the spikes stay, but I told John to turn it red. And boy, did he.

Somehow, from that, I emerged.

And John, bless him, figured out very quickly that no matter what the weather, the season, the temperatures, or my current state of affairs, it was absolutely necessary to turn the dryer on high, lower it over my face, and leave me sitting there.

Today, he added further gentleness. I think, in his quiet way, he knew I needed it.

He turned the hairdryer on ahead of time. It was already hot when it reached my scalp. He turned the chair just so, so I could reach my iced latte, sitting on his covered sink. He handed me my book. And I'm pretty sure he cranked the timer to extra minutes.

For that little bit, I was in an inner sanctum. There was heat. There was coffee. There was a good book.

There wasn't any cancer. There was just me.

I can't explain why sitting under a hairdryer means so much. There's just such comfort there. The noise that isn't a noise blocking out the rest of the world. The heat. No one and no thing can reach me when I'm in there.

Though one thing did reach me. Kindness.

Thanks, John.

And yes, that helps. Despite. Anyway.

# JULY 12, 2017

And so today's moment of happiness despite the news.
*I have seen things that you will never see*
*Leave it to memory me*
*-REM "Try Not To Breathe"*

I've been told a lot lately that I am a strong woman.

But I've also felt a lot lately that I'm not.

It makes me wonder if I'm wandering through this cancer thing the way I'm supposed to. Is there a way I'm supposed to? I've seen the commercials. Women striding through breast cancer walks, wearing pink, wearing t-shirts, raising triumphant fists in the air. I've done some striding. I've definitely raised my fists.

But there are times when I stand quietly outside on my deck, look at the sky, wrap my arms around myself, and cry.

I'm not very proud of myself then. And I look at this new club that I belong to that I never wanted to belong to and I wonder if I should be here at all.

A wonderful friend wrote me recently. In the email, he said,

*"You are a survivor, friend. I think you've actually been through worse. You are certainly no stranger to adversity, and you've weaved it all into wonderful books and poems and have shared what you've learned with writers all over the world."*

There have been a few things. I have survived. I know it.

Now I need to survive again. Battle an internal and foreign enemy. An enemy that sometimes feels huge and ferocious. And at other times, it feels like an enemy that is as common as a mosquito and I just need to smack it and then use the right repellant.

I was told this afternoon that women who go in to breast cancer with a feeling of wanting to attack it have a great recovery rate.

I want to attack it.

And I was told this evening that it's okay if I'm not strong all the time.

I listened to both of these with a great sense of relief.

I've referred to myself often as a living, breathing roller coaster.

Right now, I would much prefer being a living, breathing merry-go-round, and I'd like to be the horse that is stationary…just goes along for the ride, doesn't go up and down. But still gives rides. And still looks damn good.

After the afternoon comment and the evening comment, I took sixteen minutes out to meditate before moving on to reading and critiquing tomorrow's manuscripts. I reached 480 days in a row of meditation the other night…an accomplishment I list right up there with overcoming adversity. I'm doing one now that uses a mantra which says, "*Ananda maya moksha*". *Ananda* means bliss, what we breathe in. *Maya* means illusion, fear, false evidence. And *moksha* means liberation. So when I breathe in, I breathe in bliss. When I release the breath, I release my fear and my dis-ease. And ultimately, I reach *moksha*, which is liberation and healing. Besides doing this meditation, I am using this mantra throughout the day.

So where is my moment of happiness? It's from mixing it all together. I've dealt with difficulties. I can do it again. I will attack this, but it's okay if there are times I don't feel very strong. It's okay if there are times I feel sad. It's okay if there are times I feel scared.

And it's okay if there are times that I am so incredibly angry.

I can do this.

*Ananda maya moksha.*

At the end of his email, my friend also included a quote, which I am also using as a mantra. It's from someone named Julian of Norwich. I have no idea who that is, but I love his words:

*"And all shall be well, and all shall be well, and all manner of things shall be well."*

Today's Moment is rambling and introspective. There's no one event to point to. But I can tell you that I started the day sad, moved into ripping anger in the afternoon, and I've ended my day in peace.

And through it all, I know I am a strong woman.

And yes, that helps. Despite. Anyway.

## JULY 13, 2017

And so today's moment of happiness despite the news.

This might be offensive to some.

Today, I finally hit the internet about breast cancer.

Did I go to Web MD or one of those other places stuffed with incomprehensible and questionable and terrifying medical facts? Oh, hell, no.

I googled "breast cancer jokes."

And then I howled for the next fifteen minutes.

Maybe it's an internal conundrum. Despite being an advocate, despite raising my fist in the air and shouting for equal this and equal that, I have always and absolutely loved inappropriate, politically incorrect jokes. In high school, I had a friend whose last name carried the last three letters, "-ski", and he was forever cracking Polish jokes. I so admired him. He took the air right out of Offensiveness' tires and made it into humor. Maybe that's where this quirk of mine came from.

I love, of course, something-walks-into-a-bar jokes. My two favorites:

A priest, a minister and a rabbi walk into a bar. The bartender says, "What is this, a joke?" and

A giraffe walks into the bar. The bartender says, "What'll you have?" Giraffe says, "High balls are on me!"

I love Helen Keller jokes.

I love those awful jokes we all used to tell, like What do you call a woman with one leg? Eileen. What do you call a man with no arms and no legs who is in a swimming pool? Bob.

Ohmygod.

Two of my all-time favorite jokes ever:

Did you hear the one about the gay midget who came out of the cabinet? and

What do you call an anorexic with a yeast infection? A quarter pounder with cheese.

So now I've likely offended everyone.

Today, breast cancer jokes. I saw t-shirts that said, "Save second base!" I saw a pin that said, "If I have one more MRI, I'll stick to my fridge," and a meme that said, "I'm sick of all the jokes about breast cancer…I'm glad I got that off my chest." I saw a comic strip that said, "How to tell if your oncologist has a sense of humor," and then showed a woman with a tennis ball down the back of her shirt.

And so I laughed. Out loud. Alone in my office, I had a ball. And then I carried on with my day. Carried on. Period.

When I was walking my dogs later, and bending down to bag up the latest pile, I began to laugh all over again. Before I had breast cancer, I picked up dog shit. After diagnosis, I'm still picking up dog shit.

Life really does just go on.

I was going to end this here, but there's one other thing that I saw on the internet. It was a meme of a woman holding a coffee cup. And it said, "So apparently, God only gives us what we can handle. God must think I'm bad-ass."

If that's the case, then God's right. I am bad-ass.

And today, I'm laughing.

And yes, that helps. Despite. Anyway.

## JULY 14, 2017

And so today's moment of happiness despite the news.

Recently, I wrote about giving my daughter the gift of music – she went to her first guitar lesson last week and loved it. So she's now taking violin and guitar. On violin, she's playing Haydn and Bach. On guitar, she's playing Linkin Park and Twenty-One Pilots. But she also received another new instrument last week that I neglected to talk about.

A kazoo. It cost a buck. It wasn't pink. It was blue.

For the next several days, this sixteen-year old young woman walked around with a kazoo in her mouth like a noisy plastic cigar. She used it the appropriate way, humming and making music. She accompanied herself on the guitar. She might have accompanied herself on the violin – I'm not sure. But she also spoke through it. She used words and she used sounds to communicate. She even used it on the telephone. She laughed through it.

You know the sound a kazoo makes? That sort of annoying bee-buzzing, hoarse, humming with gravel sound? Picture it around the clock. Picture it in conversations. Picture it when all you want is a yes or no answer.

It was a looooooong couple days. But it made her happy.

Then one night, as she slid off her perpetual perch on her bed, her hip bumped the new constant companion. It fell to the floor – our floors are concrete. And it cracked.

Aw.

So she was sad.

Today, it's Friday again. She had her second guitar lesson. Before she left, I asked her if she still had a dollar from some cash I gave her last week when she went to the movies with her boyfriend. Without the kazoo.

Yes, she said.

I told her to buy another kazoo.

Fireworks!

She bought a red one. It's closer to pink. And she thinks red might make it stronger.

I'm back to having conversations with my daughter via kazoo.

But they're conversations. I'll talk to her any which way I can.

And it makes her happy. Which makes me happy.

And yes, that helps. Despite. Anyway.

## JULY 15, 2017

And so today's moment of happiness despite the news.

Today, I brought my husband alarm clock shopping.

Yes, my life is one exciting event after another.

But here, I really was excited. My husband has had the same digital alarm clock since he was in eighth grade. Michael is fifty-two years old. He received the clock as a gift for Christmas in 1977. From "Santa". That would make 40 years with this clock when we hit Christmas this year.

So first off, yes, I'm a bit weirded out about the fact that Michael was in eighth grade the year I graduated from high school (he got the clock in December 1977 – I graduated six months later in June 1978). I feel a little bit dirty now. Geez.

And second, yes, I wonder about an eighth grade boy who still believed in Santa. But this is Michael, after all.

But really. A 40-year old alarm clock?

He has a name for it. He calls it Clocky.

And it really doesn't work all that well. He's missing the plastic window in front of the numbers. His buttons are worn and half pushed in. Michael constantly thinks that he set Clocky, but it doesn't take. Which means this slow-waking man suddenly has to come zip into consciousness on some mornings and charge off to work. Michael is not a charger. He's also very used to the truly obnoxious noise Clocky vomits when he goes off. It's not a clock radio – there is only this very alarming (hence the word "alarm", I suppose) buzz/shriek/air raid siren that still makes me, after seventeen years of marriage, sometimes startle straight up in bed. But Michael sleeps through it. He automatically hits snooze without even really hearing it. He tells me he only does it a certain number of times, and he tells me this when that certain number of times is long gone.

I'm sure Clocky was a good clock. But he needs to be retired. He's put in forty years with a boy turned adolescent turned college student turned young man turned adult turned husband and stepfather turned father turned grandfather…the clock has had a good long run. He's tired. He doesn't want to wake up in the mornings anymore. He wants a life without snoozes.

And I really, really don't like the damn thing.

So today, I dragged Michael to Bed, Bath and Beyond. I told him to pick out whatever alarm clock he wanted. He chose one that looks like a big globe that changes colors. You can program it to pulse light according to music or just gently change color to color as you fall asleep. The lights will come on gradually as you wake up. It plays music. You can charge your phone with it. If it made a cup of coffee and had it piping hot and at your bedside upon waking, I would have bought two of them.

I don't think it has a name yet. And I know Michael will be a little bit sad when he plugs it in and sets it up tonight.

So I've encouraged him to leave Clocky plugged in and resting on the corner of the bedside table, next to the photo of Michael and his father when Michael was just a toddler. Clocky can still beam the time out in bright red digital letters and Michael can still see him every night, every morning.

Just like he can see me every night and every morning.

Just don't turn Clocky on.

That doesn't apply to me.

It's a compromise, the guiding light of all good solid marriages. And frankly, if Michael can hold on to a clock for forty years, even after it's not working so well, I figure he'll hold on to me too.

And yes, that helps. Despite. Anyway.

JULY 16, 2017

And so today's moment of happiness despite the news.

From the things they never tell you about breast cancer department:

I have never called my breasts "the girls". I know many women do, and I've always just rolled my eyes at that. I don't call them by slang terms – boobs, tatas, hooters, etc. – either and I definitely don't give them names. They are simply my breasts. A part of me, like my arms, legs, chin, hips, you know. They're just a part of my parts.

So today. The last thing I do at night before bed, and every morning after I shower, is climb on my bed, go on all fours and do some cat stretches to ease out my spine, then roll to my back and stretch both of my hips. I do it without thinking. It's a part of a routine and usually, I'm either counting the minutes until I can sleep or I'm already thinking through my schedule and breaking my day into clock pieces. But this morning was different.

I like doing the stretches after my shower because my body is warm and it stretches easier. I pull on underclothes and climb on the bed. This morning, when I went into my first cat stretch, I found myself face to face with…well, the girls. I've seen them every morning and every night and hundreds of millions of other times during every day and night of my life. But for whatever reason this morning, they caught my attention.

"Hi," I said out loud. "You're looking good."

With my second cat stretch, I said, "So are you two doing okay? Everything all right?"

And with the third stretch, I said, "Okay, I know it's not all right. But I'm going to take care of you."

With the fourth and final stretch, I said, "It'll be okay."

And then I rolled onto my back and stared at my ceiling while I stretched my hips, which I don't refer to in any other way. They're my hips. I wonder if they would suddenly become something else if there was an issue with them. I don't know what else I would call them anyway.

I wondered if people with cancer of other parts talk to those parts.

I realized then I was no longer talking to just myself, which I do constantly. I was talking to parts of myself as if they were separate from me, as if we could have a conversation, as if they would answer back. As if they were a person. People. A couple?

And it was right about then that I began to laugh.

When I told Michael about it later, he told me I was going to be hospitalized for something other than breast cancer if I kept that up. And I laughed all over again.

But throughout this day and into tonight, I've keep hearing myself saying, "I'm going to take care of you," and "It'll be okay." It'll be okay.

Maybe I wasn't talking to "the girls" at all. Maybe I was talking to myself. Not a couple, not people, not even a separate person. Just to myself. Me.

It'll be okay.

And yes, that helps. Despite. Anyway.

### JULY 17, 2017

And so today's moment of happiness despite the news.

Olivia and I were out running errands this afternoon. When we came back, we were about to turn onto our street when we saw a man sitting on the sidewalk in front of the entrance to the parking garage, located across from our home. I thought it was an odd place to sit, out in the bright sun and in the way of traffic, and he was hunched over, like he was looking at his phone. We do get some folks with unusual behaviors around here and I told myself to check on him when I got into the house. But then he looked up. His glasses were crooked on his face, one lens in front of an eye, the other one up on his eyebrow. His forehead looked gashed.

Olivia asked me if he was hurt.

I didn't know, but I quickly pulled the car around the corner into our garage, sent her upstairs, and then grabbed my phone and headed for the door As I walked through my classroom to the front door, I saw through the windows a couple of cars go by. So did a couple of buses. I figured by the time I went out the door, someone would likely already be helping.

But the street was empty when I stepped out. Nobody stopped.

By the time I finished dialing 911, the man was flat on his back, on the concrete.

I couldn't believe nobody stopped. Now granted, maybe someone from inside their car called 911. But nobody stopped.

As I ran, I told the dispatcher I thought the man was unconscious. "Sir!" I called ahead. "Sir! Are you all right?" Then I said into the phone, "He's not answering me." When I got to his side, he was motionless and I thought at first he wasn't breathing. But then he rolled his head toward me. "He's moving!" I said to the dispatcher.

The man made a few unintelligible sounds. He raised a finger, pointing to the sky. Then he closed his eyes again. His glasses were still crooked – I so wanted to straighten them, but I didn't know if I should. His knees were skinned. His forehead bleeding.

"It's okay," I said to him. "Someone is coming. It's okay."

It only took minutes and the police were there and then the paramedics. I offered one more, "It's okay," and then I returned home.

This was just around the corner from the spot where I was assaulted last November.

Lots of vehicles didn't stop today.

I did.

And yes, that helps. Despite. Anyway.

## JULY 18, 2017

And so today's moment of happiness despite the news.

I felt a shift today.

Yesterday, someone posted on my Facebook page that I just keep getting tested. And I suppose that is how I've been feeling, more often than not. Things have been on the crazy side since November. This latest issue, breast cancer, has been difficult on my psyche and soul. I've had moments of why me, followed by despair, followed by anger, followed by a sense of it's all going to be okay. Running up and down those steps of grief, I am.

I've had the same cleaning service for a few years, and Tracy, my cleaning person, told me about her own breast cancer experience when she learned of mine. She had a different type of cancer, much more aggressive, much further along, and she had a double mastectomy ten years ago. She lifted her shirt, showed me the scar on her stomach where they took the skin to reconstruct her breasts, showed me how they gave her a new belly button. When she tugged her shirt down, she leaned on my island and said, "When my husband and I came home after hearing the news, I took off my watch and handed it to him. I told him I was going into our room, shutting the door, and crying for an hour. He was to let me know when that hour was done. And when that hour was done, my crying would be done." She nodded. "And it was. I didn't shed a tear afterwards. I just did what needed to be done."

Well, I haven't been like that. Despite the great prognosis and what appears to be a straightforward path to recovery, there's been a lake of tears. I think I might be responsible for the flooding of the Fox River.

Fear too. I am, at heart, a big chicken.

But today, a shift. I think it actually started yesterday, when I was speaking with my nurse navigator on the phone. She was telling me that when I have my lumpectomy next week, I will be sealed together with glue, not stitches. Without even thinking first, I said, "I guess that means I'll have to start calling my right breast Elmer."

Dead silence. Then she laughed so hard, I had to hold the phone away from my ear. I laughed too, and frankly, it was good to be laughing with someone about this. Not just laughing. But about this.

One week from today, I will have the lumpectomy and thus will be officially on the start of the recovery treadmill. I watched the clock this morning into afternoon and noted when it passed 12:25, the scheduled time for the surgery. This time next week, I thought, it's all turning toward the better.

For the rest of the day, I did what I had to do, but also noted the clock. One week from today, I'll be out of surgery. One week from today, I'll be home. One week from today, this first part will be behind me.

It will all be turning toward the better.

And yes, that helps. Despite. Anyway.

## JULY 19, 2017

And so today's moment of happiness despite the news.

Ohmygosh. Today's moment of happiness is about a moment that didn't happen. I feel like the first bullet got me, but I dodged the second.

A week ago, when I had my breast MRI, a small mass was seen in the left breast. My right is the one with the confirmed cancer – the left seemed to be free and clear until the MRI. But then that very uncomfortable MRI led to even more discomfort. My surgeon called to tell me what they saw and said that she wanted me to have it biopsied.

I felt blindsided. Again.

So yesterday, I returned to the Breast Care Center. It was very disconcerting to have the staff there smiling at me and saying, "Hi, Kathie," as if I was a regular. Which I guess I am now. I very much like these people. But I never wanted to know them so well.

The radiologist and I talked for quite a while before the procedure. Back in June, I had a different radiologist and I truly didn't care for him. He basically sat down, told me he felt there was an 80% chance that I had cancer on a day I was only prepared for a routine mammogram ("Most times, I tell women they have a 20% chance. But not YOU."), and then asked if I had any questions before he got up and left the room. But this new radiologist? Calm. Relaxed. Answered every question, asked a few himself, and told me that to him, this didn't look like cancer, but that the doctor was just covering every possibility. I relaxed too.

During the biopsy itself, at one point, he shot the needle (it's like an ear-piercing gun and has the same sound) and said to the tech, "Whoa! Got it right through the middle!"

I said, "You've turned my breast into a video game."

Laughter.

Then he turned away, and for whatever reason, the gun went off while his back was to me. I said, "You missed."

More laughter. And oh, that felt good. Such a different atmosphere than the first time.

Today was the waiting game. On June 27, I was in the shower when the phone rang and I answered it without being able to read the caller ID and it was my doctor, with the news that I had cancer. Today, I was in the shower again when the phone rang. I just froze. The similarity put me into a bad moment. When I did answer the phone, it wasn't even my doctor. Finally, at four o'clock, the Breast Care Center called me and then so did the surgeon.

Benign.

I immediately looked down at my left breast and shook my finger at her. "You just couldn't stand to have your twin get all the attention, could you?"

Still, she's bruised for her effort.

The lump they found in the left breast is something that I could have removed when I have surgery next week on the right breast. There is a 90 to 95% chance that it will NEVER turn into cancer. Also, studies show that a lump like this one can be treated with the same medication that I will be on post-surgery and post-treatment. So I'm going that route. The surgery will just be on the right breast. We will move forward with the plan already in place.

And I feel like I'm standing on solid ground again. Ground that I would never have chosen to stand on, but ground that is firm.

Today proved to me that not everything is going to come up malignant. There is still benign in my life and in my body too.

And there is such richness.

And yes, that helps. Despite. Anyway.

## JULY 20, 2017

And so today's moment of happiness despite the news.

In the middle of all this breast cancer stuff, am I getting any writing done?

Yes.

But man, it's hard.

Today, I experienced the worst type of writing experience, followed immediately by the best.

This has been a crazy week. I typically write in the afternoons, after meeting with clients in the morning. Late afternoon, I leave writing behind to meet with clients again and continue through the evening, or I teach a class, or both. But my poor afternoons this week. Monday was an appointment for Olivia. Tuesday was my biopsy. Wednesday, I teach. Friday, my afternoon will end early with another appointment for me. So Thursday, glorious Thursday, all my hopes were focused on Thursday.

Thursday came. I had a phone appointment for a pre-op interview with the hospital at 1:30. It went on about a half hour, so instead of getting to my desk by one, I got there by two. By then, I was jangled. I was over-breast-cancered. I talked about it this morning with concerned clients, then had to go over the surgery with the pre-op nurse. I sat down, opened the file containing book #8, played the song I'm using to get me back into this book, did my finger labyrinth...and then stared at the screen.

And stared.

I backed up, reading over the last scene written, adding a few things. This is kind of like ready-set-go. A warm-up. Rev the engine, and then fly!

But I didn't rev.

I struggled.

I told myself it was okay, I have a lot on my mind right now, many, many distractions, this is normal. I told myself. I told myself. I told myself. And I put down a few sentences. And then a few more. And then a dialogue. And then one of my characters invited my main character to a movie...and I REVVED.

And I flew. Hard. Falling into a story is just beyond anything else I've ever experienced. If there are parallel universes, then writing fiction is the closest comparison. You're here, but you're there. You're you, but you're her, or him, or them. Your own conflict is this, but now there's that, you can worry about that, go after that...and fix it.

Fix it.

Of course, I didn't fix it today, this is a novel and I'm only on page 120. But I revved today. I lost myself. There's no breast cancer in the world I'm writing and it was such a great relief to be there.

My afternoon will be shortened tomorrow, but I'm still going to hit the desk and get some more done. I may bring my computer to the hospital on Tuesday and work until they wheel me away. Let my head work on the storyline while I'm unconscious. Wake up with my fingers already moving.

I hit the zone today and the zone is as familiar to me and as valuable to me as my own life. It was wonderful.

And yes, that helps. Despite. Anyway.

## JULY 21, 2017

And so today's moment of happiness despite the news.

Today, I was contacted out of the blue by a magazine that wants to use a blog piece I wrote back in 2014 about John Boy Walton from my favorite ever television show, *The Waltons*.

Any idea how cool that is?

Typically, you write something, you finish it, you do the market research, you send it out, and you wait. And it gets rejected and you send it out again and you wait. And it gets rejected and you send it out again and you wait. Wash. Rinse. Repeat. And then, hopefully, a piece gets accepted and published.

Woohoo!

But today, a piece I never intended for publication was asked for.

How nice is that?

It was interesting that this came up today because earlier this afternoon, in the car, I was listening to Linkin Park's CD, *A Thousand Suns*, and pondering the suicide of Chester Bennington. I wondered what regrets he had that led him to hang himself. And I wondered if he had any regrets now.

And then I wondered if I have any regrets.

Of course I do. Many.

But things I don't regret:

*having writing as the focus of my life, whether writing my own work, teaching others to write, or advocating for writers,

*starting an improbable small business, and working 85+ hours a week for over 12 years (so far),

*my first marriage (it produced three incredible children who I wouldn't have missed knowing for the world),

*getting married again and having a baby at forty – a baby who is now sixteen and provides constant joy and constant challenge,

And...I don't regret my intense love with *The Waltons*.

John Boy Walton taught me that you don't give up, even when the magazine you want to submit to only accepts typewritten manuscripts and you don't own a typewriter and don't have the bucks to buy one. He taught me that you don't go in search of the BIG story, but write all the little stories happening everywhere around you. The Walton family taught me about unconditional love, forever support, constant encouragement, and how having faith in a person can help that person harvest her own faith in herself. And Walton's Mountain taught me about community, and it's that sense of family and extended community that drives me. Almost everything I do is about me reaching out. Almost everything I do is about having someone reach back to me.

Earl Hamner Jr. friended me on Facebook a few years before he passed away. I don't think a "friending" has ever meant more.

I don't regret loving *The Waltons* one bit. Within an hour of thinking that, I came home and found the email requesting permission to publish my "I Remember John Boy" blog in a magazine.

Thank you, Earl. Thank you, John Boy.

And yes, that helps. Despite. Anyway.

## JULY 22, 2017

And so today's moment of happiness despite the news.

It's amazing to me, really, how things can happen, bing bing bing, and they all go together and create an impact that individually might have been lost. Kismet. Today was a three-bing day.

First, an AllWriters' student emailed me to let me know that her poetry chapbook was accepted by a publisher. Actually, I should amend that to say ANOTHER AllWriters' student let me know that a book was accepted. Or a story. Or a poem. Or an article. Or a memoir. I am lifted every day by watching students' dreams come true. I am delighted to play a part in that.

Second, I critiqued a student's article on what's important in running a small business. She talked about the reasons behind opening a business in the first place, and the reason that keeps you going when, undoubtedly, you find it's nowhere close to being as easy as you thought it would be.

And it's not. Trust me on that. It's grueling.

I know my reason for starting AllWriters'. Complete total and profound love of the written word and those who pound the keyboard, hold the pencil, drive the pen. I wanted to create a living, breathing, thriving, cheering community of writers. Writers who help each other. Writers who crawl out of their individual head spaces to connect and grow and, well, live a life of literary family and connection. Community. The word comes up for me again and again. We can be introverts, but we still need company. Let's be introverts together. And let's dream. Let's succeed. And let's be thrilled for each other when we do.

I can't even begin to express what AllWriters' means to me. The creation of it, the building, the watching it grow, the maintaining. The loving. My gosh, the loving. I love my work and I live it.

And then third. I was driving to Starbucks today and I had the radio on instead of the CD player. Matthew Wilder's "Break My Stride" came on and just took me over. Before I knew it, I was singing at the top of my lungs and dancing in my seat as much as driving would let me. The lyrics suddenly became my full-throated battle cry:

*"Ain't nothin' gonna break my stride,*
*Nobody's gonna slow me down,*
*Oh, no, I've got to keep on movin'."*

That might as well be my lifesong. Nothing has stopped me yet. And nothing will.

Not even breast cancer.

There's more to write, more to teach, more to do. More to dream. And I intend to write, to teach and to do.

Dream.

Bing-bing-bing kismet. Thanks for that.

And yes, that helps. Despite. Anyway.

## JULY 23, 2017

And so today's moment of happiness despite the news.

So the lumpectomy surgery is now less than 48 hours away. My anxiety is starting to ramp; fear too. Not so much for the outcome, though that's there too, but more for the procedure itself. I don't much like the idea of surgery. I've had five eye surgeries, half of my thyroid removed, and my gall bladder removed. None of those experiences left me feeling like, oh, surgery, easy peasy. So...I'm nervous.

But I really got to thinking about this whole thing today, during meditation, where I just followed my thoughts like one bubble after another up to the sky.

Meditation: I'm approaching my 500th straight day of meditation. I was skeptical for years about meditation. For some reason, 495 days ago, something clicked. And now, I can't imagine how I would have gotten through all this breast cancer stuff without it. Meditative breathing helped me through two biopsies, one malignant and one benign, a breast MRI, and many difficult days. And I figure I'll be breathing my way into the operating room.

Today's Moment: On January 23, I began writing the Today's Moment Of Happiness Despite The News, in reaction to the election and subsequent inauguration. I was overwhelmed by the negativity, overwhelmed by who won, overwhelmed by all of it. I needed to find a way to keep myself up, to keep myself positive, at least for one moment a day. And so I began to write it.

Because of the reaction, I promised to do it for at least a year.

What's resulted is a major attitude change on my part. There are days that yes, I've had to look hard for that moment. But I've always found it. It's always there.

And now? While "the news" still refers to what we see on our news feeds every day, it also applies now to the news that I'm dealing with cancer. Finding Today's Moment on the day that I was diagnosed was the hardest I've had to look. But I found it.

And I'm finding it still. It's gotten me through. It's still getting me through.

And then further, it's affected others. I've had at least twenty women tell me they went to get their put-off mammograms because of my experience. And there have been several biopsies too.

So...two things that I never believed I would do – meditating and writing about a moment of happiness every day – are in place. And they were in place and steady before I faced this challenge. And this challenge has been easier because of these two things that I never thought I would do.

I've always hated the saying, "Everything happens for a reason."

But maybe this time, it's true.

(Though I still think it would have been easier to have never had breast cancer at all.)

And yes, that helps. Despite. Anyway.

## JULY 24, 2017

And so today's moment of happiness despite the news.

So. It's the evening before surgery and I was trying to find that Moment. Not so easy, today. Today and tomorrow are packed with weirdness. Not one, but two showers with a bottle each of special yellow soap that I have to cover myself with and leave bubbling for five minutes. A radioactive seed will be planted in my breast and I have strict rules to not hug or hold a baby or child against that breast until the seed is removed with the lumpectomy. Really. I can only sleep tonight in just-laundered sheets and wear only just-laundered pajamas. I don't wear pajamas. Good thing that yellow soap is laundering me so I can sleep in my skin. The surgeon will use a special curved scalpel that will follow the shape of my breast, guaranteeing only a small scar.

As if at soon-to-be 57, I care about a scar. These breasts are retired. For the most part. When I heard that little fact, all I could think was, Use whatever works best, whatever works fastest. A steak knife. An apple corer. A hole puncher. Just GET THIS OUT OF ME.

So I was fuming today. I wasn't finding happy. I was finding anxious. I was finding scared. I was finding angry.

But while I was finding and feeling everything but happy, other things began to happen. My Facebook page was liberally peppered with comments and compassion. Encouragement. Support. Well wishes. My phone rang. My email box and snailmail box were stuffed with cards and positive messages. There have been references to lit candles, prayers, positive energy, and above all else, thinking-about-yous.

And then a package arrived from a student. In it was a card with the following words:

*We are each of us angels with only one wing and we can only fly by embracing one another.*

Within a half-hour of that, there was a message from someone on my meditation app. He sent me two prayers. One, he said, he was going to say for me. And one was for me to say for myself, if I so chose.

I choose.

It was about then that I lost it.

If we are one-winged angels, then I am surrounded by a windstorm of wings. If we can only fly by embracing one another, then I am flying high. I am flying fast. I am flying strong.

The day that my mammogram went south, my Today's Moment was that no matter what happened, I knew I wasn't going through this alone.

That's been proven to me every single day since June 20. And June 27. And now. And tomorrow.

And you know what? Even though I am terrified of birds, I collect feathers. Feathers from wings. Feathers find me in moments of need.

Today, I stepped out of my car and found a feather right next to my foot.

From one of my favorite poems, Gerard Manley Hopkins' "The Windhover":

*My heart in hiding stirred for a bird – the achieve of, the mastery of the thing.*

I feel wings. And my heart in hiding is stirring. I found Today's Moment.

I am so grateful.

And yes, that helps. Despite. Anyway.

## JULY 25, 2017

And so today's moment of happiness despite the news.

Today, I had surgery to remove the breast cancer from my body. It was a lumpectomy, and they removed a couple lymph nodes. I think. I don't remember much. The whole day, from the planting of a radioactive seed in my breast to help guide my surgeon (both radiologists argued over who got to do this for me – I think that's a good thing) to the operating room to the recovery room back to my day surgery room is a blur.

What I do know is that right now, I am sitting in my favorite chair at my favorite writing table in my favorite place ever – my home, both condo and business, under one gloriously slanted copper roof. This place provides a home for my dreams, my passions, my goals, and for so many that I love.

I'm here.

One of my ABCD mentors (After Breast Cancer Diagnosis) just texted me and said in all caps, *THE CANCER HAS LEFT UR BODY!* Shortly after, my other ABCD mentor texted and said, *You are now over that first mountain and that beautiful valley is still ahead.*

And I've been flooded with word-voices on Facebook, cheering and encouraging. I have been lifted up all day long. Even when I was unconscious in the operating room, messages continued.

Lifted up. That is exactly how I feel.

Along with sleepy and sore.

But I'm here.

One voice I heard from on Facebook was a long lost family member – that member lost to me when I divorced my ex-husband in 1998. I cannot even tell you what that meant to me!

I am lifted up. And I am here.

All I can say before I return to my recliner is I'm so, so grateful.

And I'll repeat Grandma Walton's words, from when she was in the hospital after nearly dying from a burst appendix: "I'm fixin' to feel a whole lot better."

Community. Connection. Nothing will heal me faster.

And yes, that helps. Despite. Anyway.

## JULY 26, 2017

And so today's moment of happiness despite the news.
*Keep passing the open windows.*
- *John Irving, Hotel New Hampshire*

I had a moment today that wasn't so happy. I hadn't really had a chance to see myself, to see what was done, since the surgery yesterday. When I woke up in recovery, I was in a gown and the velcroed shoulders were done up. When I dressed to go home, I was still a bit groggy and Michael had to help me. Looking down, I was able to see a bit, but not much. And there wasn't a mirror.

It's recommended after a surgery like this one that you wear a non-wired bra around the clock. The operated-upon breast feels "heavy", and the bra offers support. So even while climbing into bed last night, I was bra-ed and didn't see anything. But today, I took a shower. After undressing, I stood for a moment in front of the bathroom mirror.

And I was shocked. I look like a mess right now. The left breast is still bruised from last week's biopsy. And the right breast...well, the phrase slice and dice comes to mind. And more bruising. And then there's the area where the lymph nodes were taken too.

I don't know how women who have full mastectomies get through this. I was not prepared for the change in my appearance.

I cried in the shower.

But then some wonderful things happened and I embraced those.

First, my son went to Starbucks for me. I can drive again tomorrow, but cars were still off-limits for me today. When Andy got to the drive-thru, he ordered a grande iced cinnamon dolce latte, with just two pumps please. There was a pause and the barista asked if he was ordering the drink for someone. Andy said he was my son. When the barista handed him my drink, he told Andy to tell me they were all thinking of me. And there was a heart drawn on my cup.

Little things.

Then there was a package in my mail. I recognized the name on the return address as a student who took Michael's classes, and who I've met only once. The package contained a lovely card with a note. This student talked about the brief time we met, and that I was wearing spirals, likely a spiral necklace. I wear lots of spirals – they represent labyrinths to me. She felt from this that we were kindred spirits, something that was further solidified when she found that I collect clocks and she collects hourglasses.

We are also connected now through our cancer stories. She told me of hers and she told me that things would get better. And she sent me the loveliest ring. She said the ring was a gift of tradition among friends of hers who have dealt with various forms of cancer. It's a silver ring, with a band that spins loose between the ring borders. When I'm feeling anxious, I can spin it. It fits on my pointer finger, and my thumb can twirl the ring easily. It's like a fidget spinner, in a way! But much more beautiful.

Engraved on the ring is my favorite line from a book, a line I've pretty much adopted as my life's motto. "Keep passing the open windows," from John Irving's novel, *The Hotel New Hampshire.* The student asked Michael for a phrase I hold dear, and Michael knew the exact one.

And then the final thing happened. Someone on Facebook told me today that I am her hero, on so many levels.

I don't feel like a hero. But I'm learning more and more every day that I have made an impact. That my life does matter. That I haven't wasted it.

That's a fairly new feeling for me. I've spent most of my life worrying that I'm a failure.

But I'm not.

No matter how I look in the mirror today. Or how I looked yesterday. Or how I will look tomorrow.

And yes, that all helps. Despite. Anyway.

## JULY 27, 2017

And so today's moment of happiness despite the news.

On Thursday nights, AllWriters' offers the Teen Writing Workshop, for kids in middle school and high school. It's taught by my husband, the oldest teenager of them all, and my daughter is in it as well. Ten minutes before the workshop was to begin tonight, she emailed me her story so I could print out copies for her to share.

It was seven pages.

Yesterday, when I said to my daughter, "I'm going upstairs. I'll be writing for a bit," she answered, "Me too."

And it really hit me today, as I prepared her pages for printing: My daughter is writing. Not only that, but she writes well.

And…she writes out loud.

I didn't read her pages (yet), but the title told me enough: "Wear The

Ribbon And Make A Difference".

My daughter is writing to make a difference.

Earlier this week, we had a student call to say she had to drop out of the teen workshop. Her parents, steadfast Christians, didn't like that she was being exposed to horror. To mystery. To social activism writing. To all genres. To what the kids want to write in the class. To what this particular child wanted to write. To what my daughter writes. To what my husband writes.

To what I write.

Several weeks ago, this same girl told my daughter she got in trouble at home because she tried to write some horror. She got in trouble. For writing. Possibly for writing out loud.

My daughter is writing a story called "Wear The Ribbon And Make A Difference".

My daughter is raising her voice.

Thirty-nine years ago (yikes!), when I was a senior in high school, I wrote a short story called "In God's Name (We Trust?)". It was set in my version of Heaven, and God was a massive clanking, banging, pinging computer. Jesus was the computer's technician/maintenance man. The archangel Gabriel was a jazz-blowing drug-using trumpet player. And the archangel Michael was a frazzled overseer, trying to keep things under control as God the computer went haywire, turning Earth's skies red and raining down visions of Armageddon.

I submitted the story to my high school's creative writing magazine and it was heartily accepted. And then word leaked out to the parents. A fuss was raised. I was being irreverent. I was being sacrilegious. I needed to be stopped.

My creative writing teacher stood up for me. The principal, after hearing both my teacher and me out, stood up for me too. Despite protests, my story appeared.

I was allowed to raise my voice. I've never forgotten that.

Now, my daughter is raising hers. My students and clients are raising theirs.

My job is to help them do so.

But one young girl has been silenced. We lost one this week. Censored by a family who believes if she doesn't read whatever they find objectionable, if she doesn't write it, then it doesn't exist.

Wrong.

But so many other voices are growing. So many other voices are raising.

Writers are instruments of change.

And my daughter will write her words and wear her ribbons and she will make a difference. We all will.

And yes, that helps. Despite. Anyway.

## JULY 28, 2017

And so today's moment of happiness despite the news.

Tonight, I had coffee with a great friend and then drove home under a tilted Cheshire smile moon, a moon and a little freckle of a planet hovering down below and to the right. My right. The moon's left.

It's July and it was dark, nine o'clock at night, but I had the top down and no jacket on. I turned on my heated seat and so I was wrapped in summer above and below. Fireflies flickered out of my way. There was distant music, but also near music, my music, Linkin Park, Ten Thousand Suns, and I thought again of Chester Bennington and how he chose to end his life and he's not here anymore, to smile or frown up at a Cheshire smile moon.

I'm still here.

The music was near and far and the air was warm and the moon smiled down at me and I winked up at the freckle. As I turned onto my street, I saw lights spill from my home and I knew inside was my husband and my daughter and two dogs and two cats. And I knew they all would look up when I came inside. I knew they would look up and smile at me as I smiled at the moon. My husband might even wink.

I drove inside my garage and shut off the car and for just a few minutes, I sat. In the dark. The garage door was open and the Cheshire smile moon lit the warm air behind me and the lights from my home lit it too. I just sat in the warmth. The warmth of summer. Of family. Of quality coffee and the memory of good conversation with a great friend. My car pinged its own tune as it settled.

It's moments like this that keep me going. It's moment after moment after moment.

Warmth.

I'm still here.

And yes, that helps. Despite. Anyway.

## JULY 29, 2017

And so today's moment of happiness despite the news.

So today is my birthday. Number 57. And I will be the first to admit that this is a difficult birthday, and not because of getting a year older. I've pretty much acclimated myself to that. Dealing with cancer – not so acclimated.

I actually was looking forward to this birthday, to this year. I've been crowing for a while about how I felt things were finally falling into place – my 7th book is being released on September 7, 2017, in the year I turn 57. All those sevens – how could it be anything but lucky? I was excited, confident, raring to go.

And now…the book will be released, and then launched at Boswell Books on September 26 in Shorewood at the same time that I am dealing with breast cancer recovery and treatment. Things are moving ahead for the Midwest book tour – but I don't know if I'll be able to go. I'll know more Monday, when I meet with a team I never wanted to have – my surgeon, my radiation oncologist and my medical oncologist.

I am fighting hard to remain positive. I really am.

But frankly, this pisses me off.

And leaves me pretty sad.

I know this isn't a death sentence. And I'm very aware that it's not the common cold either. I have never liked it when things get in my way. I've never been stopped before either. But I have felt at times over these last several weeks that I am standing stock still, with no idea how to move forward.

I wanted to have a happy birthday. And I wanted that birthday followed with the build-up to the release of *In Grace's Time*, and then the debut, and then the hullabaloo of a book tour, capped by my appearance at the Southeast Wisconsin Festival of Books on November 3 and 4.

I'm not so sure I'm going to get what I want. And frankly, what I've worked really hard for. Sorry for the whine, but this just isn't fair.

So. How do I get a happy moment out of this?

My sixteen-year old daughter was eager for me to see what she made for me for my birthday. By the time I finished breakfast, had a shower, got dressed, and then came downstairs to wait for her brother and father to get home, she was practically foaming at the mouth. My sixteen-year old. You know, the one who is at the age where she's not supposed to want to be with me anymore.

When we all got together, she handed me a square of paper. On it, a drawing. The two of us. In her Manga-style artistry. My hair is red and spiky. Her arm is around my shoulders. We look alike.

And we're both wearing pink.

On the day of my surgery last week, I wore a t-shirt with a deep V, one that would be easy to pull on to go home after I was awake. Olivia pointed out that it was pink. "Like the ribbon, Mama," she said. "Are you wearing pink for breast cancer?"

She wrote a story this week, called "Wear The Ribbon And Make A Difference".

So I changed my perspective and wore pink to surgery.

And then I spent the week, my birthday week, asking that people on my Facebook page donate to ABCD; After Breast Cancer Diagnosis, an organization which has been just a lifesaver to me. I wanted something positive to come out of this birthday.

Something that I never expected. Something that I never wanted to deal with. A team I never wanted. A club I never wanted to be in.

But something positive.

I am wearing my ribbon and making a difference. I will find the positive.

And goddammit, my book is still coming out. It is still book number 7. It's still being released on 9/7, 2017, in the year I turn 57.

And it will still be a fabulous thing.

In the drawing, my daughter and I wear pink and she has her arm around my shoulder. Even though she's 16 and she's not supposed to like me anymore.

And yes, this helps. Despite. Anyway.

## JULY 30, 2017

And so today's moment of happiness despite the news.

Today ended up being a celebration of creativity, a revel in the difference. With what I do, with who I am, I am simply surrounded by creatives. I love the way some minds bend and turn around corners, when things are seen in a way they aren't usually seen, when the unimagined becomes the imagined and then the reality. Because I'm surrounded by it, there are times I grow so used to creativity that the unusual becomes the usual. And then things happen that remind me that the people around me use their heads in different ways. Wonderful ways.

The first came right out of my own home, from my husband. Since the surgery last Tuesday, I've been unable to sleep. I couldn't rest on my right side, the side that was operated on. I am a side-sleeper, and because of fibromyalgia,

I flip from side to side frequently during the night. Too long on one side and I'm in pain, particularly in my hip and shoulder. But now there was pain in my breast and on my incisions if I pressed them into the mattress. As a result, I was stuck on my left side, only sleeping about an hour to an hour and a half at a time. I'd wake up in pain and have to pace for a while, working out the complaining muscles. Then I'd return to bed for another short sleep before I had to walk again. Five nights of this left me frazzled and exhausted. "Rest!" people kept telling me. "How?" I wanted to shout back.

My husband puzzled over this with me. I tried to sleep one night on the recliner, which didn't work either. Same issue – not enough movement. But Michael got out his airplane pillow for me to use, one of those horseshoe-shaped pillows that go around your neck so you can sleep sitting up in an airplane. The night after the recliner failure, he took a second look at his pillow.

"Maybe you could use this," he said. He flattened it, and just like that, it was a different thing. I could see where my breast would fit in the horseshoe-hole, supported all around by the pillow, so that there would be no compression.

It was the birth...of the BreastRest.

Last night...oh, did I sleep. I was able to turn. I woke up pain-free.

I love my husband.

Then came creativity burst number two. I was reading a student's story, one she just started, about a woman who has an encounter with a raindrop. Yes, you read that right...a raindrop encounter. That was wonderful enough, but then I came across this sentence: "*It looked like a bird-wannabe perching on my finger in a blob sort of way.*"

And I sat straight up and laughed!

Sometimes, creativity comes out in the most straightforward, plain-speaking, just shout-it-out way. Writers especially tend to think they need to load their creativity up with fancy words and fancy sentences and multi-syllables and descriptions. This student could have said:

"*The raindrop, iridescent, ethereal, perched like a rare luminous bird on my ring finger, a wedding ring of surprise and startle. Its shape was curvaceous, its moistness saturated my skin with a tenderness like no other, and I longed to know...*" you know, what the hell a raindrop was doing on my finger.

But this writer didn't. Instead she captured an unlikely moment in lovely language that left no doubt what it was her character was seeing.

I've taught this one well, Grasshopper.

So this afternoon, I sat on my third floor deck, steeped in sunshine. My

Starbucks was to my side, I had student manuscripts in my lap, and I was well-rested. I'd slept in a BreastRest. I was reading about raindrops that wanted to be birds in a blob sort of way. I was warm and I was happy and I was delving in other's creativity and I was the beneficiary and it just felt so good.

I love my life.

And yes, that helps. Despite. Anyway.

## JULY 31, 2017

And so today's moment of happiness despite the news.

A four-hour doctor's appointment. Involving:

3 doctors – a surgeon, a medical oncologist, and a radiation oncologist

2 nurses – an oncology nurse and a nurse navigator

1 counselor – from an organization offering support to cancer patients and their families

This was my day, sandwiched in between three clients and a class. My first day back at work since surgery. And this was grueling.

But also my moment of happiness – several times over.

I feel like I've been grazed by a bullet that I quite possibly shot from my own gun.

The pathology report: there were not enough cancer cells on the lymph node for the result to be called positive. So it's a negative result, which is what we wanted. This likely means no chemo – but there is still one more hurdle to jump. The doctors decided that because of the size of the tumor – 2.6 centimeters – they want the excised lymph node to be trotted through the ONCO test – or by its formal name, the Oncotype DX Breast Cancer Test. This test will determine how likely the cancer is to travel. If it comes back low, then no chemo. If it comes back high, then chemo. If it comes back medium…then there will be a discussion.

All three of the doctors said they would be very surprised if I needed chemo. But…they're making sure. Right now, the plan is to wait for the result of the test – 8 to 9 business days – and when it comes back low (no chemo), we move into radiation. Four weeks, ten minutes a day, Monday through Friday. Then I will take an estrogen-suppressing drug for at least the next five years, and possibly up to ten years.

And…I will be done with radiation before the debut of *In Grace's Time*. And I will be able to go on tour just under a month after the debut.

As long as the ONCO test comes back low. Which they all believe it will.

Hearing this come out of the mouths of three doctors and two nurses…I cannot even begin to describe how my spirits lifted. There is a path back to normal. Even though it will always be a look-over-my-shoulder normal. A make-sure-I-keep-an-eye-out normal.

I felt good. And so appreciative of their knowledge, their compassion, their experience. My surgeon? Breast cancer survivor. The counselor? Breast cancer survivor.

Me too.

My moment of happiness.

But I have to say this…it was me that shot the gun. I went from 2013 to 2017, from the age of 53 to the age of 57, without going in for my yearly mammogram. This cancer started out as noninvasive ductal cancer in situ – meaning it was totally encased by a milk duct within my breast. 4 to 5 centimeters worth, before it burst the seam. When I went in this year and it was discovered, it had broken through the milk duct and become the tumor that was removed. If I'd only gone in for my mammograms and it was discovered, I would have had surgery to remove it…and that's it. No radiation. No possibility of chemo.

No lingering fear of the future and what-if.

I was too busy. I allowed myself to become too busy to do what I knew needed to be done, what I knew was proper vigilance, what I knew was self-care. I know what I was doing wasn't wrong – I was building a successful and transformative business, transformative for me, transformative for my students. 12 years of working at least 85 hours a week. I was using every spare moment to write. I was raising children.

I was busy.

But I held my own gun. And I shot the bullet that grazed me. Thank God for just a grazing.

So I'm learning.

BUT…

I wouldn't be me if I didn't say this. Please use me as an example. Please get your mammogram done every year. Please tell your loved ones to get their mammograms. Please say no to your schedule and your responsibilities for just one morning or one afternoon and get it done.

I'm putting down my gun. And I will learn to do the things I want to do and take care of myself at the same time.

I promise.

And yes, that helps. Despite. Anyway.

# Chapter Eight

## AUGUST 1, 2017

And so today's moment of happiness despite the news.

So imagine my surprise early this morning when, after a very positive, though grueling, appointment with the three doctors, two nurses and a counselor, an appointment that left me relieved and forward-thinking, I crashed and burned. I finished my day, spent a little bit of time decompressing in front of *Grace & Frankie* on Netflix, meditated to a guided meditation for sleep, climbed into bed…and fell apart.

Michael, saying goodnight to me, asked me what was wrong.

"I just realized," I said, "that the only Good News I get now is about the Bad News."

Yeah.

Yesterday, all day long, I was bugged by a moment in the waiting room, where Michael and I sat before being pulled into my four-hour appointment. For the first time since diagnosis, I was not sitting in the medical side of the building. I was in the Cancer Center. Everyone around me was either dealing with cancer or was there with someone who was.

An older woman wandered in, chemo port in place. She carried a basket. She stopped in the center of the waiting room and announced in a very loud voice, "I'm terminal! And I have an angel for you." She then went around the room and told everyone to pick out a handmade angel from her basket.

I was obedient. I picked out a white angel with purple wing tips. The attached card said it was the Angel of Serenity. On the back of the card, it said, "*Serenity comes when I am able to accept things as they are and trust that God will take care of me.*"

I was obedient. I tucked the angel in my purse. But every bit of me wanted to throw the angel back at the woman. Knock the basket out of her arms. Tell her to get the hell out, that the last thing a room of cancer patients needed was an angel-toting woman declaring that she was terminal.

And then right before bed early this morning, the Good News/Bad News realization.

Denial is a pretty amazing thing. You can still be in denial when you're not in denial. In a teeny little corner of my brain, even after the biopsies, the MRI, the surgery, and the four-hour appointment yesterday, there is still this hope that the phone is going to ring and someone is going to say, "Oh my god, we're so sorry, but we screwed up. Your file got mixed up with someone else's. You're fine. There never was any cancer."

You know, at this point, if someone did that, I wouldn't even sue. I would heal and move on.

I would accept it.

And now we're back to the purple-tipped serenity angel. Serenity comes when I am able to accept things as they are.

So today. Today, I was in the seething loop of this loop-de-loop roller coaster. I seethed over the angel and its terminal-announcing giver. I seethed over the Good News About The Bad News. I got the angel out and thought about doing any one of a number of things to it. Throwing it from my third floor deck. Getting a hammer. Finding a match. Tearing it fake feather by fake feather.

The phone rang and it wasn't someone telling me that everything was a mistake. Something I would accept. Something I would heal from, then move on.

Serenity.

So...I took a break and meditated.

And then I kept the angel. She is sitting on my desk lamp, next to a handmade bracelet I found in a labyrinth in Maine, that says, *Love Myself Authentically*. Next to a rosary I found and filched from a chapel in La Crosse. Near a dove Christmas ornament, given to me years ago by a good friend.

I kept it. If I see the terminal woman on my next visit to the Cancer Center, I won't thank her. I will never be that serene – that is not who I am. I will move out of her way before she has a chance to make her announcement and offer me another angel.

And I will accept. I will heal. And I will move on.

And yes, that helps. Despite. Anyway.

## AUGUST 2, 2017

And so today's moment of happiness despite the news.

Tonight, after finishing up with today's clients and before starting to read tomorrow's manuscripts, I wandered across the street to the Waukesha Metro, our city's bus depot and parking garage. At our condo, we only own two parking spaces – our single car garage and the space just outside of it. But I own three cars. Hemi (my Chrysler 300C Hemi), Semi (my Chrysler 200 convertible) and the black sheep, Starlight (the 2003 VW Beetle I bought for my daughter so she wouldn't drive my cars…and as of yet, she's not driving this one either). Starlight lives in the parking garage. Even though I pay for her space by the month, she has to be moved every 3 days or the city considers her abandoned (one would think that paying for parking for a month would be proof that she's NOT abandoned, but you know, this is the city of Waukesha). So one of my chores tonight was to move her to a different space.

As I walked up the street, I saw a young couple sitting on one of the concrete bunkers outside the garage. I knew they were a couple because I could see two heads, a tangle of four legs, and a pretzel of arms. I could not discern two bodies because they might as well have been one. This young couple obviously liked each other very, very, VERY much. As in don't-come-up-for-air much. Get-a-room much. As in sigh-very-heavily-as-you-walk-on-by-feeling-very-old much.

My heavy sigh didn't disturb them. I doubt they heard me over their mmmmmmm's.

I carried my sigh up to the second floor and moved Starlight. I parked her, patted her, told her she was a good girl, as I do every time whether she's good or not. She was face to face with a slick-looking Mustang and I said to her, "Maybe you can lock grills with that. Rev your engine a little." Then I sighed again.

Since no one was around, except for the lick-locked couple on the street, I went on up to the third floor, the roof of the parking garage. It's a nice view from up there. I wandered down to where I could see my home. I could see the couple too. As far as I could tell, they still hadn't taken a breath.

My office lights on the third floor were on. The kitchen light on the second floor. And on the first, the AllWriters' classroom was lit up bright with the Wednesday Night Workshop. My husband at the helm for this class. I couldn't see him, but saw faces turned his way, hands in animation.

I glanced back at the couple. And I remembered how I used to do things like that. Make out on park benches, big rocks, picnic tables, the middle of the street. Sometimes with people who were special. Sometimes with people who were there. I know what it's like to not need breath. To meld so completely with someone that I lose myself. When the whole world could be defined by the press of a body.

I needed to breathe now, and I did, but not a sigh. Just a breath. And I looked again into the classroom. The place that I love so much. My home, which even after eleven years of living there, I still hug around me with a joy that I've never felt anyplace else. And I looked toward the man I couldn't see, who was leading the class tonight.

I thought how in the last month, Michael came with me to my first biopsy and waited in the waiting room. How he's waited for every text from me for every other appointment. How he's come with ready arms at the odd and many moments I've just called out, "Michael, I need you." Held me at night. Accompanied me on surgery day. Insisted I rest. Brought me things. Kissed me goodnight every night. And told me over and over and over again that it's going to be okay.

In my first marriage, I was told I couldn't do anything. In my second...he believes I am capable of everything.

I glanced down at the young couple. Still at it.

But so are we. Differently. But we are no less locked together.

As I left the garage, the young woman's phone rang. She came up for air to answer it. "Oh, hi," she said. "I'm fine. Feeling a little emotional today."

Me too.

And yes, that helps. Despite. Anyway.

## AUGUST 3, 2017

And so today's moment of happiness despite the news.

I was lecturing a student today. This was a coaching client, someone who works with me one on one, and someone who I accepted as a coaching client because of her level of drive, ambition, talent and dedication. And as often happens with all writers, once we hunkered down to work, the drive, ambition and dedication was tempered by self-doubt. Words like "failure" kept showing up in our conversations. Words like "I couldn't find the time" and "distractions" and "blocked". Sentences like "I don't know if I can do this."

One of the first things students learn about me is that I don't allow negative self-talk in my classroom or in my one-on-one sessions. When Michael and I first met (online – yes, he was a student), he sent me a story to read, along with an introduction that made him sound like the worst writer since E.L. James – except that was before James, and we had no idea yet how bad writing could be. When I returned the story with my critique, my email started with, "You're absolutely right. This was crap. I wouldn't use it to line my birdcage." And I ranted on for a while, before I said, "Now that we've got that out of the way, let's get to work." Michael nearly didn't make it to the end of the email. But he did, and he learned very quickly – you don't cut yourself down around Kathie.

As students learn to cut the f-words (failure – I'm rather fond of the real f-word) and f-related words out of their vocabularies, amazing things happen. Their confidence grows. Their writing improves. Why? Because the negative expectations got in the way of the creative process. The best way to choke creativity is to stuff negativity down its throat.

So. Today, I lectured this student. We put things in place so she can succeed in the way she dreams of and that I know she is capable of. But as I listened to her, I heard myself, but my voice wasn't discussing writing.

Earlier today, I confessed to a friend how much to blame I feel for the breast cancer. I told him about how I didn't do my yearly mammogram from 2013 to 2017; I was too busy. And how this particular kind of breast cancer, if it had been caught during those years, would have been treatable with simply surgery – no radiation, no chemo, no drugs. But I didn't go. I told him how I fell out of the habit of doing monthly breast self-exams, once I was done with menopause. My breast-schedule was always to do a check three days after my period ended. Then…there were no periods. And my calendar disappeared.

I told my friend I felt like a failure. A failure at positive womanhood – doing simple, necessary things to take care of myself. Things that are a no-brainer. No-brainer – I felt like I had no brain, I felt stupid. Beyond stupid. I'd blown it in such a big way.

Well, I went on.

My friend leaned forward. "You made a mistake," he said.

I hate making mistakes.

But I realized that, just like my students, I have to change my vocabulary. I can't do anything about what I've already done, or more accurately, didn't do. I have to knock the f-word out of my mouth and out of my mind. I am doing everything I can to make this negative into a positive, by raising awareness of the importance of regular mammograms, of self-care, of treating yourself with the respect you deserve.

I'm giving myself the respect I deserve. I'm not a failure. I'm not stupid. I made a mistake.

Healer, heal thyself. Well, teacher, teach thyself.

I am.

And yes, that helps. Despite. Anyway.

## AUGUST 4, 2017

And so today's moment of happiness despite the news.

I had coffee today with my high school creative writing teacher. It's such an odd feeling, really…He was in his early years of teaching when I met him, and I was sixteen years old, so we weren't far apart in age then, and it feels like we're even less so now. At my current age of 57, to sit across from him, adult to adult, and to hear him tell me that he's amazed that I work Friday nights when for him, Friday nights were for drinking back when he was a teacher, just feels odd. And wonderful.

As I met with him today, I couldn't help but remember that he told me, way back forty years ago, that I would never be what he called "a deer and flowers writer".

He was right. I do tend to veer toward the harder subjects. Readers have told me my books are both impossible to put down and necessary to put down because of their intensity. I've been okay with that.

And then, today, when I got home from my coffee with my teacher, I found an email waiting for me from my publisher. It contained the first review for my new book, *In Grace's Time*. Do you remember how, when you got something in the mail that you weren't sure you wanted to see, you handled it with the tips of your fingers, slowly opened it, took out the letter, unfolded it, and then looked at it through one squinted eye, as if that would somehow keep you from seeing any bad news? Well, that's the way I opened this email. Considering there was nothing tangible to touch, that's no easy feat.

And this is despite having a slew of good reviews for my past books (she said modestly).

But this was a good review. A lovely review. I soon opened both my eyes wide. And then those eyes settled on one word, a word I never ever thought I would see describing something that I'd written. Ready?

*Delightful.*

Delightful? Me? Really? I checked three different times to make sure my publisher sent me the right review.

I've been called edgy. I've been called daring. Brave. Honest. In-your-face. Relentless. Unforgiving. And my personal favorite, disturbing.

*Delightful?*

I have to admit this. I saw that word and I clapped like a child at the circus. I never ever EVER in a million years would have expected to be described as such.

And I like it. I didn't expect that either. I didn't expect the whole damn book.

And to make it even better…The book I'm currently working on, my next novel, is…Ready? FUNNY.

My high school creative writing teacher knows what the novel-in-progress is about. And today, when our topic of conversation returned to breast cancer and I said that I never saw this coming, never expected it to happen, he leaned back in his chair and said, "Well, Kathie, life is not all iguanas and parakeets, you know." And he howled.

This is a direct reference to the book underway.

Delightful. Funny.

From me. Dark and disturbing me.

How about that?

And yes, that helps. Despite. Anyway.

## AUGUST 5, 2017

And so today's moment of happiness despite the news.

My grandbaby Maya Mae visited today, and I searched my memory for a bit to remember why it was I didn't want to become a grandmother. It had something to do with age, and the fact that I was still in my forties when my son married. I threatened that if he made me a grandmother before I was fifty, I would remove the apparatus that made me a grandmother before I was fifty.

My own grandmothers were gray-haired and white-haired. They wore housedresses and aprons.

Ew.

Maya was born when I was fifty-two. I am so glad I didn't remove the apparatus. There is nothing that beats the grandma gig. I learned very quickly that I could be me AND be a grandma. I took the baby Maya to the mall and I wore fuck-me thigh-high boots and a sweater to die for as I pushed her stroller. My hair didn't go white or gray, but stayed red and punked. I'm the grandmother that writes. Maya sat in the front row at the joint debuts of *Oddities & Endings* and *True Light Falls In Many Forms* last year. Her hands were folded in her lap and her eyes were wide and upraised. She was the first person to meet me when I left the stage and she hugged me around the thighs in the leg-hugging way of all children, a way that I treasure and remember through four other huggers.

I worried I would have to change if I became a grandmother. I haven't. And she loves me anyway.

Maya came with us to a bookstore today. As we walked in, Maya Mae looked up at me and said, "I want to sing a song."

"A song?" I said.

"A song for you, Gamma Kaffee." She cleared her throat, then recited very clearly, "I love you forever, I like you for always, as long as I'm living, my Gamma Kaffee you'll be."

So now picture that. We're walking into a bookstore, which is my version of heaven, and my granddaughter quotes from one of my favorite children's books, then paraphrases to include me.

Melt.

Later, we walked to downtown Waukesha to visit the Art Crawl. As we moved up the sidewalk, Maya slid her hand into mine. That unique child hand. Impossibly smooth. Chubby little palm. Fingers that grip with a tangible trust. As I rubbed her five little fingers with my thumb, I was immediately transported to each of the five hands that have held me in that way. My hand-holding leg-huggers.

Christopher.

Andy.

Katie.

Olivia.

And now, Maya Mae. Who will love me forever and like me for always. Just like I am.

I took her into an art gallery. Maya is four, and I wondered if she would be bored. But she went from exhibit to exhibit without a single whine. In front of one painting, she stood with her arms crossed, her eyebrows puckered, her face as serious as any art lover there. I stood by her and appreciated the piece too.

But I appreciated this child even more. This little one who has told me that trees talk to her. That mosquito bites make her hair fall out. That she has five toes here and five toes there, five fingers here and five fingers there, but only one head. This little one that still uses Her instead of She, and I don't correct her, I mean she, I mean her, because her is just so damn charming.

And she's mine.

After Maya and I picked out a couple books in the bookstore, and one toy too, because she wanted her My Little Pony at home to have a friend, I fanned out the pages in one of the books. "Look at all the words, Maya," I said.

"Look at all the words you'll learn."

And she held out the book to me.

Oh, this little girl. She knows exactly who I am. And she loves me anyway.

And yes, that helps. Despite. Anyway.

## AUGUST 6, 2017

And so today's moment of happiness despite the news.

I was mulling in the shower this morning. Showers are my favorite place to mull...I have a great shower, with a rainforest showerhead and body jets. I also take what I call asbestos showers – they're really, really hot. Surrounded by heat and steam and pulsating water, I can relax and let my mind wander. So it did.

And it came up with a thought that made the hot water feel cold.

*I am grateful to the Orange Asshat.*

Oh. My. God.

With a steadying hand on the shower wall, I reeled my mind backwards through the steps that landed me to...that. And then I moved it forward again. Here are the steps.

Asshat was elected.

Two days after the election, I was assaulted across the street from my home by a man wearing a red Make America Great Again ball cap.

Asshat was inaugurated.

Two days after the inauguration, I found myself in a deep spiral. In desperation, I vowed, on Facebook, to post one moment a day that made me happy, so that I could find hand-holds up and out of the spiral.

Fast-forward to June 27. I am diagnosed with breast cancer. The News in Today's Moment Of Happiness Despite The News transforms from external news – the Asshat – to internal news. Personal news. Breast cancer. By now, Today's Moment is well-established. And because it is well-established...

...I have the means necessary to keep myself positive during a time that would have normally decimated me. No, I have not skipped through the tulips during this time. I have not tra-laed. But my head has stayed well above the spiral. I'm doing fine.

If all of those steps hadn't happened, my reaction to breast cancer and treatment would have been totally different. But my path to get through this was already laid out...

…because of the Asshat. If he hadn't been elected, I would never have started Today's Moment.

Well, hell.

I spoke with a friend last week, a friend who has a weekly column. I told him I didn't know how he kept it up. He replied that he didn't know how I was keeping the Moment up, day after day. I admitted there were days that I really had to look for the positive. Days when I looked at the calendar and counted down how many more months until I reached the end of my vow. Partway into the Today's Moment trek, I started using the posts as my blog, and I added to my original vow. I said I would keep it up for at least a year. "I have to," I said to my friend. "I promised. In front of God and Facebook and everybody."

"You can change your mind," he said.

Sure. But I can't. Because writing these has really effected a change that I'm not convinced would be there without them.

An example from today. While driving this afternoon, I saw two women walking on the sidewalk to my left. Their backs were to me. From what I could tell, one was around my age, the other, a little younger. They were just walking. And then, all of a sudden, the younger woman leaped straight up in the air.

Before Today's Moment, I would have thought, Man, I wonder what kind of bug stung her. That had to hurt. I hope she's not allergic.

But today, I thought, I wonder what just happened that she's so joyful.

When I passed them, I saw that both women were smiling. So I don't think there was a bug. I grabbed my rearview mirror, turned it to my face, and said, "Who the hell are you?"

Don't know. But it made me happy.

Thank you, Orange Asshat. I guess.

And yes, that helps. Despite. Anyway.

## AUGUST 7, 2017

And so today's moment of happiness despite the news.

So here's something you might not know about recovering from breast cancer. It's something I didn't know until recently.

When you have a lumpectomy, as I did, you expect to feel some pain. You expect there to be incisions. You probably expect there to be some bruising. You might even expect there to be itching as it heals (though I swear, with the itching I have, I think someone implanted fleas below my skin's surface).

What you might not expect is that the breast feels heavy. And I mean HEAVY.

I was told that I would likely feel most comfortable wearing a bra around the clock after surgery, at least for a few weeks. I did for a while (I'm two weeks out), though when I sleep now, I'm back to free and easy. But during the day…the bra is very necessary. And I am constantly aware of the weightiness of my right breast. Unlike some women, I don't name my breasts. I don't call them the girls. But I have, in the last few days, referred to the right breast as PudgePocket, the Continental Soldier (after the girls' locker room version of Do Your Ears Hang Low: Do your boobs hang low, do they wobble to and fro, can you tie them in a knot, can you tie them in a bow, can you throw them over your shoulder like a Continental Soldier…) and YankEmUp. It feels very strange because I'm used to the two of them being in balance. But I am definitely listing to the right.

I was aware, and I wasn't, that I've begun helping out the bra by supporting my right breast in my hand. Some people walk with their hand in their pocket or they jingle their keys or some other mannerism. Right now, I hold my breast in the palm of my hand.

Which is fine, around the house, donchaknow.

Today, I went to the bank. I had to stand in line in the cow corral for quite a while. So I glazed a bit. Finally, I made it to the next available teller's window. It was Sheri, my favorite teller, someone I've known now for 12 years. She helped me with the very first deposit into my business account and she's watched the business grow with almost as much joy as I have. She's also cheered every book release. In my new novel, *In Grace's Time*, a bank teller plays a minor role. I named her Sheri.

Sheri is also aware of the breast cancer. She is a soft-hearted and quiet support.

So I stepped up today with a smile on my face and my bank bag ready to go. Sheri leaned forward. "Kathie!" she whispered. "Let it go!"

I was puzzled. "Let what go?"

She did a fast series of eye push-ups, up, down, up, down, up, down, from my face to my…right breast.

Which was held firmly and lovingly in my right hand.

"Shit!" I said, probably loudly enough to be heard. And then I howled. So did Sheri. So did the other tellers. The people in line and at the other windows, well, they weren't quite sure what to do. I mean, there was this strange woman groping her own breast in line at the bank.

When I could stand upright again, I let poor Pudgepocket go. And I turned to face the other customers. "It's okay," I said. "I'm sorry if I made you uncomfortable. See, she's in recovery. I had surgery two weeks ago for breast cancer. She's still limping a bit, and I sometimes have to give her a lift."

Lights of realization went off in everyone's faces. Some more than others, among the women. And I turned, smiling, back to Sheri.

I hope I've paved the way for other women, holding, supporting their own recovering breasts.

Last week, I found myself scratching the impossible flea-under-the-skin itch while I was in Starbucks. But we're not going to talk about that.

And yes, that helps. Despite. Anyway.

## AUGUST 8, 2017

And so today's moment of happiness despite the news.

There was a difference when I woke up this morning.

Some things were the same. The sun was in my face and baking my body, which is my favorite way to wake up. There was a small gray cat sleeping behind me, her curled back pressed between my shoulder blades. I woke with enough time to remain still for a few, eyes open, feeling the warmth.

I vaguely remembered hearing the phone ring a few minutes before. But I am protective of my time to rest and so I didn't hurtle out of bed to answer it.

The difference was that the resonance of the telephone didn't leave me soaked with the adrenaline of panic or dread, wondering what doctor or nurse was calling me over whatever test this time. And for the first time since June 20, I didn't wake with the thought, "Well, I'm still here."

Instead, my thoughts wandered around and through the remains of dreams and then cycled into an old routine…What's on the docket for today? What's the schedule?

And the thought, It's going to be a good one.

It was in the shower that I became aware of this difference, which really was a difference of familiarity. A return to normal. I looked down and saw that the deep bruises on my left breast from the biopsy three weeks ago have faded to a single dark half-circle. And on the right breast, the bruises are all but gone from the surgery two weeks ago. The incisions are dark and puckered and they feel a bit stiff, like they're protesting. If I look at the breast in full bright light, I can see that the skin is almost back to its normal color, just a shade yellow, reminiscent of all the battering this breast has gone through since June 20th. Mammograms. Ultrasounds. Biopsy. MRI. Implanted with a tag. Implanted with a nuclear seed. Operated on. Invaded. Now in recovery.

All the breast has gone through. All I have gone through.

Two weeks ago today, I was in surgery. And I realize, in the shower, that's what led to this morning's difference.

The cancer was removed.

There's still more to go through. Maybe chemo, but probably not. Definitely radiation. Medication. But the focus has shifted. It's not about search, find, destroy. It's about recovery.

It's about waking up in the morning following trails of dreams, and then moving into the day. It's about thinking, "What's next?" rather than, "Well, I'm still here." It's about breathing easy, instead of checking to make sure I am still breathing.

Oh, I felt the difference today. The difference I used to feel every day without considering it, and the difference I am so happy to welcome back.

And yes, that helps. Despite. Anyway.

## AUGUST 9, 2017

And so today's moment of happiness despite the news.

It wasn't hard to pick out today's moment. But boy, was it ever a circus to get there. You know those goofy moments in television comedies where there is a long hallway with doors on either side and one person is chasing another and they pop in and out in impossible ways and you just have to laugh?

Well, it was like that. Though I wasn't really laughing, until it was all over.

I've been waiting this week for the result of my Oncotype DX Breast Cancer Test – the Onco Test. This was the final determination for chemo or no chemo. A low score meant no chemo. A high meant chemo. And a medium meant we would talk. I didn't want to talk. I wanted a definitive answer.

And I wanted that answer to be no chemo. I've already handled surgery. I feel like I can handle radiation. I feel like I can handle taking a pill once a day for five to ten years. But chemo scares the hell out of me.

Wednesdays are always a hard day to get a hold of me. I don't write on Wednesdays because I teach all day. Clients in the morning, class in the afternoon, clients in the evening. So of course, two minutes before my first client, my cell phone rang with a number that I didn't recognize. I ignored it. When a voicemail was left, I had just enough time to check it before I signed into Skype for my client.

It was the oncology nurse. She had my result. I should call. Every time she gave the number, my cell phone burped static. After listening to it four times, I thought I had it right.

I glanced at the clock. One minute to client. I dialed the number and heard a recorded voice saying that wasn't a correct number. I listened to the voicemail again, then dialed the number again in case I dialed it wrong...still not a correct number.

Now I was two minutes late for my client. But she's a really, really nice client and I knew she wouldn't be upset if I was late, given the circumstances. So I picked up the phone, called the clinic, and began to track down the oncology nurse. Eventually, I got to an operator who found her. She patched me through...then came back and said the nurse was in with a patient.

ARGH.

So I met with my client. Who encouraged me to keep trying to reach the nurse during our call, but I demurred until we were done. With the five minutes I had before the next client, I called the clinic again, they tracked the nurse down...she was with a patient.

ARGH.

Met with my second client. Also a really, really nice client. They all are. When I finished up with her, I called the clinic...Nurse was with a patient.

"Do you want to leave a message maybe?" the receptionist said. "Maybe it would be easier for her to call you."

Fat chance, I thought, but I left the message.

I had forty-five minutes before class. I had to set up the on-site classroom, take a shower, get dressed, and quickly eat lunch. I turned to Facebook and began to vent with my status. "Oncology nurse called on a day when it's impossible to reach me. Left the wrong number. Game of cat and mouse. Please, please, please call and say, 'No chemo.'"

Just as I hit the final quotation mark, but not post, my phone rang. And it was her.

"How are you?" she asked.

"Fine." T*ellmetellmetellmetellme...*

"Well, you're about to be super-duper."

A nurse that says super-duper.

"Your test is back and you're a 9!"

"A 9! A 9! What does that mean?" I howled.

"No chemo! You're low! Anything under 16 is low! You have a very low chance that it will spread!"

I have never been so happy to get a low score on a test. I know she told me more. About radiation and the drug the medical oncologist will be putting me on to suppress my estrogen since this particular cancer feeds off of estrogen. But I haven't the slightest idea what she said. I was gone. Over the moon. Over the rainbow.

To repeat a phrase I used last week, this was the best possible news about the bad news.

The nurse will call me back tomorrow, she said, when my head comes back from the moon. But for now, all I can do is say…

NO CHEMO.

And yes, that helps. Despite. Anyway.

## AUGUST 10, 2017

And so today's moment of happiness despite the news.

It was an odd sort of day. While still elated over being told I will not need chemo, I spent the early part of my day being reminded that all has not returned to normal.

I had to go to Walgreens to pick up my new prescription, something I will be on for the next five to ten years. It will suppress the estrogen my body naturally makes. It will shut down the female hormone factory. This particular cancer feeds off of estrogen, and so the thought behind this is to not give the cancer beast anything to eat.

This still just twists my head all sorts of sideways.

Then I had to call and make my appointment for next week's "mapping". Mapping is done in preparation for radiation treatment. A form will be made of my body in the exact position required to have the radiation reach only the affected area. My arm will be up over my head. The radiation oncologist will determine what position is exactly right and then the form will ensure that is the position I will in for four weeks, Monday through Friday, for ten minutes a day. The area will also be marked with four tattoos, which will look like freckles on my skin. Yes, tattoos. Made with a needle and ink. And permanent.

After I hung up the phone, I shoved the bottle with the medication out of my line of sight. I sat for a bit and stared out my window.

Everything just feels so foreign. I am not used to knowing these things. I am having to learn a whole new vocabulary. I am not used to applying these new terms to myself. But they are now my norm. For the next several weeks. For the next five to ten years. And the tattoos are permanent.

Then this afternoon, I lost myself in writing the new book. In writing. My Normal. My Everyday. My Familiar. At one point, on the page, one of my main characters stood at a kitchen window and looked out, just to see the familiar landscape. Just to see that the world still looked the same. The snow was white, with spring's yellowed grass just piercing the surface. The sky was blue. His birdfeeders were there. His life had been odd lately and he just needed that moment of grounding, more than a moment, a few moments, to convince himself that he wasn't living in a whole new world.

I glanced down then at my own desk. I was surrounded with books on reptile care, one open to a detailed description on how to bathe an iguana, Gloria Steinem's *My Life On The Road*, a statue of an iguana, a Victoria's Secret catalog, one window on my computer open to a website on the style and design of farmhouse sinks, another window open to Amazon, showing a photograph of a t-shirt which read *A Woman Needs A Man Like A Fish Needs A Bicycle*, and to my right, a grande iced cinnamon dolce latte with only two pumps of syrup.

On my left, something new. A painted stone, painted for me by my sister, sent to me for my birthday last week. It has the breast cancer pink ribbon in it, and the words *Never Give Up*. On the back: *You've Got This!!*

And I do.

I looked at everything around me and thought, You know, your Normal isn't all that normal either, woman.

I marked down the mapping appointment on my calendar and then moved the medication bottle to where I will remember to take the pill tonight and every night. For the next five to ten years. I need to buy a pill-a-day reminder box.

And then I sat back down and got back to work.

And yes, that helps. Despite. Anyway.

## AUGUST 11, 2017

And so today's moment of happiness despite the news.

A long, long time ago in a land far away (probably 1970 and northernmost reaches of Minnesota), I was sequestered in the last stall of the girls' restroom in

Winterquist Elementary School. I was on one side of the toilet, by the flusher, and on the other side was a girl named Dawn. A couple other girls stood at the toilet's narrow nose. We listened as Dawn told us, in the most secret sacred whisper, how babies were made.

I. Was. Horrified.

I think we all were. Except for Dawn. Her face was composed as she told us the facts. She stated them flatly, without fanfare, without fantasy. No scientific terms to confuse us. No pornographic details to confound us. I can still see her round face, serious, surrounded by what we then called a pageboy haircut. We went to a school that allowed girls to wear pants on only Tuesdays and Thursdays, and only "dress" pants, not jeans or corduroys, even in the deepest Minnesota winter. This wasn't a Tuesday or Thursday, as I remember we were all wearing turtlenecks and jumpers over thick hairy tights. My jumper was navy blue, with white trim in scallops around my knees. I wore penny loafers without pennies.

It's like this postcard in my memory. A picture postcard. Of a Norman Rockwell moment about sex, and there's a toilet there too. Norman Rockwell meets Norman Lear.

I went home that day, disbelieving, and told my mother what I heard. When I asked her if it was true, my mother just stared at me. And then she said in this sarcastic voice I can still hear, "How do you think you got here?"

Overall, I much preferred Dawn's way of telling me.

I haven't seen Dawn since I was twelve years old and moved away from Minnesota. I've thought of her often, and I've told the tale of how I found out about sex often too. It might even appear in a book or a story. Unlike many memories, it is just as sharp and in full technicolor as the day it happened. I see our jumpers. I hear her voice. I feel my horror and disbelief.

Yesterday, one of my friends who stood with me around that toilet told me that she found out that Dawn passed away. She was 57 years old. My age. I haven't seen her in 45 years. Yet my feet were just yanked out from under me.

So where am I going with this?

All day today, I've replayed that memory. That earnest face, that somber whisper, telling me the facts of life. Flat-out, simple, straightforward, not prettied-up, not dirtied-down. In a way that didn't make me feel stupid, and in a way that I could understand.

She told me what I needed to know.

The next day, I went back to school and I told her she was right. I apologized for not believing her. And I very clearly remember saying to her, in my own more-serious-than-I-should-have-been ten-year old whisper, "Thank you."

Each time that memory played to its end today, I smiled. I felt warm. And each time, I said, "Thank you."

Some people step into your life for a very short time and leave a memory that doesn't fade. The memories aren't always cinema-pretty. Sometimes they offer up toilets and hairy tights and facts that seem impossible to believe. But then you find they're true and you have to believe them and they prepare you for what's ahead in your future. And sometimes those people don't ever know the impact they had.

Thank you, Dawn.

And yes, that helps. Despite. Anyway.

## AUGUST 12, 2017

And so today's moment of happiness despite the news.

Well, the day started out difficult.

I did not have a mastectomy, and I am profoundly grateful that I didn't. But the lumpectomy comes with issues of its own. I have two good-sized incisions: one crawling across the upper right side of my right breast, and one cut in a diagonal a bit below my armpit. As I said in a previous Moment, a bra is necessary right now, because of heaviness in the affected breast. But I have yet to find a comfortable bra. The side of the bra, where it glides down from the cup to the waistband, cuts directly on top of the incision below my armpit. It rubs and it hurts. I was told to try a sports bra, but that still cut across, AND it compressed too much. Around the house, I've returned to my pre-breast days and I go braless, using my hand for support. But even then, the issue is that any material, whether it's a shirt or a bra, that touches this incision irritates it. I had a new t-shirt to wear today and after about an hour, I had to yank it off because the material, despite my washing and drying it yesterday, was just too rough.

Today, I took an old bra and cut out the material that would touch the incision. But then the rest of the bra crumpled and rolled and irritated the incision on the breast.

I am tired of hurting. And I am tired of the hurt constantly reminding me of what's going on. I am tired of not being able to just roll over at night, but having to gingerly set myself down so that I don't rub the incision. I am tired of having to put the shoulder harness of my seatbelt over my head and behind my back because it hits the incision. Everything, everything hits the incision.

I am tired.

While I was attacking the bra, a commercial came on television. It was for women with the type of breast cancer I'm dealing with. It was for an aromatase inhibitor, which is the medication I'm on.

This was my first time ever seeing myself, connecting myself, to a medical-based television commercial.

And then they called the medication "a life-extender."

It was about then I had to leave the house for a while.

No one, not the three doctors, not the nurses, not the mentors, no one has referred to this medication in this way to me.

I had to cry for a while.

Later, we headed out to the mall. I was walking by a rack when I saw something tucked toward the back. It was this blue. It was that blue. It was lovely. I took it out and held it up.

I have a book launch coming up. My shopping trips for what to wear at a launch have become legendary. I usually end up with at least three, sometimes more, outfits that I can't choose between and so I get them all and then don't choose until the night of. The launch for *In Grace's Time* is a month away and I hadn't even given thought to what I would wear. I was too busy fighting all the cloth that was attacking my body. But I looked at this wisp of material, this shade of blue here, that shade of blue here, and I felt its softness.

I held it against me as I wandered the rest of the store and put together an entire outfit around it. Then I went to the dressing room and tried it all on. I turned to the mirror.

And there I was. That was me. That was how I look. That was how I wanted to look on September 26.

Everything in me that was hurting straightened up. Everything in me that was sad and frustrated straightened up. My shoulders went back. I stood as tall as five foot two can stand.

A student told me once that when I walk into a room, I own it.

In that dressing room, I owned myself. And I do not take a life-extender. Because my life has not been threatened. The threat was caught early. I have steps to get through, but I'm taking them. The incisions will heal. So will I.

There won't be multiple outfits for this launch. This is it.

Though I did buy two pairs of shoes.

And yes, that helps. Despite. Anyway.

# AUGUST 13, 2017

And so today's moment of happiness despite the news.

I started writing Today's Moment originally as a response to feeling overwhelmed after the ugliness of our last election, and over the ugliness of the man who is now in the White House. So it's impossible to keep yesterday's horrific event in Charlottesville out of this blog.

I've been to Charlottesville. I went there after visiting the real Walton's Mountain, Schuyler, Virginia. Charlottesville was featured often in the television show, The Waltons. John Boy attended a fictional Boatright University, which was, essentially, the University of Virginia. Thinking back to my visit there, over twenty years ago, I couldn't ever have imagined that yesterday's event would happen in such a gentle place.

It would be easy to get discouraged, depressed, and defeated after an event like that. But something I read in a student's manuscript caused me to lift my face away from all that and look around.

In this manuscript, one character is comforting another when both are upset over Asshat's winning the election. The comforter says that we need to remember that the election was very close. That Clinton won the popular vote. "Half of the country is still full of people who said no to the lies and the abuse," this character said. "It's not everybody."

On days when it feels like everybody, we need to look around and see that it's not.

So I looked around.

On Facebook, everywhere, people were changing their profile pictures so that they were framed with a phrase that said, "We will not let hate win." On Facebook and Twitter both, people were declaring their horror and their anger at what happened, and at Asshat's lack-of-response response to it. News articles protested. Editorials and blogs protested.

And then my own daughter spoke up on her Facebook page.

" *What happened in Charlottesville should have been taken more seriously by our 'leader',*" she said, " *yet all he had to say was it was 'sad'. Which is extremely apathetic considering the fear to those that tried to fight back against the hatred. It's devastating, sick, terrifying, nerve-wracking, disgusting, disturbing, and horrific. I could come up with more adjectives to describe what happened to Charlottesville yesterday than our 'leader'.*"

My daughter is sixteen. She is fully aware. And she is not alone.

Not everybody walked down the streets of gentle Charlottesville with their hands raised in a Nazi-esque salute, chanting hateful and racist statements. Not everybody applauded their efforts.

They were protested against and fought against every step of the way.

Not everybody is responding by speaking, but not really saying anything, like the Asshat.

Not everybody is blind to the connection between the white supremacist marchers and the Asshat who said nothing while he was speaking.

And there are so very many raising their voices now, in whatever way they can. There are so many not-everybodies.

Hate hasn't won. Even when it's encouraged and championed and embodied by That Man In The White House.

I am proud of my daughter. And I'm proud to be one of not-everybody.

And yes, that helps. Despite. Anyway.

## AUGUST 14, 2017

And so today's moment of happiness despite the news.

I spent part of my morning on the phone with a new AllWriters' student. Cora registered for an online class, but instantly became disoriented and felt like she would do better with a face to face class. Listening to her on the phone, hearing about her grandchildren and her great-grandchildren, learning of her discomfort with email and with her cell phone, I began to agree.

Then Cora told me that she'd heard about me from another woman. She said, "I've been told you can teach me. I took another class someplace else and I just ended up confused. But you…you can teach me." When I told her that my on-site classes were all filled, she said, "But I want to be in class with you. I want to see you, hear you, feel you. I can feel you over the phone!"

Well, wow.

We talked for a while longer and I suggested she take the on-site Monday Night Workshop, taught by my husband. "Really," I said, "he's just as good as I am."

"I doubt it."

She made me laugh, but I went on to explain that Michael had been a student and now, as a teacher, he knows how I liked things done, and that while he adds his own flavor to his classes, he is faithful to what I feel is important.

Cora agreed to come. We spent another little bit on figuring out how to get her here – she lives north of Milwaukee. GPS, like email and her cell phone, were confounding. We went through painstaking directions. She wrote them down. And with every direction of mine she repeated, I heard her resolve grow. When I hung up, I didn't wonder if she would make it here. I knew she would.

I love students like this. Her lack of fear, her willingness to venture out into unknown territory, without a GPS, without email, without a phone – well, she had a phone, she just didn't know how to use it – is amazing. Most of us, if we don't know how to do something, look to our technology. Cora looked to her wits. And her determination. She felt me over the phone. And I felt her: What Cora wants, Cora gets.

She wants to write a story. She will write a story. I envy Michael his new student.

I promised Cora I would stop in the classroom and see her before class began. She arrived at the studio forty-five minutes early...but she found it. Olivia let her in to the classroom as I was on the phone with a client.

Cora thought Olivia was me. I was delighted. Olivia was horrified. "Do I look like a 57-year old woman?" Olivia sputtered to me.

"No, but I guess I must sound like a very young woman on the phone," I said.

When I went downstairs to meet Cora, she greeted me with a hug as if we'd known each other for years. And somehow, I feel that we have. As I spoke with other students in the class, who asked me about how I was feeling, I had to explain to Cora about the breast cancer.

She was quiet for a bit. But before I left the room, she looked up at me and beamed. "You're going to be fine," she said. "I got the goosebumps. I know. I feel you. You're going to be fine."

You know, I think I believe her even more than I believe my doctors. Cora just KNOWS. No technology needed. And what Cora wants, Cora gets.

She found her way. She will write a story. And I'm going to be fine.

And yes, that helps. Despite. Anyway.

### AUGUST 15, 2017

And so today's moment of happiness despite the news.

Today, a woman stopped by the studio to pick up some copies of *Rise From The River*. Her book club is reading the book for their October meeting. I'll be visiting with them and joining the discussion. I love that in the middle of new book hooha, I will get to talk about an "old" book.

I stepped outside with her as she was leaving and I looked sadly at the weed-choked flowers in my little narrow strip of garden. It's supposed to have lilies and hostas in it. Now it had lilies, hostas, and weeds, weeds, weeds. This woman reads Today's Moment and she knew about the breast cancer and so I told her I haven't been able to weed.

"First, the use of my right arm was limited because of the biopsy," I said. "And now, it's been limited because of the surgery. For a month, I'm not supposed to do anything more than lift a half-gallon of milk. And no repetitive movements." I took a moment to be grateful that tapping away on the keyboard isn't considered repetitive movement. "So I can't weed," I continued. "My left hand is basically useless – I'm a righty – and these weeds typically need two hands to yank anyway."

Damned if this woman didn't just hand me the books she was carrying and then she hunkered down and weeded the whole little garden. Right then, right there. In a dress. No garden gloves. Newly coiffed hair.

I swear the hostas and the lilies stood up straighter, took a deep breath, and saluted.

"It's way more fun to do it for someone else than for yourself," the woman said as she weeded.

And then it was done. The little space is neat and tidy again, a fitting garden for beneath the AllWriters' Workplace & Workshop sign. A lovely greeting for my students. And, in this case, my readers.

I gave her back the books, took the weeds to throw in the dumpster, and watched her drive away. Then I stood for a few, the sun on my shoulders, the air warm the way I like it, and I admired my now happily uncluttered and growing plants. I admired the sky and the clouds reflected in the windows. I admired the classroom on the other side of the glass. I've always said the plants in the classroom and the ones outside grow well because of the environment of creativity and community.

The weeds grew well too, but all it took was one compassionate well-meaning woman to clear away the bad and let the good grow, grow, grow.

I thought about that too.

What a nice thing to do.

And then I reached in to my mailbox to collect today's mail and I found a Starbucks card, left there by an appreciative student.

The kindness of people continues to astound me. The simplest things can just mean so much.

And yes, that helps. Despite. Anyway.

## AUGUST 16, 2017

And so today's moment of happiness despite the news.

(Remember that old television show, *The Courtship of Eddie's Father?* Remember the theme song? *"People, let me tell ya 'bout my best friend…"* Yeah, that one. Cue that.)

This morning, during a Skype session with a client, my cat Muse jumped onto my desk and into the camera shot. This isn't the first time – she always seems sincerely interested in what's being said. My client said that Muse looked "wise."

I swear that cat's head swiveled and she leveled me with a look that said, "See? Did you hear? Did you hear what she said?"

I've been surrounded by animals for my entire life. There was a dog, Cindy, in my house when I was born. I helped to put myself through college by working at the local humane society – my old boss is still there and he waves at me every time he drives by in the shelter's van. I've owned fish, hamsters, guinea pigs, parakeets, cats and dogs, and when I was at the humane society, I handled pretty much every animal known to man. Including a kangaroo, that escaped from a local traveling circus. Currently, there are two beagles and two cats under my roof. I love them all, but Muse, my Muse, is definitely a writer's cat.

So what's a writer's cat? A cat that keeps the writer company.

Before Muse, there was Einstein. When he was a kitten, he sat on my shoulder while I worked. He started curled up on my left shoulder, then as he grew, he draped from shoulder to shoulder like a stole. As age set in, he settled for sleeping in a bed directly behind my desk. He listened to every word, every key clack, every sigh of frustration and fist-pumped "Yes!" of success.

Muse came along before Einstein passed away. She was born in an RV, traveling from California to the east coast. Her family was visiting one of my students when I complained in class one night about having too much testosterone among the pets in my house – at the time, I had two male cats and a male dog. The next week, in came my student with this family and a box full of kittens – one of whom was female. She and I locked eyes and that was all she wrote.

Well, not me, I kept writing, and Muse took over as the writer's cat. She's a tiny girl, weighing in at six pounds. She fits nicely next to my computer, a purring, warm paperweight. And like Einstein, she listens to every word.

But she's become more than that too. She sleeps with me at night. Since the onset of fibromyalgia, she has the uncanny ability to know where the pain is and she often settles herself down on that exact spot, and her light pressure and warmth eases it away. She gets up in the morning when I do, follows me wherever I go. She meditates with me, in the afternoon and again at night, before I go to sleep. When I shower, she sits on the floor beside the tub, or on the back of the toilet. She joins me for breakfast and supper, usually at my computer, and she's always nearby at lunch, which I try to take at the kitchen island, giving myself a moment to read for enjoyment.

The day I came home from the lumpectomy, she was on my lap as soon as I was settled. She stayed with me that whole day, only leaving to get her dinner when it was served, and then she was back again. She bathed my arm over and over. If she could have checked my pulse, she would have. But she couldn't, so she provided comfort.

As she has throughout this current ordeal, and any that have come before.

Muse is thirteen years old now. When my client called her wise, it made me laugh. But I've looked at her with different eyes throughout this day. This little cat knows what I need when I need it.

Yes, she's wise.

And yes, that helps. Despite. Anyway.

### AUGUST 17, 2017

And so today's moment of happiness despite the news.

Today was the day I was "mapped" for my radiation treatments. This meant I went in to the cancer center, turned down a new hallway, and after changing into a stylin' robe, I was ushered into the radiation machine room.

I met the machine for the first time. I named him Xappa, pronounced Zappa. "Hello, Xappa. I'm Kathie. Looks like we're going to have an intimate relationship."

After getting on the table, I had to lay back on this thing that looked like a beanbag chair. I put my hands over my head (assume the position) and the nurse began to scrunch the beanbag all around me, and pushing a button that took air out of it as she went. But the time she was done, this thing was molded to me, and to me alone. From this point on, the beanbag me will be waiting on the table for each treatment and I will always be in the exact same position when Xappa does his stuff.

Then the doctor and the nurse worked together to draw all over me with a purple sharpie. Xappa was used to find certain points, though no radiation was used on me today. And then the nurse tattooed me in five different spots. Four on my right breast, and one on my left side. She explained that the tattoos will be used to further line me up correctly in Xappa. Only one tattoo hurt enough to make me gasp; it was directly in my sternum.

You know, I would find all of this so interesting, if it wasn't happening to me. I wish it was a documentary. I wish I wasn't the documentary.

Where I made my mistake was after it was all over and I went back to the changing room. I slipped the robe off and then, instead of just dressing, I turned toward the mirror. And there I was, all marked up with purple lines and dashes and dots, and the five new tattoos. And of course, the incisions were there too.

You know those diagrams of beef cows, where they draw dotted lines to show where the different cuts of meat are? That's what I looked like.

Earlier today, a student told me she admired how I was handling all of this. She said, "I think I'd be sitting in a dark corner for days."

Oh, I've had dark corner days, believe me. But as time has gone on, the days have dwindled and I have infrequent dark corner moments now. This was one of those moments. A dark corner beef cow moment.

I got dressed and stepped out of the dressing room. But the dark corner moment was draped over me, heavy as a lead cape, and I knew I couldn't walk through the door to the waiting room and then the exit. Not yet. So I sat down on a chair by the lockers. I just sat and spun the spinner ring given to me by a student who has dealt with cancer. The ring helps with anxiety. And she had it engraved with, "Keep passing the open windows."

In this dark corner moment, I was stuck in front of the open window. All I could think of was, What is happening to me?

The nurse came back in. She sat down beside me and put her hand over mine. "It's all good, Kathie," she said. "You're doing great. You are great. And we're all making sure that you are through all of this by the time your book comes out. When you drive off on your tour, you can look over your shoulder and see it disappear behind you."

She saw me. Not the beef cow. She squeezed my hand.

And the lead cape dark moment slipped off and fell away.

Being treated as a person. Being treated as an individual. Being treated with respect. That's all it took. I walked past the window.

And yes, that helps. Despite. Anyway.

## AUGUST 18, 2017

And so today's moment of happiness despite the news.

On an evening, oh, on a lovely evening when you hold an event and you never can predict how such events will turn out, but when you hold an event and the room is full and the voices are full and the spirits are full and then, on top of it all, you witness the following:

*a student gets up and reads her poetry with such heart, with such strength, with such confidence and poise and power,

*another student gets up and reads something she never thought she could think, and she never thought she could write, and she never thought she could read aloud, and she never ever thought she could be the person she is today, but there she is for everyone to see and she's glorious,

*a third student gets up and reads from a book that he sweat blood and bullets and brain cells to write and to write and to write again and to write well and when he reads, he hears the audience's reaction and you just know that he knows it's so damn good, and it was all worth it,

*and then a new friend gets up and he reads his work and his words twist your heart and your mind fifty thousand different ways and you just want to open all of his books all at once on a table and move around reading them, turning page after page after page (hell, you'd like to roll in them too, but who is gonna admit that?),

*and then you get up and you read and as you read, you hear it, that moment, the moment when they stop hearing you and they stop seeing you and they only exist in the story and that story has vacuumed them in with the suction that only words have, that only imagination has, that only creativity and lyricism and, gosh, the everything that it has, it has all that you wanted to say and you are the one who wrote it, and, well, hallelujah...

...when that happens, you just feel soaked through with right. Not righteousness, and not right, as in I'm-right-and-you're-wrong, but right as in all is right with your world.

In this moment, right here, right now, I am happy and content and full and satisfied and convinced that my choices were the choices I needed to make.

Oh, baby. Amen.

And thank you.

And yes, that helps. Despite. Anyway.

## AUGUST 19, 2017

And so today's moment of happiness despite the news.

It seems that when large numbers of people get all het up over watching something, I'm usually on the outside. I never watched *Downton Abbey*, and in fact, for the longest time, I thought it was Downtown Abbey. I've never seen *Game of Thrones*. I haven't watched *A Handmaid's Tale*, although I love Margaret Atwood. *Cat's Eye* is my favorite. Usually, if the television is on, it's set to HGTV. I also guiltily enjoy *Say Yes To The Dress*, as my daughter is engaged and I am so looking forward to dress-shopping with her. Michael and I, right now, are watching an episode of *Grace & Frankie* and then an episode of the old *Bob Newhart Show* every night before bed.

But now there's watching in real life and I'm watching people getting ready to watch and I'm not planning on joining in.

The solar eclipse.

People are buying special glasses to view the eclipse on Monday. They're traveling to special places where the view is supposed to be better. Bonnie Tyler is singing "Total Eclipse Of the Heart". I did a little research and found that the next total eclipse visible from the United States will be in 2024, over parts of Texas and Mexico. The entire eclipse this time is supposed to last for 2 minutes and 40 seconds. And it is supposed to be the worst travel day of the year as people try to drive into places where you can better see it.

Okay. My plan? I'll glance outside every now and then to see if it's gotten darker.

I don't know why I'm not more excited. I should probably remove the "more" from that sentence. I'm not excited at all.

Today, while I was out driving in the convertible, I basked in the sun. I am a sun-lover. There are no window treatments in my home – I don't want to block the light.

I thought back to the last total eclipse that I can remember. Through research again, it must have been the one on March 7, 1970. I was nine years old, not to turn ten until July. In Minnesota, it was all they talked about in school. And it came fraught with warnings. "If you look up, you'll go blind! You can't look up all day, if you do, even for one second, you'll never see again!" We were taught how to poke a hole in a piece of typing paper and hold it over another piece of typing paper while standing out in the snow with the darkened sun back over our shoulders, and that was supposed to project a safe image for us to watch. This was a Saturday, and on Friday, we were sent home with our dire warnings, two pieces of typing paper, one pin-pricked, and some weird box thing that we made that was also supposed to make viewing safe. I threw my weird box thing away on the way home. My mother wanted the typing paper.

I was totally freaked out. I didn't want to go blind. I didn't want the world to go dark in the middle of the day. I didn't like the dark. What if it stayed dark forever?

The dark. I didn't like it then. I don't like it now.

Which is why, on that winter day in 1970, my mother went out in the snow to see if my typing paper worked, and I went down in the basement and stayed there until it was all over. A few names were tossed down the stairs at me, but I didn't care. I didn't want to see the sun disappear.

Now, I suppose I can't say I totally dislike the dark. But the best dark for me is when the moon is bright. My bedroom window allows the light of the moon to fall in, and when it does and adds a silver blanket to my bed, I get my best sleep.

Today, in my car, stopped in line at Starbucks, I closed my eyes and tilted my head back against the seat. The sun turned my eyelids rosy; even my closed eyes didn't bring the dark. The sun kept it away. The warmth draped over my face and down my neck and chest into my lap. My arms were warmed. And I realized that I don't have to watch what others are watching. I can sit quietly and wait for the light to return. And this time, I know it will. When it does, I will go out in the convertible, find a sunny place to park, tilt my head up, and bask. Welcome bask, Sun.

I don't have to hide in a basement to be myself anymore, do I.

And yes, that helps. Despite. Anyway.

## AUGUST 20, 2017

And so today's moment of happiness despite the news.

I know well the phrase, "Happiness is a warm puppy," and in fact owned that book when I was a child. The book's cover, showing Lucy from the Charles Schulz Peanuts series hugging Snoopy is a classic picture-perfect depiction of happiness. Which is interesting, really, given that throughout the Peanuts series, Lucy battled Snoopy, often falling victim to his tongue and collapsing to shrieks of "Blech! Ugh! I've been kissed by a dog! Get boiling water! Get iodine! Dog germs!" But on the cover of that particular book, it is the dog-germ hating Lucy who is beaming from ear to ear as she hugs a beagle.

Today, my happiness didn't come from a warm puppy, despite owning two beagles. My Lucy-smile came from the following:

Happiness is a Sunday morning sleep-in (afternoon!) follow-your-nose coffee, created by a coffeepot that brews before you wake breakfast in a recliner coffee in your favorite mug to your right doughnuts to your left maple-frosted and stuffed-with-raspberry white-frosted three sections of the Sunday paper, stacked and read in order comics entertainment food/house & garden pajama-clad all the while then a shower that lasts till the hot water runs out oldest jeans ever favorite t-shirt

And the best: seeing a Sunday in every week of your future.


And yes, that helps. Despite. Anyway.

## AUGUST 21, 2017

And so today's moment of happiness despite the news.

Today was Total Eclipse Day. And it was an Eclipse Day for me too, as my spirits and mood started out damn dark.

Typically, during the summer, I go away for two weeks on retreat. This gives me solid time to reflect, recharge and, above everything else, write. I've discovered during my almost thirteen years in business that the only way to get myself out of small business chaos is to put myself as far across country as I can. If I'm too far away, I can't do anything. Except focus on myself. And write. Oregon is my place of choice, the same house, the same beach, a place that feels like home deep in my bones. Maine is my second choice – opposite coast, opposite ocean, but lovely.

And this summer – nowhere. Breast cancer interruptis. Mammogram, ultrasound, biopsy, diagnosis, MRI, biopsy, surgery, prognosis (a GREAT one!), medication, and soon, four weeks of radiation. And then I'm done. But so is summer.

Facebook, every day, notifies me through its On This Day feature of posts and photographs from years gone by. And right now, since I usually take my retreat in July or August, every day is a reminder of what I'm missing. Today, every single past post was of Oregon. Every single one.

So this morning – total eclipse.

But then the sun started coming back.

## FROM TOTAL ECLIPSE TO 66.6% ECLIPSE:

Any time I came downstairs today, I was barreled into by my sixteen-year old. Hugs, hugs, and more hugs. And always, a gentle kiss on my cheek. She knew. And she set to work at cheering her mother up. Glimmer.

## FROM 66.6% ECLIPSE TO 33.3% ECLIPSE:

I sank into my novel-in-progress this afternoon. Concentration was difficult at first. I just wanted to go take a nap. I told myself I could – after all, I'm in recovery from breast cancer. I can nap, right? I should nap, right? I deserve to nap. But my fingers wouldn't pull themselves away from the keyboard. And then I slipped fully under the surface of story.

It's really hard to be sad when you're writing about an iguana, wearing a leather bomber jacket and racing cap, touching grass for the first time. In the sunshine. In spring. With the promise of summer ahead. I rejoiced with the iguana. And with my characters, watching him. I know – writers are weird. We find our joy in strange places. And often those strange places are within secret compartments in our minds. Glow.

## FROM 33.3% ECLIPSE TO FULL-BLOWN SUN!

And then tonight. My granddaughter, Maya Mae, was here for a little bit. I didn't see too much of her because I was meeting with clients and teaching, but my daughter Olivia babysat. And right in the middle of a client meeting, I heard it. It came bounding up the stairs and shot round the corner and landed firmly on my desk.

That laugh.

That little four-year old girl laugh.

That soprano trill, all peach cheeks and silky hair, pink dress and scuffed knees, tickle-toes and glitter-eyes. All joy. All happiness. Just...pure. Better than any birdsong. Better than any symphony.

That laughter blew the last of the shadow away. GLOW.

No more eclipse.

And yes, that helps. Despite. Anyway.

# AUGUST 22, 2017

And so today's moment of happiness despite the news.

*I hear my battle symphony*
*All the world in front of me*
*If my armor breaks*
*I'll fuse it back together*
*Battle symphony*
*Please just don't give up on me*
*And my eyes are wide awake*
*--Linkin Park, "Battle Symphony"*

I wasn't prepared for how I was going to feel about the scarring caused by the breast cancer surgery. I was told by several that the scars would be small and so I really never stopped to consider it. But now, a month later, I find myself examining the scars, both of them, every morning and every night. The one from the sentinel lymph node removal is relatively small. But the one where the tumor was removed…well, not so small. And they're not disappearing. They aren't fading. In my mind, they're neon and they're blinking. And they're a reminder that, without my being aware of it, something had been going on inside me that was very wrong. That was dangerous.

A reminder. And it mars what I see when I think of my own reflection.

Now, granted, these scars are going to be seen by a relative few. But for whatever reason, I've found myself fixating on them. They make me feel ugly.

Not something I was expecting.

So today, I took Olivia to her new high school, which happens to be my old high school. We walked her schedule. With every turn down a hallway and peek into a classroom, I was inundated by memories. Good memories. Here's where I took creative writing. Here's where I took Psych. I took care of the rabbits in the bio lab. Here's where the typewriters used to be. And here…and here…and here…

I loved that school. It was my third high school and when I arrived in those particular hallways, I bloomed. I don't usually use flowery (ha!) language, but there's no other word to describe it. I came home. I took courses called Growing Up In Literature & Reality, Mystery & The Macabre, Sci Fi and Fantasy, and of course, creative writing. Sociology. Psychology. Women's History. Every class just pulled my mind up higher. Every class made me excited.

As I walked the halls with Olivia, I saw myself all over again, at her age. Sixteen. And then seventeen. Long straight hair that required no blowdryer or curling iron. No make-up. Jeans and a t-shirt or jeans and a sweater with no real thought to fashion. When I got up in the morning, I didn't hustle to the bathroom to spend incredible time changing my appearance. I just wanted to get to school. I just wanted to talk, discuss, debate. I just wanted to learn.

It's not all that different now. I still don't use a blow dryer or a curling iron, though the hair is short now. I don't wear make-up. I wear clothes that I like, not clothes that I see in magazines. I get up in the morning and then spend hours teaching and hours writing and talking, discussing, debating. And learning. Always, always learning.

Then is now. Just like my years in that high school, where I learned how happy I could be living a cerebral lifestyle, an intellectual lifestyle, a life celebrated and danced in words, that's who I am. That's who I want to be. How I live, how I love, how I learn, has absolutely nothing to do with how I look. How my breast looks.

So as we left the school this afternoon, I gave my breast a subtle, quiet pat and an apology. She's a part of me, she's come along for the roller coaster ride, and the scars simply don't matter. They aren't who I am. They're not what I'm about.

I'm sure I'll still sting a bit when I look in the mirror tonight before bed. But you know what?

They're battle scars.

And I won.

And yes, that helps. Despite. Anyway.

## AUGUST 23, 2017

And so today's moment of happiness despite the news.

I know absolutely nothing about the scientific configurations of air current and wind and how they are affected by the objects they swirl in and around.

But I was enthralled today.

In the middle of the afternoon, I drove topless (in my convertible) on my usual trip to Starbucks. When I receive my latte, I don't even wait until I'm out of the drive-thru lane before I rip open my straw and stick it into the cup. As a result, the little tray by my knee is filled with crumpled-up straw wrappers and the tippy tops that I tear off of those wrappers.

Today, as I flung the wrapper tip toward the tray, the wind caught it. And it began to flap and flutter all around my front seat. From my face to the floor through the steering wheel to the windshield to the passenger seat to the rearview, up, down, around, and twirl, this little piece of paper became my own personal butterfly for a few minutes. And it never left the car. Instead, it eventually came to rest on my knee.

I was delighted – there is no other word I can use. The paper butterfly made me laugh as it did its tricks in the air. All for me. The whole show was for my eyes alone.

In those minutes, I became a little girl again, chasing a white butterfly. A little northern Minnesota girl, running alongside the creek (pronounce it crick, please) that ran through my back yard, a place where I pretended to fish with a stick and a string and a bent nail, where I sailed schooners made from paper and splintered pieces of wood, where I swung on what we called Tarzan swings up and over the little flow of water. Little creek; in my eyes, a mighty river.

I chased white butterflies. And yellow butterflies. As an adult, I know, of course, that these were moths. But then, they were butterflies and they were as beautiful as the multicolored wings that appeared from time to time too. The white was like Minnesota snow in the summertime or lace that lived. And the yellow was breathing bits of sunshine that fell to the earth for the sole purpose of visiting with me.

When I would catch one of these white or yellow butterflies and I would open my cupped hands and the little creature would sit there, on my palm, the wings moving so slowly that I could see every curve, every vein, every ephemeral cell, it was magic. These were no moths.

Any fairy-winged creature with silky thread legs that sits like air on a child's palm is a butterfly.

And today, with the flitting tip of my straw wrapper, a butterfly came back to me and rested on my knee. In my laughter, there was the trill of that little Minnesota girl, chasing snow in the summertime, sunshine from the sky, and butterflies along the edge of a creek (pronounced crick, please).

And yes, that helps. Despite. Anyway.

### AUGUST 24, 2017

And so today's moment of happiness despite the news.

Today, I had to bring Hemi, my Chrysler 300C Hemi, in for a recalled airbag replacement. When I called to make the appointment, I was told it would take up to four hours. Four hours! And this had to be done at the Chrysler dealership, not my beloved CarMax, where they would have set me up in a cubicle and plied me with privacy and fresh-made coffee and a treat or two.

So I prepared for four hours. In the middle of the afternoon. I packed my computer, my mousepad, my mouse, my power cord, my phone, and I thought, my flash drive. I dropped the car off with a pat of encouragement and then walked across the street to Culver's, a not-so-fast fast food place. After placing my order, I scouted the seating and found the one spot that had an electric socket.

I soon had my own little workstation in the middle of a busy restaurant. And it's about then that I discovered I didn't have my flash drive with me.

I sighed a few times, but then decided there was a bright side. My flash drive is for student manuscripts. Not having student manuscripts with me meant I could devote the whole time – without guilt – to my own writing.

So I did.

Partway through, I was well-immersed (and well-fed with a deluxe burger and coleslaw), and only barely noticed the two taking a seat at the table next to me. I registered that it was a little boy and a grandfatherly man. Their voices, the boy's a chipmunk chatter, the grandfather's a bass interruption, provided me with a pleasant accompaniment. At one point, I heard the grandfather reminding the boy that he could only have one cup of soda – express orders from Mama – and so he should wait to drink until his food arrived. Which of course, the boy didn't. Soon the straw was doing that sucking slurping sound that straws do when there is only ice and dregs left. And the ice melts slowly enough that the dregs keep reappearing.

The food arrived. And then it started.

SLUUUUUUUUUUUUUURP! <giggle>

"Buddy, don't do that," Grandpa said.

SLUUUUUUUUUUUUUURP! <giggle>

"Buddy, eat your cheeseburger now."

SLUUUUUUUUUUUUUURP! <giggle>

"How about some of this water? I got you water."

SLUUUUUUUUUUUUUURP! <giggle>

"Your fries, Buddy! Eat your fries!"

SLUUUUUUUUUUUUUURP! <giggle>

Grandpa was getting frustrated. People around us were beginning to shift in their seats. I hadn't written a word for five slurps.

So I considered my soda. I rarely drink soda and so I'd only filled my cup halfway and it was just about gone. I turned to the little boy, raised my cup in a toast and...

SLUUUUUUUUUUUUURP! <adult giggle>

And ohmygod. This little guy and I created a slurp symphony. And a laughter fest. Grandpa was drinking coffee, or I'm pretty sure he would have joined in.

And then...the drinks were all gone. The slurp symphony, done in quick bursts, used up all the soda, all the ice. Nothing left. There was a method to my madness.

"Buddy," I said, "eat your cheeseburger and fries. Drink your water. Make Grandpa – and Mama – happy."

He did. I returned to writing. The din in the restaurant returned to normal proportions.

I earned a hug from Buddy before he left. And a whispered thank you from Grandpa.

And my car only took an hour and a half, not four hours. I swear, the Culvers people probably called the dealership and said, "Fix her car NOW! Get her out of here before she slurps again!"

But that's okay. Grandpa didn't lose his temper. Mama would be happy. Buddy had fun.

I had fun.

And yes, that helps. Despite. Anyway.

### AUGUST 25, 2017

And so today's moment of happiness despite the news.

Today's Moment is written basically in anticipation...because the moment won't happen until approximately 11:00 tonight. But the happiness is rising steadily until I can soak up to my neck in it. Literally.

Tonight, at around 11:00, after I'm done with all my clients (my last client is at 10:00), after this week is declared done-finished-bam, I get to take a BATH!

No small thing. I haven't climbed into our jetted tub since a couple days before my breast cancer surgery on July 25. I haven't been allowed. "Don't you even think about it," my surgeon said. But this week...the restrictions were lifted.

A lot feels lifted this week. I no longer have restrictions on how much weight I can lift with my right arm. It no longer hurts when I lay on my right side. I can wear the shoulder harness of my seatbelt again. My daughter is no longer hugging me at arm's length, her hands and wrists clamped to my neck, the rest of her body held away from me by locked elbows, because she was afraid of hurting me. And I can wear regular everyday bras again! Goodbye, ugly sports bras! Sayonara, uglier post-op bras!

And a bath. I can have a bath.

Water to me means relaxation, whether it's a pond, river, lake, ocean, swimming pool, hot tub…or bathtub. Though I will admit, the hotter the water, the better. I love to melt.

When Michael and I built this place, most of our neighbors-under-construction were eyeing building allowances and their kitchen dreams. I dreamed of my bathroom. This was 2006, and ever since my first son was born in 1984, I lived in houses with only one bathroom and shared it with children, plus an assortment of rubber duckies and letters that would stick to the walls when they got wet. They were supposed to teach the children a soggy alphabet, and then spelling, but sometimes, they became a form of wet magnetic poetry. Or wet magnetic sarcasm. When we moved here, I'd been living for almost six years in a one-bathroom house with two adults, three teenagers, and one growing baby. The bathroom was tiny and our hot water heater didn't give out enough heat to fill the tub. Traveling meant looking for hotels with hot tubs.

But now…two full baths. One just for me and Michael. And he very willingly turned the planning over to me. And I planned.

A shower with a rainforest showerhead that has several settings, plus two body jets with even more settings. In the bathroom showroom, I was measured so that one jet would hit me squarely at the base of my neck, and the other would hit me in the small of my back.

A jetted soaker tub. Deep enough to sink in up to my neck. Six powerful pulsating jets.

We installed a great water heater too.

Oh, heaven. On move-in day, exhaustion set in and I fell into bed without trying my new adults-only sanctuary. But our first morning here, I took a long shower. A loooooooong shower, Our second night here, I took a bath and discovered the miracle of more hot water at my command when the first batch grew cold. And the second. Sometimes the third.

I love this place. I love my home.

And tonight…I will be reunited with my bathtub and supreme relaxation.

All of this, the bath, the lifted restrictions, the seatbelt, the hugs, the bra, all of it expresses signs of healing, of course.

But it's more than that. These all express signs of a life going back to normal. A life that is chaotic enough, noisy enough, crazy enough, to require every Friday night soaks in a tub whose surging hot waters ease me back into energy and enthusiasm. Like my home, a life that I love. And appreciate, now, more than ever.

Tonight, I bathe!

And yes, that helps. Despite. Anyway.

### AUGUST 26, 2017

And so today's moment of happiness despite the news.

Today, we checked out a new mall that opened up in our area. It's nowhere close to full yet, but has already developed the reputation of being a bit high-falutin'. I don't consider myself high falutin', but you know, I was curious. Figured I wouldn't fit in with the high falutin' crowd, but I would just keep a low falutin' profile while I admired the view.

We went into the anchor department store first. Olivia went to the juniors department, I went to the women's. Within a few minutes, I decided it was time I became high falutin'. The fabrics were amazing, and while I found three things on the clearance rack, I also found two that were still full-priced. One called my name. The other called my name and said it would love me forever. A sales clerk going by said, "Isn't that gorgeous? We just put it out last week."

So I answered the call. Besides the store itself being beautiful and the try-on rooms large and comfortable, besides the fabrics being lovely and the chorus of name-calling, I also wore a size smaller there. High falutin' siren song.

I began to think that maybe, just maybe, I did fit in here.

While I waited for the purchases to be wrapped up in high falutin' tissue paper, I mentioned that the clothes would likely be worn during upcoming presentations. A woman behind me said, "Oh!" and came to my side. "You're a writer?" she said. "My nieces are writers!" And we talked about writing. As we talked, two other clerks came over and joined in. By the time I walked out, I'd given away six business cards – three to the woman with the nieces. "One is for me!" she said.

Then we wandered into a high falutin' furniture and home goods store. Holy cow. This was HGTV on steroids. As we prepared to leave, I came across an extremely high-backed wooden chair that looked like something a king would sit in at a hunting lodge. "That," I said, "would make for a fantastic teacher's chair in the classroom."

My current teacher's chair was bought at Salvation Army twelve years ago. I love it. But it's getting a bit...worn out. And this new one...well, it demanded respect, lemme tell ya. I could RULE.

The manager came over. Told me the price. I laughed. I couldn't help myself. She said, "I could give you ten percent off." I laughed again and told her to call me if it ever came down by 50%. She told me they do sell the floor models from time to time and asked to take down my name and number. I gave her, you guessed it, my card.

"You're a writer?" she said. "I'm a poet!"

And we talked writing. And talked writing some more.

I've no doubt that she, and that chair, will end up in my classroom.

Wherever I go, I run into writers. It's the weirdest thing. I've found students in baristas, fast food clerks, gas station attendants, bookstore clerks, waysides, while walking the dogs. Michael often says, "How do you DO that?" when I go out for a bit and come home with new students.

I don't know. But I love it.

And you know what? High falutin', low falutin', and everywhere in between...I guess I fit in. I've always felt that I don't. I've always felt like the odd one out, the square peg, the one who just hovers on the outskirts.

But really, the world just seems to keep fitting itself around me. Giving me community. No matter where I am.

I like that.

And yes, that helps. Despite. Anyway.

### AUGUST 27, 2017

And so today's moment of happiness despite the news.

I had a difficult night last night. It was not expected. It took a while for me to unravel it today, to go after its source, and then to find today's moment in the realization.

I have a book launch coming up on September 26. I have always, always dreamed of being brought to a book launch in a limo. Yesterday morning, I called down to Michael and asked him if he thought it would be terrible if I rented a limo to bring me to my launch. I said, "I just don't think it's ever going to be done for me. And I feel like I'm running out of time."

It seems to me Michael answered that I deserved that indulgence, but I wasn't really listening anymore. I had to find a seat, fast. My breath was gone. Where did THAT thought come from?

A student once told me that he wanted to know when Death was coming. He wanted to see it, face it head on, watch it hit with wide open eyes. I've thought of that often since June 27th. And I've wondered if I've met now what will eventually take me from this world.

It's disconcerting.

I felt a little off for the rest of the day. Then, last night, we were watching an episode of Netflix's *Grace & Frankie*. It's from this past season, and in it, Frankie, played by Lily Tomlin, experiences a small stroke. Tomlin is an excellent actress, and in that moment, when she turns to Jane Fonda, unable to speak intelligibly and with one side of her mouth drooping, her eyes said it all. I have no control over what's happening to my body. Help me.

And I knew just how that felt. Tomlin's face nailed me between the eyes.

It's interesting, isn't it, that someone who has fought since she was a teenager for women to have the right to control their own bodies is now experiencing something within her body she has no control over?

Oh, how we deceive ourselves.

I meditated before bed last night. But instead of relaxing, I suddenly found myself in the midst of a panic attack. With my eyes closed, the voice of the guided meditation faded and all I could see, in all-capital huge purple letters, and I could hear it being shouted in my voice too, was WAIT...I HAD CANCER???????????

I don't use multiple punctuation marks. But behind my eyelids, there they were.

Another student last week, a doctor, when I told him that I was feeling more like myself, asked, "Who were you feeling like before?" He chuckled and said he always says that when someone says, "I'm just not feeling like myself." So who are you feeling like?

Before I began to feel like myself again, I was feeling like someone who was blindsided by cancer. And I was trying so very hard to get back to feeling like someone who doesn't have cancer. Someone who never had cancer.

Well, then. I am someone now who doesn't have cancer. I am someone who no longer has cancer. I will never ever be someone who has never had cancer again.

It all led to last night's big purple letters. And to no sleep until around six this morning.

And to a realization. I have always twitched when someone says, "I shouldn't feel bad. There are people who have it worse than I do." Of course there are. If you break your leg in two places, there's someone out there who broke it in three. If your home is destroyed by fire, there is someone out there whose home and family were destroyed by fire. If you were abandoned by your husband, there is someone out there who was abandoned by their mother…in the freezing cold…in the middle of the woods…which are infested with wolves.

Just because someone may have it worse doesn't invalidate what you're feeling.

I know I've been incredibly lucky since June 27th. The cancer was caught early. I didn't need a mastectomy. I don't need chemo. I've had a lumpectomy, I'm on medication to block estrogen for the next five to ten years, and tomorrow, I embark on four weeks of radiation. Compared to what some women go through, this is a cake walk.

But it's a cake walk with the worst-tasting cake ever. I'm not exactly digging into chocolate layer cake topped with coffee-flavored frosting here.

I've been doing quite the job of beating myself up when I've felt sad or overwhelmed or angry over all this, despite acknowledging that there are people who have it worse. I've been doing what I tell people not to do. And I've been doing it to the point of denial, telling myself I'm lucky to have it as good as I have, so soon, I will return to being someone who has never had cancer.

No, I won't.

A friend told me a while ago, "Everyone is telling you you're strong. You know you don't have to be, right?"

I do now.

Today is not a strong day. And I'm okay with that.

And yes, that helps. Despite. Anyway.

## AUGUST 28, 2017

And so today's moment of happiness despite the news.

Today was my first day of radiation. That sounds very weird to say. There are so many other firsts that sound better. My first day of school. My first day on the job. My first day as a wife, or my first day as a mother. Today is the first day of the rest of my life.

Boy, let's hope so.

Well, it was the first day of radiation. I have 19 more. I will have off on Saturdays and Sundays and on Labor Day. And I will be done on September 25.

The day before the *In Grace's Time* launch.

Whew.

It wasn't a bad experience, overall, except for the knowledge of what I was there for. A woman in the dressing room admired my hair and then asked if I wore it this way because it was growing back from chemo. I said no. She asked to touch it. I said sure. I think I made her day. "I'm going to do mine that way!" she said. She wore a baseball cap.

In the treatment room, I had to state my full name and my birthdate. They will ask me that each and every time, even though they will be seeing me almost every day over the next month. The treatment machine was not the same one I met a couple weeks ago. I introduced myself. I'm still calling it Xappa and chalking it up to a case of mistaken identity. It's an odd and eerie-looking machine, animalistic, with a long neck and a round head. It twists all around me, starting from below my right shoulder to up above my left. It gets pretty close – the technicians assured me it would not touch me – so that it can reach its target, the spots designated by complex computer calculations. It hums while it works and I decided that was charming. It – He – was busy and focused.

I will admit to starting to hyperventilate partway through. I closed my eyes then, fell into my own hum, breathed deeply.

And then it was over.

For the day. 19 more times.

Tomorrow, after saying hello to Xappa, I will start with my eyes closed. He and I will hum together. We'll get this done.

I had to stop on my way out to get a print-out of my 19 appointments. When I gave my name, I thought the receptionist was going to squeal her way past the sound barrier. "It's YOU!" she said. "You're THAT one! You're THAT one!"

I will admit to wanting to duck and cover. "Um…what one?" I asked.

"The writer! You're the one with the book coming out!"

And I was suddenly surrounded by nurses and technicians and receptionists. Oh, my.

"Tell us about your book!" they all said.

So I did. And I felt myself come fully back into my skin as I did so. No hyperventilation. No duck and cover. Just me. THAT one.

And then I thanked them all for whatever part they played in getting my care and treatment done in time for the launch on September 26.

You know, I've always wanted to be THAT one. There have been other times I've been identified as THAT one. But I don't know that I ever wanted to be THAT one in a cancer treatment center. But now I am.

I walked out smiling.

And yes, that helps. Despite. Anyway.

## AUGUST 29, 2017

And so today's moment of happiness despite the news.

I don't know when the last time was that I was out on a weeknight. Out meaning out…not working, not at home. Having…what's that called? Fun.

I also don't know when the last time was that I attended a Milwaukee Brewers game. I do know that we did the Macarena in the stands. Several times. And somehow it became better choreographed with every drink…oh, wait, I mean inning.

Michael's employer hosted a picnic and ball game tonight. It caused me to do something I don't think I've ever done. I canceled evening clients and class. To go to a ball game with my family.

I very nearly didn't go. I woke up out of sorts this morning. I don't know if it was because yesterday was the first day of radiation (and today was the second), or if it was because of our condo garbage being picked up right outside my open bedroom window at five-thirty in the morning when I'd only been asleep since three, and the special truck that picks up the dumpster and empties it seemed to think it had to shake the damn thing several times before letting go, or if it was that I got up an hour earlier than usual for a client. I was tired. I was crabby. My stomach was a little messed up. And I just felt a bit down. While I am on the last step of breast cancer treatment, this is the first time I've dealt with it on an everyday in-your-face level, as every day, I get bare and my breast and I stare a radiation machine in its Star Wars face. At the same time that I see a definite end date, it also just feels relentless.

I tried to get someone else to take my place at the game. No one would. In the end, I decided to go.

It was worth it.

While I don't like baseball, I do enjoy going to games. I like to watch the people, I like the music, and while I don't understand what they're doing, I do admire athleticism. Tonight, I had all of that, and I had all of that under a beautiful open-roof sky. Fireworks went off and I love fireworks. I had nachos. I bought my daughter a Milwaukee Brewers pink and white unicorn. Really. My husband had a sundae in a miniature helmet. And on one side of me was my daughter and the other side was my husband. I sang along to the Turtles' "Happy Together", directing one lyric in particular to Michael while my daughter cringed in embarrassment and I didn't care:

*I can't see me lovin' nobody but you*
*For all my life*
*When you're with me, baby the skies'll be blue*
*For all my life*

The skies were blue. On a night when I am typically at work in the classroom and on the computer.

Oh, and I fell in love with a player named Domingo Santana, just because of his name.

The Brewers were playing the Cardinals, and I was born in St. Louis and lived there for my first six years. Partway through the game, my daughter asked me who I was rooting for.

"The Brewers," I said.

"Why not the Cardinals? That's your hometown," she said.

"This is my hometown."

"You weren't born here."

No, I wasn't. And after leaving St. Louis, I moved to northern Minnesota for six years. But from twelve years old on, I've been in Wisconsin.

"This is home," I said.

I put my arm around my daughter. My husband put his arm around me. Home.

The Brewers lost. I didn't.

And yes, that helps. Despite. Anyway.

### AUGUST 30, 2017

And so today's moment of happiness despite the news.

A few days ago, Michael and Olivia were over at Walgreens, buying Olivia first-day-of-school supplies. In high school, you don't get your supply list until you get your syllabi for each class, so we just wanted to make sure she went with the basics – notebooks, folders, pencils, highlighters. They forgot the list and so Olivia texted me, asking for a few details. And then she texted,

"Dad got Orange Oreos. ☺"

My response: "ORANGE OREOS??????"

As I've said before, I do not write in multiple punctuation marks. But this warranted it. My first thought was absolute wordless joy. My second thought was, This is August. They can't possibly be ripe.

Orange Oreos are an October food. But…oh. Orange Oreos!

You know how sometimes there are themes or common occurrences in a writer's work? Anyone who has read my stories or novels has seen a prevalence of Oreos. And in particular, the Orange Oreo. In my novel, *The Home For Wayward Clocks*, there is a story/chapter titled Marriage in Orange, in which Orange Oreos are practically a character. And they're even used in a, well, intimate, erotic sort of way.

<blush>

Now here's the thing. I don't know why Orange Oreos affect me the way that they do.

Does the orange stuff in the middle taste like orange?

No.

Do the Oreos, even though they are orange, taste like any other type of plain Oreo?

Some would say so, but I would argue that they do not.

Why?

I don't have the damnedest idea. They're just the absolute BEST.

I don't want Chips Ahoy. I don't want Nutter Butters (oh, ick – and remember the commercials? *Have a 'nother Nutter Butter Peanut Butter Sandwich Cookie!* No, thank you.) I don't want Fig Newtons (*Ooey-gooey rich and chewy insides! Soft and cakey tender flakey outsides!*), Fudge Stripes, or those weird (though yummy) neapolitan-striped wafer cookies. I don't want any of the other special color or special flavor Oreos. Whoever came up with the Swedish Fish Oreo was certifiably insane.

But Orange Oreos. Oh, baby. Curl my toes.

I should probably mention that the Orange Oreo is commonly called the Halloween Oreo – especially by its maker, Nabisco. The chocolate cookie part has Halloween-type creatures stamped into it. I don't care. That's not what makes it special. It's the ORANGE.

So my moment of happiness today. Right now.

Michael is downstairs, teaching a class.

Olivia is at a friend's house.

The dogs are asleep. The cats are asleep. I'm done with clients for the day.

It's quiet. My deck door is open and while I hear the sounds of the city, I also hear night-bug type noises. There is a rain-fresh breeze.

And by my side: a stack of Orange Oreos and a cup of hot, strong black coffee.

No, I don't share.

And yes, that helps. Despite. Anyway.

## AUGUST 31, 2017

And so today's moment of happiness despite the news.

Today, I realized that, in the middle of all this hot mess breast cancer, I forgot my daughter. And in that realization, I just wanted to wave the white flag and fall to my knees.

My daughter and I walked her schedule at her new high school again today. School starts tomorrow. It was partway through our walk-through that I realized.

"Olivia," I said, "what time does school get out?"

"3:05," she said.

When I had to work with the Cancer Center to set up my 20 days of radiation, I gave them a window of 1 to 5. My writing time. My meditation time. But radiation needs to be done. I worked it around classes. I worked it around clients. The majority of my appointments were set at 3:30.

I forgot about Olivia. I forgot about school.

For a 3:30 appointment, I have to check in at 3:15. There is no way her final bell can ring at 3:05, she can pack up and run out, and I can get her home and then be at the Cancer Center by 3:15.

And it was about then my overwhelm valve blew.

Oh, this week. What a dose of reality. All along, I was told radiation was easy. Just lay down for ten minutes a day. Meditate. Take a nap. Simple!

It's not easy.

Every day, I face that machine. Every day, I lay there while everyone else runs from the room to avoid what the machine is doing to me. Destroying unhealthy tissue and healthy tissue to make sure that unhealthy tissue can't come back. And every day, I have to face, for ten minutes, this new reality. Cancer invaded my life.

Every day, I walk under a sign that says Cancer Center. And I see people wearing baseball caps and head scarves. People who look like they would wisp in a fan-breeze down the hallway if the nurse didn't anchor them by the arm. I heard one woman coming before I even saw her – her breathing sounded like she was underwater. I heard her breathe past me and I heard her breathe down the hall.

I tell myself every day how lucky I am.

But then today, I realized I forgot my own daughter in the middle of this hot mess breast cancer.

The technician came to get me. Her name is Denise. She started to say, "Hey, Kathie, how are –" and then I looked at her. In an instant, she was holding me, rocking me, and I just completely blew apart. That's not something I do. The other technician came in and hugged and rocked me from behind and I became the stuffing in a huge comfort sandwich. My own Orange Oreo, though I was wearing gray.

When Denise asked me what was wrong, I still couldn't find my voice. I just motioned around the room. And she said, "It's just all this, isn't it."

Yes. Just all this. And then I said, "I forgot my daughter! How could I forget my daughter!"

And I was sandwiched again. There was no hurry. There was no glancing at the clock, even though I'm sure I messed up their schedule. There was just soothing and comfort and compassion and care. And lots and lots of kleenex.

And then they left the room so I could be zapped. I watched Xappa move around me and hum and I felt remainder tears roll from the corners of my eyes, over my temples and into my ears. I thought of the woman with the drowning lungs and I wondered if that's where her tears went.

As I was helped off the table, Denise said, "You didn't forget your daughter. You never ever would. You're just full to the brim right now. It will get better. This will be over. You're okay."

And she hugged me again. Which was just what I needed. That hug pulled me back together. At least for now.

And yes, that helps. Despite. Anyway.

# Chapter Nine

## SEPTEMBER 1, 2017

And so today's moment of happiness despite the news.

This morning, after waking, I walked downstairs to get some breakfast.

It was very quiet.

The dishwasher was already emptied, dishes put away. For the first time in a couple months, I retrieved my morning coffee mug from the cupboard, not from the dishwasher.

The counters were cleared – no dirty breakfast dishes waiting to go in the dishwasher. It was all already done.

I went to the second floor deck to open the door and let the fresh air in. I glanced in Olivia's room; I was ABLE to glance in Olivia's room. The door wasn't tightly shut to protect a sleeping-in girl. Her bed was made. Her room was (relatively) picked up.

She was at school. First day of junior year, in a new school for her, an old school for me. The school I graduated from, and so did my three older children. I went to three different high schools. But this school, the one she walked into today, is the one I consider MY school.

Michael was at work.

I prepared for my own workday, and it was quiet, and it felt normal.

Oh, it felt normal.

Last year, in her old school, a school we chose to send her to, taking her outside of her district, Olivia fell victim to cyberbullying, and also traditional "live" bullying within the school walls. It was a horrible experience for the whole family. Every morning, she went to school with dread hanging over her like a black cloak, and every morning, I looked in her empty bedroom and draped the maternal version of that cloak over my own shoulders. I watched the clock and counted the hours until she got home, when I would have her safe again. But with cyberbullying, there is no safe. Even with supposed school "consequences", it kept going. There are no walls on the internet. No doors to close.

So we pulled her from that school and put her into her district school. The school I went to, The school her siblings went to. The one I love. When I have dreams of high school, that's where I am. And now, so is she. They took such good care of me there. I have faith they will take care of her too.

Normal.

When I glanced in her room today, it was with a sense of hope.

Olivia came home chattering about kids who just sat down and started talking with her at lunch. About the boy who was nice to her in art class. About the friend from elementary school who recognized her and hugged her in the hallway. She's been invited to the football game tonight.

A quiet house. A sense of hope. A child who is chattering at breakneck speed and happy.

Normal.

And yes, there was another dose of radiation for me in the afternoon.

But I am focusing on the normal. And on my daughter who deserves to be treated with respect, with kindness, and with care. And who deserves every happiness.

And yes, that helps. Despite. Anyway.

## SEPTEMBER 2, 2017

And so today's moment of happiness despite the news.

Today was a day off in many ways. No radiation. Holiday on Monday, so I don't need to start reading manuscripts for next week until tomorrow. I not only slept in, but I stayed in bed for a while after waking, just…lolling. What a great word. And that's what it felt like. Lolling.

After an afternoon of gloriously not–much, I started poking around the movie theater sites. Maybe a movie, I thought. A movie would be nice.

And that's when I saw it.

*Close Encounters of the Third Kind.*

It's the 40th anniversary. And one theatre here has it on the Ultrascreen.

There were no Ultrascreens when I fell in love with that movie when I was seventeen years old. While everyone else was going crazy over this movie called *Star Wars*, babbling about alien bar scenes, light sabers, young heroes named Han Solo, old men named Obi–Wan Kenobe, I was going crazy over a musical spaceship rising over Devil's Tower. Richard Dreyfus becoming obsessed with sculpting mashed potatoes. A missing child. A clanging railroad signal.

I don't know how many times I went to see it. I had *Close Encounters* t–shirts. Posters. Books with the movie's storyline and books describing how the movie was made. I remember the first time I realized that spaceships came zipping out of each of the stars in the Big Dipper. "Wait!" I wanted to yell. "Rewind! I never saw that before! Let me see it again!" My mother even painted the scene of the ship coming over Devil's Tower for me. On black velvet. It hung proudly in my living room for years, until it was punctured in a move.

Some people have Elvis on black velvet. I had *Close Encounters*.

To this day, I don't know why that movie grabbed me so much. All I know is that it did. I dreamt it, read it, watched it, breathed it.

Maybe tonight, seeing it at 57 years old, I'll be able to figure out the connection. But even if I don't, I don't care. I can't wait to see it. And on the Ultrascreen!

Yesterday, my almost 17-year old daughter started school at the same high school I went to at 17. I started there as a junior. She is starting there as a junior.

I fell in love with *Close Encounters* when I was 17. Tonight, I will bring my almost 17-year old daughter to see it, on the movie's 40th anniversary.

Earlier today, I went shopping with my almost 17-year old daughter. At one point, I looked at her in a drop-dead amazing dress, and I thought, I don't know if I really remember what it feels like to be 17 anymore. I look at her and I think, Holy cow! I don't remember feeling Holy cow. Maybe I need to remember.

Tonight, I'm going back to 17.

And yes, that helps. Despite. Anyway.

### SEPTEMBER 3, 2017

And so today's moment of happiness despite the news.

It's that time of year again. As a Starbucks fanatic (some would say addict), I know it well. Your streamlined Starbucks goes all to hell. Seasoned baristas go off to college. Some, finished with college, go off to other full-time jobs. Unseasoned baristas, who will become seasoned baristas, move in. And what it all means is an extended waiting time in the drive-thru lane. And a few mistakes here and there. Nothing earth-shattering. The other day, instead of my usual grande iced cinnamon dolce latte with only two pumps of syrup, I received a venti iced coffee, heavy on cream and sugar. Yuk. My daughter ordered a cinnamon dolce frappuccino and received an all-white concoction that clearly had no coffee in it.

Basically, this is the time of year when you prepare for your coffee break to be a break in and of itself, before ordering your coffee, after you order your coffee, and after you've received your coffee. Make your car comfortable. And doublecheck your order. It's no biggie. Though of course, it is, to some people.

Today was a wait-in-line day, even though it was Sunday. The weather was lovely. I was in the convertible. I had Linkin Park's new CD in the player. So I tilted my head back and relaxed. There were cars in front of me. There were cars behind me. There really was no choice. The Starbucks I go to has the drive-thru built in such a way, with high curbs and hedges, there is no way out once you're in line.

Well, others felt differently. I heard one man yelling from three cars up. Some people honked. Engines revved. I felt like fuming at those that were fuming, but I just kept listening to the music and soaking in the sun and pleasant breeze.

Finally, there was just one car in front of me. I couldn't hear what the woman was saying, but I could hear the tone in her voice. I watched as drinks were handed to her, and I watched as drinks were shoved back. I kept count. After a total of four drinks were passed and rejected, the fifth one seemed to be correct. "I'm so sorry –" I heard the young barista say, but the driver hit the accelerator and she squealed away.

I drove up. The young barista was staring at the counter. I wondered if I should take a photo of her, to put in my own personal dictionary, to define dejection. Cross-referenced with frustration. And desperation. Then she looked at me. "I'm sorry for the wait," she said. I heard fear.

"It's okay," I said. "It's not a problem."

She looked back at the counter and I saw a line-up of drinks waiting there. She glanced at her screen. "You had the cinnamon latte, right?" she asked.

There are a few cinnamon-type drinks at Starbucks, so I said, as gently as I could, "A grande iced cinnamon dolce latte with two pumps."

She studied the drinks again, then picked one up. "There's no sticker on this," she said, referring to the stickers identifying each drink typically stuck to the side of the cup. "Does this look like the right drink to you?"

Now, I suppose maybe this could be seen as rude, but I began to laugh. Starbucks drinks don't usually have too many physically defining characteristics, other than brown, and this just struck me as so funny. But when I began to laugh, the young barista's mouth quirked. And then she began to laugh too.

New photo, new definition. Relief. Cross-referenced with gratitude.

I glanced at the long line behind me. "It looks just right," I said, though I wasn't sure at all. "I'll take it."

"Thank you!" she said, and it was the most impassioned thank you I've heard in a long time.

"You're going to be just fine," I said, and then I drove off.

Turns out it was my drink. But I wouldn't have gone back and complained if it wasn't.

Sometimes giving someone a break lowers your own blood pressure, as well as his or hers.

I made a new friend today. At least until she goes off to college.

And yes, that helps. Despite. Anyway.

## SEPTEMBER 4, 2017

And so today's moment of happiness despite the news.

*DENIM: Noun. A heavy, Z-twist, twill cotton for jeans, overalls, and other work and leisure garments.*

HAPPY JEANS: pants made of denim that, over the years, have softened to more than quilt, more than blanket, more than cottonballs, more than clouds. Just soft. And thin. And threadbare. And more than likely destined for the ragbag or the dumpster, except for the sentiment and comfort in the barely-there almost-gone weave.

Just before my shower this morning, I yelled down the stairs to Michael and Livvy. "Can you bring up my holey, barely-there, almost-gone, almost-dead happy jeans?"

They knew exactly which pair I meant. The jeans were fresh out of the dryer, and every time they're fresh out of the dryer, I'm afraid that most of them will be left behind in the lint filter.

It takes a while to become happy jeans. They definitely don't start that way. They start out stiff and new from the store. And then gradually, as the line of happy jeans before them are worn and sadly discarded, through a time of being worn in public and then thrown in the washer and dryer, through years of threads coming loose and holes beginning to appear and the gentling of the stiffness and the softening of material, they get promoted to happy jeans.

It takes history to become a pair of happy jeans.

These are jeans that can no longer be worn out in public because they are more hole than jean. And these are not fashionable holes. These are not the strategically placed holes you see worn in the mall or to school or to more liberal workplaces. There's nothing strategically placed about these holes. These holes are life-placed.

But when I pull them on, they cover me in soft, in gentle, in comfort and soothe, in consolation, in relief, in mollify in pacify, in oh-so-good that moves beyond even pajamas.

I don't like pajamas. They're for sleep, though I don't wear them then either. But happy jeans are for living. For being awake and being happy to be so.

This is the third day of a three-day weekend. I've slept in every day (without pajamas). On Saturday, I didn't do a bit of work. And I didn't have to go to radiation.

On Friday, when I had my Weekly Review with the radiation oncologist, I mentioned that my final day of treatment would be a Monday, the day before the launch of *In Grace's Time* at a bookstore in Milwaukee. Since my diagnosis on June 27th, my three doctors, surgeon, radiation oncologist and medical oncologist, have put their heads together to create a schedule that would get me through treatment by the book's launch.

"You really brought it down to the wire," I said. "The day before!"

Dr. Jones laughed, but then he said, "You know, we have three people coming in on Monday (Labor Day). They can't go a day without treatment, so we'll be here, and if we're doing three, we can do four. Do you want to come in so that you can be done on the Friday before the launch? Then you'd have the weekend and Monday to be out of treatment before the big day." He shrugged. "It won't make any difference medically, but emotionally…"

I considered it. But then I said no. Since there wasn't any difference medically, I figured I needed three days off more now than then. The adrenalin of the launch event will get me through.

But today, the last day of the three days, the day before I return to radiation tomorrow, I reached for those happy jeans. Those jeans and a gray t-shirt that has the silhouette of Wisconsin on it, with the word "home" in script over the state.

Like their predecessors before them, the happy jeans worked their magic. I'm ready for tomorrow. I'm ready for the rest of it.

And I'm looking toward September 26th with so much anticipation. Maybe I'll wear my happy jeans.

And yes, that helps. Despite. Anyway.

## SEPTEMBER 5, 2017

And so today's moment of happiness despite the news.

Sometimes, moments of happiness are tinged with moments of absolute snark.

Several months ago, a theatre company in Colorado contacted my publicist. They wanted to see some of my stories for possible inclusion in a series called Stories On Stage.

Short stories brought to life.

My publicist sent them my collections, *Oddities & Endings* and *Enlarged Hearts*, and the short story that appeared in Prairie Schooner, "Clean", nominated for a Pushcart Prize.

And then, well, it was months.

Today, my publicist emailed me, with the header, "Ready to smile?" She told me they decided to do one of my stories, "Snap Dragon", a story that appears in *Oddities & Endings* and is a commentary on social media.

I was, and am, ecstatic.

Fiction writers, memoirists, essayists, poets don't often get to see an audience response to our work. If we're lucky, we run into someone who happens to be reading our work. Soon after *The Home For Wayward Clocks* was released, I was at the Starbucks drive-thru (of course) and the barista leaned way out of the window. "Kathie!" she whispered. "Someone is in here, reading your book!"

Well, you know I had to park and go in and see. And I analyzed everything, from the way she held the book to her posture to how often she stopped to sip from her latte or check her phone. The pink on her cheeks. The curve of her fingers.

I decided she liked my book. I went home, beaming.

And now…my characters are going to be on stage. These particular characters are nameless…but they're going to take form. And they're going to be seen by between 200 and 300 people per show and there will be two shows.

Ohmygosh. How cool is that?

Months ago, I told my publicist, "If this happens, I'm going. I want to see it." I volunteered to do an author talkback.

And now…well, now breast cancer. When my characters step onto the stage, I will still be having radiation treatments. I will still be staring up at

Xappa once a day, Monday through Friday, for ten minutes.

Can I say this? Fuck.

I am tired of being tethered. I am tired of first cancer and now cancer recovery being the center of my orbit. What did George Jetson say on the treadmill at the end of the cartoon show, *The Jetsons*? Get me off of this crazy thing!

And…I am getting off of this crazy thing. In fourteen more treatments. September 25. I know that.

But today, I lay beneath Xappa and I listened to his now familiar hum and watched his rise and fall from my left to my right and I telepathically threw every four-letter word I could think of at him. And I know a lot of them. And I'm a writer – I can make up new ones and create new combinations.

But when I got off the table, I said, "Thank you, Xappa."

Because fourteen more treatments.

And whether or not I'm in Colorado, my characters will step onto the stage. They are going to take form. They are going to be seen by 200 to 300 people. Per show. Two shows.

My publicist emailed, "Ready to smile?"

Oh, I am.

And yes, that helps. Despite. Anyway.

### SEPTEMBER 6, 2017

And so today's moment of happiness despite the news.

Today, when I walked into the Cancer Center, I was bummed. Today's treatment was scheduled smack-dab during a class that I teach, the AllWriters' Wednesday Afternoon Women Writers' Workshop. It started at 1:00; my treatment was at 1:30. I set up the classroom, which includes coffee and treats, greeted my arriving students, then left them on their own as I ran out the door.

Not the way I like to teach. Not the way I like to run my business. And once again, I felt like cancer was calling the shots for me.

I lectured myself all the way there. This is going to end. This will be all right. You are all right. On September 26, your life will return to normal. You're one of the lucky ones.

And all the way there, as I droned to myself, I became more and more bummed. Bummed, bummedier, bummediest.

I'm a writer. I'm allowed to make up words.

So I was dragging when I walked through the doors. By now, I know the routine. I read the positive message on the blackboard, I receive a cheery greeting, I'm walked to the changing area and waiting room, I strip from the waist up, pull on a robe, lock up my stuff, and wait for the technician to bring me back to Xappa's lair.

Today, the technician greeted me with a huge grin. "Hey!" she said. "It's the day before your release!"

I was startled. Today was treatment #7 out of 20. For a moment, I wondered if I'd been granted a miraculous reprieve. "No," I said. "This is only Day 7."

She laughed. "Not this," she said. "Your book!"

My book!

*In Grace's Time* will be released tomorrow, September 7th. It's my 7th book, being released on the 7th, in 2017, the year I turned 57.

But that's not my moment of happiness.

My moment is that in the middle of their workday, a day like all of their days which are full from morning to evening with man after woman after man after woman coming in for cancer treatments, this technician, and the others that I spoke to, remembered. Not only did they remember, but they remembered and talked to me about it on a day when I was bummed, bummedier, bummediest. On a day when I felt that I wasn't living up to my responsibilities, my students' expectations, and my own expectations. On a day when I felt that cancer was calling the shots and I was sinking.

I didn't feel like that when I left. I was smiling. I sang all the way home and walked into my classroom and taught my heart out.

At the Cancer Center, they know who I am and they reminded me today of just who that is.

And...as long as we're counting, the day that they reminded me that my 7th book will be released tomorrow on the 7th, in 2017, in the year I turn 57 was Day 7 of radiation.

They remembered. And they cared. They saw me.

And yes, that helps. Despite. Anyway.


### SEPTEMBER 7, 2017

And so today's moment of happiness despite the news.

I've been sort of geeking out over the number 7. Maybe geeking out isn't the right word – but I like it, so I'm going to use it. But the number 7 has been pointing out joy to me lately, and as a word person, I'm surprised to find a number that is making me happy.

I'm not into numbers or numerology. I did win the opportunity to have my numerology chart done once and the woman who did it was amazing. She was an old lady – and I say that with the utmost respect. She was old and she said so. I gave her the information she needed and she had me to her house to go over the results.

When I stepped in her doorway, she grabbed me by the hand. The eyes that looked at me were not old. If blue can blaze, they did. "You are the one I'm supposed to have as my last reading," she said. "I know I can be done now. I'm so glad to meet you."

She died less than a month later. I was her last reading.

The things she told me were incredible, to the point I stopped taking notes and just listened. I still have all the pages of her work and I wish now I'd taken those notes because I haven't the faintest idea what it all means. I mostly remember being stunned.

So I have a healthy respect for numbers, even as I don't understand them.

So the 7 thing started coming up last winter, when my new novel was accepted by a new publisher. One of the things he offered me was the ability to choose my own release date. "September," I said. "September 7." I knew I wanted September, and 7 just seemed like a good date.

But then I sat down and thought about it. This was my 7th book. Being released on the 7th, in 2017, in the year I turned 57. 7 is supposed to be lucky, right? I felt very lucky.

I wrote yesterday about the technicians lifting my spirits by reminding me, actually remembering themselves despite dealing with hundreds of patients, that my book was being released today. They did this on Day 7 of radiation.

And I also wrote about how a theatre in Denver is going to put one of my stories on stage. Guess what day the show will happen? September 17.

So I was having fun today, reveling in the 7s, when my mind suddenly popped over to the day of diagnosis with breast cancer. The day I consider one of the worst days of my life.

June 27.

I sat with that 7 for a while. And I thought that perhaps my joy in 7s was going to disappear. Despite all those wonderful 7s I'd been experiencing, there was THAT 7. That awful 7. The worst-day-of-my-life 7.

But then I turned it around.

June 27 was the day that the cancer was caught early. It was the day that began the process to stop it in its tracks and then to wipe it out of my system. It was the day my life was saved.

It was the day I was saved.

I was damn lucky.

The joy is still here.

And yes, that helps. Despite. Anyway.

## SEPTEMBER 8, 2017

And so today's moment of happiness despite the news.

*But I always find my way back to story. And I always find my way home.*
*–Sherman Alexie, "Words" from You Don't Have To Say You Love Me*

I started my 20-day stint of radiation treatments for breast cancer on August 28th. Today was Day #9. Since August 28th, I haven't written a word, beyond this blog. My novel-in-progress has ground to a halt.

The dry spell is mostly because of practical reasons. I write in the afternoons. My mornings are for clients, and my evenings, from 5:00 on, are for more clients and for classes. Radiation has been plunked into my afternoons, typically with my having to leave the house at 3:00. By the time I finish with morning clients, it's noon, and then there's the dogs to walk, the bed to make, lunch to eat, phone calls and emails to catch up on for the studio…and by the time I sit down at my desk to write, I have barely an hour to do so. I'm usually pretty good at cramming a lot into an hour, but with this situation, my eyes keep shifting to the clock, watching 3:00 move closer, and feeling my anxiety ramp up. I worry about the radiation itself, I worry about falling too far into my storyline to notice the time passing and then running late, messing up the Cancer Center's tight schedule, I worry, I worry, I worry. And I don't get anything done.

By the time I get back from radiation, it's usually 4:00 and I have an hour before client time again. I've also learned, the hard way, that within a half-hour of receiving radiation, I crash. So it's a good time to meditate, which lately has become a really nice word for nap.

I am not one of those people that declares with passion, "I have to write! It's like…like BREATHING to me!"

Writing is not like breathing to me. I don't often think about breathing. It comes automatically. I do think about writing – a lot – and it doesn't come automatically. It takes work. The only time breathing is as hard for me as writing is in the middle of an asthma attack.

When I don't have time to write, when writing is taken away from me for an extended period, I get sad. I've tried taking full vacations – time away without teaching OR writing – and it doesn't work, because I don't feel rested, I don't feel relaxed, I don't feel happy. So I write.

I hadn't written since August 28th. And I'd been staring Xappa the Radiation Monster in the face every day since August 28th, during time that I normally spend writing.

I was getting sad. Even finding my Today's Moment was getting harder and harder. I'd have the Moment, be happy I had the Moment, then return to sadness.

Then, this week, a writing trifecta:

1) A new magazine contacted me, praising a story the editor saw in another magazine, and asking me if I would please consider submitting to them. They wanted "a Kathie Giorgio story."

2) Book #7, Novel #4, *In Grace's Time*, was released. The reviews have been calling it delightful, wonderful, beautiful.

3) A theatre in Denver, Colorado, selected one of my short stories to put on stage for their Stories On Stage series.

And while I was thrilled, I also grew a bit sadder. I wasn't writing. I likely wouldn't write until September 26, my first day without radiation. I wanted to write NOW. I wanted to be the writer who earned the trifecta above.

At lunch today, I read from Sherman Alexie's new memoir, *You Don't Have To Say You Love Me*. And I read those words above. *But I always find my way back to story. And I always find my way home.*

I bolted my lunch. And I went upstairs to my desk and I opened up the file containing the novel-in-progress. And then I looked at the clock.

An hour and fifteen minutes. What if I sank? What if I lost myself? What if I was late?

What if I wasn't?

I tore my eyes from the clock and grabbed my cell phone. I set the alarm for an hour and fifteen minutes from then.

And then yes, I sank. I lost myself. And ohmygod, it felt good.

I didn't finish an entire scene. Which disturbs the hyper-organized part of my brain. But…I wrote.

I found my way back to story. And because I found my way back to story, I found my way home.

And yes, that helps. Despite. Anyway.

And so today's moment of happiness despite the news.

I had a discussion with a woman this morning, someone I never met before, but who was talking to me because she was a breast cancer survivor. She asked me how I was doing with the radiation. She asked if I'd been burned yet. She asked if I was itching to the point I couldn't stand it anymore yet. She asked if I was so tired, all I wanted to do was sleep, but I couldn't sleep…yet.

I said no. But then I told her I was having difficulty with the radiation on an emotional level.

She said, Aren't you about halfway done?

I said yes, that I just finished day #9 and I had 11 treatments yet.

And then she basically told me to just suck it up.

Apparently, I'm only allowed to have difficulty with radiation if I'm burned, crazy-itchy, exhausted, and unable to sleep.

I ended the conversation quickly.

Later, Michael, Olivia and I were at Home Depot. We were trying to get a key made for Olivia. While Olivia and I were waiting, she spotted a keychain with a pink ribbon on it. "Look, Mama," she said.

I looked. And then I looked away.

She asked if I was looking forward to Pinktober, the month of October, which is Breast Cancer Awareness month and many businesses turn their lights and signs pink. She said she would wear pink for me in October. She said she would show me support.

I told her that I wasn't looking forward to Pinktober. That maybe I would next year, when this is all behind me. But that right now, everywhere I look, there's cancer. Turn on the TV, there's commercials about cancer. Go on the computer, there's articles about cancer. Go get a key made, there's a keychain about cancer.

"I'm just so tired of it, Livvy," I said. "I can't get out from under it. Radiation every day. Cancer Center every day. Look here, look there, see pink ribbons and cancer. Cancer, cancer everywhere."

When I went in for my initial surgical consultation, I was given this huge binder, tucked into a bag that looked like the black and white of a cowskin. The binder had so much stuff in it – resources, magazines, booklets, slots for places to keep track of my appointments and test results and medications and recommendations. A pink notebook. A pink pen. It's been sitting on the floor by my reading chair since I got it and I could see it, every day, from my desk. Earlier this week, I took the whole thing and stuffed it under all the clothes in my closet.

Olivia said that she loves Autism Awareness Month and when everything is lit up blue. I told her that this might be because she has such a good handle on her own autism, that she deals with it with grace and intelligence and compassion.

"I might feel better about Pinktober when I get to that point too," I said. But right now, I'm not there. I wish I was. But I'm not.

And then I thought of the woman I talked with today and I immediately felt guilty, because I'm not burned, I'm not crazy-itchy, I'm not exhausted and I am able to sleep. I wanted to put my head through a wall and scream, Why aren't you handling this better?

And then Olivia said, "Oh, Mama," and she flung her arms around my neck. This almost-seventeen year old young woman, who typically walks ten feet in front of me in public, who won't hug me outside of our house and who rolls her eyes if I hug her, well, she threw her arms around me in the middle of Home Depot and hugged the stuffing out of me. She planted a solid kiss on my cheek.

And that was just what I needed.

I thought of the woman I talked to this morning and I decided she needs to meet my daughter and learn just a bit of her grace and intelligence and compassion.

Olivia will wear pink in October. And I will wear blue in April.

And yes, that helps. Despite. Anyway.


### SEPTEMBER 10, 2017

And so today's moment of happiness despite the news.

When I was first diagnosed with breast cancer, I had two major fears. Dying, of course. But also medical bills. And well, actually, there have been about a bajillion fears, I guess. But those are the ones that ranked highest.

Last year, Michael lost his job. Which meant we lost our insurance. I own my own business, and so our only options were Cobra, which was ridiculous, and private insurance through Obamacare, which we couldn't afford. I have to say, though, that this in no way reflects how I feel about Obamacare and the Affordable Care Act. Obamacare wasn't perfect – but it was a step in the right direction. If anything, I think our situation at that time only expresses how much our country needs an Obamacare that reaches even further than it did. So...for a few weeks, we were without insurance. And it was terrifying.

But then Michael landed a job and within a few weeks, we were insured again. At first, I wasn't so sure about it – the insurance company mistakenly told us we had what seemed to be an insurmountable deductible. But I put it out of my mind. We'd be okay.

Fast forward several months, and I was blindsided at my mammogram. Let me tell you, that deductible loomed large – as did the 80/20 split that followed after the deductible was met. I actually considered not going through surgery and not receiving treatment, because of the debt I would put my family – and my business – into.

Then we discovered that while it was a large family deductible, we also had a $5000 individual deductible. I met that before I even got to surgery. And then...and then...insurance took over.

Last night, I said to Michael that I was still worried, because the bills from radiation hadn't started coming in yet. So Michael went on the insurance website and looked.

My bill so far (and I'm not quite halfway through radiation): just over $8000.

What insurance has taken care of: just over $8000.

My bill: zip.

My knees actually went weak. I had to sit down.

Nobody – NOBODY – should have to choose between healthcare and family. The last thing a person dealing with a crisis needs to worry about is how to pay the bills. One of the first things I was told when the diagnosis hit was that I needed to find a way to reduce stress and relax. My response was immediate: "How can I do that when I'm afraid this will cost me my business, my home, everything my family needs?"

The worry was phenomenal.

It's not over yet, but the worry isn't as intense anymore. I know – again – that I'm one of the lucky ones.

My happiness today was swirled with a big helping of anger. Quality healthcare should be available to everyone.

My happiness today was also swirled with a feeling of selfishness – I'm happy we were saved by a great job for Michael and insurance that was there when we needed it. But I know that doesn't solve the problem at large.

My knees went weak. And a huge burden was lifted from my shoulders.

And yes, that helps. Despite Anyway.

### SEPTEMBER 11, 2017

And so today's moment of happiness despite the news.

In the last 48 hours, I had two women, breast cancer survivors, ask me, "So…have you gotten burned yet?"

Burned?

They were referring to receiving radiation therapy, something I'm in the middle of. Day #10, with 10 to go. I'd been told that the skin might get a little pink. But these women were talking burns. Blistering, peeling, painful burns.

No, I haven't been burned. I haven't even looked pink. Yet.

"Oh," one of the women said. "You're just hitting day 10. It should happen any day now. It's all downhill from here."

The other woman said, "I began to itch so badly, I literally couldn't stand it another second. I called my doctor and demanded a prescription anti-itch cream."

I felt sick. I was already having issues dealing with the emotional impact of radiation. Heaping on more made me feel like I was being nudged steadily toward a cliff.

So when I went in for radiation today, I asked one of the nurses about it, while I waited to see the doctor for my weekly review. "Oh, yeah," she said. "Happens to everyone." When I told her I was heading out of state this weekend to Denver and I was now worried about what would happen if I erupted while far from home, she left the room and came back with a baggie of different creams.

I now had an arsenal for an enemy I don't want to face.

Then my doctor came in. "Oh," he said. "You just did Day 10! Halfway! It's all downhill from here."

I did a pretty major flinch at the echo of those words.

He noticed. "No!" he said, leaning forward and grabbing my hand. "I mean that in a good way. You've made it through the first ten days. You're at the peak. Now you're going to coast downhill."

I told him what I'd been told. I held up the arsenal.

He frowned. "Honestly," he said, "bad skin issues are just not the norm. They're unusual. Usually, you see a little pink, like a light sunburn, that's all. Really," he said, leaning forward again. "You're doing great. Your skin is holding up. You aren't showing any signs of having problems."

So what do you do when you're faced with different stories, from women who've experienced it firsthand, nurses who've witnessed it firsthand, doctors who've treated it firsthand?

You wait. And you hang on tight to your arsenal.

I felt really discouraged.

"Kathie," he said, and I so appreciated his using my name. "No matter what, you're going to be fine."

And then he asked to shake my hand. I gave it to him, but asked why.

"I heard about your story going on stage in Denver," he said. "That is so amazing. I'm proud to know you."

This past weekend, I looked on the website for Stories On Stage in Denver at the Su Teatro theatre, where my story Snap Dragon is going to be performed. I saw my name. And I saw other names. Names that I recognize and admire. Among others:

Louise Erdrich. Joan Didion. Amy Bloom.

Writers who I would ask to shake my hand. Writers that I would call amazing, and who I would say, "I'm proud to know you."

I left the Cancer Center today, clutching my arsenal. But I also went glowing, and not just from the radiation.

And yes, that helps. Despite. Anyway.

### SEPTEMBER 12, 2017

And so today's moment of happiness despite the news.

Over the last couple weeks, temperatures have been dropping. We've followed the summer to fall cycle of air conditioning, then windows open night and day, then windows open during the day, but closed at night because it's cold. I had our gas fireplace maintained, which involved the technician climbing to the vent sticking out of the second story of our condo and clearing out a massive bird's nest that was stuck down deep. The fireplace has been on every evening since, and we haven't roasted a birdie yet. Our windows were washed today, all three stories, clearing away more evidence of summer birds, increasing our visibility to predict the inches of snowfall when the first storm hits. And, instead of parking Hemi and driving only Semi, the convertible, I've been splitting my time between the two. When I've driven Semi, the heated seats are on.

I even had a Starbucks grande cinnamon dolce latte, extra hot, instead of iced.

So I thought summer was on the way out. It made me sad, as summer is my favorite season, and I feel I've missed most of it this year. It's been breast cancer season, spent in and out of a variety of doctors' offices, having mammograms and MRI's and ultrasounds, surgery, then recovery from surgery, then radiation. When I was told originally that the radiation might make me look a little sunburned, I laughed. I am normally thoroughly browned by now, from driving around in Semi and spending time walking the river and reading on the deck. This year, I'm not so brown and so the radiation could be a form of tanning bed for me, I guess.

But I am heading toward the end of breast cancer season, and to the sunset of a positive outcome, and I've told myself over and over, it's worth having to miss just one summer if it means many more summers to come.

But while I tell myself that, I have to admit, I don't often feel it. I feel angry and sad during the winter. This year, I've felt angry and sad during the missing summer too.

But today, summer came back.

Brilliant blue sky, full-out sun. Heat. The grass is still green and the trees are too, even though some streaks of color are sneaking in. Flowers. I've been hearing geese almost every day lately, but there were no honks today, and I definitely heard a robin. Even when I was inside, working, I turned my computer and my face toward my deck door, soaking in as much as I could.

I drove Semi to my radiation treatment. As I was walked out, the technician said to me, "Enjoy the rest of your day, in what is probably the last summer day of the season."

When I got to my car, I didn't start him right away. I sat down behind the wheel and then rolled my short sleeves up until my shoulders were bare. I unbuttoned my shirt as far as I dared to go in public and opened it to the left; I have to protect the right from sun during radiation. I put on my sunglasses and leaned my head back against the seat. One arm rested on the open window, the other stretched across the console. Sun embraced me.

And I soaked summer in. I soaked summer in as hard as I could for about fifteen minutes. I cooked myself in July and August, beaches, white clouds, sun-streaked skies, ice cream cones, sandals. Hamburgers, hot dogs, brats on the grill. Corn on the cob at the county fair. Fireworks. Iced tea, iced coffee, iced sangria, Icees. I jam-packed it. It was a flash-summer, similar to flash fiction, complete with a beginning, middle, end. With conflict and resolution.

A satisfying end. A positive resolution.

And then I drove home, in a breeze that was just beginning to cool.

And yes, that helps. Despite. Anyway.

# SEPTEMBER 13, 2017

And so today's moment of happiness despite the news.

A student told me this traditional Jewish story today, over Skype, from most of the way around the world:

A man was very unhappy. He lived in a small one-room house with his wife and six children. It was so small and so crowded and he just couldn't take it anymore. So he went to the rabbi and confessed how very unhappy he was. He said, "Life couldn't possibly get worse."

The rabbi said, "Do exactly as I tell you and things will get better. Do you promise?"

The man promised.

The rabbi said, "Go home and bring a goat into your house."

The man was stunned, but he'd promised, so he did exactly as he was told. The next day, he went back to the rabbi and told him he'd moved a goat into his house.

The rabbi said, "Good. Now go move a second goat in your house."

And the next day, he told the man to add a third goat. And then a fourth.

Finally, the rabbi told the man he could let the goats go back outside. The man did so. When he came back to the rabbi, he said, "Life is so much better! We have so much more room in our house without the goats there!"

I was charmed, of course.

Later, I went in for my radiation treatment, Treatment #12, with 8 to go. I was feeling fine until I climbed onto the table, lay back in the mold of my own body that holds me still and in place, put my hands over my head, and felt them bind my feet together. As the two technicians trotted from the room and Xappa The External Beam Radiation Machine moved himself into place, I suddenly felt myself totally awash in sadness. It was actually a physical sensation, an empty warmth filling my eyes and then rolling down over my whole body. I felt like I must have just changed color with the force of it.

I don't think I can take this anymore, I thought.

And Xappa began to hum.

I thought of my student and her story. And then I spoke to Xappa, silently, of course, as I'm not allowed to emit any sound as that might move my body and throw off the course of the radiation. Xappa and I speak telepathically.

"Xappa," I said, "you're a goat. You're a goat in my house."

I thought of the other goats that had been in my house recently. Tests, surgery, and now Xappa. Only Xappa was left. My house was already getting roomier.

"When you're gone, Xappa," I said, "my normal life will be so much better."

I think, when Xappa goes, I won't complain nearly as much. I think, when Xappa goes, I will no longer have to struggle so hard to find one happy moment a day.

Things will return to normal. But I will be different.

And yes, that helps. Despite. Anyway.

### SEPTEMBER 14, 2017

And so today's moment of happiness despite the news.

This may be the shortest entry ever.

Today zipped by fast. And all the way through, ALL the way through, there was conversation about my story going on stage in Denver on Sunday, my book being launched in a little over a week, what I'm writing now, what I wrote then, what students are doing, and what's next, what's next, what's next.

What's next. There's a next!

There's so much more to come.

Then tonight, at the end of a conversation with a coaching client, he said, "The next time I talk to you (in one week), you'll have only two treatments left."

Only. I'll be that close to being finished.

There's a finished!

Some days are just about the complete and utter joy you feel because you're alive. Some days are about the complete and utter joy you feel over what you've accomplished. And some days are about the complete and utter joy because you know you aren't done yet. Not by a long shot.

Today, as I kept up the pace with meeting morning clients, walking the dogs, writing an essay, running to radiation, running to an appointment, meeting with evening clients, I just felt happy. There was joy in every step forward.

It's been a while.

This time next week, there will only be two treatments left. And then there's what's next.

My what's next is still alive and well.

When I sat down tonight to write the Today's Moment, I thought, how the hell do I do this? How do I write about a feeling that created a day, and that day is the Moment? Nothing concrete, but something ethereal. Just. Feeling. Good.

How do I write about it? I just did.

And yes, that helps. Despite. Anyway.

## SEPTEMBER 15, 2017

And so today's moment of happiness despite the news.

They threw a curveball at me in radiation today. I think it's a good curveball, but I don't know that for sure, and I am always frustrated when there are things I don't know or don't understand.

One of the things that I feel medical professionals need to understand is that routine and familiar help. Even when you're going through something difficult, if you can make a routine of it, it becomes a path that you walk. Not a strange stumble down a strange back road in a strange country.

While I hate it, I've grown used to radiation. I walk in the same door every day, meet the same receptionists, get walked to the same dressing room, put on the same robe, put my things in the same locker, wait in the same chair, walk to the same radiation room, say hello to Xappa, announce my name and birthdate, take off the robe, lie down, get zapped, and get walked out.

Today, my technician said, "So did they tell you that we'd be measuring you today for (something unintelligible)?"

"No," I said. "What's that?"

I was told that an attachment would be added to Xappa, and that he would be drawn very, very close to me, though he would not touch me. And then they would be putting radiation, not very deeply, but directly into the spot where the tumor was. They would no longer be treating the whole area, but just that one spot. "You have two more of the regular treatments, and then four of (something unintelligible). And then you're done," the technician said.

4 + 2 = 6. Today was day 14, and yes, I'd been expecting 6 more. But I wasn't expecting (something unintelligible). Or that Xappa would be getting even closer to me.

Nor was I expecting that, when the treatment was done today, I'd have to continue laying in that awful position while they drew again on my breast. I didn't turn into a diagram of the parts of the cow this time. Instead, there is a big black circle. I've become a target.

I'm sure this is part of my plan. I'm sure it was intended all along. I'm sure it's a good thing, because the explanation ended with, "and then you're done." But it's DIFFERENT.

I am amazed right now at how easily DIFFERENT can topple me over. I wanted to cry. And when I got out to my car, I did. All the way Starbucks.

Where I ordered the same drink I order every day. Where I spoke with baristas that I know. Then I drove home and called out a hello as I walked in the door. Familiar bounded out of Olivia's bedroom, in the form of Olivia herself, and I got the hug and the kiss and the school run-down I get every day. Then I met with a client, meditated, and then met with two more clients.

Familiar. The world is solid again beneath my feet. Sameness, everydayness, acting on what I know and doing the things I understand. Oh, the relief in that.

And remembering those words: "And then you're done."

Whew.

And yes, that helps. Despite. Anyway.

## SEPTEMBER 16, 2017

And so today's moment of happiness despite the news.

I've never written a Today's Moment while sitting in an airport before. Nor while sitting in an airport in Dallas, which I've only been in once before, on my way to lecture at Dallas' Big Read when they were doing Bradbury's *Fahrenheit 451*. And I am eating at Au Bon Pain, where I've never eaten before.

It seems to be a moment of firsts.

I had difficulty sleeping last night. I went to bed after two and was up again at seven, worrying. Thinking I probably shouldn't be doing this trip right now. The stress, the cost, the stress. I've been dealing with breast cancer (and paying for it) for three months. Radiation is beating me up. My immune system is likely down and I'm going to be in a total of three enclosed tubes, filled with whatever bugs people are carrying and coughing. I'm tired.

I had a ridiculous conversation with Michael before I left, in which I said, "I won't have a car while I'm there. What if something happens? What if I get sick? What if I have to go to the hospital?"

Michael rolled his eyes and said, "There's this thing called an ambulance."

And I answered, "But what if I'm unconscious and can't call for the ambulance!"

He said, "Well, then you wouldn't be able to drive either."

There are times when having an imagination isn't such a good thing.

What if, what if, what if.

So it was in that mood I taught a workshop this morning, then packed up and got the hell out of Dodge. And it was in that mood that I sat in the Milwaukee airport and thought, You know, you only have to call Uber and you can go home. You're still conscious.

But I got on the plane. I sat down, belted in, and tried to breathe.

As we flew toward Dallas on my way to Denver, which makes sense to no one, I read from Sherman Alexie's new memoir, *You Don't Have To Tell Me You Love Me*. At one point, Alexie wrote, *"During my twenty-four year literary career, I'd earned nearly two million frequent flyer miles and performed at more than three-hundred colleges."*

I closed the book for a bit. I closed my eyes too. And I thought, My literary career has spanned forty years. I don't collect frequent flyer miles. I've presented and taught many places, but not three-hundred colleges.

Sherman is a few years younger than I am.

So I heaved a sigh.

But then I opened one eye and looked at the little television screen in front of me. It showed a silhouette of the plane and where we were in the country just then. We were over Oklahoma. When it panned out, I could see Milwaukee, I could see Dallas, and I could see Denver. Where I was going.

Where my story is going to be on stage tomorrow.

And I sat straight up. I opened both eyes wide.

Story on stage tomorrow. Book #7 launched in a little over a week. I say that my literary career started when I was fifteen years old and my first story was accepted and published – hence just over forty years. I've taught for twenty-one years and I've launched so many writers, I've lost count. My literary career is kind of like flying from Milwaukee to Denver, via Dallas. Doesn't matter how I get there as long as I get there.

I'm there.

My story is on stage tomorrow.

Oh, I wanted to go. I wanted to be right where I was. There were no should nots here. There were shoulds. I should go. I should see.

And I should freaking revel.

On to Denver.

And yes, that helps. Despite. Anyway.

And so today's moment of happiness despite the news.

Tonight, I sat in the audience at a theatre in Denver, Colorado, and I watched and listened as an actress performed my short story, "Snap Dragon". Do I need to go any further with saying what my Moment was?

Actually, I do.

It was incredible watching an actress do my story. Hearing my words come out of her mouth, hearing her intonation, her pauses, watching her face and her hands as her whole body took on the story, was just stunning. I don't think I breathed through the whole thing. But what was most stunning to me was that it wasn't my voice coming out of her. And it wasn't her voice either.

It was the story's. It was my character's. He was there, loud and true and real.

Holy cow. When you write fiction, that's what you're going for. It's not about expressing who you are, it's not about having your voice heard. It's about having your story heard.

My story was heard tonight.

But even more...What led to the Moment was that I sat in that audience and heard their reaction. I heard when they laughed. I also heard the tone of the laughter change when they began to recognize themselves in the story. And when the impact came, near the end, the impact that wasn't so funny anymore – I felt as that impact hit the audience. I felt the gasp and the held breath, the sudden stillness. The silence that hung over the theatre for just a moment.

That story had impact, and it sunk in.

And it sunk in to me too. This Moment isn't particularly artfully written. But it is FELT.

So many times in the last couple years, I've wondered if my work has any impact. If it reaches anyone. If anyone cares, if anyone is moved, if it makes a difference...and ultimately, if the work is worth doing.

I don't have to wonder anymore. I felt the answer tonight.

Oh, there's impact.

Holy cow.

And yes, that helps. Despite. Anyway.

## SEPTEMBER 18, 2017

And so today's moment of happiness despite the news.

I came home from Denver today. I was still flying high from yesterday's performance of my short story on stage. But as I wandered through the airport, stopping to buy my daughter a stuffed donkey with "Colorado" stitched on his hooves, stopping again at a counter where I could plug in my computer and work for a bit, and finally, stopping at my gate, where "Milwaukee" was lit up in red in a theatre-like marquee, my heels began to drag some.

I was flying to home and studio. To husband, children, grandchild, dogs, cats, students, students, students, a radio interview tomorrow, a book launch in a week and one day.

And I was flying home to Xappa and radiation. Within a couple hours of placing my feet firmly back in my home state, I would be placing my body firmly under an external beam radiation machine.

And I didn't want to.

I stood there, just a few feet away from the counter at my gate. I didn't realize I was staring at the screen until the woman behind the counter asked if she could help me. I shook away Xappa- fog and said, "Yes. You know what? Do you have any upgrades available?"

She was training a new attendant and she set him to looking. Then she noticed the book under my arm and she asked what I was reading. I told her it was Sherman Alexie's *You Don't Have To Tell Me You Love Me*. She wrote the title down. "I'm always looking for a good book," she said.

"Well..." I said.

As I turned to the new attendant to see what he came up with, this woman's fingers flew over her cell's keyboard. "I'm stalking you on the internet," she said.

While she did that, I decided to fly home first class.

Just as the new attendant was handing me my receipt and new boarding pass, the woman flipped her phone toward me. "I just ordered Alexie's memoir," she said. "And I ordered *In Grace's Time* too."

I walked over to the line for Zone 1 – first class – with my heels not dragging anymore.

On board, first class was definitely first class. Roomy comfortable seats.

Our own bathroom. A large console between me and the other rowmate. Drinks served before take-off. Jackets taken and hung up. Help stowing my carry-on. After take-off, one of the attendants brought out hot towels, handed to us with salad tongs. I thought this was odd, but I watched my fellow first classers and then I wiped my hands and face with the towel. It smelled good. I was tempted to raise my shirt and treat the beaten-up breast, but I didn't think the guy next to me would appreciate that.

And then…well, I became me.

While others had drinks with complicated alcoholic ingredients, I had a Sprite, then a cup of coffee. I was delighted that the Sprite was not in a can, but in a very nice glass with ice, and the coffee was in a ceramic mug.

Then, when we were offered our meal, the choice was a barbecue brisket or a spinach ravioli, along with a list of fru-fru this and blahdeblah that. I politely said no thank you, and then pulled a package of cheese crackers with peanut butter out of my purse. I did, however, munch on the little bowl of mixed nuts they brought. They were warm! I never had warm mixed nuts before.

Then I studied the little television in front of me. I plugged in my headphones. I furtively looked over my shoulder – there was a wall between me and the people in coach. My rowmate had his eyes closed. No one was watching.

So I put on *Say Yes To The Dress*.

It was a happy couple hours.

And yes, I came home to radiation. One of the technicians hugged me and told me how wonderful I smelled. It had to be the hot towel.

And yes, that helps. Despite. Anyway.

### SEPTEMBER 19, 2017

And so today's moment of happiness despite the news.

I am four treatments away from the end of radiation. I know the grand finale is coming. I know it will be better soon. I know most of it is behind me. But I am still gritting my teeth.

The fatigue hit this morning. I've been feeling gradually more tired, but this morning, it was a wall. Overnight, I began to feel some pain just below my armpit. So this morning, I looked, and yep, the warned-about red is there.

I was told this would come near the end. They were right. I'd pretty much started to believe myself when I said that I was apparently going to escape this part. It is not the first time during this new journey that I've managed to fool myself.

So I was dragging a bit today. Despite it being Treatment #16 of 20, almost the end. Despite being interviewed on the radio this morning. Despite a photograph showing up of my book in Australia. Despite the book launch being a week away. I was just flat.

When I went in for radiation, it took me a little while to go into the Cancer Center. I leaned against my car's hood and looked down the hill at the little lake that's there. I listened to the geese. And I told myself that I couldn't do this. That ending four days early likely wouldn't make any difference anyway. But then I told myself not to fool myself again and I went in.

When I was finished, I returned to the dressing room. I glanced at myself in the mirror – I think I still keep hoping that I'll find myself magically restored to how I looked pre-operation – fooling myself -- and then I got dressed. As I was putting in my earrings, I heard the receptionist open the door and usher someone in.

"So will I see the doctor first?" a woman said.

"Yes," the receptionist said, "but you can still go ahead and change into a robe." She showed her how to use the lockers. I heard the woman go in the dressing room next door.

And then I heard her start to cry.

She was at the start of her treatment. I was near the end.

My eyes welled up too.

I stepped out of my room and tapped on her door. I heard her gasp, but she slowly slid the door to the side. She was holding her robe, using it to wipe at her eyes.

I thought of all the things I could say. It will get better. The machine is scary, but it won't hurt. It will get better. The people here are really nice. It will get better.

But then I said, "I know this is really, really hard."

And she fell into my arms and sobbed.

I never once said that it would get better or any of those other things. I just kept saying, "I know, I know, I know, I know." One of the technicians peeked around the corner, likely looking for this woman, and I just held up one finger – just a moment.

I think, sometimes, we need to hear about what's happening right now. An acknowledgment. We don't need to hear about the future, because at that particular moment, it seems very, very far away, whether it's nineteen treatments away or four or one. I told her what I said to myself as I leaned against my car, looking at the geese, looking at the lake.

This is really, really hard.

When the woman calmed, she said thank you, and then she went back into her dressing room. I left. I didn't tell her my name. She didn't tell me hers. I don't know that I'll ever see her again. But I hope, as she comes in each day, she takes the time to lean on her car and look at the lake and the geese, and that she acknowledges to herself, This is really, really hard. And then she grits her teeth and goes inside. Maybe she'll say it to someone else too.

They say what doesn't kill you makes you stronger.

Well, I'm still standing, aren't I.

And yes, that helps. Despite. Anyway.

### SEPTEMBER 20, 2017

And so today's moment of happiness despite the news.

I've been reading Sherman Alexie's new memoir, *You Don't Have To Say You Love Me*. It's a BIG book and with my limited time for leisure reading, it's taken me a while to get through it. But I found I didn't mind; it's one of those books that takes time to ponder. You read, you think, you read, you think. It's an oddly constructed book too, combined of poetry, essays, and chapters. And it's lovely.

At the end, Alexie writes a poem about a bird that hits his window pane. Alexie thinks the bird is dead, but then, it lifts its head up. It goes through an odd number of actions, shaking one wing, the other, shaking its whole body, walking in circles. Eventually, it flies away. When Alexie tells his therapist about this, his therapist, a birder, explains that when birds have this kind of shock, the shaking and pacing in circles brings them back to their bodies. They teach themselves to be birds again; they shake off the trauma. Much of Alexie's book has been about trauma. He goes home and tries the bird's method. Then he writes:

*And as I continued to shake, I felt*
*A sparrow-sized pain rise*
*From my body and – wait, wait, wait.*
*Listen. I don't know how or when*
*My grieving will end, but I'm always*
*Relearning how to be human again.*

I've been disturbed since Saturday morning, when I taught a workshop where we got into a discussion on kindness. We talked about people who are unkind to themselves and to others because they were raised in an unkind way and so they don't know how to be, well, kind.

I asked about those who were treated unkindly, who are unkind to themselves, but are kind to others. And I was pretty much shot down by the class. They didn't seem to think this was possible. When I protested, I was told that those who have this background and who believe they treat others kindly often don't realize that they are being unkind. So I fell silent. And began to worry.

I was treated unkindly. I've been known to be unkind to myself.

But I believe I am kind to others. I try really hard to make a practice of it. So was I fooling myself again?

I've been second-guessing myself since Saturday. Questioning my motives. Looking at what I do, how I do it, why I do it. Looking for unkindness. Looking for possible.

And then I read Alexie's words today. I'm always relearning how to be human again.

I thought of the anonymous woman in yesterday's Today's Moment. The one I heard crying in her dressing room. I could have walked out without saying a word. I could have left her to her privacy. Or I could have knocked and then reminded her that there are many people who are worse off than she is. I could have called her a crybaby and told her to suck it up. I could have told her that this will end, and things will get better.

But I didn't. I acknowledged that this time, this moment, was hard. And I held her while she cried.

You know what? I'm a kind person. And I'm possible.

And I'm always relearning how to be human again.

Thanks, Sherman. Thanks, Words.

And yes, that helps. Despite. Anyway.

## SEPTEMBER 21, 2017

And so today's moment of happiness despite the news.

When I walked outside this afternoon to take the dogs on their after-lunch constitutional, I found a brown paper bag waiting at my door. It had my name on it. I wondered what it was as I alternately followed and dragged the dogs around the block – the dogs' potty break waits for nothing, so that had to be first.

Back at home, I opened the bag and found a bottle of cooling mist, along with a note from a wonderful student who said she thought this might help with my "hot flashing".

Right before I started radiation for breast cancer, I was also put on a medication which I'll have to take for the next five to ten years. This particular breast cancer feeds off of estrogen, and so the medication suppresses estrogen production in my body.

Which means, essentially, that I'm back in menopause. Which as we all know is the exact phase of life that most women would just love to relive again. I'm so delighted. And my husband is thrilled too.

Not.

I am usually a cold person. Not cold personality, but I feel cold all the time. I have a desk-top space heater that I use year around, especially when the air conditioning is on. During the summer, while my husband and daughter revel in the a/c, I turn the fireplace on and cuddle up under my electric throw. I drive topless in my convertible with the heated seat turned on high. At night, I sleep with at least three blankets pulled up to my nose. My husband will say that I steal his, blankets, but he lies. He tosses them off during the night and over me and I happily accept them. There are times I move my little space heater over to my bedside table so that I have heat blowing directly on me all night.

Well…no more. I'm HOT. All the TIME!

It's now me that throws the covers off at night – my husband complains that I throw the covers on him (he's never happy). I've turned the heating element off on my space heater and I use it as a fan instead. Another small fan is sitting on the kitchen island where I eat lunch, so that I can have cool air blowing on me while I eat. I've done coaching sessions with clients while mopping sweat off my forehead and neck. Instead of turning on my heated seat in my convertible, I'm driving topless with the a/c on.

I'm HOT. I'm DRENCHED. I'm HOT.

And not hot in the way I used to be. Sigh.

So when I received my little bottle of cooling mist, I ripped the protective wrapping off that sucker with my teeth and I choked the lid off like I was killing a chicken and I threw it across the room. I sprayed myself, liberally sprayed myself, and I wanted to howl like a wolf. So I did. Ooooooooooooooh, yeah, baby. I swear steam rose from my skin and piled around me in clouds of angst and frustration and stupid stupid Menopause Round Number Two which isn't menopause at all, but cancer-inflicted ridiculousness.

Oh, what a lovely gift this is. It WORKS!

Please send me cases of this stuff. In gallon-sized bottles. It's going to be a long five to ten years.

But for today, for this moment...Ahhhhhhhhhhhh. Thank you, thank you, thank you. I've been saved by a bottle.

And yes, that helps. Despite. Anyway.

## SEPTEMBER 22, 2017

And so today's moment of happiness despite the news.

*"And when {birds} hit a window like that, or get hurt in any significant way, they have this ritual. They shake off the pain. They shake off the trauma. And they walk in circles to reconnect their brain and body and soul. When your bird was walking and shaking, it was remembering and relearning how to be a bird."*

*--Sherman Alexie, You Don't Have To Say You Love Me*

Today was my second to last day of radiation treatment for breast cancer. My final day is Monday. And on Tuesday...my seventh book has its official launch event.

I sat back today and thought of the metaphor of these two days on the calendar. On Monday, I walk away from breast cancer. On Tuesday, with a book event, I walk back into my life, MY life.

And that just made me cry. I've been given to tears more in the last few months than I think I have in my entire life. I was ridiculed for crying as a child which led to sad-expression stoicism as an adult and now...well, I don't think I'd be ridiculed for the tears I've shed this summer. Today's tears were about relief and happiness and looking-forward. I thought again of Sherman Alexie's book, *You Don't Have To Say You Love Me*, and the scene where the bird who bashed himself in a window shakes himself and paces in circles to connect himself with himself again. Between Monday at 3:45 p.m. and Tuesday at 7:00 p.m., I plan to shake myself out like a favorite shirt that was pushed for a season to the back of the closet. And then I'm putting myself on again.

A phrase that popped up in my head right after diagnosis and that has sat on my shoulder throughout this whole experience is "What doesn't kill you makes you stronger." When the diagnosis hit, and it hit out of nowhere, with no warning, no foreshadowing, it was a semi coming out of my blind spot, I didn't know at first that this wouldn't kill me. But as time went on and positive upon positive was stacked upon the original negative, that phrase on my shoulder kept yanking me by the earlobe. On days I felt particularly weak, it yanked me particularly hard and reminded me of the word "makes". What doesn't kill you MAKES you stronger. It's a process. Not an immediate morphing.

So far, I've only written, outside of this blog, two things about dealing with breast cancer. The first was a poem, called "What Doesn't Kill You". The second is an essay.

I don't know if there will be any more. Maybe. We'll see how my head and heart feel as time goes on.

But today, as I walked out of the Cancer Center and thought, One more, just one more, I realized I was looking forward again. Not just to the next horrified glimpse in the mirror. The next step, the next test, the next treatment, the next appointment. But forward. And into my life.

Monday, the last day of radiation, is big. But Tuesday, opening the door of the bookstore and stepping into my book launch, is even bigger.

I'm shaking cancer's dirt off of my shoes. For that matter, I'm taking off the shoes entirely, my socks too, and leaving them behind in the ditch. And then, I'm pulling out my favorite shirt, shaking it, shaking it, and putting it on.

As I walked out of the Cancer Center today, there was a parade of geese crossing the parking lot, right next to my car. A couple stopped to look at me. "You're early," I said. "Come back and give me a parade on Monday."

I don't think I've ever wanted so much for a weekend to pass quickly.

Let's go, let's go. I'm ready. Shaking, shaking and pacing. Remembering and relearning how to be me.

And yes, that helps. Despite. Anyway.

### SEPTEMBER 23, 2017

And so today's moment of happiness despite the news.

In the middle of a batch of errands today, I stopped at Office Depot. I was on a mission. I needed a signing pen for *In Grace's Time*. The launch is this coming Tuesday.

When *The Home For Wayward Clocks* came out in 2011, I picked out a pen. It's a Sharpie, ultra fine point. And it's black. But when *Enlarged Hearts* came out a year later, it didn't seem right to keep using the same pen. So I picked out another. Purple. Then, 2013, *Learning To Tell (A Life) Time*. Blue, to match the cover. 2015, *Rise From The River.* Orange. 2016 was a challenge – two books released! *Oddities & Endings; The Collected Stories of Kathie Giorgio* and *True Light Falls In Many Forms*, a poetry chapbook. *Oddities*: Green. *True Light*: Blue, but a lighter, more sky blue shade than Lifetime.

OCD has a really odd way of coming out sometimes. But hey, it just makes me happy.

And then today, I stood in front of the huge Sharpie display at Office Depot. With each subsequent book, I have fewer choices if I don't want any duplicates. I looked from the cover to the colors. Green. Been done before. Blue, been done before TWICE. And then I looked at the car on the cover.

When my publisher asked me if I had any ideas on what I wanted on the cover, I said the only thing I felt very strongly about was that it had to include a tan 1969 Chrysler Newport 4-door sedan. I searched for images on the internet and when I found the car, I sent it on to the cover artist, so he could see exactly what I meant.

My first car, sold to me for a dollar by my father in 1980, was a tan 1969 Chrysler Newport 4-door sedan. The car had been in the family for some time and my dad was ready to move on. I needed a car. So the big tanky vehicle, which really didn't leave any impression on me before, became mine.

And with that, he became special. He became Chrys. And he was the best damn car ever.

I loved him. He was like driving a sofa. He was a bitch to park because he was so huge, so I headed to the far end of the parking lot so I wouldn't have to figure out where his magnificent hood ended. After my first husband and I were married, we were plowed into by a car trying to pass us. That driver didn't see our left turn blinker as we were turning at an intersection. I can still feel the impact, still see that other car bounce off Chrys' driver's side door like he hit a rubber wall. I swear I saw every line as the windshield of that other car shattered.

That car was totaled. Chrys' door was bent in, but my ex-husband wasn't even bruised. Chrys was declared totaled too, because of his age. We drove to a junkyard, found another 1969 Chrysler Newport and bought the driver's side door, replacing ours. Chrys no longer matched – his door was green and the rest of his body was tan. But we drove that car for another two years.

When we finally junked him, it was because his muffler was gone and we were pulled over for a noise violation. It just wasn't worth replacing it. We bought a 1979 Plymouth Volare, which I hated. We left Chrys at the auto graveyard. I cried all the way home.

This is why I still drive Chryslers. I've owned a 1994 Chrysler LeBaron convertible, a 2003 Chrysler Sebring Lxi convertible, and now a 2006 Chrysler 300C Hemi and 2012 Chrysler 200 convertible. And I've loved them all. LeB, SeB, Hemi and Semi.

But when I needed a car for this book – a car with a personality, a car with a long life, a car that would protect the people tucked within its doors – there was no doubt. Chrys came back to life on my own pages.

Today, I bought a pen that matches him. And it's for my seventh book. I brought the pen home and laid it reverently on my own copy of *In Grace's Time*.

Perfect.

And yes, that helps. Despite. Anyway.

## SEPTEMBER 24, 2017

And so today's moment of happiness despite the news.

I'm feeling the tide beginning to turn. This is a good thing.

Late last night, I had an email from my publisher, letting me know that *In Grace's Time* is now available as an e-book. I've not had an e-book before – my first publisher wasn't interested in them. As a writer, I am – I don't read them myself, but I know plenty who do, and I'm interested in anything that means my book(s) are available to as many readers as possible. So my excitement went up a notch.

Then this morning, I saw a photo posted by an AllWriters' student which showed *In Grace's Time* in the window of the bookstore where the launch will take place on Tuesday. And my excitement went up another notch.

And finally, when I popped over to Amazon to see that my book was indeed listed as an e-book as well as a print, I saw a new review. It was five stars. And it had only two sentences: "Novel takes reader on a tumultuous ride of a mother's suffering. Not to be missed."

Not to be missed. Well, HELL, YES!

Under the book's description, where it shows what other books were viewed by customers looking at that book, there were the covers of four other books. All mine.

So this by itself would be enough to make it a moment of happiness. But there's more.

In the middle of the day, I was coming back home from dropping Michael off at the grocery store. As I walked through my garage, I noticed a really, really large spider on the wall. Really, really large by my standards means…well, honestly, any spider at all. I moved as far against my car as I could, to maintain as much distance as possible between me and the spider, and promptly walked into my car's sideview mirror. With my right breast. THE breast. The one that has been poked, squashed, squeezed, biopsied, operated on, and fried from the inside out.

I let loose with a stream of profanity and vulgarity that I didn't even know I knew. It's probably still around, in a great blue storm cloud over Wisconsin, maybe making its way over Lake Michigan. As for the spider, I don't know where he went. If he was smart, he got the hell out of there.

So for those moments, I saw stars. I saw more than stars. I saw and felt pain that encapsulated my entire summer, from June 20th to now. It bent me double. There were tears and there was anger and there was nothing else in the world but that. Nothing else mattered. And I just shrieked. I'm kinda surprised my neighbors didn't call an ambulance. Or for the men in the white coats, given the language I was using.

But then the world came back. The pain dissipated. I straightened up, wiped away my tears, made sure I wasn't bleeding, took some deep breaths. And I went back inside and continued reveling in the discoveries above.

Moment of happiness? Again, HELL, YES! Because that whole scenario represents tomorrow and Tuesday and the rest of my life. Tomorrow, I walk into the Cancer Center, receive my last dose of radiation, and walk out. I will not be going back. And on Tuesday, I launch the book.

The moments of tears and anger have been absolutely encompassing and overwhelming and blinding and deafening and world-suppressing. But after tomorrow…

I'm back.

And (hell) yes, that helps. Despite. Anyway.


### SEPTEMBER 25, 2017


And so today's moment of happiness despite the news.

Today was my last day of radiation. 20 treatments, done. 16 covered the spot where the tumor was, the surrounding area, and the lymph nodes. 4 were what they call a booster, with all of the radiation just focused on the tumor's spot. All of them were grueling emotionally. The last week was grueling physically, and from what I understand, I will be feeling the effects for a few more weeks. The fatigue, my doctor said, will peak and dissipate over the next two weeks, the fried skin will get worse for a bit, then heal over the next three.

But no more assuming the position. No more shrinking under Xappa the Radioactive Hulk. No more hearing his hum and knowing that while he sounded cheerful, he was shredding my cells and causing damage that was ultimately going to be healing. No more, no more.

After the treatment, I had to return to the waiting room until someone came for me to take me to the weekly review with the radiation oncologist. I was expecting to feel elated, way up, unable to stay in my seat. Instead, I leaped out of my seat to grab some tissues because I fell into a teary meltdown. I was so surprised. I never thought I would fall apart at the end. I fell apart at the beginning. I fell apart in the middle. Now the end too?

When the nurse came to get me, she sat down beside me. "Feeling overwhelmed?" she asked.

I nodded, unable to speak.

"That's really common," she said. "Everyone expects to skip out of here, to dance a jig, to cheer. But instead, it's like the enormity of it all just lands on your shoulders. When you're in treatment, you're so busy looking ahead, you're not looking at what is happening right now, or at the experience as a whole. But then suddenly, you're not looking ahead anymore."

No. I was just there. And it was like this entire three months just crashed over me. From that first day, the mammogram radiologist telling me that he thought I had an 80% chance that this was cancer, to today, being told that I'm done. Yes, I am returning to my normal life. But I am not who I was before.

As we sat there, I saw one of the technicians walk by, carrying my molded beanbag body form. It was made right before I started radiation. When I was a cancer victim. Now it was being thrown away. It's not necessary anymore. Because I'm a cancer survivor.

I never wanted to be either of those things. Those characters in my story. But in the end, I had no choice.

The cancer wrote me.

Before I walked out of the Cancer Center, I was given a Certificate of Achievement. It was signed by all the nurses, the technicians, and the front desk receptionists. It said:

*Kathleen Giorgio has completed the prescribed course of radiation therapy, with the highest degree of courage, determination, and good nature.*

Well, I know the truth of this, of course. Courage? I was terrified.

Determination? Well, I gritted my teeth through my tears a lot. Good nature? Well, some days. Maybe. I put on my public face. Though some days, I just couldn't.

But I made it through. I said goodbye to Xappa, the external beam radiation machine, and told him I'd immortalized him forever in a poem. I hugged those that helped me. Which means everyone.

And then I walked out that door, clutching my certificate. It was a warm sunny day and I drove in my convertible to Starbucks, where the barista called through the drive-thru mike, "Your usual, Kathie?" and I said yes, please. Please, the usual. Then I drove home, hugged my daughter, and sat down at my desk. My desk. My life.

Changed. But still mine.

And yes, that helps. Despite. Anyway.

### SEPTEMBER 26, 2017

And so today's moment of happiness despite the news.

Today was the official launch of my new book, *In Grace's Time*. Well, you just know that's got to be The Moment.

Of course it was.

There is nothing, nothing like reading your own words in front of an appreciative crowd. Hearing their response. Or hearing their lack of response when they're all holding their collective breaths. Answering their questions afterward. Signing books. Oh my gosh. It's what I live for.

It's what I live for. I'm going to come back to that.

But I had one major wish for tonight. A hope. No, not for world peace. Not that Steven Spielberg and Oprah Winfrey would be in the audience and that afterward, they would say, "We want to make a movie of your book!" Well, maybe that, a little. What I wished and hoped for was this:

That more chairs would have to be brought out because they ran out of seating room.

And…they did.

Oh, yes.

But back to that "It's what I live for."

The first night that I was in Denver, I partook in a guilty pleasure: watching *Say Yes To The Dress*. On the show that night, a father, diagnosed with cancer, said, "When you have cancer, you begin to make every moment count. Every day becomes important. And you make sure you don't waste your time anymore; you try to do what really counts."

Since diagnosis, I really have tried to think that way. I've sat and I've pondered and I've perseverated and ruminated on what is important in life, on what gives it meaning, and I've said, "I really have to focus on this now. I really have to spend my time wisely."

But tonight, at the podium, I realized that I am already doing what I most want to do in this world. And all I want is to be able to do more of it. I want to write. I want to teach.

It's what I live for.

I've said it before. I love what I do. I do what I love. If I'm not writing, I'm teaching. If I'm not teaching, I'm editing. If I'm not editing, I'm advocating.

It's what I live for.

Tonight's audience was filled with all sorts of pie slices from my life. Students were there. Readers were there. Friends and family were there. My high school creative writing teacher. My radiation oncologist. People I knew. People I didn't. And they had to bring out more chairs.

I do what I love. I love what I do. It's what I live for.

Ohmygod, tonight felt good.

And yes, that helps. Despite. Anyway.

### SEPTEMBER 27, 2017

And so today's moment of happiness despite the news.

I took off work for the rest of the week, to give myself some time to decompress and recover, from both the radiation treatments and the book launch and just from the whole cancer kit and caboodle. I needed a break. I didn't have much scheduled for today, but I did have to go to the post office and to Walgreens. My skin on the right breast and side is still a mess. Wearing anything hurts. I decided to venture out braless. My t-shirt would suffice. I'd be fine. Who would notice? Who would care?

I was at the self-help kiosk in the post office lobby when an older woman sidled up next to me. "A woman your age," she said in a voice that I think she intended as a whisper, but wasn't, "shouldn't be out in public without a bra."

I didn't remove my eyes from the screen, where I punched in a zip code, a street number, the first letter of the street name. "I'm in recovery from breast cancer," I said, keeping my voice even. "I just finished 20 days of radiation. My skin is burned. I can't tolerate a bra. I can barely tolerate this t-shirt." I looked directly at her. "You might want to think before you speak. You might want to think before you assume."

Her jaw hung somewhere around her amply brassiered chest. Then she hurried away. I finished my business and went to Walgreens, trying hard to not be self-conscious.

At Walgreens, a clerk I know introduced me to another clerk. Her head was covered with a bright pink scarf and her eyebrows were drawn in. She asked me what stage I'd been in (2), and if I'd done chemo yet. I said I didn't have to have chemo, just radiation. She rolled her eyes. "I was Stage 3," she said. "I had surgery and radiation. Then they found a spot in my shoulder bone. And on my ribcage. Now I have chemo." She nodded at me. "You should have chemo. Your doctors, they're not right."

I thanked her, held my tongue because she's another breast cancer victim, and I went on my way. And I began to think about the assumptions we make.

Post office lady assumed that because I was a late-fifties woman out without a bra, I was trying to be something I wasn't. Walgreens clerk assumed that because my breast cancer case is different than hers, my doctors are wrong.

We make so many assumptions.

I've been watching, quietly, this whole Take A Knee thing. Some assume that the NFL players who took a knee during the National Anthem were doing so because they disrespect our flag, or our country, or our military.

It could be that they're taking a knee because they're protesting what's being done to the country they respect and love. They could be protesting those in power. They could be protesting bigotry or racism.

The other day, when the Orange Asshat said that NFL owners should fire those that are "disrespecting our country," I thought, quietly, It could be that they're disrespecting you, Asshat. You and this country are not synonymous. I'm thankful for that.

Eventually, I found myself in the drive-thru at Starbucks. When I pulled up to the window, several of the baristas called out a hello. Then the one who took my order handed me my drink and leaned out the window. "Are you doing okay, Kathie?" he asked. "Are you all right?"

And I smiled. There were no assumptions here. Just genuine care. A moment of offering compassion. "I'm just fine," I said. "Thank you for asking."

And then I took my braless self home.

I don't really know the point of this ramble. I just know there were some assumptions made today, some judgements, that made me unhappy and uncomfortable. But a simple moment of compassion, which would really be easy enough for us all to offer each other, lifted me up.

And yes, that helps. Despite. Anyway.

## SEPTEMBER 28, 2017

And so today's moment of happiness despite the news.

*The world should know that she is infinite and not limited*
*She has never-ending abilities in a never ending crazy infinite world of*
hers
*−Olivia Giorgio, She Holds The Infinite World*

Today, I helped my 16-year old (almost 17!) daughter prepare manuscripts for submission to two magazines. One magazine received a short story in the horror genre. And the other received two poems, including one that I called a Memoir Built With Poetry, as it's about Olivia's experience with growing up autistic.

When a child decides she wants to do what her parents do, it's just so mind-blowing on a number of levels. I have four children. One doesn't write at all. One was working on a novel and writes an active blog. One writes poetry when she takes breaks from getting her PhD in math (that's mind-blowing too). And now this one, who flat-out says she wants to be a writer.

*Her parents write*
*They have their colorful worlds*
*Their worlds get published*
*She doesn't understand how publishing works*
*But all she knows is that she wants to be like them*

In particular, Olivia's poem about growing up autistic gets to me. I can't read it without tearing up. Her experiences of trying to marry her rich interior world with the real outer world are just visceral. Olivia went from nonverbal for her first three years to trying to communicate by memorizing massive amounts of television show scripts to being beautifully well-spoken with a vocabulary that would put most to shame. She also automatically adds twists to words that are at times funny, but are mostly soul-reaching and artful.

*But the words wouldn't come*

*Yet her head is filled with wonderful words that no one seems to understand*

For me, one of Olivia's most stunning moments came in first grade, when I tried to calm her dancing, stimming hands. "I need my hands, Mama," she said. "Sometimes my brain slips sideways, and my hands bring it back."

I knew then that I had a child who would use her words to speak of her inner world to the rest of the world.

*She also wishes to give others this gift of the infinite world through song, art, and words*

Today, Olivia showed me the fainted remnants of a pink ribbon she drew on her hand. "I wanted to show you support, Mama," she said. She told me that the swim team at school is creating Pinktober shirts and she wants to buy one. "I want to show you support, Mama."

We told Olivia that she is autistic when she was in the sixth grade. As she struggled to understand this new definition, she became obsessed with anything with the autism symbol – a rainbow-colored puzzle piece. T-shirts, jewelry, stickers. "I want support, Mama!" she cried.

Under her words, I heard the need. For support, of course. For acceptance. For love.

And now, "I want to show you support, Mama."

Support. Acceptance. Love.

I love you too, Olivia. So incredibly much. *because she knows the truth*
*Her world is infinite*
*She contains it all*

And yes, that helps. Despite Anyway.

### SEPTEMBER 29, 2017

And so today's moment of happiness despite the news.

Over the last 21 years, I've taught writers. Beginning writers, advanced writers, writers of all genres and writers of some genres that haven't even been invented yet. For the last 13 years, I've taught at my own studio, AllWriters' Workplace & Workshop. AllWriters' is named deliberately... ALL writers are accepted here, all genres, all abilities. All everything. And here is one thing I've learned over and over again about ALL writers:

Writers are the most discombobulating combination of huge ego and crippling insecurity.

And yes, ALL writers. Including me.

Over the last several months, I've had some amazing highs as a writer.

*a publisher came after me.

*several magazines asked me for a "Kathie Giorgio story".

*I was nominated for a Pushcart.

*My short story, "Snap Dragon", was chosen to be put on stage in a lovely theatre in Denver.

*And my book launched, to many lovely reviews and a great debut event which required the bookstore to bring out more chairs...because they all filled.

Amazing. Ego flying to new heights. You couldn't touch the soles of my shoes, I was up so high.

Then yesterday, I found that there was a new review on a reader review site – a site where the reviews aren't professional, but done by readers. In it, this reviewer said the writing was "average."

Average. My writing has never been called average in my LIFE.

Ego: smashed. Insecurity: pushing me underground up to my neck.

Average?

Granted, this book does leave me a little insecure. It's different than what I usually do. It's gentler. It's quieter. It's not "dark and disturbing". But...average?

So I pitched a fit. Internally, anyway. I was going to quit writing the current novel, which is also different. I was going to quit writing, period. I was going to throw myself off the highest bridge I could find. But I'm scared of bridges, so instead, I was going to go straight to bed and never get up.

Oh, it wasn't pretty. Fits generally aren't. That's why I tend to keep mine internal.

Thing is, while I've had a lot of positive reviews on *Grace*, this was the second negative one. The first one, I laughed off. It was from a young guy in Nebraska, who said that Grace's grief was tiresome (sorta the point of the book, bud – that people want you to get over your grief quickly), that a gay man would never be attracted to a woman (wake up to the world, darlin') and that the book failed to present grief in a unique way (oh, I know...there have been so many books on grief where the grieving person runs off with the town's gay doll salesman). This review was so ludicrous, I shook it off in a matter of minutes and I congratulated myself on doing so.

But average...that punctured me. And so I had a fit and I licked my wounds and swore they were never going to heal again.

Huge ego. Crippling insecurity. All writers.

But then tonight. Michael and I attended the opening night of a new play at a theatre in downtown Milwaukee. We were accompanied by two writers from AllWriters'. We had four tickets.

Why?

Because two weeks ago, the theatre wrote ME. They invited me to attend the opening night with guests because...are you ready? Because I am "a leader among Wisconsin writing organizations."

A leader. I like that word. So much better than "average".

And you know what? I am.

So I attended tonight, as Kathie Giorgio. Leader among Wisconsin writing organizations. Author of seven books and tons of short stories. I walked in with my feet off the ground again. Partly because of two key lime martinis. But mostly because I threw that second review out the door with the first one.

Huge ego intact, thank you. Crippling insecurity – back under control.

It's how writers survive. ALL writers.

And yes, that helps. Despite. Anyway.

### SEPTEMBER 30, 2017

And so today's moment of happiness despite the news.

Last June, it was announced that Stephen King and his son, Owen, were coming to Milwaukee, pushing their new book, a collaboration, called *Sleeping Beauties*. The event, while being hosted by the same local independent bookstore that hosted my launch earlier this week, was to take place in the Riverside Theatre. A theatre. A huge, gigantic, lovely theatre. A theater where I saw the Moody Blues perform. A theatre. For an author and his son.

Michael, who writes mystery and horror, loves Stephen King. I don't care for horror, but for Father's Day, I bought Michael two tickets. By the time I ordered them, I was lucky to get any – the event was sold out within days.

We decided to make a weekend of it in Milwaukee, celebrating Father's Day and my birthday late, the end of radiation now, and then our anniversary early. We walked to the theatre, leaving the hotel when the theatre doors were opening, thinking that by the time we got there, we'd be able to walk right in.

The line stretched to the next intersection and around the corner.

Eventually, we got in and moved up to our nosebleed seats. Still, we could see. And I looked around and marveled. Every seat was filled.

For an author event.

When the Kings were introduced, it was mentioned that our books, purchased with our tickets, would be handed to us on our way out. All 2400 of them.

2400 books. 2400 readers.

I wondered, as I looked around, how many people there actually read King's books, or if they were there as movie fans. But as the audience was allowed to ask questions, it was clear that majority of the attendees were readers. The few questions that were asked about the movies always connected the movie to the book.

Holy cow. 2400 readers in one place.

We read studies all the time that say Americans aren't reading. I saw impressive evidence tonight that we are. And I was thrilled.

When it was all over and we worked our way out, which was horrific as 2400 people tried to get down the stairs and to the front where the books were being handed out one by one, I stopped to let an older couple take their last final steps down from their seats to join the line.

"You can go ahead," the woman said.

"No," I said, and waved in front of me. "Come on."

They stepped carefully down and the woman thanked me.

"It's not a problem," I said. "No matter what, this is going to be slow. So we might as well be polite."

She lit up. "Exactly!" she said and patted me on the arm. "Let's be polite!"

So. Americans are reading. And we're even polite. As we walked back to our hotel, looking for a spot for a late dinner, we saw clubbers and theatre-goers, couples hand in hand to take a moonlight cruise on the Milwaukee River, bachelorette parties and bachelor parties. And lots and lots of people, carrying Stephen King's and Owen King's new book. 2400 of them. We dominated the night.

Hard to believe, from what we see on the news every day. Remember covfefe? Remember braggadocious?

But I was a believer tonight.

And yes, that helps. Despite. Anyway.

# Chapter Ten

## OCTOBER 1, 2017

And so today's moment of happiness despite the news.

I've spent most of the day trying on metaphors. Trying on metaphors like trying on a pile of not-quite-right dresses in a fitting room. (Did you see what I did there? I talked about metaphors by using a simile. It made me laugh. Writers have strange senses of humor.)

So here's the thing. Ever since diagnosis, I have used metaphor or symbolism to help me get through the situation and whatever step was necessary to take next, as well as the results of the steps. While waiting for surgery, the tumor became a big blue tick-spider with blue legs that somehow buried itself under my skin – not cancer at all. During surgery recovery, I decided that any poison in my life, personified by this now-gone lump in my breast, was excavated out of my body. During radiation, Xappa, the external beam radiation machine, was a scary monster with a heart of gold and a positive mission – zapping me clean. The radiation itself became a positive energy beam.

It's been harder since radiation ended. It's very difficult to come up with a metaphor or a symbol to help make fatigue and painful fried skin into a positive.

And now...and now...I'm peeling. Oh, what fresh hell is this? I had difficulty looking in the mirror before. Now, I'm shredding. And I'm in need of a new metaphor. A metaphor to make impossibly itchy, peeling skin into a positive.

Here's something that isn't talked about much. Most of what I've seen about breast cancer on television shows or in the movies or in literature concerns mastectomies. A common storyline is the woman's difficulty getting used to her new appearance. When you say you have a lumpectomy, I think the general idea is that just a teeny tiny piece of your breast is removed, and other than a few stitches, you're still as you were. Well, not in all cases. And not in my case. I did several double-takes whenever my surgeon referred to my lumpectomy as a "partial mastectomy". The result: the right side of my right breast sags, as if it's been cut loose from the whole. My breast is no longer round. I think my surgeon used an ice cream scoop to remove the lump. And I'm scarred.

And now…I'm peeling.

When it came to the metaphors, of course I came up with the obvious. I'm a butterfly emerging from a chrysalis. Well, that made me gag – I'm just not a butterfly kind of person. Then I came up with the unfortunate comparisons – I'm an onion. I'm a snake. Ew, ew, ew.

On the way home from our weekend away in Milwaukee, I told Michael about this. Turning to me, he said, "I don't see any of that when I look at you."

I stopped talking. Sometimes, words fail me.

"You're just beautiful," he said.

I'm pretty sure that when I look in the mirror tomorrow, I will still see what I saw today. But I will also hear his voice.

And yes, that helps. Despite. Anyway.

## OCTOBER 2, 2017

And so today's moment of happiness despite the news.

Dark day today. Like everyone else, I woke to news of the mass shooting in Las Vegas. A shooting that breaks the old record for being the deadliest. So far, 58 people have died. The record that was broken came from the Pulse Nightclub shooting in Florida, barely a year ago. 49 people died there. What horrible records. What horrible news. What a dark day.

So when I left this afternoon for a trip to the bank, my mood matched the day. I tried sitting down this afternoon to work on the new book, but I kept drifting off into the blank stares. I switched to trying to start a new short story from an idea that hit this weekend, but after typing NO TITLE YET, the blank stares returned. Not only no title, but no story, I thought. No motivation. No energy. No nothing. So I gave up, shut down, and pointed my convertible Semi's nose toward the bank.

I'd only gone a short distance when I noticed the police car in my rearview mirror. I checked my speed – I was fine, and I made sure I stayed there. My right hand was on the wheel, my left arm rested on the open window, so it was clear I wasn't doing anything with my phone. Even though the police car followed me through several turns, I was relatively relaxed – I wasn't doing anything wrong. My license plate had current stickers. All was well.

But then he flashed his lights at me. No siren, but the red and blue flicker of doom.

A dark day. I pulled over.

He waited for a bit before getting out of his car and approaching me. He rested both of his hands on my driver's side door. "Ma'am," he said, "why don't you have your seatbelt on?"

I glanced down. "I do," I said, and I showed him my lap belt. Then I leaned forward so he could see that the shoulder harness was behind my back. "I just don't have the shoulder part on," I said.

His eyebrows quirked. He straightened. "Why not? You're required to have the whole seatbelt on, ma'am. It's the law."

I nodded. "Yes, sir, I know. But I'm in recovery from breast cancer," I said. "I finished four weeks of radiation treatments a week ago. My right breast is burned, and the shoulder harness hits me on one of the most painful spots. I've blistered and I'm peeling." I gestured at my shirt. "It's all I can do to wear clothes right now. The harness is excruciating."

He stood there for a moment. I wondered if I was going to get a ticket. Then he said in a soft voice that transformed him from policeman to boy, "I remember. My mother had breast cancer. She couldn't wear the shoulder harness for a while either." Then he patted my shoulder. "I'm sorry if I just added to your stress. Keep the lap belt on, please. Be safe. And feel better." He returned to his car.

I counted to ten, took some deep breaths. Then I pulled out into traffic again. He followed behind me. When he turned right at the next intersection, he waved.

It was a dark day. But there are kind people in this world. Kind, kind people.

And yes, that helps. Despite. Anyway.

### OCTOBER 3, 2017

And so today's moment of happiness despite the news.

*MY SEASONS ARE MOVING BACKWARDS the sting of new skin
like Spring pushing up through radiation's
    Summer burn.*

When I got out of bed this morning, I felt a new type of pain. Lighter. A pinch, a poke. A tickle of an itch. But not searing. Right at the moment, right where I am in the process, any new pain creates inroads of fear anFd fury, even when it's not as sharp, not as encompassing. My new involuntary mantra, what the hell is this then what the hell is this then woke up with me; I rose in full chant. Going into the bathroom, I turned on the lights and faced the mirror, right arm straight up.

Peeling. The peeling of my radiation–burned skin started yesterday, with puckers and little tiny tears. But now, huge sections of the dead skin were gone. And ohmygod, peeking out was…pink.

Skin that twinged with newness. Skin that only knew the dark undersurface of burn now felt cool air.

Light pain. But a positive pain.

I turned this way and that, lifted my breast, checked every curve. And everywhere, new skin shone through. Pink. Sensitive. Gentle. New. Untouched.

I touched.

Soft. I remembered touching my babies. I thought of flower petals, and the thought gave way to my favorite flower, daffodils, which dropped me headlong into Spring.

We are moving into Fall. I've just gone through the Summer of Breast Cancer. But now, my skin, my body, turned the calendar back.

Spring. New. Soft.

Every year, when Winter passes, I welcome Spring. This Fall, I welcome Spring in me.

And yes, that helps. Despite. Anyway.

## OCTOBER 4, 2017

*Special note: This was the one day I deliberately did not write about a moment. For the second time this year, Michael lost his job. And with it, our health insurance. And I was in recovery from breast cancer. There was no moment.*

## OCTOBER 5, 2017

And so today's moment of happiness despite the news.

Yesterday, for the first time since I started this blog in January, I didn't post a Moment. I just couldn't. And yet I've managed to post on the worst possible days. The day my mammogram went unexpectedly south. The day I received my diagnosis of breast cancer. I even managed to post this past Monday, while the world reeled from the shooting in Las Vegas.

Doing these blogs has been a solid lesson for me. If I look hard enough, I'll find the Moment. Sometimes, it's so big, I can't help but see it. Other days, so tiny, I have to search with a magnifying glass, and a magnifying heart.

But yesterday was an Oh, hell no! day. I didn't post. And I feel badly about that. I promised publicly that I would do it every day for a year. And now my every day has been broken. I'm feeling broken too.

Years and years ago, when I was about to turn 21, I was driving my 1969 Chrysler Newport 4-door sedan home from my summer job. I was in between my junior and senior year of college. I'd just gotten married for the first time. I was young and even at that age, I was already skeptical. But that day, it was summer and all four windows were open and the radio was on (WKTI, 94.5 FM). I was driving down a heavily treed lane and the cornfields were tall and green, going to golden. I was following, respectfully, a motorcycle.

Ahead of us and to the right, a young cat suddenly sprang from the cornfield. She sprinted quickly across the center line and I thought, Oh, whew, good, she's not going to get hit. And then I saw the motorcyclist cross the center line and deliberately run over the cat.

Even now, 36 years later, I can still see that little cat, body flat, but her head up, watching the motorcyclist drive away. That little cat was thinking, What the hell just happened?

Yesterday, I was that little cat.

Michael's new employer, out of the blue, decided they didn't want a Senior Accountant. They're going the bookkeeper route, and they didn't want to "insult" him by offering him that position.

Oh, insult him. Insult him please. The title doesn't matter. The money is something we can deal with. But now, with breast cancer, we can't lose the insurance.

Michael's employer is aware of the breast cancer. And it's interesting how they've used that awareness, this being breast cancer awareness month.

So, the little cat. I hit the brakes on the big Chrysler and wrestled it to the side of the road. Then I went and stood over that little cat, making sure other cars that came along swung around. I talked to her the whole time. "Are you okay? Can you move? Are you going to be all right?" She swiveled her head from watching the departing motorcycle and looked up at me instead. I didn't know cats could look so shocked. And so, so hurt.

Pretty much, I'm sure, how I looked yesterday.

Oh, I don't know if he saw, but I flipped my middle finger at the departing motorcycle. I didn't yell. I didn't want to scare the cat.

Eventually, she started trying to get up. She got her legs under her. I bent and held my hands to her sides, so she could bounce gently against me as she gained her balance. She was feral and I got some hisses, but I wasn't about to quit. She began to move across the street toward the cornfield and I bent over her the whole way.

*Are you okay? Are you going to be all right?*

Her back had a sway that worried me, but she kept moving and by the time we hit gravel, she broke into a slow trot and disappeared into the cornfield.

Early this morning, I wanted to disappear into a cornfield. I got into my Chrysler 300C Hemi and I drove for a couple hours, until almost two in the morning. Aimlessly. I was so shocked. And so, so hurt. Like that motorcyclist, like that little cat, someone had absolutely no regard for my life.

This morning, though, I felt people standing over me. Making sure that other cars would go around. I heard them asking me, *Are you okay? Can you move? Are you going to be all right?* I felt their hands to my sides as I got to my feet and began to move again. But I didn't go into the cornfield.

I kept moving down the road.

Oh, and Michael's old workplace? You've been flipped the bird.

And yes, that helps. Despite. Anyway.

## OCTOBER 6, 2017

And so today's moment of happiness despite the news.

The last 48 hours have been just a shitstorm of shock, sadness, and anger. And then, suddenly, I found myself this afternoon putting something into place that I have wanted to do for years.

I was sitting in Starbucks (of course), surrounded by school teachers, and to my left sat my own creative writing teacher from eons ago. On November 3rd, as part of a local book festival, I am sending a mass of writers, REAL writers, into the schools. 11 writers spread out over 8 high schools, 6 traditional and 2 non-traditional, and 1 middle school. All of the writers are traditionally published. All of them have novels, book-length memoirs, or book-length poetry collections. And all of them, ALL of them are connected to AllWriters'. They will be talking to the kids about the writing life, sharing their experiences, answering questions.

BAM.

I couldn't help but think about the event I attended last weekend for Stephen King and Owen King. 2400 people came. And at one point, Stephen King answered a question with, "Because I'm old and I'm rich and I can do what I want." A student of mine attended an event for Alan Alda last night. Another 2400 people. I wondered how many high school writers attended those events, and came away with the idea that what they saw and heard represented the writer's life.

It didn't. Those two events represented the exception.

As I sat in Starbucks and shaped, sculpted and delighted in putting together this program, I also thought about a comment I received on Facebook right before I left. Someone suggested I apply for jobs that provide insurance, and I put the studio on hold. The single one-word answer hit me hard as I sat there.

NO.

I've put 13 years of hard work into building AllWriters' Workplace & Workshop. It's gone international; I can no longer count how many countries our students represent. We've served thousands of writers. It is the most frustrating, godawful hard, bloodsweatandtears, back-breaking, amazing wonderful incredible thing I've ever done in my life. When I explained this, the person said that she understood, but that no business is worth a life.

Yes, there is a business worth a life. I will do my damnedest to get insurance in place so that I can continue being treated for breast cancer. But I will not walk away from the studio.

I think everyone has a line. That one is mine.

I looked around at the circle of teachers at Starbucks and I could have cried. Which I've been doing way too much of lately, but this would have been different. This would have been with the absolute joy of bringing something to high school students that I desperately wanted when I was that age. And that joy increased a hundred fold when I glanced to my left and realized I was doing it alongside the teacher that gave me everything he had when I was that age, and now was helping me create what I needed then.

I did offer up on Facebook yesterday that if any college or university wanted to hire me and give me insurance, they could. And quite honestly, and ego-y, they should. I can pretty much guarantee that I would increase their student success in the publication field. I am, for whatever reason, freakishly good at that. But even if that happened, it would be in addition to running the studio. Never ever EVER leaving it behind.

I felt such an incredible sense of rightness as I sat in my comfy Starbucks chair this afternoon. Not rightness, as in "I'm right and you're wrong," but rightness as in This is who I am, what I do, where I'm needed. I was exhausted, I was stressed, one particular burn on my right breast was making me want to scream, but I'm pretty sure that anyone looking at me would only have seen the glow of great energy.

In my collection, *Enlarged Hearts*, in the final story, there is a scene with the manager of Large & Luscious all alone late at night in her store. And I can tell you, in absolute honesty, that when I wrote this passage, I was writing about me and AllWriters':

*"And at night, like this, tucked away in her chair, alone in her store, the manager just felt safe. Content. She protected the store; the store protected her. The rest of the world was locked outside. At night, segregation felt good. There were no voices to hear, no faces to see. No one to bolster, to encourage and cheer. There was no need here. There was just the manager and the store. The manager felt her edges blur, and the store's edges blur. And they blended, the two of them. Partners. She couldn't explain it. But the store had a being all its own. On Sunday nights, when there was just silence and color and gentle light, the manager felt her hand held, her shoulders squeezed. The manager took care of everyone, but on Sunday nights, the store took care of her."*

We talk a lot about faith. I have absolute faith. I am taken care of. I will be all right.

And yes, that helps. Despite. Anyway.

## OCTOBER 7, 2017

And so today's moment of happiness despite the news.

Today is Homecoming at my daughter's high school. Which is also my high school – the one I graduated from. Olivia has a new boyfriend, Isaiah, and the two of them were planning a night of romance: dinner at the New China Buffet, then the dance, and maybe Denny's afterwards. I thought I had everything under control. Dress – check. Wrap – check. Shoes – check. Jewelry – check.

Then, at about 2:30 this afternoon, four and a half hours away from the big event, I walked into our local grocery store, in search of doughnuts for tomorrow's breakfast. Passing through the automatic doors, I remembered doing this last year, for Livvy's first Homecoming, at a different school, with a different boy, and I walked through these doors to pick up a...

...boutonniere. Oh, no! Uncheck, uncheck, uncheck!

I hadn't ordered it. I hadn't thought of it. And they usually needed a week or so in advance.

I flew through produce toward the floral section. My son, who works in the bakery, intercepted me. When I told him what I did, or didn't do, he said, "Go talk to Colleen. Tell her you're my mom. She'll help."

Colleen was just handing off a plastic box with a gorgeous boutonniere in it to another woman. A woman who thought ahead, who remembered, who ordered the damn thing. When Colleen turned to me, I explained who I was and my dilemma. And then I said, "I haven't been the best mother lately," and my tears rose with the truth of it.

She hugged me, then asked me the color of my daughter's dress, which was seafoam green. Then she smiled and grabbed my hand. "Come here," she said, and pulled me in to the refrigerated section. In a bucket of many-colored roses, all of which clashed with seafoam green, there was one perfect white rose. "Look," she said. "That one was waiting here for you."

If it wasn't so cold in the refrigerator, I likely would have dissolved.

Together, she and I picked out the ribbon, a lovely thing that would match the sparkle of my daughter's shoes. "Come back in twenty minutes," she said.

I did, and it was done, and it was perfect. Again, Colleen hugged me. "You're a great mother," she whispered in my ear.

She knows my son.

Last week, when I wrote about the policeman who didn't ticket me after he found me driving without the shoulder harness of my seatbelt, I said that there are kind people in this world. Kind, kind people. In a way, I think I've been a bit prejudiced. I've always believed that the kindest, most compassionate people exist in the arts. And maybe they do, but I allowed my belief to extend into the thought that all people in the arts are kind and compassionate.

Michael's now nonexistent job was in the arts, at a local theatre. When I pleaded with them to please either give my husband his job back, or give him the lesser position that was replacing his spot, or to at least give us a few more months of insurance so my breast cancer medication would be covered while he looked for other work, I was told that while they knew this was a difficult time, they wouldn't do it. They knew about the breast cancer. They didn't care.

But today, this woman in a grocery store florist department went out of her way to make me feel better. And she presented my daughter with the most beautiful boutonniere to give to the new love in her life. Despite my distraction. Despite my lack of attention.

And she told me I was a great mother.

And later, when we stood in the new boyfriend's living room and admired how color-coordinated the couple was, his mother whispered to me, "I just got the shirt this morning."

There are kind people in this world. Kind, kind people.

And yes, that helps. Despite. Anyway.

## OCTOBER 8, 2017

And so today's moment of happiness despite the news.

This afternoon, I presented on a poetry and prose panel with three lovely poets. I was prose (though I'm poetry too). We offered up an amazing amount of information and experience to the audience. For me, that's an ideal way to spend a Sunday afternoon.

For a few moments, we discussed how writers often have a second or even a third creative passion that they use to express themselves. I thought about my own, which is painting, and which is something I haven't done since my last trip to Oregon, during the summer of 2016.

I started painting years ago. I approached it cautiously, as if it was something I shouldn't be doing, almost like I was cheating on writing, as if writing was my lover and not my calling. I also wanted to chuck aside my tendency to perfectionism – I wasn't planning on doing anything professional with the painting, so I didn't want to take the time to learn technique. I just wanted to paint. Not for the world; for me.

I signed up for a class. The studio was amazing – the walls were floor to ceiling dry erase boards, and we taped our big heavy sheets of paper on these without care of making a mess or going off the paper. The paint was held on a trough that ran down the center of the room. The purpose was to allow us just to paint, to create what we saw in our heads, and not worry about making mistakes. There weren't mistakes.

Imagine.

I loved it. I used brushes. I used my hands, my fingers. I got flat-out messy. And…I didn't make any mistakes.

At the end of the year, the teacher had me come in on a Saturday. She hung all of my paintings around the room. I stood there in the middle and gaped. What was up there…was me.

I haven't painted now in over a year.

When I got home from the panel today, I found that my daughter was locked in her walk-in closet. The walk-in closet is Olivia's safe place. When the world is overwhelming, she goes in to the dark and quiet and she waits it out. My husband said she'd been working on a painting for her art class. She was using acrylics for the first time and she glopped on the background and of course it dried fast and now she didn't know how to fix it.

I stood outside the wall that was the kitchen on my side and Olivia's closet on the other. "I know you're upset," I called. "But if you want me to try to help, I'd be happy to try."

About a half-hour later, she came out. She said she needed white paint to tone down the bright red she'd spilled. We studied the painting together, and we studied the paints I had in my cabinet. "What if you made the pink parts darker, like the red you spilled?" I asked. "And here…I have a darker color. You can put that at the top, fade to the red, then fade to the pink at the bottom."

Have you ever felt a child light up? Not just see it, but feel it? I did.

"Why don't you paint anymore?" my daughter asked me as I handed her the paints.

I shrugged. "I don't have the time." And I thought about that. I've been thinking about that a lot; not having time for things. Like going to my daughter's orchestra concerts. Like painting. Like getting my mammograms. I suppose it's common to think about your lack of time when that lack of time bit you in the ass. Or in the breast, actually. I've been thinking about mistakes I've made.

I let her use my portable easel, so she could paint a little easier (and not on the rug in her room). I told her she could keep the easel if she wanted.

"No," she said. "I'll use it when I need it. And I don't have the space in my closet."

No, because that's her space.

Painting is mine, isn't it.

The world has been very overwhelming lately. It's time for me to find time.

And yes, that helps. Despite. Anyway.

## OCTOBER 9, 2017

And so today's moment of happiness despite the news.

Today is Michael's and my 18th wedding anniversary. When I was married the first time, it lasted for 17 years, and Michael made me promise, on our wedding day, that I would remain married to him for at least 17 years and 1 day, so that he would smash my first husband's record.

Well, it's smashed, by way more than a day. It's made it longer by a year.

I wanted today to be special, to be a celebration of getting through 18 years, but also a celebration of making it over what I thought was the latest hurdle. I didn't know breast cancer was going to manacle my ankles and make sure that my future would remain uncertain, and I didn't know the manacles would be handed to Cancer by my husband's previous employer.

A little over a week ago, Michael and I spent the weekend in a lovely hotel in Milwaukee. We took a couple students to see a play. We went to see Stephen King and his son Owen present their new book. Part of our celebration was our anniversary. We didn't know that my husband was soon to be unemployed again. And that his employer would only give us until the end of the month before our health insurance is cut off.

I am so livid and so hurt, I just don't know what to do with myself. So this afternoon, I did nothing. I went back to bed. I am not a go-back-to-bed person. I am a what's-next-on-the-list person. But I didn't care.

I guess I am still that squashed kitten, looking after the motorcycle that just hit her.

I am surrounded by good people who are making it very clear that they care for me, and for what I do. But this outpouring of support is caused by another group of people demonstrating that they have no regard for my life, and no care for my family. This is a sobering thought.

I spoke with someone from ABCD today, and when I said I guessed I was lucky that this didn't happen right before surgery or during radiation, that it happened after treatment, she said, "Kathie, you are still in treatment. And you will be for years. Treatment includes medication and preventative care." And I realized that I was in a situation where I might not be able to take the medication anymore that keeps the cancer at bay, that I might not know if the cancer is back because I won't be able to have the tests that will look for it, and even if I do find out that it's back, I won't be able to do a damn thing about it. That was also very sobering.

Manacled. Flattened like a small cat run over by a motorcycle.

And so I went back to bed.

When I got back up, I found a message request on Facebook. A woman I don't know said, "I enjoy your moments of happiness posts. No matter how my day is going, when I see one of those, I know I will always come away with a better perspective." And I thought (think sarcasm here), Well, today's is really going to lift her up.

And then I laughed.

Hey, I laughed. I wiggled the manacles. And that's something.

And yes, that helps. Despite. Anyway.

## OCTOBER 10, 2017

And so today's moment of happiness despite the news.

Last night, Grandbaby Maya Mae was here. Olivia provided the babysitting while I was teaching a class online, and throughout the class, two voices that I love so well piped and laughed and drifted up the stairs to my office.

When class was done, it was time for me to pack up Maya Mae and go get her mother for the drive home. I admired Maya Mae's leopard-print dress draped gracefully over hot pink leggings, the leggings ending over beaded flip-flops. "You look beautiful, Maya Mae," I said. "You make a fashion statement."

She looked up at me, eyes wide. "Whaaaaaaaaaaat?"

Oboy. "A fashion statement. It means that you choose to wear what makes you feel beautiful. You wear stuff that you like and that makes you happy. You wear what makes you Maya Mae."

She thumped her chest. "I am ME!"

Indeed.

On the way to pick up her mother, Maya Mae suddenly said from the back seat, "Guess what?"

"What?"

"We have swocolate milk!"

Swocolate? "You have chocolate milk?'"

"Yes! It is a powder and you put it in milk and you stir and you stir and it makes swocolate milk!" Deep breath. "It's MAGIC!"

I looked in my rearview mirror. I swear the entire mirror was filled with big brown eyes. Big sparkling amazed brown eyes. Oh, there was the magic.

"Well, guess what, Maya Mae?"

"What?"

"There's a powder that makes strawberry milk too."

"WEALLY?" Then her voice dropped, and she spoke more to herself than to me. "Stwabewwy milk. I like stwawbewwies. Stwawbewwies are sweet."

Like you, I thought.

Remember the magic of powder in your milk? The metal container with the rabbit on the front and the big letter Q, and you had to pry the form-fitting lid off with a knife or yank your fingernails backwards, trying? The discussion over whether you poured the milk over the powder, or if you scooped the powder into the milk. And, when your mother wasn't looking, you added two more scoops. Maybe three, if you were lucky and she was distracted. Four. Your milk became a candy bar. And, if you were me, you stirred and stirred and then scooped the milk into your mouth with the spoon, like soup, and then you stirred and stirred again and you filled your ears and the kitchen with the clankety-clank of the spoon against the glass. And the sweet. Oh, the sweet.

I glanced in the rearview mirror again, where the big brown eyes, still wide, still sparkling, now contemplated stwabewwy milk.

Oh, there was the sweet.

Throughout my day today, as I bounced between frustrations, aggravations, unhappinesses, busynesses, and oh yes, good things too, the sweet, I took the time to glance in my rearview mirror and remember those big brown ⟨bwown⟩ eyes from the night before. Swocolate milk. Stwabewwy milk. I am ME!

There's the sweet. There's the magic. Leopard print. Pink leggings. Beaded flip-flops.

And yes, that helps. Despite. Anyway.

## OCTOBER 11, 2017

And so today's moment of happiness despite the news.

Last night, my daughter Olivia attended her first concert. She went to see a band called I Prevail at Milwaukee's Turner Hall Ballroom. This was a present for her birthday, and not just her birthday, but her GOLDEN birthday, and not just her GOLDEN birthday, but the birthday where she will be 17 on the 17th…in 2017.

Of course, she went to the concert on the 10th – I've already said I'm not good with numbers.

The concert was on a school night, and because of the golden issue and the fact that the child's grades are golden too, we allowed it. We bought two tickets and hoped that at least one other parent would understand our concert-on-a-school-night reasoning.

Nope.

So Olivia went with her father.

When I picked them up, driving through a pounding rain that left me white-knuckled, Olivia came bouncing toward me, all energy and happiness and excitement. She bubbled all the way home.

Michael, on the other hand, looked like he'd been standing for hours in the rain I just drove in. "The first band," he said, "was so loud, it drove all the snot out of my sinuses. I had to keep going to the bathroom to blow my nose." He's had a cold, so this is a good thing, but he kept on about how the band screamed and he had no idea what they were saying, though he did recognize the explosion of many, many f-bombs.

It made me remember my own mother, freaking out over my brother playing his Yoko Ono album. "Noise!" my mother said. Once, when I was playing an LP by the Moody Blues, my mother magically showed up in my doorway bedroom and shrieked, "What did they just say?" I picked up the needle of my stereo and thought back, reciting the lyrics. When I got to, "New mother picks up and suckles her son," my mother withered. "Oh," she said. "I thought they said, "New mother cuts up her circumcised son." And she walked away.

Well, yeah, that would change the meaning a bit.

There have been confusions and irritations over other people's musical tastes throughout history. I can remember the fuss over Springsteen's "Blinded By The Light", which he claims uses the word "deuce", but which the entire world heard as, "…wrapped up like a douche, another roller in the night." For years, my first husband and I fought over Genesis' "She Seems To Have An Invisible Touch". I heard it as, "She seems to have a physical attraction!" I didn't care what the title was. And my own personal favorite, Til Tuesday's "Voices Carry", which both Michael and I lustily sing as, "Hush, hush, keep it downtown, this is Gary!" What a nice advertisement for Indiana.

But you know, music has soothed throughout history too. I've used music for years, assigning a song to every novel I write, so that when I sit down to work, I can listen to the song and be transported out of my world and into the novel's. And I use music all the time to calm myself down, to pick myself up, to get myself through things.

Today, I thought of all this as I got into my car to run errands. Throughout radiation, I played the same song every day as I drove to the Cancer Center: "Battle Symphony" by Linkin Park. I haven't played it since September 25th, the last day I was zapped.

It was returned to my CD player today. And I sang. And my shoulders went back, I sat straight, and my voice rose.

So did I.

*"This is my battle symphony, all the world in front of me, if my armor breaks, I'll fuse it back together..."*

I understood every word. And I felt fused.

And yes, that helps. Despite. Anyway.

## OCTOBER 12, 2017

And so today's moment of happiness despite the news.

So I've suddenly developed a new form of insomnia. I've always had trouble falling asleep, but since beginning meditation 576 days ago, I conk almost immediately. For the last week, I've been going to bed between two and three, as usual, but then I'm awake again at four, until around six. I lay in bed and I ruminate, perseverate, mull, and generally stew.

This morning, I kept thinking about how some have said that Michael's employer's decision to let him go wasn't "personal".

And I realized that that's just my point. It SHOULD have been personal.

When we lose sight that there are human faces behind most everything that gets done in our world, when we lose sight that there are human lives, human needs, hell, just HUMANS, then we all get in trouble.

Years and years ago, when Olivia was still a newborn, Michael was let go from the advertising agency where he was working. We had a new baby and three teenagers. I didn't have the studio yet, instead teaching anywhere and everywhere in community and continuing education that would take me. Money wasn't just tight, it was gone. We had one week where we had $30 to feed the family – and Olivia's formula cost $20.

That was not pretty.

But the advertising agency, who had to lay people off because of losing a big account, didn't just show people the door. The ones that remained began to network and network and they didn't stop until everyone who lost their jobs had a new jobs. Michael was working within a month.

That company saw the humans behind the numbers, the additions, the subtractions, the ins and outs of a business.

At AllWriters', I keep close tabs on everyone. Sometimes, I have a student who can't quite afford to pay for what he or she needs. Sometimes, I have a student who needs a little extra help. They get it.

I know that some would say that this is why I am 57 years old, in charge of a successful business, and unable to afford to buy health insurance. That could be. But you know what? I don't regret it. And I would do it again. I do it still. Because it's the right thing to do.

So I kept mulling. And at around 5:30, I suddenly heard two words, loud and clear:

Oh, well.

And I thought, what?

Oh, well.

And then I figured out what I was trying to tell myself. I am doing everything I can to combat this, but there is only so much I can do. And in the end, what's going to change? Even if months go by and I use up the funds that are in the fundraising campaign and I do, ultimately, lose my health insurance, what am I going to do? Jump in front of a bus?

Of course not. I would get out of bed the next morning and go to work. Reading manuscripts. Meeting with students. Helping them get to where they want to be. Cheering for them when they do.

Just like I did this morning. Just like I've done for the last thirteen years. Well, actually, 21 years, if you take in my whole teaching career.

Seeing the human faces of every single person I work with. And taking them personally.

Because that's what I do. I'd keep living...until I'm not anymore.

And then I fell asleep, harder and deeper than I have for a week. Maybe longer.

Oh, well. It's my new mantra.

And yes, that helps. Despite. Anyway.

### OCTOBER 13, 2017

And so today's moment of happiness despite the news.

I wore a bra today!

Okay, so that has not been an accomplishment since I was eleven years old and my mother grudgingly handed me a white chest band with a little pink rose in the middle, which I think was supposed to signify where my future cleavage would be. My mother really didn't want me to start wearing a bra – she held off for as long as possible. I'm not exactly sure why, but she did prescribe to the "Once you start shaving, your hair grows in thicker and you can never ever stop" theory. So maybe she thought bra–ing those budding breasts meant they would get bigger faster and cause all sorts of problems.

Well, you know. There were a few.

The bra has been an on-and-off thing – literally – since my breast cancer diagnosis on June 27th. For a while, after surgery, the incisions hurt, and the lymph node one was just below the underarm strap, causing irritation and pain. It was painful not to wear one too, which made it an awful tit-for-tat situation (yes, that's deliberate). And then, just as bras became comfortable again, radiation began. I was doing okay until near the end, but then the burns showed up, followed by the peeling, and bras again went out the window. Not literally.

As I've spent the last month braless, it's brought back many memories. College years, vacillating between being a wild child while I thought I was being a wild woman, breasts loose and free and easy beneath my t-shirts and sweaters (and yes, I chose my words very carefully), and being a radical feminist, convinced that my participating in marches with my fist high in the air, my breasts marching with me beneath my "A woman needs a man like a fish needs a bicycle" t-shirt would somehow free the masses, especially the female masses. Not wearing a bra then was a sign of freedom, of individuality, of not being under the thumb of the Man.

But for the last month of my 57-year old life, being braless has been a sign of annoyance and anger and wondering if life was ever going to be normal again.

This morning, facing a day where my clients were all either on Skype (seeing me from the shoulders up) or the phone, I dressed with the abandon of not really needing to see anyone. My favorite ripped and threadbare happy jeans (Michael saw them draped over the loveseat the other day and he said, "Aren't these the jeans you were going to throw out?" I just can't.) and my Ray Bradbury t-shirt, soft with frequent wears and trips through the washing machine. But before I pulled Ray over my head, I cautiously put on a bra. I walked around the room. I twisted to the left and right.

No pain.

When I was fully dressed, I stopped for a moment in front of our full-length mirror. "Well, okay now," I said, a variation of yesterday's mantra, "Oh, well."

I believe the operative word here is "well." Because that's what I'm moving steadily toward.

Wearing a bra today is an accomplishment. A sign of recovery. I suppose it's possible that my mother's prediction that wearing a bra could only lead to trouble was true, given what was in my future. But my words today are true too.

Well, okay now. I'm well. I'm okay. Now.

And yes, that helps. Despite. Anyway.

## OCTOBER 14, 2017

And so today's moment of happiness despite the news.

Grandbaby Maya Mae was over again today, so we took her out to dinner at her favorite restaurant: Applebees. Maya Mae is a great connoisseur of macaroni and cheese, applesauce and apple juice.

As the four of us, Michael, me, Olivia and Maya Mae, sat and waited for our food, and I nursed the vat of watermelon sangria in front of me, I couldn't help but notice the variety of topics that bounced around our table. *The Spoon River Anthology.* Whether or not girls should be allowed into the Boy Scouts and if boys should be allowed into the Girl Scouts. Fashion, particularly admiring the fringe vest that Maya wore. My upcoming visit to Olivia's high school, talking about the writing life with the students there, and then on the computer with students at the online school .Best friends, boyfriends. Maya listed seven kids that are her closest friends in 4K, including a boy named Scofield. We discussed the name Scofield.

At one point, Maya Mae put her hands on her hips and declared, "You know what, Gamma Kaffee? Dey don't even haf show'n'tell yet!"

Wait, what? No show'n'tell? The horror! The horror! "No show'n'tell?" I raved, appropriately shocked.

"No! An' I haf stuff to SHOW!"

I've no doubt about that.

She also told us that there are two playgrounds at school...the big one and the little one. "You haf to walk to da big one from da little one," she informed. "And you haf to walk to da little one from da big one."

Makes perfect sense to me. But no show'n'tell?

From there, we somehow got on the subject of banned books. I googled for Olivia "banned books in the Waukesha school district", and we pored over the variety of articles on parents trying to get certain books removed from the shelves of school libraries. We weren't able to find one article where the book was actually removed; the banning was always shot down.

Still, Olivia huffed and took down the names of the books that were threatened. She vowed to read every one.

I remembered and talked about my own time in this high school, with one of my favorite classes, which was called Growing Up In Literature And Reality. We read *The Catcher In The Rye, To Kill A Mockingbird, Dinky Hocker Shoots Smack, Tell Me That You Love Me, Junie Moon, Wanda Hickey's Night Of Golden Memories*. I hope beyond hope that my daughter and granddaughter are exposed to these books in school. If not, they're all on my own shelves in the AllWriters' classroom.

I found an article on the 10 most commonly banned books in public schools and Olivia pored over that one too, while I played peekaboo with a jack-in-the-box Maya Mae. Often the only part of her I could see was her splayed-fingered little hand on the surface of the table, while the rest of her ducked under.

When we walked out to the car, that same warm little hand tucked itself into mine without my asking and I smiled in the starry dark. I love that little hand.

As we drove home, I listened to the two of them in the back seat, seventeen-next-week Olivia and five-in-January Maya. Chirpy voices. Olivia went to her first concert last week, to see a band called I Prevail, which I've never heard of. Turns out Maya Mae sings a song by them. 12 years between them, they synced with music.

I thought of them, each with their hands on their hips. Maya outraged that her school hadn't offered show'n'tell yet when she had things to show, and Olivia outraged over banned books when she has a desire to read. Maya wants to SHOW! and Olivia wants to KNOW! Neither one of them shy about expressing their feelings or their needs. Neither one shy about making demands and standing up for her rights.

I smiled in the starry dark. And kept on listening.

And yes, that helps. Despite. Anyway.

### OCTOBER 15, 2017

And so today's moment of happiness despite the news.

Today, I introduced one of my students at the launch of her first novel. This has become a not-so-uncommon thing at AllWriters', but it is no less extraordinary than the first time I did it. In the last four years, almost 100 AllWriters' writers have landed traditional book-publishing contracts. In that same four years, we've not gone a single week without an AllWriters' acceptance in a magazine or an anthology. It's amazing, and no one is more amazed than I am.

Helping students to reach their goals and their dreams is a primary joy in my life. Watching them step headlong into their success is another.

I've heard lots of thank-yous. That's also not-so-uncommon, but always extraordinary. Each one bowls me over. Today's student said, "I wouldn't be standing here today if it wasn't for Kathie."

But it's a partnership. If I had a student that didn't have the drive to remain standing, there would be nothing I could do to keep his or her feet on this earth. But those students who want to remain standing even as they question if they can, well, I can join forces with them and help raise them up strong.

My favorite moments? When I look at a student, see him or her holding their published poem, published story, published book, and I lean in and say, "I told you so."

I said it to a student whose book was accepted last week. I said it to a student whose book was accepted a month ago. And I said it to this student whose book launched today. I said it and I will say it again.

The student today signed her book for me with, "You kick ass."

Yes, I do.

When I came home from the event, I tucked this student's book with the others on the special shelf that showcases AllWriters' authors. Then I tucked a second copy into our Little Free Library, doing my own little launch ceremony, celebrating another AllWriters' success, sending that student's work out into the world.

As I walked up the stairs to my office, where I will settle for the rest of the night, reading manuscripts, critiquing, editing, it was with a great sense of satisfaction.

And you know what? Satisfaction gets you through.

There's been a lot of crap in my life lately. From breast cancer to my husband's job loss to the threat of no insurance and breast cancer treatment screeching to a halt and one of our dogs today ripping a claw out of her foot and spouting blood like a demon and requiring a sudden trip to the emergency vet and god knows what else, a day like today makes one thing ring loud and clear in my mind and my heart and my soul.

I love my life. I love what I do. I regret nothing.

And yes, that helps. Despite. Anyway.

## OCTOBER 16, 2017

And so today's moment of happiness despite the news.

I took a sort of unintentional mini roadtrip today. I'll be appearing at a bookstore just short of an hour from here in November, and they wanted five copies of *In Grace's Time* for promotional purposes. My publicist could have mailed them, but I decided to take them out there myself, as I'd not seen this particular bookstore.

It was a lovely day, one of those days that reminds you not only of the summer days you just had, but of the winter days to come, because you can just feel the last-minute of it. So I took Semi, my convertible, put the top down, turned the heated seat on, turned the temperature control on the heat to 78 degrees, put on a jacket, and I headed down the freeway. I'd been told that I would just exit the freeway and go straight to the store...but Naggie, my GPS, had other ideas.

I have a strange GPS. I have had her since the early 2000s, and I haven't replaced her because she has a way of sending me on journeys. I've known other people with the same model GPS, but when we go to the same place, Naggie takes me a different way. She always gets me where I'm supposed to be, though, so I've learned to trust her. And somehow, she seems to always know just what I need.

So I was tooling down the freeway, wind whipping, heat on, music up, singing, when Naggie yelled over it all, insisting that I exit in an unexpected place. There hadn't even been signs for my destination yet, not even on those signs that tell you how far away different cities are. But I did as I was told. And after just a couple of orders to "Turn left here, then right," and "turn right here, then left," I found myself in absolutely stunning middle-of-nowhereness. I shut off the music and Semi and I just scrolled the two-lane roads. We saw:

*cornfields gone to gold and trees gone to orange and yellow,

*barns that whispered their red and barns that boasted it,

*farms and farms and farms. Some with names like Homeview and Sweetsong,

*cows and horses and goats. When the big kids were young and Olivia was younger, it was our tradition to make the sounds of all the animals we passed. I honored that tradition,

*two small tilted-headstone graveyards. I wanted to stop and pay my respects, but there was no time, so I bowed my head as I drove by. I did the same with the two dead deer,

*a little clear-glass lake, crowned with a rusted bridge,

*pumpkins for sale, displayed on picnic tables, around trees, on old, old wagons, and a lucky few that became the heads of scarecrows,

*a man mowing his lawn on an old John Deere, who waved at me as I

passed (the man did, not the tractor),

*and quiet. Just the purr of my engine, the hum of tires, and the rustle of trees. Quiet.

It was lovely. And it was just what I needed.

Thank you, Naggie.

And yes, that helps. Despite. Anyway.

## OCTOBER 17, 2017

And so today's moment of happiness despite the news.

Seventeen years ago today, at the age of 40 years old, I gave birth to my fourth child, my second girl, and the only child from my second marriage. Because of my age, and because she was my fourth, I thought I had everything under control. I'd seen it all, I thought. A son who couldn't stand to touch jello or shaving cream or mud or grass or to wear blue jeans or t-shirts with the tag on the inside. Another son who became so obsessed with maps that we canceled our AAA and used him to get us from Waukesha, WI to Washington DC...at the age of five. A daughter who learned after only one repetition, they told us, when the average person takes at least five, and who they wanted to skip at least two grades (we said no, thank you). Map son also a boy who was scared of EVERYTHING...cars, trucks, airplanes, sirens, trains, lawn mowers, fish, exposed rafters (yes, rafters – only kid I know who was terrified of Toys R Us). Don't-touch-me son who became so enraptured with dinosaurs that at the age of four, he led a presentation on the topic to a group of first-graders, complete with Q & A and the ease of a seasoned speaker. Learns-fast daughter who wanted to do all things boy while wearing a dress and tights, and who soaked her socks because she wanted to pee like her brothers.

I'd seen a lot. Olivia couldn't be that different.

Right.

When the word autism was handed to us, I didn't know what to think. Olivia was difficult at times. She was nonverbal until she was three. But I always thought of her as just Olivia. She was herself. She was quirky. My quirky (exhausting), quirky (creative), quirky (sees the world in her own way) girl.

Her presents today, at seventeen: a pink ukulele. A multi-medium combination painting of a VW Beetle. A necklace of a skeleton of a mermaid, and skeletons for her ears too. Infinity bracelets. A shirt that says, "Uke, I am your father," with a picture of a guitar and a ukele on it. And a few other things for my quirky (goofy) girl.

Tonight, I appeared at a local library. They had a nice reception and then I read from *In Grace's Time*. Taking questions afterwards, a woman raised her hand and told me she was currently reading *Oddities & Endings*. "I've only read a few stories so far," she said, "but it's clear you write…quirky."

And I do. I'm known for quirky characters. Characters that aren't like anybody…but are also just like somebody you know.

And then I realized. Inside (my mind when I'm writing, my body when I'm pregnant), I produce quirk. And outside (my stories and my children), I produce quirk. Quirk, for me, is normal.

Must be that quirkiness is genetic.

But I look at these four children, three who are now amazing adults, one who is an almost-adult and well on her way to amazing, and I love them for their differences. I had to give up on reading parenting books because my kids were never ever represented in those pages. But mothering now for thirty-three years, almost thirty-four, it's been an incredibly rich experience. And when I look behind me on my desk, at the seven books lined up there, each one the first out of the box when my copies were sent to me by my publisher, I love each and every one of my characters too, for their differences. I also gave up, early on, on reading how-to-write books, because what I wanted to say, and how I wanted to say it, was never ever there.

My kids accept their differences. And I accept mine.

So I guess I love the difference in me too.

Happy birthday to my youngest baby.

And yes, that helps. Despite. Anyway.

## OCTOBER 18, 2017

And so today's moment of happiness despite the news.

Last night, I presented *In Grace's Time* at a local library for a Meet-The-Author event. When I finished reading, I took in a breath, about to ask if anyone had any questions. But before I could, a woman in the front row leaned forward.

"And you got all that," she said, "ALL that…just from your mind?"

And I beamed. Because it is an amazing thing, isn't it.

This magic of putting down a word and then another and finally a sentence and then you do it again and again and soon there's a paragraph and a page and then a story and somehow it all comes together even though you likely started it all with a barely coherent thought…well, this has been a part of my life for as long as I can remember. It's just such a wonder.

"All from my mind," I answered. "Yes."

The woman sat back and said, "Wow."

I loved that wow.

I would like to say that, as the one writing the words, the one performing the magic, I'm the magician and I know how the trick works. But I don't. The trick works me. And it surprises me every time.

Sometimes the magic hits a clunker. Remember Rocky and Bullwinkle? One of the segues in their show was when Bullwinkle says, "Hey, Rocky, watch me pull a rabbit out of my hat!" Rocky answers, "Again?" Bullwinkle persists, says, "Nothing up my sleeve…", reaches into the hat and pulls out any number of non-rabbity things. Still magic, because how did that lion/monster/whatever get into the hat, but not the intended magic.

I was just reading a student's manuscript and this student had a very Bullwinkle moment. This student is typically a magic master and so I was enthralled as I read. And then I hit the final line. And something very non-rabbity happened. Oh, dear.

But here's more magic. I know we're going to talk tomorrow and she's going to make an unhappy face at me and then she's going to get it right. And the story will get so rabbity, there will be a magic explosion. Complete with a handkerchief that never ends, a white dove, and a woman sawed in half.

Words are magic.

Over the last couple days, words proved their magic and their impact all over social media, on Facebook, on Twitter. A phenomenon. The motivation was to simply acknowledge if you were a woman who had been sexually harassed or assaulted in your lifetime. Two words, a total of five letters, smacked the face of the earth.

"Me too."

I marveled.

I think, though, that I might have wondered something a little different than most. From comments that I read and articles that came too, it seemed like most of the intent was behind waking up the male gender to what they were doing. But I wondered if this would wake some of the female gender up as well.

The women who rushed to the movie theatres to see *50 Shades Of Gray*, a movie that glorified rape and abuse and called it romance, based on a book that glorified rape and abuse and called it romance. The women who read that book in their book clubs, particularly those who did it in their mother and daughter book clubs.

Women who voted for the Orange Asshat, even after he admitted to assaulting women. Women who, after that admission, came to his rallies wearing printed t-shirts proclaiming, "Donald! Grab this pussy!"

The words on those t-shirts were not magic. They were the lion/monster/whatever that has given me nightmares ever since.

But now I'm dreaming. Hopeful dreams.

Because there is magic in two words. Five letters.

Me too.

And yes, that helps. Despite. Anyway.

### OCTOBER 19, 2017

And so today's moment of happiness despite the news.

Which one do I choose?

I met over lunch with a book club that read *Rise From The River*, which was published in 2015. This was a wonderful change of pace for me; with a new book out, you typically end up talking about nothing but the new book. But here, I was able to go back and discuss the novel that took me 20 years to build up the courage to complete. And the discussion happened during the week of the #MeToo phenomenon, which was beyond kismet, as *River* is about what happens to a woman who becomes pregnant as the result of a rape. The book takes place during the first trimester.

This book club was an amazing collection of intelligent, articulate women. The discussion was thorough; the comments thought-out and sincere. Two women said that they are anti-abortion, but that this book opened their eyes to a situation where abortion needs to be an option. One said, "I always thought that abortion was a black or white issue; but after reading your book, I can see now that it's not. It's gray."

As I sat and listened and sat and spoke, I was filled with that one moment that writers live for: the book spoke, it spoke clearly, and it said just what I wanted it to say. These women were touched, these women were moved, and these women understood. There is absolutely nothing like that moment. My book made a difference. Rainey and Doris, my two main characters, made a difference.

I made a difference.

*In Grace's Time* was not ignored as the newcomer. The women asked about it and at the end, most everyone bought a copy. I did lots and lots of signing today.

When I left, I was exhausted and happy. The women gave me a couple envelopes which

I figured were thank-you notes and I didn't open them until I got home. When I did, I was bowled over. I didn't know that the book club knew about my breast cancer and the issues I've faced since Michael lost his job. But those envelopes were stuffed with cash and two pre-paid gas cards.

I was beyond stunned.

And then…and then…

Last week, I had the happy accident of learning about the Authors League Fund. The ALF is associated with the Authors' Guild, of which I'm a member, and it's been around since 1917. I've never heard of it before. But it exists for the sole purpose of helping writers in financial distress, especially those with medical issues. Writers donate to it, and those funds are used to help writers who need it. I filled out the application, sent it in, and within 24 hours, found myself talking to someone about my situation.

When I got into my car after the book club today, carrying my envelopes and feeling happier than I have since Michael lost his job, I found an email from ALF. They are sending me a check which, when combined with the money raised by the GoFundMe campaign, will allow me to afford the six months of Cobra insurance I was asking for.

In my car, top down, sun everywhere, blue sky and autumn leaves offering a palette of color that didn't have the word pastel in its vocabulary, two unopened envelopes in one hand, my phone displaying the email in the other, my ears still ringing with the discussion of *River*, I became totally unraveled.

You know what? For the first time since October 4, I think I'm going to be okay.

I am being lifted up by the kindness of students and readers. Writers. Friends and family. And I am being lifted up by the kindness of strangers.

I don't even know what to say.

Yes, I do.

Thank you. Thank you, thank you, thank you, thank you.

And yes, that helps. Despite. Anyway.

## OCTOBER 20, 2018

And so today's moment of happiness despite the news.

Generally, when I walk the dogs after lunch, I'm not particularly happy to be doing so. People use the phrase "herding cats" when something is difficult. "Trying to get everyone together for this meeting is like herding cats!" But you know what? I have two cats and I have two beagles. Herding cats is easy peasy compared to herding beagles.

The noses. The stomachs. The BADD – Beagle Attention Deficit Disorder. They go here, they go there, they stop and dig their feet into the ground and refuse to move until their noses have sniffed out every scent left in just that spot since the earth was formed. And there is always another spot just a step way. Trust me, I outweigh my beagles by quite a bit. But when they don't want to move, I can't move them.

But today was different. Today was quite possibly the most perfect capture of an in-between season. It was Summer/Fall. It's October 20th, but I was wearing a t-shirt, capris, and sandals. It was sunny and warm. All around us, the leaves were falling. The trees were red and gold and orange. When we walked, there was that wonderful scuff-scuff sound that you get when you step through fallen leaves…but it was accompanied by the slapping flip-flop of my sandals. Summer! Fall! Summer/Fall!

It was glorious.

Even beagle-braking didn't make me upset (yes, I meant braking, not barking). I didn't mind braking. I didn't mind standing for moment and watching the leaves and feeling the sun and just…aaaaaaaaaaaaaaah.

Over the last couple weeks, well, ever since Michael lost his job on October 4th, I've been saying and thinking that I want to get back to June 19th. On June 19th, I didn't know yet about the breast cancer. I knew I had an appointment the next day for my regular mammogram, but it was barely a blip on my radar as I figured out how the day was going to go, how I was going to rearrange my usual schedule before and after the appointment so that everything could still get done.

On June 20th, it all went according to plan until the mammogram. And then my world blew apart. I've been trying to put it back together ever since.

Standing in the sun today, feeling summer's heat while fall leaves swirled around me and gathered at my sandal-clad feet, I felt it and saw it all. I saw the past: Summer. I saw the future: Fall. And I stood in the middle of them both in today.

Because I meditate, I get barraged with a lot of platitudes telling me to stay in the Now, be in the Present, Om, Namaste and so on. And I do think it's important to be aware of the present – that's sort of what the Today's Moment is all about. But I also think that being aware of the past and the future is important too. We learn from the past. We take our experience into the future.

Today, I reveled in the past – the heat and light of a summer almost gone. But I also rejoiced in the future – the colors, the swish and swirl of this not-quite-warm, not-quite-cold fall-about-to-be. And I stood in today, planted firmly by two stubborn beagles.

I am definitely learning from this past summer – the importance of self-care, the fragility of life, and I will never ever again go for four years without a mammogram. I am taking those lessons into the future, looking forward to all the bright colors and sounds, but also aware that things can change in a flat second.

And I am grateful for today. Even while dragging beagles around the block, and then having them drag me.

The things I learn from herding beagles. Don't tell the cats.

And yes, that helps. Despite. Anyway.

### OCTOBER 21, 2017

And so today's moment of happiness despite the news.

My daughter's birthday was last Tuesday and a loving uncle sent her a gift card for the store Forever 21. When a girl turns 17 and someone sends her a gift card, do you know what happens? The gift card follows her around on secret little feet and shrieks, "Use me use me use me use me!" until she can't stand it anymore and so she convinces her mother that she has to go right now right now right now right now.

So we went.

When you are fifty-seven years old and your nerves have been a bit shot lately due to happenings in your life and you've always been sensitive to noise and to crowds and you like things orderly and neat, stores like Forever 21 are a nightmare. Narrow aisles. Clothes not just hung, but heaped spilling from piles on tables and racks and shelves and floors. Loud relentless music. Teenage girls and young women in high-pitched staccato conversation punctuated with shrieking laughter, barreling through the store with vaulting strides. Noise, noise, noise. People, people, people. Stuff, stuff, stuff.

But I love my daughter, so I took a deep breath and dove in.

And she loved EVERYTHING.

"Ohmygod! This is so poofy! And so soft! And ohmygod, I LOVE these! And look, the Care Bears! Ohmygod! Mario! Ohmygodohmygod, puffy camo! Oh, WOW! Rainbows!"

All at three thousand miles per hour with nary a breath in between sentences. Everything she loved got thrown over my extended arms. I soon became one of the messy racks.

Eventually, I followed her voice to the fitting rooms. The nice woman there put us in the furthest back room, a large room, with a great bench and faux stone wallpaper. As Livvy tried on clothes, she jabbered nonstop, and I got a few words in edgewise. I noticed her belt, bought for her when she was around 12, was getting more than a little frayed. "A new belt?" I asked.

"YES!"

I'd recently been in Claire's, looking for jewelry for this child for her birthday (she got a necklace that is an iridescent skeleton of a mermaid - really) and noticed that there were displays of suspenders, thus announcing their return to the fashion scene. So I said, "Would you like suspenders?" She gasped, I thought in a positive way. "You'd have to wear your shirts tucked in though."

"Ohmygod, NO!" she shrieked. "I don't want to be a farmer! I'd be all, like, farmer's market and 'Hey, you wanna buy my potatoes?'"

And then she was gone in a gale of giggles. No, not giggles. Not for this kid. Guffaws. Howling happy totally in the here and now belly laughs at her very own self, at her own humor, and at the audacity of a mother suggesting suspenders.

Since she was a baby, Olivia's laugh has been joyfully infectious. Whenever she laughed, people around her joined in. And so did I. Hearing her laugh today, seeing her laugh personified, her arms hugging herself in a fuzzy rainbow sweater, her head tossed back, in full roar, she shot me through with the joy she's given me since she was born.

So I joined in.

When Olivia was around three, one of the therapists in the Birth To Three program said, "Even though she's not speaking, there's no doubt what

Olivia is feeling. She IS her emotion. She embodies it."

Today, she embodied joy and she threw it at me, drowning out the din of the store and the chaos of the last couple weeks.

Smart move. Because of course she got more than what her gift card covered.

So worth it.

And yes, that helps. Despite. Anyway.

## OCTOBER 22, 2017

And so today's moment of happiness despite the news.

I've learned that there are some definite pluses to my accountant husband working in the deli of a grocery store.

*He comes home smelling like the 35 pounds of salami he sliced. World's best cologne! Just ask our beagle.

*He brings home deli fried chicken for dinner, and he remembers that I love the BLT salad.

*And the stories. Oh, the stories. Really, really interesting people come to grocery stores.

But still. On Sunday mornings, it's tradition for Michael and me to sleep in. When we wander downstairs, we sit side by side in our reclining loveseat. During the fall and winter, we turn the fireplace on. During the spring and summer, the windows are open and a breeze slips through, along with the sounds of a city on Sunday. There are usually two snoozing beagles on the couch, a snoozing gigantic orange cat on the chair across the room, and a little gray cat sleeping between us. I have a cup of the hottest coffee I can muster, and a doughnut or two from the bakery (from the same store where my husband now works). He has whatever he's in the mood for – usually some form of dry cereal. His crunching accompanies my slurping my coffee.

When we're settled, I read the Sunday paper, always in the same order. The comics. The arts section. The home and garden section. And this week's house sales. I show Michael the comics that make me laugh. From the arts section, I let him know which writers are coming to town and I read out loud my favorite columns. The home and garden section gives us this week's recipes and we either find them interesting or ew in unison over those that have ingredients we've never heard of, don't know how to pronounce or would just never touch.

And then we go about our day.

I love Sunday mornings.

I felt strongly today the drawbacks to my accountant husband working in the deli of a grocery store.

*Weekends are no longer "off". I woke up alone.

*Half of the loveseat was empty. I still had the dogs, the cats, the newspaper, the fireplace, the coffee and the doughnuts, but…half the loveseat was empty.

*The comics didn't make me laugh even when they were funny.

*I read through my favorite columns in silence.

*Even the recipes that were appetizing weren't appetizing.

*I went about my day, but I kept an eye on the clock.

At 4:00, I had my Today's Moment Of Happiness Despite The News.

He came home, smelling of salami and carrying a bag of fried chicken and a plastic container of BLT salad.

He came home.

And yes, that helps. Despite. Anyway.

## OCTOBER 23, 2017

And so today's moment of happiness despite the news.

I'm still working this one through in my head, so bear with me please.

I had to run errands this afternoon. When I was through at the post office, I turned Hemi toward the grocery store, to pick Michael up at the end of his shift. As I idled at a stoplight, I watched a couple walking away from me on the other side of the intersection. The man was clearly in pain. He would take a step, then swing his other leg, held straight, in an arc, and then gingerly put his foot down. Every now and then, his torso began to twist and torque and the woman beside him placed a hand on his elbow to steady him. They stopped, then moved forward. And again.

When the light turned green, I pulled up alongside them and rolled down my window. "Sir," I called, "sir, would you like a ride somewhere? Can I help you?"

He and the woman peered in at me. And when he smiled, it felt like the rainy day became sunny. "Thank you, ma'am," he said. "Thank you so much. I appreciate it. But we're just going to the bank there." He motioned to the next building. The woman smiled too, and patted his arm.

So I drove on.

When I pulled up to the grocery store, I looked around for Michael. There are no benches outside the store, so he was sitting on the sidewalk, leaning against the building. He looked tired. It was now 2:30 in the afternoon – he'd been on his feet at work since six in the morning. When you're used to working in an office, switching suddenly to eight hour shifts all on your feet takes a physical toll.

When he got into the car, he pointed to an older couple a few parking rows over, loading bags into their large pick-up truck. "See them?" he said.

He then went on to tell me how he was sitting there, waiting for me, when this couple came out. They looked at him and one said to the other, "I wonder why he's sitting on the sidewalk."

"Must be he can't afford a car, working here," the other said.

And then they walked off, as if Michael couldn't hear them as he sat there.

So I drove Hemi down one aisle and up the other, so we could be in direct eyeshot of this couple as they sat down in their truck. I stopped and idled, Hemi's wonderful engine making our presence known. And we looked at each other. They could clearly see Michael. The man who was sitting on the sidewalk.

I thought about what to do. Roll down my window. Yell, "This man sitting on the sidewalk? Could be because he's been on his feet since six this morning and he's tired. Could be that he doesn't drive because of a disability. Could be that he's waiting for his wife, who drives this pristine Chrysler 300C Hemi. Could be you are absolute clueless idiots." I thought about it.

But then I just drove away.

I simmered through the trip to the bank, the drive-thru at Starbucks, picking up our daughter from school and then our drive home. I thought about all that I could have said, could have shouted, and I regretted not saying it.

But then I thought of the man with the sunny day smile, and his "Thank you, ma'am, I appreciate it."

One thing that I have learned over and over since I took up this blog is that there are kind people in this world. I've seen kindness extended over and over and over again. And I've come to the conclusion that despite the ugliness we witness every day, kind people outnumber the hateful people. The hate-filled people.

I thought of the man I offered to help, of the woman by his side.

And I thought of the couple I glared at in silence, but then moved on.

There is kindness in me too.

And yes, that helps. Despite. Anyway.

# OCTOBER 24, 2017

And so today's moment of happiness despite the news.

You know, it's always good when you find out you're not crazy.

When I started the Today's Moment in January, I said it was a way to keep me from feeling like I was drowning in our current political climate. By finding one moment a day that made me happy, I was able to realize that the gloom and doom of the news wasn't all there was in life.

The last few months have been difficult, and current times are difficult too. But that aside…Today's Moment has been invaluable to me.

Today, I read an article in the Washington Post. It was by a breast cancer survivor and it talked about how, when the whole ordeal was over, she was…sad. The more I read, the more it resonated. Eventually, I stopped reading the article and cried. Again.

All I want to do is sleep. Moving through my day right now requires the greatest effort. And for the first time in my life, I am not writing. Except for The Moment.

Last week, I said to a friend, "I know I survived breast cancer. But I feel like I didn't. I feel like it killed me."

Who knew that the aftermath was going to be as hard as the during? The discovery, the biopsy, the waiting for diagnosis, the diagnosis, the tests after diagnosis, the surgery, the medication, the radiation after radiation after radiation…Recovery and healing was supposed to be the spa that followed the <insert your most difficult physical accomplishment here>.

This ain't no spa. Though maybe a warm stone massage would help…

So why is reading this article my Today's Moment Of Happiness? Because I know that the commercials that show glowing haloed women feeling grateful for every moment, women wh suddenly have all the answers, women who leap out of bed, dance a jig, and proclaim, "I am so happy to be alive!" isn't real. At least not right away. In fact, it presents an unreachable role model. And it leaves you awash in grief and guilt that maybe those women were the ones who were supposed to survive and they're surviving correctly, and maybe you weren't. Maybe I can stop yelling at myself now. Stop berating myself, saying, "You're one of the lucky ones! Start feeling lucky! Be happy! Wear pink! Skip!"

Can you picture me skipping? Me?

Why the hell was I yelling at myself to skip? I didn't freaking skip

BEFORE breast cancer, why would I do so after?

So Today's Moment Of Brutal Honesty Despite The News: I'm sad. I'm really, really sad, mixed every now and then with rage. Not anger. Rage.

Yes, I'm dealing with depression.

But Today's Moment Of Happiness Despite The News: I'm not crazy. It's not hopeless. I put my own survival guide in place before I even knew I needed one. Somewhere deep inside, I must have known a change was coming and I put Today's Moment in place.

To me, the Today's Moment Of Happiness Despite The News is my own personal miracle. The television commercials are fake news. I will not watch them and feel badly. I will write my Moment and get through.

Bottom line: I'll be okay, in time.

And yes, that helps. Despite. Anyway.

## OCTOBER 25, 2017

And so today's moment of happiness despite the news.

Today, I found out that crumpets are real.

Really. I always thought they were fiction. I thought they were a fairy-tale delicacy of the Hansel and Gretel specially-made variety that only royalty nibbled on while drinking tea with their little pinky fingers extended. They would be impossibly delicious – because they're fiction – and I figured they were shaped sort of like Bugles, those corn-flavored crunchy snacks, but bigger and flakier and just the loveliest shade of golden brown. Why Bugles? Because crumpet rhymes with trumpet so they would be trumpet-shaped.

Hey. That's just how my imagination works. It doesn't have to make sense.

So I have this wonderful client who is a poet-essayist-journalist. She has a British accent that puts me immediately into memories of watching *Upstairs, Downstairs* when I was in high school. I especially liked the character Rose and the butler, whose name I can't remember. Joanna, my client, lives in Israel and when I Skype with her, she sits in Wednesday evening, while I sit in Wednesday morning, and the magic of this time-shift-and-share still makes me amazed, even though I've been meeting with international students for over 20 years. Now, thanks to Skype, I can see them too, and greet their family members as they walk in and out, and say hello to their dogs and cats. The clients I Skype with are immediately inspected by my cat, Muse, who insists on being a part of the conversation.

So Joanna had crumpets in her manuscript this week. And I about fell off the page. I wrote in her margin, THEY'RE REAL? and when I met with her this morning, the first thing I said was, "Crumpets are a real thing?"

"Yes," she said and went on to describe how you bake them and then, when you're ready to eat one, you pop it in the toaster and then lather it up with butter and eat it while it's still hot.

I was both enchanted and devastated. A TOASTER? You put the fairy-tale crispy golden magical crumpet in any old toaster sitting on any old counter in any old place? I like my toaster, it's bright red, but really. For a crumpet? A crumpet should be baked in a regal rare golden brick oven made especially for royalty.

"No," she said. "A toaster."

And she promised to send me a recipe. I don't bake, so Michael will have to make them and then I will toast one and I will eat a crumpet. With tea. Pinky finger extended.

I will feel royal. And fiction will become fact.

How amazing is all this. I am of an age where technology does not feel like a given. It's as magical as crumpets. I can turn on my computer and speak to my student in Israel and listen to her lilting British accent and be transported back to high school when I sat on the floor in front of my family's console TV and admired a British housemaid named Rose. I can make another call and speak to another student living in Israel and listen to her still-there it-will-never-go-away New York City accent and remember *Barney Miller.* A student who lives in Illinois can travel to France and still meet with me while her baby grandson pouts and waves. And I can admire another grandson when a student in an on-site class, who typically sits right there with me at the classroom table, flies to Portland, Oregon to visit and still sits at the table with the rest of us, looking out at us from a screen.

And through all of it, ALL of it, I can keep learning. Last week, I learned from an Australian student that a common phrase there is, "It's time to pull my finger out of the hole." Dear God, I said. WHAT hole? And she said she thought it had to do with the hole in the dike in Copenhagen. This week, I learned that crumpets are real and I'm going to be able to taste one.

I can keep on learning and looking around, amazed.

So I do.

And yes, that helps. Despite. Anyway.

And so today's moment of happiness despite the news.

Tonight, I drove my daughter and her boyfriend to his house, to drop him off after their date. As we rounded a curve in the early-dark fall evening, I peered through the black to find what for me is a sure sign of home. It was quiet in the back seat too and then suddenly, Olivia's boyfriend cried out, "Where is the cow? The cow is gone!"

But then I found her. Her soothing brown eyes held their always steady gaze, twelve feet up in the air.

"She's there," I said. "They just don't have her night lights on."

I heard a collective sigh of relief from the back seat and I smiled. It makes me happy that today's seventeen-year olds look for the cow just as much as I did when I was seventeen. And still do, at fifty-seven.

At a certain point in Waukesha, where Northview Road curves one way and a new curve becomes Delafield Street, there is a gigantic cow. She used to stand in front of the Golden Guernsey Dairy, but a few years ago, it became Lifeway, an organic-based dairy. The cow is made of fiberglass and she stands twelve feet tall and weighs around five-hundred pounds. She cost $3000 when she was originally purchased around 1970. According to an article I read tonight, her name is Gertrude Basse The Cow. I never knew that. To me, she's always been Bessie.

I moved to Waukesha in 1977. I was sixteen and a junior in high school. Soon after moving here, I landed a job as a kennelworker at the Humane Animal Welfare Society, a job I loved and held throughout the rest of high school and partway through college. Whenever I went to work to tend the dogs and cats and all manner of small animals, I passed Bessie and I waved and whispered, "Hi, Bessie." Whispered so she could hear, but whispered so no one else could.

I can't explain why she made home Home to me, but she did. My parents moved away from Waukesha while I was in college and I didn't return here until 1987. One of the first things I did was drive to the odd intersection to find her. I was Home.

Every Halloween, the dairy dresses her up. She's usually a witch, but this year, she looks more like a wizard. At Christmas, a gigantic wreath hangs from her shoulders. But the rest of the year, she is a strong, tall brown and white cow, holding her gaze and her stance steady through all sorts of weather, all sorts of world events, all sorts of life.

I think of her as a strong woman and even now, at 57, I wave at her and whisper, "Hi, Bessie."

There was a night, a long, long time ago, when I was seventeen, a very tumultuous time. I was removed from my house for one night, I was told for my own safety, and placed in a house that was for such situations. There were all sorts of kids there, for all sorts of reasons, and I was terrified and sad. But this house was right across the street from Bessie. In the middle of the night, in a room with eight beds, I was surrounded by sleeping strangers and I was wide awake. The window had a wide sill. I got up and sat on the sill, looking out at Bessie the Big Cow. The strong woman with a gentle steady gaze. She was Home. She kept me company.

I look for her now too. She is on the path to and from the grocery store where Michael is working. I see her often, and I see her at a time when I need to be reminded of safety, of strength, of endurance, and of a steady gaze.

Home.

"Hi, Bessie," I whispered on the way to my daughter's boyfriend's house tonight. And "Goodnight, Bessie," on the way Home.

Her gaze followed me as I went around the curve. And I know she'll be watching for me tomorrow.

And yes, that helps. Despite. Anyway.

## OCTOBER 27, 2017

And so today's moment of happiness despite the news.

I was on the phone tonight with a client from Massachusetts. We finished discussing his pages and he said, "Oh, I have to tell you…"

He works as an ER doctor and he was talking to a radiation oncologist at his hospital. My student said to me, "You know all about radiation oncologists now."

Yes, I do.

Well, this radiation oncologist has an obsession with watches. He collects them, reads about them, knows all about them. So my student said to him, "You should read this book by my writing coach. It's called *The Home For Wayward Clocks*—"

"Oh!" the radiation oncologist said. "I've been told about that book! I need to get it!"

He's been told about that book. A radiation oncologist out in Massachusetts who has never met me or heard of me has been told about that book.

Heeeeeeeeeeeeeeee!

This came on top of receiving another review of *In Grace's Time* today. This reader said:

*This was a lovely book about a pain that goes beyond the norm, and of finally coming to grips with it – in the right time... With a different style of writing, this book could easily have slid into sappiness, corniness or drivel, but it didn't. It was well-written, and I can only imagine how real it must be to find yourself drowning in pain so deep that you're helpless to reach out to save others who are drowning with you. A beautiful story.*

And again:

Heeeeeeeeeeeeeeee!

I was often told, and I often tell others, that we have to develop a tough skin as writers. And we do. There's a lot of rejection in this life. But here's the trick. While we need to develop a tough skin for the negatives, we need to keep our skin soft for the positive. We need to soak it in. Take a bath in it. Revel. When those positive comments come, it's wonderful.

Two examples of how the negative tends to stick harder to our toughened skin than the positive tends to soak in to the softened skin:

1) In all my years of writing and presenting, there has only been that one time in Green Bay that no one showed up for the event. Just once. So despite it only happening once, despite my usually filling rooms, guess what I always think about the night before an appearance? Uh-huh.

2) The reviews on In Grace's Time have almost all been positive. There have been two negatives. Both by men, interestingly enough, and both who felt that the grieving went on too long, that Grace needed to just get over the death of her child. One man wondered why someone who identifies as gay would ever be attracted to the opposite sex. The other called my writing "average". So despite the fact that I am receiving positive review after positive review, guess which ones I think the most about. Uh-huh.

So. I have to practice what I preach. I fully intend on taking a long hot bath tonight in the words, "lovely book" and "beautiful story", and there will be bubbles filled with, "I've been told about that book!"

And yes, I also flinched a bit at "You know all about radiation oncologists now." Yes, I do. But I forced myself to turn that phrase around.

Yes, I know all about radiation oncologists now. But if I didn't, I wouldn't have survived. Not knowing about radiation oncologists wouldn't have taken away the cancer lurking in my body. Knowing about them, and knowing about medication oncologists and surgeons, means that it's all been taken care of and I'm just fine.

I'm going to plunk that into my bathwater too.

Heeeeeeeeeeeeeeeeeee!

And yes, that helps. Despite. Anyway.

## OCTOBER 28, 2017

And so today's moment of happiness despite the news.

I had Grandbaby Maya Mae today for eight hours. Michael was at work and Olivia had a friend over, so it was pretty much just me and Maya. I'd hoped to take her to the Domes, but then when Olivia invited a friend over, I had to pick the friend up in the middle of the afternoon, and with the Domes' closing time of 4:00, our visit wasn't going to work out. Then I was going to take her to a pumpkin farm, but with temperatures in the upper thirties and drizzly rain and Maya already sniffling with a cold, well, that wasn't going to work either.

So since I knew that Maya is a huge fan of My Little Pony, I decided to take her to the theatre to see the movie.

Me. My Little Pony. Oboy.

It was an adventure for Maya, her first experience in our theatre's new Dream Loungers. She learned very quickly how to push the button that made the seat recline and come back up…and she discovered that when done just right, the leather makes a lovely kid-comedy farting sound. This sent her into gales of giggles which sent every child in the theatre into gales of giggles, and soon, even though the sweet Little Ponies were being threatened by these monster-looking things (they really were scary), the theatre was rocking with child-laughter…and some adult-laughter too, actually.

As the movie went on, I couldn't help but notice that one pony, a rock star named Songbird Serenade, looked a lot like Sia, one of my favorite female vocal artists. When Songbird Serenade finally opened her pony mouth to sing, I knew without a doubt that this was Sia. That voice!

I contemplated this for the rest of the movie. Sia is not known as a bouncy-jouncy happy-happy Pony-song type singer. Her songs are serious and moody, and that's part of the reason I like them. But here she was, as a pony singing about rainbows.

After the movie, Maya and I went to pick up Michael from work, and then there was a break for a bit. When it was time for me to run to McDonalds to get our supper, Maya asked if she could come with me, rather than staying home with Grandpa Mike and Aunt Olivia.

"Sure," I said. "You can come. But why?"

"Because you're fun, Gamma Kaffee," she said.

I'm…fun. Fun?

I don't think I've ever been called fun in my entire life.

A couple months ago, when *In Grace's Time* was released, I was startled when it was called "delightful." My work has been described with other d-words, like dark and disturbing, but never delightful.

Fun. Delightful.

As I buckled Maya into the back seat of Hemi, and received a Grandbaby kiss on the nose for my efforts, I contemplated this too.

Sia can be a My Little Pony, singing about rainbows.

And I can be fun, and my work can be delightful.

How about that?

If I ever meet Sia, I'm going to give her a high five. And I'm going to hug her tight and whisper in her ear, "Isn't it great when people begin to realize you're three-dimensional?

Isn't it great when you yourself realize it?

It is.

And yes, that helps. Despite. Anyway.

### OCTOBER 29, 2017

And so today's moment of happiness despite the news.

I have two places on this earth (so far) that feel like home even though I've never lived there. I don't know why these places call to me, but they do. The first is definitely Waldport, Oregon. I go there as often as I can, on retreat, usually for two weeks at a time. The little house I stay in has the ocean out the back door. The house, the ocean, the beach, the town itself…there is something about the whole package that just makes the world drop off my shoulders and my breath come easier. I don't understand the attraction, as it's colder there than I would like. But it feels like home. I often dream of it.

I wasn't able to go this past summer, because of dealing with breast cancer.

I've been feeling its absence. The reason I needed it more than ever was the reason I couldn't go.

But I have another spot, an Oregon for me in Wisconsin. And that's La Crosse. I think it's primarily the Mississippi River that calls me here. I am happy when I'm next to it, happier still when I wade in. And so, with a visit to a book club in La Crosse on Wednesday, I decided to make up for my lack of Pacific Ocean by coming early to La Crosse and hovering as near to the river as I can.

It's water for me. And that's something else I don't understand, because I don't know how to swim. You'd think I'd be scared, but I have no fear of water whatsoever. When I am near water, whether it's the Fox River, Lake Michigan, the mighty Mississippi or the temperamental Pacific, something in me eases.

And I've been needing easing.

As I drove here today, I was waiting for one particular spot. I can't pinpoint it exactly, but as I drive over a hill, Wisconsin suddenly changes her personality and erupts from the earth. Our gently rolling hills become flat-top bluffs and there is a long-distance vista of rising curves and I know the river is close by. Just as the land surges skyward, so does my heart. I was tired today as I hit that point, tired with the fatigue still left over from radiation, but I felt that surge. My foot pressed involuntarily down on the gas pedal and Hemi carried me faster.

I felt a lightening in me. The beginning of the ease.

It took me a little bit to find my hotel – I'm staying in a different place this time, choosing a hotel right on the river so that I could have her right there, right there, right outside my door. The Mississippi exerted a magnet pull as I unloaded the car, but I insisted on self-discipline. I believe in finishing work before pleasure, and so I unpacked, put away my clothes, set up my toiletries, my computer, put the book I'm reading by the chair, set out my headphones for meditation, plugged in my sound machine. Then and only then did I grab my coat and run to the river.

And I mean run.

It was raining. It was cold. I didn't care. I ran to where the walkway stopped and the next step would have dropped me into to the water. I was all alone and the evening light cast everything in my favorite shade of blue. The river was quiet tonight and she whispered, so I whispered too.

"Hi. I'm back. I'm so glad to see you."

I was getting soaked in the rain, but it was the river I soaked in. Her sound, her perfume, the curves and bends to my right, the bridge like a necklace to my left. And just like when I stand by the Pacific Ocean, the world dropped off my shoulders and I breathed easier.

Tomorrow, I am heading across the river to Pettibone Park, and I don't care how cold it is, I am walking in to the river and taking her into my pores. I will wash my face with her.

I can't wait.

And yes, that helps. Despite. Anyway.

## OCTOBER 30, 2017

And so today's moment of happiness despite the news.

This afternoon, as I moved around my hotel room, I made a concerted effort not to make the bed. I'm not crazy about having someone come into my room when I'm traveling, preferring instead to have everything set up the way I like it and not having to worry about it being touched or moved. I am territorial to a fault, I know. While I'm here, this is MY place. Entrance is by invitation only.

But making the bed. When I travel with my husband or daughter, they both make fun of me for making the bed. I'm supposed to be on vacation; I'm supposed to be relaxing; I'm supposed to not do any work. So why make the bed?

Don't make the bed, I said to myself. Relax.

When I left home yesterday, I also deliberately did not make the bed. My husband claims he makes the bed every day when I'm gone, but well, I figure that's one of those white lies that spouses tell each other. I knew the bed wouldn't be made again until Thursday morning, so that when I returned to our bedroom, the bed would be tidy and his secret would be kept. But why make it before I left, since he didn't care one way or the other?

So I left it, even though it made me feel itchy.

And now, today, I found myself averting my eyes whenever I walked by the bed. Which, in a hotel room, is often.

As I got ready to leave my room for a trip over the river to my favorite park, I forgot to avert my eyes and I glanced at the bed. I became suddenly awash in a memory.

During a visit from my parents years and years ago, I became sick with the stomach flu. I was very pregnant with my second child and my first child, just turned two years old, was sick with the flu before me. It was the first time he was sick with such a thing and as a still young and very worried mother, I spent two nights sleeping on the floor by his crib, to make sure he was all right. The morning after that second night, I woke up and immediately fell ill.

Having the stomach flu is a horrible thing. Having it when you are very, very pregnant is a nightmare.

My parents, both terrified they were going to get it too, stayed as far away from me as they could. Twenty-four hours later, when I dragged myself out of bed, I was staring at my ugly self in the bathroom mirror when my mother called through the door.

"Is there anything I can do for you, honey?" she called. She didn't say it, but I knew she wanted to add, "Without actually touching you, of course."

My mother insisted my siblings and I make our beds every day. By 9:00 a.m., even during school vacations and weekends. Even when we were sick. She at least made our beds for us if we were sick – we just had to be out of bed and onto the living room couch by 9:00 so she could do so.

Despite the discomfort of getting out of bed and moving to a couch throughout all the years of my childhood, through the flu, strep throat, bronchitis, mono, I will be the first to say that when I would get back into bed that night, the smoothed-out bed, the plumped pillows, the freshened blankets, always felt amazing.

"Mom," I said, staring into the mirror that day, "would you please make my bed?"

And then I wrapped my pregnant self into a robe that no longer fit and went downstairs to the couch. When I returned to the bed several hours later, and I slid between the cool smooth sheets, tugged the blanket up to my chin, rested my head on a pillow that wasn't squashed and sweaty, I knew I was taken care of.

So today, I made my hotel bed. When I climb into bed tonight, it will be with that same feel of being taken care of and watched over. Even if it's me that's doing the caring and watching.

And yes, that helps. Despite. Anyway.

## OCTOBER 31, 2017

And so today's moment of happiness despite the news.

For years now, I've walked labyrinths. I believe they helped me to meditate before I was meditating. There's just something about setting my feet onto a path where I know I can't become lost.

I've used labyrinths for help with creativity and in times of emotional uncertainty. I often walk in feeling scrambled, and then walk out, not with a solution, but with a feeling of steadiness and the sense of a solid path in front of me.

There is a labyrinth in La Crosse that I discovered my first time here and that I've walked each time I've come. Last year, I taught a class on creativity and the labyrinth, setting students walking that certain path, and then letting them rip on a story or piece of artwork. It remains one of my most joyful teaching experiences. When I made my plans to come to La Crosse this year, I knew I'd be walking the labyrinth. But then I realized it would be different this time.

The labyrinth is located outside of a cancer center. Its intended purpose is to bring peace to cancer patients and survivors. This year, that's how I would be walking it.

It didn't take very many steps before the tears came. I wasn't surprised by them, but I was surprised by the force. I felt like I was being wrung out. You know how you can wring out a towel, then loosen it, then wring it again and still get more water from it? That was me this afternoon. Wring and pause, wring and pause.

When I got to the center, I stood and folded my hands. There is no bench at this labyrinth, so I just stood in the exact center. Folded hands, bowed head.

I receive three emails every day, just for fun. One is a fortune cookie, which you click on to crack open. One is an astrological forecast. I'm a Leo. And one is "A Note From The Universe". This morning, each and every one had the same message: *"Don't be afraid to ask for help."*

I've often been told that I seem like I'm not afraid of anything. Seem is an important word.

In the center of the labyrinth, head bowed, hands folded, I decided to not be afraid and I asked for help. I have no idea who I asked, but I asked. I asked for help in recovery. I asked for help finding Michael a job. I asked for a return to a feeling of safety.

Someone told me, right after diagnosis, that I would never feel safe again. I find that hard to accept.

So I asked for help.

Then I started the walk back out.

Throughout the walk, on the way in and on the way out, the same red leaf kept skittering into my path. It was directly in front of me when I started, and I stepped carefully around it. Each time I started to cry, that red leaf moved in front of me. I stopped my walk, noted it and moved on.

Red is one of my favorite colors. It's a color of strength.

As I stood in the center of the labyrinth, the red leaf blew in front of me again, stopping by my toes.

And right before I stepped off the labyrinth, it blew in front of me again.

By the time I stepped off the labyrinth, I was no longer crying. My shoulders were relaxed. My head was up. Despite the cold air, I was breathing steadily. I didn't feel wrung out. I actually felt pretty good.

The windows of the cancer center line the wall behind the labyrinth. When I looked inside as I was stepping off the labyrinth, I saw a row of five women standing there. One raised her hand with the thumb and first finger together, in the A–OK sign, and then she pointed at me. I nodded and smiled. All five women raised their fists in the air and smiled back.

An old labyrinth walked with new intention. A persistent bright red leaf. A group of five anonymous women who took the time to make sure I was all right and who raised their fists in triumph and strength and solidarity.

Today's moment of happiness.

And yes, that helps. Despite. Anyway.

# Chapter Eleven

## NOVEMBER 1, 2017

And so today's moment of happiness despite the news.

This was my last full day here. When I looked out of my hotel window this morning, I saw more rain, which changed to snow, which changed to sleet, which changed to rain. I decided to stay in. And I decided to face the challenge of the screen.

I haven't written, except for the Today's Moments, since midway through radiation. It wasn't that I couldn't, that I ran out of time. It wasn't that I had writer's block, which I don't believe in. It was that I simply didn't want to.

I have never ever in my life not wanted to write.

I had a horrible case of What's The Point. This was the worst ever, because it had the worst ending to that sentence: What's the point, because I'm just going to die anyway.

Even with the treatments over, even with the low score on the Oncotype DX Breast Cancer Test, I still heard myself saying that.

Now it's not like I ever expected that I would live forever. It's not like I never knew that someday, somehow, I was going to die. But suddenly death seemed larger than life. And I was frozen in its grip.

Honestly, truly, I thought I was done writing. It wasn't that I'd said everything I wanted to say. It was that I didn't see the point in saying it.

A good friend dared to advise the advisor. "Just write down a sentence you find interesting," he said. "And follow it. It's what you've told me to do."

I've said that a thousand times.

So I wrote down the opening sentence last week:

*Faith wished for a prayer, and then wondered if, by wishing, she was already praying.*

It wasn't from the book I was working on before I was diagnosed. It was totally new. For the next several days, I stared at the sentence and I added a few more. Each day, I went back to the beginning and started again. And started again. And started again.

Yesterday, when I worked on it again, I came to what I thought was an ending, even though I hated it. That's just stupid, I thought. It doesn't make any sense.

So. This morning, when I sat down to look at it again, I heard those words, *That's just stupid,* and then I heard the words I tell my students: *Write the stupid. Sometimes what you think is stupid and far out is actually the best thing ever.*

Back to the beginning. Work it through. Add a little, add a little, add a little...

And it wasn't stupid.

I finished my first first draft since diagnosis. There's a mirror in front of this desk I'm working on, and when I finished that first draft, I looked into the mirror and I recognized myself all over again. All over again! And I did what I've done since practically day one, when I hit that moment when it feels so right and I know who I am and I know what I'm doing and I am just drenched with skin that is on the right body and graced with a mind that is firing synapses in the best possible rhythm and ohmygod, I did it.

What did I do? I stood up, raised both fists in the air, and said, "Damn, I'm good."

It'll be stupid again tomorrow, but that's all right, that's just the way of things. It will make me fight for that *Damn I'm good* moment again, through a second draft and a third and a fourth, and more than likely a fifth and a sixth.

I remember very clearly what it was like to write my first story when I gained control of a pencil and paper and letters and words when I was six. I remember what it felt like to sell my first story when I was fifteen. I remember the day my first book was accepted. Hell, I remember what it was like to sell all of the stories I've sold, and the births of books two, three, four, five, six and seven.

And I will remember today too. The day What's The Point went back to whatever dark part of me it usually hides in.

And ohmygod yes, that helps. Despite. Anyway.

### NOVEMBER 2, 2017

And so today's moment of happiness despite the news.

Well, holy cow.

So a couple of days ago, a student from the studio called me several times, leaving messages, telling me that she had a "special surprise visitor" for me and when would I be around on Thursday? That's today, of course, and it was the day I was coming home. I called her, confused, and told her I'd be home around 6:30, but that I had a client at 7:00.

"That's perfect!" she said. "I promise it won't take long."

I puzzled over this. Could it be Oprah? I've always wanted to meet Oprah. Maybe President Obama? I've always wanted to meet President Obama. I puzzled and I puzzled.

But it was even better. Better than I could have ever imagined.

I waited in the studio, and saw my student Kris walk by the windows, a woman following her. It wasn't someone I recognized, and I went into an immediate panic that it was a student I no longer remembered. But they came in, sat down on either side of me, and the woman introduced herself. She said that Kris showed her my story on the Today's Moment blog. And she just wanted to give me a present.

It was a lovely plaque, that said, "You never know how strong you are until being strong is the only choice you have."

We talked a little bit about my past summer, the diagnosis, the surgery, the treatments and Michael's job loss. Suddenly, a group of four people walked by the windows and they all turned into the studio.

Okay…

They introduced themselves as part of the This Time Tomorrow Foundation. One talked to me about the history of the foundation, and then they said that I was nominated to be gifted with a RAK – Random Act of Kindness. They handed me two gift bags, filled with natural body soaps and a coffee mug that said #cancersucks and a t-shirt that said the same, and a bunch of other goodies. And then one of them handed me an envelope. "And we wanted to give you this," he said.

I opened it and peeked inside.

A check. A check made out to me, with funds that equate to two more months of insurance.

That's about when I froze. Trust me, inside, there were tears, there were the shakes, but I think there have been so many tears, there have been so many shakes, there just weren't any left right at that moment.

They've come since.

And then the group told me that Michael and I are going to be guests with others that received RAKs at a gala at the Pfister on November 18th. We will walk in on a red carpet. There will be music. And…and…and…

Ohmygod.

Kindness. Kindness and caring. I just can't believe how much has been shared with me.

I just don't know how I can ever feel that the world is dark again. There are dark places…but there is so much light.

I don't know how I can ever give back enough.

Thank you, Kris. Thank you, Time For Tomorrow.

I'm just overcome.

And yes, that helps. Despite. Anyway.

## NOVEMBER 3, 2017

And so today's moment of happiness despite the news.

It's been a literary day.

This morning, I had the opportunity to put into action something I've wanted to do since I started AllWriters' almost 13 years ago. I sent professional writers into high schools, middle schools, and an online school to talk to kids about what the writing life is really like. I'm hoping to get a student count from all involved soon, so that I can say just how many kids were affected by AllWriters' writers today. From the reports I've received from my authors, it was a wonderful experience. All of the writers today were either on the AllWriters' faculty or are students, or, in one case, both.

I went into my own alma mater, Waukesha North High School, and as I did so, I knew other school doors were being opened and writers were striding on through. While I attended three different high schools, Waukesha North holds my heart. I credit it with saving my life. And today, I was able to start giving back, as I've wanted to do for the longest time. The giving back expanded well past the walls of my own school into other schools in Waukesha, Muskego, New Berlin and Hartland, and online. It is my hope that next year, we push into more communities, more schools, and send in more writers.

Later in the day, I hugged the stuffing out of my high school creative writing teacher, who works alongside me in the planning of this local book festival. I hugged him for now; I hugged him for then.

Tonight was the keynote of the festival, and I sat with the audience and watched Nickolas Butler speak and read. At one point, Nickolas looked into the audience and said that my community had to understand and be grateful for what they have in me. Someone who loves writers, who loves writing, who loves reading, and who loves her community.

It was so nice to be acknowledged. But particularly wonderful to be acknowledged by someone I know shares my passion and dedication and drive.

As I listened to Nick speak about writing, I thought back to all the questions and comments made by the young writers this morning at Waukesha North and at E-Achieve Academy. What I heard in their voices, I also heard in Nick's, and I hear in my own. That need, that desire, that siren call to create, to speak, to make a difference.

Community is such an amazing thing.

This morning, before any of this happened, I received an email with an assignment from a brand new student, taking my online Starting – And Finishing! –The Novel class. In her email, this woman said, "How can anything be so fun and painful at the same time?" It made me laugh, and I wanted to open my computer screen like a big barn door and reach inside and grab her by the shoulders and say, "Look! Look at who all you have to keep you company! Look who is laughing with you and saying ouch, all of you, all at the same time. And look, look, look! I'm right there with you. Welcome to the family. We understand."

Slid right in to where I belong today.

Oh, so good.

And yes, that helps. Despite. Anyway.

### NOVEMBER 4, 2017

And so today's moment of happiness despite the news.

Today was the local book festival. AllWriters' is a co-sponsor and I've been involved with the development of the festival since day one. Typically, I'm everywhere at the festival – on panels, doing my own presentations, moderating. This year, I purposely cut back after I was diagnosed with breast cancer. I wasn't sure what shape I would be in by the time the festival rolled around. So I interviewed our keynote onstage this morning for a casual breakfast event, I presented *In Grace's Time* in combination with a discussion on how this book has bookended my career, and I taught a class in how to market your book.

I was feeling pretty discouraged in the morning. I did the breakfast keynote, but found myself absolutely dragging by the end of it. My next event wasn't until 2:30 so I reluctantly decided to go back home and sleep for a couple hours.

I have never left an event to sleep. I have never left an event. By the time I got home and upstairs to my bedroom, I was desperate for sleep. Instead of unmaking the bed (yes, I made it this morning), I took my side of the bedspread and flung it in half to the other side, and then just crawled under the covers. I don't think I was awake for more than another minute. I did set an alarm and then…darkness. I don't remember dreaming. When I woke up two hours later, I hadn't moved.

This fatigue. This desperation for rest. It's really getting to me. I want my energy back.

When I returned to the festival, I moved pretty quickly into action. My presentation of *Grace* went beautifully. The marketing class – intense, fast and satisfying. I signed quite a few books. And in between…five women came up to me at separate times. Some were in my presentations, some came to me at the AllWriters' table, some came to me at the book-signing area. All told me they were following me with the Today's Moment. All had experienced breast cancer.

"I'm five years out," one woman said.

"Eleven years out," said another.

"Fifteen," said a third.

"Twenty-five."

One had been diagnosed just a couple weeks before me.

I asked all of them the same question. "Will this fatigue ever go away?"

"Yes."

I was told I was doing fine. I was told I was amazing. I was told I would make it through this. And I was hugged over and over again.

I needed that today.

One of the women repeated to me something that appeared last week, on the same day, in three separate emails: one a fortune cookie, one an astrological forecast, and one a "note from the universe". "Don't be afraid to ask for help," she said.

I asked. These women answered. And I was hugged and held up strong

And now I'm going to sleep.

And yes, that helps. Despite. Anyway.


### NOVEMBER 5, 2017

And so today's moment of happiness despite the news.

Back on June 7, I wrote about a woman I met years ago, when she lived down the hall from my daughter in her dorm at the University of Wisconsin – Madison. Carla was determined to make it through college, despite having Cystic Fibrosis. When I met her that day, while I know it sounds trite, the young woman had fire in her eyes. You know how you can just feel strength emanating from someone? I was warmed by it as I stood by her.

Carla ended up going home before she received her degree. But that hasn't stopped her.

My daughter is 30 now, and I believe Carla is about the same age. She's continued to plow through her life, getting married, making the most beautiful crafts, running her Etsy store, and traveling. And checking in and out of the hospital. Her Facebook profile says that she's a professional patient. But she's so much more.

While I was in La Crosse last week, I received a text full of exclamation points from my daughter: "Carla got lungs!!!" Carla had been at the top of the list for a lung transplant for several months, and, if you'll pardon the expression, everyone who knew her was holding our breath for this moment.

I've watched her Facebook page since and kept up with all the medical moving-forwards. The coming out of surgery, the wiggling of her toes and saying coherent sentences, the going on a c-pap machine and then being extubated. Every single update, I just feel my heart and soul swell. I feel the warmth of her strength and determination and perseverance all over again. She's a fireball.

What an amazing thing medicine is. What an amazing person Carla is. What a chance she's been given. And oh, how much she deserves it.

Carla has wanted to write a book about her life and experiences for a long time. And I've wanted to help her with it. Maybe now, we can get down to it. The world needs to know her.

My Today's Moment Of Happiness is simply this: Carla can breathe. Carla can breathe. Carla can breathe.

Oh, thank you.

And yes, that helps. Despite. Anyway.

### NOVEMBER 6, 2017

And so today's moment of happiness despite the news.

Over the weekend, at the book festival, there was a great raffle. Signed books from participating authors, of course. Brandy. Wine. Gift certificates. Tickets. Food. But that wasn't what sucked me in.

Oh, no. It was a large photograph of an iguana. On metal.

So there's a story behind the photo, of course.

I've spoken often of my high school creative writing teacher, Duane. He and I work together on the book festival. I am about, oh, thirty some years older than he was when he taught me. Which makes us both feel old. But this man had my back when I was in high school. And he still has my back now.

I told him quite a while ago that my novel-in-progress features an iguana named Newt. So when he was on a trip to Costa Rica, he took this photograph, and it's lovely – for an iguana. Our discussion, and his trip, happened before the breast cancer hit.

It has, of course, hit since.

Partway through radiation treatments, my motivation to write completely up and left. I'd managed to write through the diagnosis, the biopsies, even the surgery. But the radiation just was insidious. I've never experienced anything quite like this malaise. I became my own coach, my own cheerleader, getting myself up out of bed in the morning, getting through my day, and then crawling gratefully back into bed at night.

But writing? No go. No desire. Plenty of ideas. But I looked at the book on my screen and just thought, No. No. No, I just don't want to.

In La Crosse last week, I finally broke out of that and managed to write a short story – I'm now on subsequent drafts and I actually like it. But even as I worked on the story, I wasn't sure I would ever return to the iguana novel, or to any novel.

A novel takes determination, perseverance, discipline, commitment…and time. And I guess, when I allowed myself to peek into the dark recesses of the back of my mind, I wondered if I was running out of time. I wondered if I would be around to finish the novel.

Yeah.

Through it all, Duane kept talking to me. Sending emails: How are you doing? Want to go to coffee? Want to talk? How's the book? How're you? How're you? How're you?

It meant the world.

And then I walked into the reception for the festival this past Friday night, where the raffle items were on display for the first time, and came face to face with an iguana. MY iguana.

Duane hadn't told any of us on the planning committee what the photo was. He just kept saying, "It's gonna be BIG!"

And it was. It tugged at me.

So I bought raffle tickets. And I won.

Kismet, one of the book festival organizers said.

I brought the photo home today. I have to get someone to hang it for me, as I want it over my stairwell, facing me, so that when I look up from my computer, I see this big ass iguana. And so I hear, How are you doing? How's the book?

How's the book. I've always done what Duane – Mr. Stein – told me to do. And he's always known and had absolute faith in what I can do.

Last week in La Crosse, I told myself that while I was writing again, I was going to abandon the book. I would simply write stories and essays from now on. It would mean, in my mind, that I would have a better chance of not leaving any work unfinished.

But now, I have a big ass iguana glaring at me.

Back to work.

And yes, that helps. Despite. Anyway.

### NOVEMBER 7, 2017

And so today's moment of happiness despite the news.

Tonight, I was in the AllWriters' online classroom, meeting a student who sat in tomorrow morning and looked out her window at spring cusping into summer. Outside my window, it was dark and an earlier trek outdoors promised me that winter was on the way.

My student made me feel like July.

Before we started in on her pages, my student talked about the Today's Moment. We touched on the Moments from last week and how I had been feeling and how I feel now. How I felt like I was never going to write again. How I'm writing now.

My student confessed that she wanted to quit writing herself, a short time ago.

I knew that. She's been going through a very difficult time.

"But the thing is," she said, "you kept writing those Moments. You kept writing...something. Which is what I tried to keep doing. Even though a lot of it is a mess, it's better than nothing. Even this week's story. It was a mess. But it's turned into something."

Oh, I agreed. What a lovely story it's become.

"And you've kept me motivated too," she said. "I had to write."

She did.

This was one of those times I was glad for the chatroom and not the in-your-face of Skype. On my side of the computer screen, I was choked up.

I have felt so phenomenally useless over the last few months. I've been tired, I've been sad, I haven't been writing, I've had to count on the kindness of friends and strangers instead of on my own strength. I didn't feel strong. I wasn't standing on my own two feet. I was leaning on the shoulders of others.

I. Felt. Useless.

And then today, I found out that even while I felt useless, I wasn't. I was making a difference. Granted, it was happening in a way that I never could have predicted.

These damn Moments, as I call them around my home. Well, sometimes with a little more colorful language than that.

I told my student that she had to write because she was too good to quit.

She said, "No, I had to write because otherwise, you would be cross with me."

There is that.

From one side of the world to the other, from fall into winter, spring into summer, night and day, we both laughed.

I was also reminded, again, to say that I had breast cancer, not have. Had. Had. Had, had, had.

If you've worked with me, you know how I feel about the word had. "Had is bad, and would and could are not good."

But in this case, I love the word had. And yes, I will start making a conscious effort to use it.

I had breast cancer. I don't now. It's just me in here.

And yes, that helps. Despite. Anyway.

### NOVEMBER 8, 2017

And so today's moment of happiness despite the news.

Over the last week, discussions of titles have been happening all around me, and today, it popped up three separate times.

This morning, a client told me that the title she loves for her book, a title I love too and one that she's used since I started working with her, was put down by someone who she loves and respects. And now she's second-guessing. To the point where I saw tears in her eyes.

This afternoon, in class, two different titles for two different student works were questioned. One, the writer wasn't sold on. One, the writer was.

A few nights ago, over a dinnertime discussion with friends, students and faculty members, someone said to me, "You have the best titles!"

I can remember only twice being contentious over a title. The first was eons ago, before I was even Kathie Giorgio, and it was over a short story published in Wisconsin Magazine, which used to appear in the Sunday Milwaukee Journal. They didn't publish much fiction, but they published mine. This story, about a woman who loses a massive amount of weight, was titled "Fits Like Silk". The day the story came out, I sat down in the morning with my then-husband and reverently opened the magazine, paging through to find my story. It really looked lovely, complete with an original illustration. But they didn't use my title. What did they use?

"Dieting".

Blech. I was horrified. Scratch that. I still am horrified.

Years later, my third book was about to be published. It's a novel called *Learning To Tell (A Life)Time*. The phrase "learning to tell time" is important, but so is "a lifetime", and there is a reason for the parenthesis. Every time I exchanged correspondence with my publisher, he identified the book as *Learning To Tell Time*. I finally reminded him of the (A Life). He didn't like it, he said. But because it was my third book, he was willing to let me use it. Later, when I saw the first attempt at a cover, the words (A Life) were in teeny tiny letters, compared to the rest. I complained. Eventually, we reached an agreement. It was done my way.

Last week, I got into a discussion with a friend over how I tend to think of myself in what are essentially titles too. Kathie Giorgio, Author. Kathie Giorgio, Teacher. Kathie Giorgio, Small Business Owner. And so on, to the newest, most reluctant title: Kathie Giorgio, Breast Cancer Recoverer. Reluctant, because it was never a dream or a goal to be this. And Recoverer, because I am not yet comfortable with calling myself a Survivor. As more time moves behind me, I'm sure I will take that title on. But not now.

Titles are like the names we give our babies. We struggle over identifying personality, meaning, definition. What we call our children doesn't come without a struggle. Neither does what we call our poems, our stories, our novels, memoirs, essays. These are our babies too.

Neither does what we call ourselves, giving great thought over identifying personality, meaning, and definition.

Going back to my client from this morning, I want to tell her to keep her title for her book. Her name for her baby. She struggled through writing the book, and she struggled to find the right name. She wrote it. She found it.

It's her baby. And it's an expression of who she is.

That's what titles are all about, Charlie Brown.

And yes, that helps. Despite. Anyway.

## NOVEMBER 9, 2017

And so today's moment of happiness despite the news.

What are the most terrifying words a homeowner can hear? I think "Your roof needs replacing" or "Your furnace is shot" are right up there.

Add the fact that one of the homeowners was recently let go from his job, and man, do you up the terror.

Our furnace wasn't working. And the temperatures were steadily dropping.

In the last month, three furnaces in our condo complex have been replaced. We only have nine units. The complex is now eleven years old. All appliances have hit and/or passed that dreaded ten-year mark. We've replaced, thus far, our washer and dryer, our refrigerator and our dishwasher. Our garbage disposal too, if that counts – we've done that twice.

But a furnace...oh, a furnace is a BIG ticket item.

And so terror descended. I called our favorite heating/cooling company and asked them to stop in for a visit. And then I began a steady internal mantra of "Please, please, please, please..."

Our condos were built oddly. We have two furnaces, one for the studio on the first floor and one for the living space on the second and third floor. It was the living space furnace that was fritzing. Our furnaces were built into closets, one on the second floor, one on the third. The one on the third is a closet within our closet. We have to empty out Michael's clothes closet to get to the door, and then squeeze our way to the back corner, open the secret door, and there's the furnace. The little closet it's in isn't insulated and it's vented right to the outside, so you're essentially hanging over the parking lot when you get to it.

And the kicker – the furnace was put in before our closets were built. Why? Because we couldn't have gotten the furnace in AFTER the closet was built. So when our furnace is replaced, the closets will have to be torn down, the new furnace put in, and then the closets rebuilt.

"Please, please, please, please..."

My friendly furnace guy showed up – they're all friendly. I love this company. But it was one who hadn't been here before. His eyes widened as I showed him the path he would have to take. "Oh, boy," he said.

"Oh, boy," is kind of like hearing "oops" when you're at the hair salon.

For the next ten minutes, he wandered from the furnace to the second floor where the thermostat is, to the furnace, to his truck, to the thermostat, and my internal mantra began to ramp its amps.

"Please, please, please, please…"

Eventually, he parked himself in front of my desk. "Who installed that thermostat?" he asked.

"My husband did," I said. "Last summer, when the a/c wouldn't turn on. I bought the thermostat and he put it in."

"Ah," he said. "He didn't put the wires in the right place. He did the cooling one right. But the heating one wasn't where it was supposed to be. So the furnace wasn't getting any signal to start."

I sat quietly for a moment. "So…" I said cautiously, "the furnace is okay?"

"It is. You've taken very good care of it. All the components are just fine."

"So…this is all my husband's fault?"

His immediate grin lit my entire office. "Yes," he said. "But I won't put that in writing. For his protection."

Oh, the relief. I only had to pay for diagnostics and for the service call.

Michael made a mistake. The furnace is just fine. Tonight, the house is warm. Outside, we're reaching new lows.

This may be the only time ever that my husband making a mistake becomes my Today's Moment Of Happiness. As soon as he comes upstairs from teaching, I am going to hug the stuffing out of him.

WHOOPEE!

Now tomorrow, I have to bring Hemi in for service. He's making a banging noise. Michael hasn't touched him.

Please, please, please, please…

And yes, that helps. Despite. Anyway.


## NOVEMBER 10, 2017

And so today's moment of happiness despite the news.

Today, I had to bring my beloved car, Hemi, a 2006 Chrysler 300C Hemi, in for service. It was time for an oil transfusion, and in the last week or so, his powerful engine was being overpowered by a loud noise of another sort. So in we went.

I may be the only person in the world that looks forward to having her car serviced. I am always treated well there. They know who I am and they know I'm coming, so they set up a private cubicle out on the sales floor where I can set up my computer and work in peace. They bring me fresh hot coffee. And they call my cars by their names: Hemi and Semi.

My little cubicle is in a back corner. Unless the sales team comes swinging back there, they don't know I'm there. I sat there today, my coffee to my right, steaming (they made it fresh right after I got there), a package of oatmeal raisin cookies to my left, my new story up on my computer screen, and I was just happy. There was nothing here to interrupt me, except for the occasional update on my car. I was conscious that there was music playing over the store's speakers. And I heard the deep voices of the salesmen as they joked and talked with each other, punctuated at times by a saleswoman. But I didn't really pay any attention to it. I was deep into my own words.

Then the Righteous Brothers and "Lost That Loving Feeling" came on.

From the sales floor, a voice joined in.

*You lost that lovin' feelin'*
*Whoa, that lovin' feelin'*
*You lost that lovin' feelin'*
*Now it's gone, gone, gone, whoa-oh-oh.*

Another voice jumped in and I looked up from my screen. I couldn't see the salesmen, and they couldn't see me, but oh, could I hear them!

*Baby, baby, I'd get down on my knees for you*
*If you would only love me like you used to do,*
*(love me, love me)*

More voices, more voices, and soon it seemed the entire salesmen staff became a chorus. A boy band with deep and expressive voices. They sang with gusto. They sang with grace. They harmonized. And emotion blended easily through their lyrics.

*We had a love, a love, a love you don't find everyday*
*So don't, don't, don't, don't let it slip away*

Don't! Don't! Don't! In my seat, I began to sway with the rhythm. When they got to this part:

*Baby (baby!), baby, (baby!!!)*
*I beg you please (please!), please (please!!!)*
*I need your love (I need your love)*
*I need your love (I need your love)*
*So bring it on back, so bring it on back*
*Bring it on back, bring it on back!*

Bring it on back! I wanted to leap up and sing with them. In the middle of this snowy gray November afternoon, in a car dealership in Waukesha, Wisconsin, I wanted to wail the heat of the song and blend my voice and heart with theirs and feel the rhythm join us and the music move us...

...but I didn't want to ruin this. Their glorious, un-self conscious performance they thought was only in front of each other and the cars lucky enough to be inside the showroom.

So I hummed. And enjoyed. Bring back...that lovin' feeling!

When the song was over, they went back to talking and I went back to writing in my hidden-away corner, and it was as if nothing ever happened.

But my humming, "Whoa, that loving feeling..." as I walked out the door to my rental (Hemi is being held over for new muffler-related parts on Monday) and my humming it still, swaying in my chair here at home, shows that it really, really did.

Love me! Love me!

And yes, that helps. Despite. Anyway.

### NOVEMBER 11, 2017

And so today's moment of happiness despite the news.

One year ago today.

One year ago today was the start of what was to be a very difficult year. One year ago today, I was assaulted as I walked my dogs around the block for their just-after-lunch outing. It was something I'd done every day for ten years. It was such an everyday activity that I didn't even think about it as I did it. But that day, things ended up very differently.

A man came toward me and I tried to pull my dogs off the sidewalk. They didn't move fast enough and he swung his leg back to kick my oldest dog, who is very frail with advanced kidney disease. I put myself between him and Blossom and he kicked me instead. Then he grabbed my shoulders and threw me off the sidewalk. When I looked up from the grass, he said, "You need to get in your place now, woman." And then he walked away.

It was three days after the election. I can still hear his voice, still hear those words.

I got up, gathered the dogs and we walked home. I don't remember being afraid. I only remember thinking that I had to get home and I had to do the next thing on my list. I gave the dogs their treat, poured myself a glass of water. I can see myself doing this, as if I'm watching from a distance. Then I went to my computer, posted what happened on Facebook and was told that I was in shock and should call the police. So I did as I was told. It was when I showed the police officer the bruise that was turning a deep purple on my calf that I began to shake.

The aftermath was worse than the assault. It was soon all over the media and I received death threats. My family received death threats. They came from all over the country, via Facebook private messages, or posted directly on my page, or through Twitter. I was told I should die. I was told I should go to jail. I was told I should be raped and beaten.

Why?

Because I reported that the man wore a red Make America Great Again hat.

I tried to explain several times that if he'd been wearing a Hillary hat, I would have reported it. A Badgers hat, a Packers hat, whatever kind of hat he wore, I would have reported it. It wasn't just a red baseball cap. It had gold letters that said Make America Great Again.

On one hate-talk radio show, I was discussed. I tuned in just in time to hear them say, "Well, she writes fiction. So she's probably lying about this too." When I called in, they wouldn't let me speak.

What followed was months of being afraid to walk my dogs. Months of walking them with a cell phone pressed to my ear, my husband talking to me as we went. Months of locking my classroom door as soon as I knew all my students were present. Months of jumping and shaking at every loud noise, at the phone ringing, and the doorbell. Months of being irrationally afraid to travel.

My post on Facebook that day was passed around to extreme proportions. 1.3 thousand reactions. Over 1 thousand shares.

Today, it's one year ago. So why is this day, with this awful memory, my moment of happiness?

Because I'm still here. Because I'm traveling again. Because I can walk the dogs without fear, though I do still try to impossibly look around the corner before I turn it.

And because I've learned, over and over again, as this dreadful year continued, that there are more kind and compassionate people out there than there are mean, angry, hateful ones. Because I've learned that when something bad happens, there are wonderful people who sweep in to restore the good. To more than restore it. To double, triple, quadruple it.

Today's Moment Of Happiness: I'm just fine. And I'm here.
And yes, that helps. Despite. Anyway.

## NOVEMBER 12, 2017

And so today's moment of happiness despite the news.

The last 24 hours were really all about reflection and introspection. Realizing that yesterday was the one-year anniversary of the assault hit me pretty hard. I've been so focused on the latest assault, the breast cancer, that I'd relegated that event to the back of my mind, even as tendrils of that attack still worked their way through my mind, through my body. There they were, the assault by the man in the Make America Great Again hat and the aftermath, and breast cancer and its aftermath, side by side. Both assaults. Both attacks. One external. One internal.

In both cases, I've said to people, "I didn't expect the aftermath to be as hard as the {assault}{breast cancer}."

But it was. In both cases.

Last night, middle of the night, I felt the impact of both. And it wasn't inconsiderable.

I was told last week by a friend that I'd "overstated" the impact breast cancer has had on me.

Well, you know what? I don't agree.

This whole year, these two assaults have had a huge impact on me. Inside and out.

Every day, on Facebook, you get a reminder of what has happened on that day in the years before. I looked at it today, and so much of it held responses to what happened to me on that sidewalk. There was so much support, so much incredulous disbelief (not that it happened, but that it COULD happen) and so many offers of help. From people I knew. From strangers. Yes, there were those that threatened me. But there were so many more that lifted me up.

And then there was one of my own statuses, from that day after:

*NOVEMBER 12, 2016 8:02 p.m.*

*He said I needed to be put back into my place.*

*His definition, of course.*

*But I am already in my place.*

*And it's my definition that matters.*

*I've worked very hard to get here.*

*Word by word by word.*
*There is no "putting back".*
*There is only moving forward.*
*And that is what I will do.*
*Word by word by word.*

And that is exactly what did, isn't it. I moved forward, word by word. Writing these Moments. Writing my own creative work. Teaching others. Word by word by word.

I did not "overstate" the impact. It is my definition that matters.

And I've recovered.

I did it.

My Moment today: Reading this status, from just over 24 hours after the assault, and seeing that I had every intention of surviving. And realizing today, that I have.

I'm taking on the title of survivor. I am not just in recovery. I am fully here.

Survivor.

And yes, that helps. Despite. Anyway.

## NOVEMBER 13, 2017

And so today's moment of happiness despite the news.

Hemi, my Chrysler 300C Hemi, is still in intensive care at the car shop, receiving a muffler and assorted connected parts transplant and an oil transfusion. When they called me today to give me an update, I was tempted to ask if I could come visit him. But even I figured that might be going too far.

Because I have an extended warranty, I get a rental to drive in while Hemi is gone. Last time, they gave me a burly Dodge Charger, which seduced me. This time, I have a Hyundai Accent. I was in too much of a hurry on Friday to shriek, "You're giving me a WHAT?" So she and I drove off the lot together.

Yes, she. On Saturday, when Michael, Olivia and I walked to the car to go out to dinner, I said something like, "She's in the back."

In unison, Michael and Olivia screeched to a halt. In unison, they said, "SHE?"

I drive boy cars.

Almost all of my cars have been male. And named.

1969 Chrysler Newport 4-door sedan. (Chrys)

Plymouth Volare (Sergio)
Original Toyota minivan. (Toycar)
Dodge Neon (NEEEEEon)
Chrylser LeBaron convertible (LeB)
Nissan Frontier crew cab pick-up (Fronty)
Chrysler Sebring convertible (SeB)
Chrysler 300C Hemi (Hemi)
Chrysler 200 convertible (Semi)

There was a female vehicle before Fronty. It was a Dodge Windstar minivan. Named Windy. When Michael and I were pregnant with Olivia, we realized that NEEEEEon was not going to work with two adults, three teenagers, and a baby. So we bought a mom-mobile. I hated her.

And now...this temporary Accent. "Yes," I said. "A girl."

"Why?" Michael and Olivia said, again in unison.

I shrugged. I don't know why. She's petite. She's curvy, where my boys have sleek straight lines. She doesn't roar. She has a very nice purr.

"Her name is Zizzy," I said. Before they could ask, I said, "The last three letters on her license plate are ZZY."

So I've been driving this little girl. And missing Hemi. Hemi is my bodyguard. He's big and strong. The Hemi engine tends to make people jump away. He has memory seats, so he puts me in the right place every time. He has a thermostat and keeps the interior at a steady 78 degrees. He has heated seats too. He tells me when a tire is low and he tells me which one. And he has a great sound system. I swear he sings with me.

This little girl car...not so much. I sigh every time I look at her.

But this morning, everything was wet. There'd been a heavy fog and a little snow and freezing temperatures. I didn't know it yet, but there was black ice. As Zizzy and I pulled out, she sang a little chime. A bright light came on in her dashboard. It looked like a two-lane road, with an X at the beginning.

Not recognizing that light, I pulled over and dug out her manual.

"The roads are icy," Zizzy told me. "Drive carefully."

Wow.

"Thank you, Zizzy," I said. I patted her wheel. I felt cared for. Watched over.

All of my CDs are in Hemi, so I put on the radio and fumbled around until I found a decent station. And then I began to sing. I think Zizzy did too. And we drove very carefully.

She doesn't have heated seats, but she kept me warm.

Hemi should be home tomorrow. In the meantime, this little girl and I will be BFFs.

And yes, that helps. Despite. Anyway.

## NOVEMBER 14, 2017

And so today's moment of happiness despite the news.

Oh, it was just one of those days. THOSE days. Those days where you want to rip your hair out and shriek about a dozen different times before noon. When, if you were five years old, you would have stomped your feet and held your breath until you turned blue, but you're fifty-seven, and then you decide to hell with it and stomp your feet anyway, but you don't hold your breath because you're asthmatic. Ooooooooooh…one of THOSE days.

At first, it was just interruptions. Everything that I wanted and needed to get done didn't get done because more stuff got added that needed to be done too, even though next to nothing was stuff that involved my job – running AllWriters'. One or two things, fine. Ten, eleven, twelve, and I start to get a bit huffy.

But then came the big one.

My phone rang and it was my car place. Which still has Hemi. They'd already called me earlier in the day and said that because they are doing so many big jobs, they wondered if I was okay with staying in the rental until tomorrow. Well, Zizzy and I are doing fine now, so I said sure. And now here they were again, and I thought maybe it was, Surprise! We got your car done!

Well, it was Surprise!, but not that. They'd found that my car's catalytic converters (Hemi has two) had cracked pipes and needed replacing. It wasn't covered by the extended warranty because it was the result of rust. And so my bill, which was $0, went to $1400.

$1400. About the same cost as one month of our health insurance. About the same cost as our mortgage. So, essentially, it will be like we paid our mortgage three times this month.

That number, 1400, is the bane of my existence.

My car lady said, when she told me about the warranty, "When I called them, they said that the repairs we're doing already shouldn't have been covered either. The person that gave the okay made a mistake. But they're honoring it because you were already told, we already agreed, and the work is being done. So consider that a Christmas present."

Merry Christmas.

So…the work is being done. And I won't have the car until Friday.

I stewed until it was time to cook dinner. I don't cook. The only things I know how to cook are spaghetti and meatloaf and baked potatoes and lasagna. But with Michael working these crazy hours at the grocery store, sometimes the cooking is now falling on me. He didn't leave me spaghetti or meatloaf and baked potatoes or lasagna to cook. He left me La Choy Chow Mein. I'm sure he thought it was easy. Cook the rice, open the two cans, heat them up. Sure.

Those two cans. One stuck on top of the other with some kind of blue tape that would keep any bank vault safe from entry. I attacked it with my fingernails. I attacked it with scissors. Then my sharpest knife. I hit the damn thing with a hammer. Then I lost total control and screamed like a banshee as I walloped the can over and over against my countertop.

Nothing. It's still together.

So I threw it back in the cupboard and I cried. Total waste of about five minutes.

When I pulled myself together, I poked my head in to Olivia. "I'm going to get McDonalds," I said. "I've been defeated by chow mein."

She was wise not to say anything.

As I gathered together my purse and keys and my equilibrium, I saw an envelope from the mail the day before. It was addressed to me and I forgot to open it. It was much easier to open than the chow mein. No blue tape here. I popped the opening and out slid a car decal that I'd forgotten I ordered.

Just Breathe, it said, in sky blue curly cursive

Oooooooooooh, what exquisite timing. I laughed. And then I took a deep breath. And another.

Well played, Universe. Well played.

And yes, that helps. Despite. Anyway.

### NOVEMBER 15, 2017

And so today's moment of happiness despite the news.

I have absolutely no sense of direction. If people tell me to go north or south, I have to ask them to please use left or right. I just have no clue. I've never used the GPS on my phone – it's too hard to see the screen. So despite these things now being at a tap of a phone screen, I still use a separate GPS monitor.

So imagine my horror this morning when I realized that I had to drive

Michael from Waukesha to Whitewater to teach at a high school creative writing festival – about a 45 minute drive – and Naggie, my GPS, is sitting in Hemi at the car shop. Still.

Yes, I'd made the drive several times before. That doesn't mean I know where I'm going!

When you go to bed at four and then have to be on the road by eight, there's already the issue of grogginess. But fear works really well, along with caffeine. Michael used his phone to guide my way to UW – Whitewater's Visitor's Center, where I let him off for the day. I figured I'd only have to backtrack the way I came. I took Highway 59 to Second Street to Starin to Prairie. Easy.

Uh-huh.

I was facing the wrong way on Prairie to get back to Starin. There were school buses everywhere, and cars pulling into parking lots and college kids who felt sufficiently safe that those yellow "people crossing" signs would protect them from getting hit, so they streamed across the street without looking. And there were so many! At 9:00 in the morning! When I was in college, I learned quickly to not schedule anything before 10:00, or I'd sleep right through it. What were they all doing awake?

Eventually, through a couple right turns, I found myself back on Starin. I congratulated myself as I crossed back over Prairie. Things looked familiar. There was the old farmhouse with the lavish porch I commented on. There was the field with newly turned soil that Michael cried out in his early-morning-yapper way, "Look how rich that soil looks!" before turning to me and asking, "That is what I'm supposed to be saying, right?" There were cows.

And then…I was in an industrial park. Starin ended and there'd been no Second Street. It disappeared, along with the cows and rich soil. Instead there were streets like Enterprise and Technology.

What the hell?

In a panic, I made a few turns, hoping to find Second Street, or at least a numbered street that would bring me back. Eventually, I just pulled over. Now what? I didn't have Naggie. I had no one to call. I looked at my phone.

Now bear in mind that I also have no idea how to navigate technology, just as I have no sense of direction. My phone is basically for calls, texting, and checking email. I have apps, but I don't know what they are. My phone is new from last week, so I'm amazed I know how to turn the damn thing on. I scrolled through apps until I found one that looked like it had Google stuff in it. I tapped on it and found, among other things, Google Maps. So I tapped on that.

Lo and behold, magic of all magic, this little blue dot appeared that was supposed to be me, and it was on a map with streets that matched where I was, and if I turned left, I would run right into Highway 59.

The blue dot and I turned left. Highway 59! Highway 59 West was to my left. Highway 59 East was to my right. Wasn't Lake Michigan east? Maybe?

I turned right. And I found my way home. I felt like I was planting my flag on the moon. I was never so happy to be a little blue dot on a Google map.

(And it made me feel good that when my son went to pick up Michael later in the day, he got lost too.)

And yes, that helps. Despite. Anyway.

### NOVEMBER 16, 2017

And so today's moment of happiness despite the news.

Yesterday, when I picked Olivia up from school, I told her how I'd just heard the song "Red, Red Wine" performed by the group UB40. That song always makes me smile because it was the first song that my oldest child, Christopher, went whacko for. When he was 4 years old. Imagine a 4-year old sitting in the back seat of your car, singing in a piping young voice:

*Red, red wine*
*Stay close to me*
*Don't let me be alone*
*It's tearin' apart*
*My blue, blue heart*

That boy will be 34 soon, and he grew up to be someone who rarely ever has a drink. I think he's the only one I know to get his degree at UW – Madison without ever going once to a let's-get-totally-plastered party at that famous-for-drinking school. He certainly didn't follow his mother's example.

Olivia laughed and asked what song she went crazy over. "'Gloria,'" I said. "Laura Branigan." Again, little voice in the back seat, this time of a convertible, singing at full volume:

*Gloria, how's it gonna go down?*
*Will you meet him on the main line, or will you catch him on the rebound?*
*Will you marry for the money, take a lover in the afternoon?*
*Feel your innocence slipping away, don't believe it's comin' back soon.*

Olivia laughed again and then said, "Do you miss me as a little girl, Mama?"

I didn't even stop to think about it. I said, "No."

Well, of course I do. I miss all my babies. I had my first three within four years, when I was very young – 24, 26, and 27. I had Olivia 13 years later, when I turned 40. With the kids currently at 33, 31, 30 and 17, I've now reached a time when I interact with my kids as adults. And I find it amazing. They aren't just my babies, though I see those baby faces as I look at them now. I hear those voices. I remember the exuberant hugs, the little hands that held mine, I remember all of it. But they're PEOPLE now. And I think I'm PEOPLE to them now too.

Today, I had lunch with my 30-year old, my daughter, Katie. She's almost done with earning her PhD in math from the University of Wisconsin – Milwaukee. Among the things we talked about:

*the new (horrible) proposed tax bill
*the orange Asshat
*the next election
*breast cancer
*her relationship
*my relationship
*how to raise a girl
*boots (ohmygod, we love'em)
*teaching

And more. But see? If she was still my little girl, which she is, which she will always be, we wouldn't have had any of those discussions. Well maybe boots. And while I have always looked on her with pride, it wasn't like the pride I felt today, looking across the table at her, hearing her intelligence, witnessing her open and gracious mind, seeing the incredible woman I always knew she'd be. While at the same time remembering the intense little girl that parked herself directly in front of her dance teacher's feet so she could watch every move. Who wanted to learn everything rightnowthisverysecond. And who loved a stuffed sheepdog named Bowser.

See, it's all so FULL now. It's like having your cake and eating it too. I can still see and hear my little ones, but there's also the glory of having them standing side by side with me now. Of their being PEOPLE.

And besides, I get my young'un-fix with Grandbaby Maya Mae.

And yes, that helps. Despite. Anyway.

# NOVEMBER 17, 2017

And so today's moment of happiness despite the news.

This morning, when my alarm went off, I rolled onto my back, stretched, and stared at the ceiling. Which is what I do most mornings. Usually, in my new breast-cancer-usuallyness, I immediately do the math that allows me to know just how many hours it is before I can fall asleep again. But today, I didn't.

I looked up and thought, Huh – I feel pretty awake today.

Yesterday, when I finally settled down to meditate at about five o'clock, I realized I just spent the afternoon with my daughter, walking through a mall, trying on clothes, having lunch, having coffee, and I didn't feel that tug to be home, to be in bed, to take a nap. When I meditated, I didn't fall asleep.

Wow.

On Wednesday, as a student was on her way out the door, she turned and said, "I have to say this…it's so good to have you back."

Have me back. I haven't been gone. But…I understood what she meant. I was fully there, in that classroom.

And again, back to this morning. When my phone rang at 10:00 with my first client, we greeted each other and she said, "You sound really awake this morning!"

Which, on the one hand, makes me think, Good lord, how tired was I? How much did I let show?

And on the other hand, it makes me think that maybe the fatigue is finally going away. Maybe I'm fully back in my skin, my body, my mind, my heart, my soul.

Let me tell you, that one hand, and then the other hand, well, they started clapping.

This afternoon, I sat down in front of my computer and opened the file for my novel-in-progress. My novel-abandoned. Left behind in the blur and grief and pain and fatigue that was recovery from surgery followed by radiation treatment. I didn't think I'd ever work on this book again. I thought I was done. Literally. The End.

Because, honestly, I wasn't sure if I'd be around long enough to finish it.

Writing is who I am. Writing is what puts iron in my blood.

And so I lost myself for a while.

But now… "It's so good to have you back."

Days in a row without naps.

Meditation that is really meditation and not unconsciousness.

Waking up, looking at the ceiling and making a mental list of what I need to get accomplished that day, not a list of hours before I can sleep again.

And writing. Writing!

I opened the novel-in-progress file and I decided, instead of starting where I left off, to go back to page one. Start moving through it again with what I knew then…and what I know now.

That novel looked right back at me and it ROARED.

Throughout this whole ordeal, beginning on June 20, I have been obsessively playing Linkin Park's new CD, *One More Light*. And the one line that has gone through and through and through my head for months now is "I wanna fall wide awake." I didn't know, when I first began to listen, when I first began to hear, how much I was going to feel that line. What all it was going to mean to me.

Well, now, I've fallen wide awake. And I am so grateful to those who pointed it out to me. I'm always so busy looking out that I sometimes don't notice what's going on in here. But I greeted the ceiling this morning. And I felt ready to get up.

Hello. I'm here.

And yes, that helps. Despite. Anyway.

### NOVEMBER 18, 2017

And so today's moment of happiness despite the news.

Tonight was a very different night for me. I went to the This Time Tomorrow gala at the fabulous Pfister Hotel in Milwaukee. I was a guest, because I was a recipient of a TTT Random Act Of Kindness, something I wrote about a couple weeks ago.

It's hard to describe what it feels like to have strangers show up at your door with a check for you…and something more too. Compassion. Care. Concern. An understanding that a diagnosis like this, and going through treatment like that, does more than affect the body. It affects everything, from how you view the world, to how you think and feel, and extends to worry not just for yourself, but for your family too.

It was interesting, watching a video they showed of some recipients receiving their surprise checks. Most recipients burst into tears. I didn't. I very distinctly remember freezing because of an instant case of overwhelm. It was like my mind and body were wrapped in Holy Cow. I hope I was appropriately grateful. I honestly don't remember much.

So tonight was the gala, and RAK recipients were asked to attend. Now I normally dress well, I'm very conscious of that, but this was a different kind of "well". This was, as the invite said, "dress to impress". So I put on the floor-length black velvet dress, the sparkly shoes and matching handbag, the really nice jewelry. I even broke down and wore make-up. Which was when I discovered that I no longer see well enough without my glasses to put on eye make-up. I flustered about that for a few minutes, but then pitched the fluster over my shoulder. I see what I need to see.

When we arrived at the Pfister, I was given a very pretty wrist corsage. We walked a red carpet and had our photos taken. Then we went into the grand ballroom for a very nice dinner, one of those that looks like artwork on a plate.

But as the evening slid on and we listened to presentations, I began to realize my own discomfort. There was a video shot of a list of names of people who died of cancer. The list scrolled by for ten minutes. There were presentations by people who talked about how cancer affected them and their families, and there were many, many well-earned tears.

It was a lovely, touching, poignant evening. But as it went on and my discomfort grew, I realized this: I wasn't yet ready to be in a group, of any size, that was talking about cancer. Right here, right now, I've only just begun to get a handle on the fact that breast cancer is a part of my experience. My history. I'm still learning to sit beside this experience and own it, relate to it, the put it away and move on. Hearing about deaths, about horrible experiences, is just not in my ability. Yet. It will be. But not now.

And yet in the last week, I've interacted with a good friend, another writer, who was diagnosed with my type of breast cancer and who just went through her surgery. I didn't interact with her on Facebook, with everyone watching. I interacted with her privately. I was able to share her grief and her fear. And tonight, I received an email from her saying that she'd gotten the All Clear from her surgeon – no need for chemo, no need for radiation, she just needs to recover. With her, I was able share joy. Overjoy.

But in that large ballroom tonight – overwhelm.

So…during a break, Michael and I got up and left. I needed to go home.

And so this is my Moment Of Happiness. I was able to put aside what I felt was my public and social responsibility – go to the gala, share experiences with others, and acknowledge my gratitude – and do what I personally needed to do. Go home. And continue to deal with this thing my way.

The dress is back in the closet, along with the sparkly shoes and purse. I gave my new make-up to my daughter. My jewelry is tucked away in my jewelry cabinet – yes, I have a cabinet. I. Love. Jewelry. I put on pajama pants and a too-big shirt.

As I took off one necklace, the shorter one that didn't garner much attention, I ran my finger over the engraved words. I did the same with the ring I pulled off and set on my dresser, because I will put it on again tomorrow morning.

On the necklace: *You were given this life because you are strong enough to live it.*

On the ring: *Keep passing the open windows.*

I am. And I will.

And yes, that helps. Despite. Anyway.

## NOVEMBER 19, 2017

And so today's moment of happiness despite the news.

I've been feeling restless and edgy as a reader lately. I finished a novel a couple weeks ago, and while I liked it, and it was the second book I read by this author, I just didn't feel compelled to read the third book, a story collection, that I'd bought and had at the ready. I also had another book, a new book by an old friend, and I read the first part and then put it down.

It was frustrating. It doesn't usually take much to pull me into a new book, but I found myself just bogged. Almost like reader's block, I guess.

I typically read recreationally at lunchtime. Because of what I do, I read all the time. There are always a stack of student manuscripts and editing projects for me to work through. And there's my own work as well. But lunch – lunch is reading without editing. Much. I don't know that I can ever completely put that purple pen down.

So in this interim, this I-have-stuff-to-read-but-I-don't-wanna phase, I've taken to having my lunch in my recliner while watching an episode of something on HGTV. But I've missed reading. There's something amazing about losing yourself in someone else's words, particularly when you are a writer yourself. You know the work behind the words.

Last night, when I wrote The Moment, I mentioned pulling off a ring engraved with the words Keep passing the open windows. The ring is a gift from an AllWriters' writer, sent to me shortly after diagnosis. The phrase is my all-time favorite from literature, John Irving's novel, *The Hotel New*

*Hampshire*. I've been asked the question of what book would I choose if I was stranded on a desert island. This book. Irving is also one of two of my favorite writers, with the second being Ellen Gilchrist.

A couple Christmases ago, Michael gave me a signed *Hotel New Hampshire*. My original copy, read for the first time so long ago, is down in my classroom. But the signed copy stays up here, with me, right behind my writing desk.

And it was the "so long ago" that got me. I realized that while I still readily respond to the desert island question the way I always have, and that I've yet to read a book that has replaced this one at the top of my list, I no longer fully remember what it was about. Well, I do, I could give a one-sentence synopsis. But as in all Irving books, there are plots upon plots upon plots and delicious details I've undoubtedly forgotten.

When I sat down at my desk today, I pulled my signed copy from its spot. I opened it and stopped for a moment at the signature page, running my finger over Irving's scrawly letters, just as I ran my finger yesterday over the ring's engraving. And then I turned to the first page and read the opening sentence.

*"The summer my father bought the bear, none of us was born – we weren't even conceived: not Frank, the oldest; not Franny, the loudest; not me, the next; and not the youngest of us, Lilly and Egg."*

Smitten. All over again. And memories came back too.

I was a brand new mother when I read this novel for the first time. A brand new mother trying to figure out how to write around the schedule of a new baby who refused to have a schedule that had anything to do with what I wanted to do. Naptime quickly became the two hours that I resisted sleep myself and I wrote what was to be my first novel (now buried in a box in my closet, though it earned me my first agent). But reading…what was I to do with reading!

I found ways.

I pushed my son on long afternoon walks in the stroller, bracing the open book on the stroller's canopy. I tripped often. The book waited by the toilet for necessary breaks. I read at night, when husband and baby slept. I put my son in his swing and I read him the book too. I read, I read, I read and I couldn't put the book down.

It would be my desert island book.

So I decided today that it is time to revisit an old hero, embrace an old friend.

Lunchtime tomorrow: *The Hotel New Hampshire.*

I can't wait.

And yes, that helps. Despite. Anyway.

### NOVEMBER 20, 2017

And so today's moment of happiness despite the news.

Right before I went to bed last night, a commercial came on television and told me that we've officially started the holiday season.

I thought of the Christmas decorations up in Walgreens right after Halloween, the Christmas parades that were done over this past weekend when we haven't even had Thanksgiving yet, my turning on the radio in my car last week and hearing Christmas music, and my visiting the mall last Thursday, where I waved at Santa and he waved back.

"No kidding," I said to the television.

I am not a fan of Christmas. I used to be. I actually used to decorate my house from top to bottom, filling shelves, counters, walls, even the bathroom with Santas and snowmen and reindeer. Now…yuk. Christmas to me is just more work.

Last year was a difficult Christmas. It was a little over a month after the assault. I didn't want to celebrate anything, let alone peace on earth, good will to men who threw women off the sidewalk after attempting to kick their dogs. I didn't want to decorate anything. I didn't want to do anything.

It's not like we do much. When we moved to the condo, we discovered we really don't have the space to set up a tree. So we bought a four-foot tree and set it up on the kitchen island, which divides the kitchen and living room. It was a loaded four-foot tree, having to heft the sentimental ornaments of an 8-footer. We don't have a basement here, so all Christmas decorations are kept off site in a storage unit, which means a trip out there and back, and then repeat on New Year's Day.

I wanted none of it. But I have a child still at home. Eventually, I broke down and bought a teeny tiny tree from Walgreens, decorated it with some of Walgreen's ornaments, bought a wreath and used it as a tree skirt. Instead of putting the presents under the tree last year, we put them under, around, and over the tree. It worked.

Well, I'm no more enthused about Christmas this year. But then I saw a photo. Of a shiny silver aluminum Christmas tree. Ugly. Ugly, ugly, ugly.

I WANT ONE.

When I was somewhere around eight years old and living in northern Minnesota, my parents bought a shiny silver aluminum Christmas tree. It came with a bunch of red velvet ornaments. And there were plug-in color wheels to set up on either side of the tree, changing it to green, red, orange, and blue. Sometimes my father timed the wheels so that the tree changed colors all at once, and other times, he staggered them, so the tree would wash from left to right. It was set up in front of our picture window for all the world to see. The real tree was put in the basement rec room with our usual ornaments and such. But I loved to lay with my head under that shiny silver aluminum Christmas tree. I looked up into the fluttering branches. The silver seemed to be made of a type of tinsel and so any breath of air caused it to tremble. And I watched with wonder as the tree turned impossible colors. It was an impossible thing. It was a phenomenally ugly thing. But it was magic.

"Michael," I said last night, "I need a shiny aluminum Christmas tree."

"Maybe painted pink!" he said in a perfect imitation of Lucy from a Charlie Brown Christmas.

All Charlie Brown's little tree needed was some love.

And I've decided I need some wonder. Some magic. Some impossible. All from something phenomenally ugly.

Sorta sounds like a metaphor for my 2017, doesn't it.

So my Moment Of Happiness? I've found a way to look forward to Christmas. I'm gonna find me a tree. Hopefully with color wheels and red velvet ornaments. I want to poke my head under it and look up.

Look up!

And yes, that helps. Despite. Anyway.


## NOVEMBER 21, 2017

And so today's moment of happiness despite the news.

This one might be a little more political than most of my posts. But I've been thinking about this all day.

With today's announcement of Disney/Pixar executive John Lasseter taking a leave of absence because of what he calls "missteps" (i.e. inappropriate behavior), and coming right on top of Charlie Rose's firing, I put up a Facebook status that said, "Ohmygod, it's raining dirty old men."

It was meant to be funny, but also a statement of reality. One after another, bam, bam, bam, we're all getting soaked with news releases about rapes, assaults, inappropriate touching, inappropriate language, and on and on and on, all involving older men.

Kinda like our president. Remember the "Grab'em by the pussy. You can do anything," videotape?

I've watched this rainstorm with some stoicism. Several people expressed shock over Charlie Rose. I haven't expressed shock over any of it. Why? Because we are the country that elected a man to the presidency who openly admitted that he didn't like women and to assaulting women as well.

Have any of us forgotten the night of the debate where the Orange Asshat stood directly behind Clinton as she spoke and he glared and he glared and you just knew what he wanted to do to her.

Many applauded that.

No, not everyone, and no, we didn't all vote for him. But enough of us did that he's there.

Maybe this means that over the years, many of us have consciously or subconsciously released approval for that this kind of behavior. It's normal. It's okay. It's just boys being boys. Maybe we've even tolerated it ourselves.

Years and years ago, I got into a discussion (argument) with my father. He was totally incredulous that I would say that patting a female co-worker on her ass was inappropriate. "I was just appreciating her!" he said. "I was just telling her she did a good job!"

"Would you tell a man he did a good job by patting him on the butt?" I was only fifteen. I couldn't use the word ass in my parents' house.

"No," my father said. "It's just a woman thing. They like it."

Ah.

I bit my tongue then. My father was not someone you argued with. But I remember a few months later, as I walked through a shopping mall, a group of about six young men approached me. I thought it was odd that they lined up one right after the other as they got closer. And then, as I moved past, every single one smacked me across my ass. One grabbed my breast.

The boys laughed and cheered. I didn't say a word. I didn't scream. But I had tears in my eyes. I couldn't have vocalized why I was upset. It was, after all, what men did to women. When they appreciated her. When they just wanted to say Good job! I was appreciated! I was supposed to like it!

I've battled a lot of appreciation.

Today, the realization that we're in a rainstorm of dirty old men, dirty old men washing into the gutters and from there to the sewers made me happy. We have a misogynist in the White House. We have a sexual predator in the White House. At first, I worried that this might be a sign that this type of behavior was forever going to be given a go-ahead, it was forever going to be seen as all right, boys will be boys, they're just showing their appreciation, and women like it. Good job! But now, it seems like we're raising our hands and saying, "Hey, wait a minute." Maybe something will finally be done.

It means we'll see some heroes fall, along with the villains. But it's a start. I hope.

Maybe it means that my daughters and my granddaughter will be able to walk the malls without having to keep an eye out for overappreciative men.

Keep raining. Clean the air. Let all the dirt wash to the sewer where it belongs.

And by the way – those men that don't behave this way? Because I am well aware that not all men do. But these nice guys? The guys that truly know what appreciate and respect means? Well, they're just going to shine like beacons in the clean air.

And yes, that helps. Despite. Anyway.

### NOVEMBER 22, 2017

And so today's moment of happiness despite the news.

Tonight, as we ate an impromptu dinner at Culver's, I behaved like my mother. I performed a behavior I swore I would never ever do, because it was just too "old lady".

I was freezing. So I draped my coat over my shoulders, pulled the collar tight to my throat, but left my arms free of the sleeves. As I watched my hands wave like disenfranchised limbs over my dinner (where are the sleeves? we need the sleeves!), I had an instant vision of my mother. Sitting in nice restaurants with her coat draped over whatever fancy dress she was wearing. Sitting at our own kitchen table at lunch with her eternal white sweater draped over her shoulders, even in summer, when her shoulders were bare. Riding in the car with her light coat draped over her shoulders and the seat belt strapping it to her body.

Each time, she looked like an old lady to me, even though she was likely in her forties the first time I saw her do it. And each time, I thought, Put your arms in your sleeves! Why are you wearing your coat like an old lady shawl?

Tonight, I was cold. Tonight, I draped my coat like a shawl over my shoulders. Tonight, I felt old. Like my mother.

Michael has been telling tales of the grocery store where he works, and one that pops up frequently is a customer complaining about being carded in the liquor department when the customer is clearly over 21. Sometimes the customer is closer to 81 than 21. But the grocery store's policy is that everyone needs to be carded, and there are several security cameras trained on the cashier to prove that he or she follows that policy. I don't understand the customer complaint. I love to be carded. I can pretend it's because I'm so young-looking.

Last week, in the mall with my daughter, we were approaching one of those kiosks where they sell sea-salt skin products. The young man there stood, appraising us, rubbing his chin with one finger. "Hmmm," he said as we drew near, "Are you two sisters?"

I laughed and patted his arm as we passed. "No thank you," I said, "but very nice try."

Afterwards, I thought that line was really akin to shooting himself in the foot. If I look like my 30-year old daughter already, without using his products, what did I need them for? His line should have been, to my daughter, "Dear, help your great-grandmother over here and we'll fix her up with a lotion that will remove her elephant skin."

Of course, I would have decked him.

Somewhere along the line last week, a young student complained to me about turning 37. "That's practically 40!" she said.

And I answered, "Try 57. That's practically 60."

And it was like reverse déjà vu. I'd had this conversation before, only it was me complaining about turning 30. A mentor was turning 60 and she chided me the way I just did this young student. I remembered rolling my eyes and thinking, Wow, 60. That IS old. You must feel lucky to be alive.

My mother and her draped cardigans and coats. Being carded. An attempted seduction into skin products. Practically 60. I thought of all this tonight as I sat at Culvers, with my coat draped around my shoulders. Because it was cold. And the lack of sleeves allowed me better movement.

Oh. THAT'S why she did it.

But I still heard myself loud and clear as I thought, You must feel lucky to be alive.

Yes. I surely do.

And yes, that helps. Despite. Anyway.

### NOVEMBER 23, 2017

And so today's moment of happiness despite the news.

Well, Thanksgiving, of course. I spoke with a friend last week who told me that the whole "attitude is everything" deal is actually false. That there are studies that show people with cancer or other issues heal and survive just the same whether or not they have a great attitude or a toilet attitude.

I can see that, I guess. The body does what the body does. But I know that trying to find a moment of happiness each day has been a big part of my recovery and getting through 2017.

There was chaos in the house as all four kids, one daughter-in-law, one future son-in-law, one granddaughter and one boyfriend descended. But it was a good chaos. Having them all under one roof doesn't happen much anymore. I'm happy when they're here.

As I made two pumpkin pies, two pecan pies, fruit fluff and green bean casserole (my contribution to the meal), I thought about this year and about gratitude. It's no exaggeration to say that 2017 has been hellish for me. It started with the assault just a couple months before 2017 began, From there, I plowed through Olivia experiencing bullying so extreme, we had to switch schools, to Michael losing not one, but two jobs, to my diagnosis of breast cancer and all that entailed. Ultrasounds, biopsies, MRI, surgery, radiation, medication.

It's been a rough year. It's been a sad year.

So I thought about that today and figured I could easily focus on what I'm not grateful for. Which is all of the above. And there have been days that's exactly where my focus was. All the what-if's, all the why-me's, all the why-now's. I'm sure there will be more as I continue to move through recovery and learn to acclimate myself to what is now my life. With recovery, I really have my feet on two different paths – physical recovery and emotional recovery.

But I don't want my focus to be on what I'm not grateful for. Because of that same not-grateful-for list, a whole lot happened that I am grateful for. I felt the circling of the wagons around me. Such intense and complete community. Family, friends, students, readers, writers, and absolute strangers.

The one thing I've learned over and over and over this year: kindness exists. Goodness exists. What is most often shoved in our faces is not what is most prevalent in this world. You have to push aside that ridiculous and maddening roar and listen to the quiet and persistent hum.

I'm listening.

More than anything, I'm grateful to be alive. I'm grateful the cancer was found when it was. I'm grateful it could be taken care of, despite all that entailed. My radiation oncologist said to me once, "You're one of the lucky ones who is going to be okay." And I am. I still have at least five years of medication to get through, with all the attending side effects, and the more frequent fearful mammograms, but ultimately, everything points toward my being just fine.

I am grateful to be alive. And I'm grateful that I can hear the hum.

I thought I lost myself there for a while. But as I looked around my living room today, saw my son hugging my granddaughter while my daughter-in-law laughed, saw my daughter holding hands with her fiancé who treats her like the amazing woman she is, saw my son teasing everyone, but still finding a moment to hug me, saw my daughter laughing with her new boyfriend who seems oh, so nice, and looked at my husband who was reassuring one of our naughty dogs that he wasn't naughty at all, I realized I'm not lost at all. I'm right here. And I'm who I've always been, with just a few adjustments and awakenings. Improvements, really.

I'm grateful to be who I am.

I'm grateful for everyone who circled and stood firm. Thank you.

And yes, that helps. Despite. Anyway.

## NOVEMBER 24, 2017

And so today's moment of happiness despite the news.

Today was closet-cleaning day. I had to switch out my Spring/Summer clothes for my Fall/Winter clothes. Olivia got into the mood too and she plowed her way into her walk-in closet, going through clothes and old toys all at once. This prompted several runs up the stairs to show me something she'd found. "Oh, look, Mama!" she said over and over again, holding up a treasure from her childhood.

Several times, she said, "Oooooooooh...I miss the early 2000's. It was such a simpler time."

A simpler time.

In the early 2000's, I gave birth to my fourth child after a gap of 13 years. I was forty years old, and I suddenly had three teenagers and a baby who shrieked inconsolably much of the time. I was teaching 65 hours a week in a bunch of different places online and "live". And on top of it, I decided to go to grad school to earn my MFA in fiction.

Oh, and then in 2005, I decided to start the studio.

Simpler. Uh-huh.

Another time, Olivia ran up the stairs and said, "Look, Mama! It's like the predecessor to virtual reality!" She carried a 3-D Viewmaster, given to her somewhere around 2005.

A Viewmaster. The predecessor to virtual reality.

Well, maybe. As I folded clothes, I thought back over my own walk through technological predecessors. Manual typewriter to electric typewriter to word processor to desktop computer to laptop. My first cell phone. I remember holding it and realizing, with a sense of both wonder and absolute horror, that I was now able to be reached no matter where I was, no matter what I was doing. LP to cassette to CDs, with a hiccup in there for 8-traks, to MP3 players. Sitting down at a certain time on a certain day of the week to watch a certain channel which had a certain television series, to now sitting down whenever I want and finding it streaming.

Olivia held her Viewmaster in amazement. I felt like a dinosaur.

But we worked steadily through the afternoon into the evening, each of us gathering bags of donations that filled Hemi's trunk and his back seat. I decided to be vicious with myself this year. As I pulled out sweaters and shirts of similar colors, I chose only one and got rid of the rest, with the exception of burgundy. I love burgundy. As my closet gained space and the empty hangers on the floor grew, I felt lighter and could breathe easier. Olivia was giving away treasures from her childhood. I was getting rid of what I didn't need.

And then, as I pulled clothes out and exposed the floor of my closet, I saw what I shoved there earlier, in an attempt to get it out of my sight, out of my mind, out of my life. The cow-patterned bag that contained the binder full of information about breast cancer.

I no longer have breast cancer.

I carried it, bag and all, out to the dumpster and pitched it in. I am not in denial. But I deal with things my own way. And that bag wasn't my way.

Olivia sorted through her treasures that she was happy to keep as memories of a simpler time now. And I got rid of what was weighing me down.

And yes, that helps. Despite. Anyway.

### NOVEMBER 25, 2017

And so today's moment of happiness despite the news.

Olivia and I drove out to Bay View, Wisconsin, to pick up the shiny silver aluminum Christmas tree I wrote about a few days ago. Well, not that exact same tree. But after that tree's memory was a part of my Today's Moment, a poet friend found one for me through a friend of his…and so I am suddenly the proud owner of a phenomenally ugly shiny silver aluminum Christmas tree. It was in an old warehouse. First, I got lost, of course. Naggie, my GPS, kept saying, "It's HERE, it's HERE, it's right HERE, ya dipshit!", but I sure didn't see it. Okay, she didn't really call me a dipshit, but it was the attitude. I called the woman selling me the tree and for a bit, that didn't help either, because she kept saying words like north and east, and we already know that doesn't mean diddly to me. But eventually, we got there.

The building was amazing…old, old brick, maybe cream city. We had to climb up two flights of those see-through metal stairs. Olivia asked me if I was all right, but then she had to quickly wonder if she was all right. It was a little disorienting. When we finally accomplished the see-through climb, we followed signs…and suddenly found ourselves in a room that housed everything my parents and my childhood friends' parents ever owned.

Ohmygod. The lamps. The sharp-lined, skinny-legged furniture. Ashtrays made out of little tiles. Exaggerated figurines, all politically incorrect. Ceramic poodles. Wall hangings of the four seasons.

And then Olivia discovered a rotary phone. She tried to put her fingers in it. "Mama, how does this work?" she asked.

And so I showed her. As I stuck my fingers in the appropriate holes and dialed out our number, I might as well have stepped firmly into my past. Oh, that ratchet purr of the dial. Winding it up, watching it roll back. And the time it took!

I handed her the receiver and told her to try. I watched my girl of today dial our number like the girl of yesterday –me. And then I showed her how you hung up. I remembered the utter satisfaction of slamming down the receiver when I was angry. You can't do that with a cell phone.

"Weird," she said.

Yep. And still so familiar.

My cell phone, tucked in my purse, sang its fairy sound and let me know I had an email or a Facebook notification or a tweet. Olivia dialed and the rotary phone purred.

It was such an odd moment of here and there, then and now. Watching her in my past while I checked my present.

In the end, I didn't buy anything. I only brought home the shiny silver aluminum Christmas tree. Olivia and I rode down the warehouse elevator, one with big double gates and lots of noise, and that was an experience in itself.

And then we left my past behind, in that warehouse, although a piece of it came with me; a bright shiny aluminum piece.

And I'm okay with that.

At dinner tonight, Olivia told her father about dialing the rotary phone and they laughed. All three of us had our cell phones next to our plates. I remembered how, at home, if the phone rang at dinnertime, it was ignored. Now, our phones have a place right next to the silverware.

And I know I should complain about that, but I won't. Because while our phones were present, we still talked to each other. Just as much as we did at the dinner table of my past.

I'm not quite sure where this piece is going. Except there was just something about that moment, watching my daughter dial a phone, that made me happy. She was doing something that I did. She was learning a piece of my past while I had my hand firmly on the present. And I was here to show it to her.

It made me smile. For who I was then. At my daughter, now.

And yes, that helps. Despite. Anyway.

### NOVEMBER 26, 2017

And so today's moment of happiness despite the news.

One of the hardest things about the writing life is dealing with rejection. I recently bought the latest edition of the Pushcart Prize anthology, primarily because I wanted to see if I'd won, since how the winners are announced seems to be the biggest mystery in the literary world. I have a friend who didn't know he'd won a Pushcart Prize for seventeen years. I always wondered how this could happen. Now, being a nominee myself from 2016, I understand. No one knows when, where or how the winners are announced. The dates on the anthologies are also misleading. The 2017 anthology has winners from 2015 in it. So I'm assuming the 2018 anthology has winners from 2016 in it, though you sure wouldn't know from the book, which only tells you what magazines the stories were published in, not when.

Anyway, I was talking about rejection, and what I noticed as I looked through this anthology is all the names of the writers listed under the "Worth Mentioning" section. So many fabulous names! Writers I adore! But not winners. Oh, and if this is the appropriate anthology, I'm not a winner either. I'm not even Worth Mentioning.

But hey, I was nominated!

So writers are often told early on in writing that they have to develop a tough skin. I don't quite believe that. A tough skin keeps you from being open to all that happens in the world worth writing about. A tough skin repels empathy, a fiction writer's greatest tool. But writers do have to learn to feel the sting of rejection and then shake it off. Move on. And revel in the acceptances.

I'm not sure what the opposite of sting is – maybe zing? – okay, we'll go with zing. The zing of acceptance doesn't usually happen on a Sunday, a sleepy day in the literary world. Everyone is home reading the Sunday paper, not making decisions for magazines or publishing houses. But today, when I was home reading my Sunday paper, I got a zing when I discovered that my novel, *In Grace's Time*, was selected as one of the top 47 Books For Holiday Gift-Giving by the Milwaukee Journal Sentinel. I was in my recliner, doughnut to my right, coffee to my left, surrounded by sleeping beagles and sleeping cats, and I was definitely zinged into a straight-up position.

What a lovely way to start the day!

Then, when I returned to my desk and opened my email, I found a note from a magazine editor who was working on acceptances and rejections on a Sunday. My poem, "Rapture", was accepted for a special theme issue on Love. I submitted it three days ago.

Zing!

And in the meantime, Michael received a Twitter email, telling him he might want to check into what Kathie Giorgio, Harlan Coben and Ken Follett are tweeting.

Well, wow. What nice company to be in. Zing!

From the writer side of things, this was a great zingy Sunday. My skin didn't need to be tough at all. It almost makes me look forward to Monday.

Almost.

And yes, that helps. Despite. Anyway.

### NOVEMBER 27, 2017

And so today's moment of happiness despite the news.

Words are important. Poetry and Story is important. Books are important. It's amazing to me how often I wrap words around me. Like a blanket when I was a child. Like a showstopper black dress as I grew. Like a shawl now, not around stooped shoulders, but around a need for comfort and companionship and a sense of being all of a piece.

Today, harried, I ran downstairs to my mailbox and found an unexpected envelope. It was from Birchbark Books, Louise Erdrich's bookstore in Minnesota. I love Louise Erdrich and I love her store and the deli right beside it. I set everything I was carrying down and opened the envelope. Inside, Erdrich's new novel, and it was signed.

Years and years ago, I attended a luncheon at the Milwaukee Public Library, where Erdrich was the special guest. She had a new book out then too, and I stood in line to have it signed. When I got to her table, I told her my name, so she could personalize the book.

"Wait," she said. "Are you the Kathie Giorgio who wrote…" and she pulled out a literary magazine from her bag that, yes, indeed, had a story of mine in it. "This is lovely," she said.

And today, as I held Erdrich's new book, I held that moment in my hands as well. I wrapped myself in a moment of personal history that made me stand straighter, look up, and realize even more deeply who I am.

There was no card, but I knew where the book came from. A student who traveled from Minnesota to the book club I visited in La Crosse brought me a beautiful wall hanging of a turtle from Birchbark. She confirmed her gift tonight.

I have amazing students.

Then after I taught an online workshop tonight, I found an email from the writer who used to be my student, is now on my faculty, and is also my personal assistant. There was an attachment, and she told me she made me a present.

I opened it and watched in stunned delight as a graphic of the covers of books traditionally published by AllWriters' writers lit up my screen. 60 covers so far…More are already under contract and we're just waiting for the cover designs.

With these books, I wrapped myself in accomplishment and pride. Look at my students. Look at them go and grow and fulfill their dreams and goals and wishes. And you know what?

I had a part in that.

I'm wrapped up tight in words tonight. I wouldn't have it any other way.

And yes, that helps. Despite. Anyway.

## NOVEMBER 28, 2017

And so today's moment of happiness despite the news.

This morning, I sat with a student and we talked for a bit before getting into her pages. She'd just finished reading *The Home For Wayward Clocks*.

"I think you wrote this book just for me," she said.

In a way, I did. For her. For everyone.

Every week, I talk with students who try to place the value of writing on the number of words they produce each week, the number of pages written, or the possible pie-in-the-sky amount they might someday make on their books (despite the multitude of studies out there that tell us that just over 50% of traditionally published writers and 85% of self-published writers make less than $1000 a year on their books).

But see, that's not the value. That's not the worth. That's not what makes the writing life so incredibly rich.

*"I think you wrote the book just for me."*

There's the richness. That's why I write.

I've had students say to me, "I just want enough to pay off my mortgage," and "I want to be able to stay at home and live off my writing."

Oh, trust me. You can live off your writing. Please focus on the meaning of the word "live".

For me, my writing has absolutely nothing to do with the number of words I write each day, the number of pages I produce each week, or the amount on my royalty checks. I asked my first publisher to please never ever tell me how many books were sold; I didn't want to know. Writing isn't about numbers. It's about words.

*"I think you wrote the book just for me."*

And it's about impact. I had my moment of happiness by 9:30 this morning.

But then this afternoon, in the AllWriters' online chatroom with another student, I mentioned that I had a poem accepted for a magazine's theme issue on love and I joked, "Yes, me. Someone who writes poetry about peeing beagles. I wrote a love poem."

"But you write about love all the time," my student said.

That one took me aback. This is a student who has read the majority of my books. I don't think most people would say that I write about love all the time. They would cite some of my topics, which some consider dark (I consider it real) (though my latest novel has been described as "delightful!"). But you know what?

This student is right. I do write about love all the time. ALL the time. I learned something today.

Which is also why I write. That's the value. The worth. The richness.

Richness not from dollar signs or numbers. But from words. The words I write, and the ones brought back to me. The lessons learned.

*"I think you wrote this book just for me." "You write about love all the time."*

And I live off my writing.

And yes, that helps. Despite. Anyway.

### NOVEMBER 29, 2017

And so today's moment of happiness despite the news.

In the shower today, I realized that my right armpit appears to be permanently bald.

Not your usual showertime discovery, that's for sure.

My right lymph nodes were involved in the partial mastectomy and in the subsequent radiation treatments. I admit, I haven't paid much attention to that area, or the area on the other side. Most of my summer was spent in sleeved shirts due to the surgery and treatment. Shaving was the least of my worries.

Then today...I noticed the difference between left and right armpits.

Well, how bizarre. I haven't read of this side effect. And I suppose it's not necessarily a bad one.

I began to think of all the time I could save from now on, with only the left armpit to shave. This past Sunday, in a fit of frustration and too-much-to-do, I yelled at Michael, "I don't even have time to clip my own toenails! That's how busy I am!"

Well, now, the gift of time. Armpit-shaving cut in half. So to speak.

Standing under the warm water, I tried to calculate just how much time this would save me over the course of a year. Let's see...let's say it takes me 5 seconds to do one armpit, and I do it twice a month. That would be 24 times a year. 5 seconds times 24 times would be 120 seconds. 120 seconds equals two minutes.

This was in my head, mind you. I didn't have a calculator in the shower.

I could have two extra minutes a year from now on! If I live another 30 years, that's 60 minutes, which is a whole hour! The year I turn 87, I could have a whole hour of free time, if I stockpiled those minutes, and...

It was round about then that I began to laugh.

Ten seconds a month is not even enough time to get my toenails clipped.

I guess I'll just have to keep on being busy.

And honestly, except for the days I yell about it, which are infrequent, I'm perfectly fine with that. I yell about it only once in a while. Maybe once a month. And the yelling only lasts about two minutes.

So if I stop yelling about it, that would save me two minutes a month. If I combine that with the ten seconds a month I'm going to save by not shaving my right armpit, then I'll have two minutes and ten seconds extra each month. If I live for another thirty years…

And I didn't even figure in how much cash I'm going to save in razor blades! Bonus!

And yes, that helps. Despite. Anyway.

## NOVEMBER 30, 2017

And so today's moment of happiness despite the news.

Some days, it's really, really hard to find that damn moment. The whole needle in a haystack image comes to mind. I had a haystack sort of day.

My day ended yesterday with an email from a writers' retreat I really, really, really want to get into, and I didn't. Again. It felt doubly hard because I didn't get to go on retreat this last summer, due to breast cancer. I usually take a couple weeks each year to just get away, be a writer, and drop all of my other roles. That didn't happen this year, and I added another role to my long list: breast cancer patient to breast cancer survivor. So I went to bed grumpy.

Then during a Skype visit with my first client of the day, there was a resounding crash from downstairs. I knew what it was before I ran to the stairs. Below, two beagles looked up and wagged their tails next to the wreckage of the Christmas tree, now sprawled like a chalk outline on the floor. I finished with my client and went downstairs and lifted the tree back up. It was already an ugly tree, but now it was worse – bent and misshapen even more than it was originally. A beagle crime victim.

To clean up from the tree, I first had to pick my way around assorted accidents. The dogs are becoming ancient – 16 and 14. Both have bladder issues – one is in advanced kidney disease. One is growing more senile every day and seems to have forgotten all housebreaking training. So my second floor was a disaster.

After all was in order, I went back upstairs to make the bed and shower. And then I heard the tree go over again. I told myself I would not go downstairs until I was at least showered and fully dressed. When I did, I found yet another puddle.

So the shiny silver aluminum tree is gone. It's packed away, along with the ornaments, the garland, the tree skirt, the star and the special red lights I bought for it. I never even got the chance to use the color wheels. Through it all, the dogs wagged.

Sigh.

I was just closing the last box when I looked at the clock. 3:16. My daughter gets out of school at 3:05, but on Thursdays, she usually has orchestra rehearsal. I'd texted her, asking her to tell me when to pick her up and she never answered. Figuring she must be in rehearsal or she would have let me know, I called just to make sure. Nope, no rehearsal. She was outside the school, in the cold, abandoned. I asked her why she didn't text me. "You texted when I was in class, Mom," she said. And after school? "I didn't think of it."

Sigh.

Bear in mind that all of this happened during the time I set aside in my day to write.

I went to pick her up. Glum. Grumpy. Pissed off at the world in general. Even Starbucks didn't pick me up. The barista chirped at me through the speaker and as I pulled away and went around the corner, I muttered, "Oh, shut the fuck up."

Yes. That kind of day.

When I got home, I found a Facebook notification that someone was trying to connect with me. I looked and it was a message from a girl who attends the high school where I presented a few weeks ago. She said, "Your stories that you told were really inspiring to me. I have now read all of the books you donated to our school. They are amazing books."

I thanked her, and told her I was so glad she liked the books.

She said, "I'm so glad you wrote them!"

Smashed tree to no tree to dog poop to dog pee to unscheduled pick-up to way-too-cheerful barista to…"I'm so glad you wrote them."

ZING!

And yes, that helps. Despite. Anyway.

# Chapter Twelve

## DECEMBER 1, 2017

And so today's moment of happiness despite the news.

My daughter Katie was married today.

And yes, that's a pretty big moment of happiness! But there's more to it than that.

Katie and her fiancé Nick have been engaged for quite some time. Katie is earning her PhD in math at the University of Wisconsin – Milwaukee and she wanted to wait to have the wedding until after she graduated. Katie is a hard worker, a perfectionist, and someone who always wants to invest herself totally in her goal. She wants a beautiful wedding. She wants her PhD and to perform admirably as she does so. She couldn't do both to the extent of her dreams unless she focused on one at a time. So we all settled down to a long happy engagement, knowing the wedding would get there when it was time.

Then…Governor Scott Walker and 2017 Wisconsin Act 59.

Because of Walker and the 2017 Wisconsin Act 59, people who receive state insurance will no longer be able to list a domestic partner on that insurance. My daughter receives state insurance as part of her program at UWM. She and Nick, who is self-employed, were domestic partners and planned to be until they married after her graduation.

They were being level-headed, fiscally mindful, responsible and patient.

And today, so they could maintain their insurance, they cast aside the big wedding they were waiting for and got married at a courthouse. It was only the two of them; none of us were present. We didn't know until afterwards. Because this was not the wedding they dreamed of, they decided to do it on their own.

I've missed the opportunity to be with my daughter as she commits herself to her husband.

While I have a moment of happiness, I also have a moment of anger. And it's not at my daughter. It's at Scott Walker.

My moment of happiness? I am beyond proud of my daughter. She didn't sit back and take the sanctimonious holier-than-thou crap Walker is puking out. She found a way to keep herself and her husband safe. She set aside the wedding for the marriage.

And the other moment of happiness? My daughter has found someone she loves that much. And he loves her right back.

Oh, we'll still find ways. I will make sure my daughter has her bridal showers. She and I will shop for the wedding dress. She will have her full ceremony and reception and she will be the most stunning woman I've ever seen. Even if she's already been married for a while.

She will have it all, despite Scott Walker.

I love my daughter.

Congratulations, Katie and Nick Boddie.

And yes, that helps. Despite. Anyway.

## DECEMBER 2, 2017

And so today's moment of happiness despite the news.

Michael was carrying a bag when he came out of work at the grocery store today. "I got you something," he said.

A present from a grocery store? I pictured a candy bar, maybe, a Baby Ruth, which I've been craving lately. But he peeled back the bag and I saw glimpses of red and purple paper, and green, and a rosie pink.

"It's a blooming Christmas cactus," he said. "Like from *The Homecoming.*"

Oh, *The Homecoming*. The made-for-tv movie that launched my favorite show, *The Waltons*. The show that, within a minute of an episode starting, I can tell you what it's about, just based on Earl Hamner's voiceover narration. The show I can recite the script right along with the actors and actresses, all through its nine seasons. The show whose memorabilia fills space in my office – the board game, the dolls, the books, the lunchbox, the viewmaster reels, the LP, the paper dolls, and more. There is, as far as I know, only one piece of *The Waltons* memorabilia that I don't own – the dollhouse replica of the Walton home. I covet it.

And now, in my car, a blooming Christmas cactus. I could immediately hear the original Olivia Walton's voice, in *The Homecoming*. She was played by Patricia Neal, a somewhat rougher-around-the-edges version of the mother of the Walton clan, as compared to Michael Learned's interpretation of the part in the series. In *The Homecoming*, as the family eats lunch, Olivia goes down the basement to collect some apples to make some of her famous applesauce cake for Christmas Eve. She wasn't going to make it – her husband hasn't returned home from his job in the city with his paycheck and she needs sugar, but money is running low. Then she decides to make it anyway. As she turns from the apples, she spies her Christmas cactus, put away since the fall, just blooming away. She bursts into song, "I Heard The Bells On Christmas Day", then brings the plant up the stairs, pokes her head around the door, and says, "Who wants to see something pretty?" All the Walton children cheer with excitement.

Imagine a world where children are excited to see something pretty, something like a blooming Christmas cactus.

Today, in my car, Michael smiled at me and said, "Who wants to see something pretty?"

I did.

Near the end of the scene, after Olivia has taken her place at the table, she says that the Christmas cactus was grown from a cutting from her own mother's plant, that she did the cutting the year she married John, and that the plant is now seventeen years old. Mary Ellen, the oldest daughter, asks, "Why'd you marry Daddy, Mama?"

Olivia answers, "The same reason anybody gets married, baby." She pauses, then intones. "Love." This is echoed at the end of the movie when Olivia, sitting on the couch with her finally-returned-home husband, says, "John, you must have spent most all of your paycheck. What are we going to live on?" And John answers, "Love, woman. Love."

The cactus in the episode is 17 years old and John and Olivia have been married 17 years at that point. Michael and I have been married for 18 years. We have a daughter named Olivia. Every Christmas Eve, we watch The Homecoming.

"Who wants to see something pretty?" Michael asked me today.

I did. And he knew I did.

Well, I do vow.

And yes, that helps. Despite. Anyway.

### DECEMBER 3, 2017

And so today's moment of happiness despite the news.

My search for feeling okay about Christmas continues.

The experiment with the shiny silver aluminum Christmas tree failed big-time, due to the backs of beagles. I was excited about the tree, excited about bringing back a magical moment from my childhood: lying beneath an ugly silver aluminum Christmas tree, watching it turn impossible colors due to the crazy color wheels, and looking up into the utter impossibility of a tree that went from orange to green to blue to red. But the beagles took care of that (see 11/30/17). It made me sad.

So I've worked at picking myself back up. I brought out the little tabletop tree from Walgreens I purchased last year and we set it up on the island between the living room and kitchen. That helped. And then yesterday, while working at my desk, I kept glancing at my hibiscus, brought inside for the winter. I popped up the idea of maybe decorating it, with lightweight lights and ornaments. And then I thought of the Starbucks ornaments I've collected for years. Starbucks puts out little ceramic miniatures of their cups to hang on your tree. I've never done that – I had them hung on my wall for a while, until I collected too many. They've been stuck away in a credenza for a few years now.

So I brought them out. And now...I have a Starbucks tree in my office. I might get some lights too. It's helped.

Today, as I drove toward home, I noticed all the trees appearing in people's windows and the outdoor lights that have gone up. Bessie, the gigantic dairy cow statue I wrote about a while back, is sporting a Santa coat and hat and a lit wreath around her neck. All the glitter and light made me think of *The Grinch That Stole Christmas*. Despite the Grinch stealing everything away from the Whos in Whoville, they still celebrated Christmas. They were still happy. They still rejoiced.

Kinda like Asshat, I thought. Over and over, he is beating this country down, most recently with the worst possible tax reform which is going to leave many of us crippled and broken. But despite that being all over the news this week, along with the constant deluge of dirty old men, we are putting up Christmas lights. Christmas trees. We are setting up Nativity sets and lighting the menorahs. Kids are practicing for holiday concerts. Santa, the very same Santa that my daughter has visited for all of her seventeen years, is waiting at the mall. He waved at me the other day. I know he's waiting for his visit. Olivia, while she shrieks that she's seventeen now and while her Christmas list is filled with t-shirts printed with feminist slogans, will go to see him just the same.

We're just like the Whos. And that made me hurry home to my teeny Walgreens Christmas tree and my Starbucks hibiscus. And my family.

And yes, that helps. Despite. Anyway.

# DECEMBER 4, 2017

And so today's moment of happiness despite the news.

I think of all the roles I play, the most difficult is as a parent. I've been a parent for almost 34 years now and you would think I would have gained some confidence in my ability. Well, not really.

I felt like a horrible failure today. A little over a year ago, I bought an old Volkswagen Beetle for my daughter Olivia. She'd been in love with the little buggy car for years; her entire room is decorated in Beetle – posters, artwork, rug, model cars, and she owns every Herbie movie. When it came time for Olivia to learn to drive, I jokingly said (okay, I was dead serious), "This girl is NOT going to learn how to drive in my cars." So I found this Beetle. Olivia promptly put pink eyelashes on the headlights and named her Starlight Lashes.

Today, Starlight Lashes was towed away, pink eyelashes and all, as a donation to Rawhide Boys' Ranch.

In the little over a year since I bought her, I put more money into Starlight Lashes than I paid for her. She broke down. And broke down. And broke down. She was broken down more than she was running. She broke down when she was holding absolutely still with her key hanging on a hook in my kitchen. The final straw came on the Saturday after Thanksgiving when she wouldn't start and her warning lights went crazy, flickering and jumping. ALL of her warning lights.

So the donation. Off she went to Rawhide. I saved, for Olivia, the little vase with the flower in it that all Beetles have. And the Starbucks keychain I gave her. And I promised her that there will be another Beetle soon.

But here's the bigger thing. Olivia still isn't driving. Not through any fault of her own. She wants to drive. But as the sole driver in this household, I didn't have any time to take her driving. 85 hours a week of work sort of puts a crimp on your free time.

So. I am the one who bought the lemon Beetle without having a mechanic look at her first. And I am the only one who can take Olivia driving and I can't. It's my fault that my daughter's car was towed away today. And it's my fault that she's still not driving.

I have three other kids. I took them driving and I provided them with beater cars that survived until they killed them. But I didn't have my own business then. I didn't work 85 hours a week then. Thirteen years after my third child was born, Olivia came along to a life with an older mother. A more

Kathie Giorgio   411

established mother. And a more divided mother.

So I was feeling pretty awful when I left today to do errands. On my way back home, I had to pull over for at least a dozen blazing police cars. As I waited for them to pass, my phone pinged with an email from Olivia's school. It was on lockout. There was a "situation" in the area and no one was allowed to leave the school or come into the school, no matter what.

All those police cars.

I didn't know whether to barrel to the school, where they wouldn't let me in, or barrel home and try to get information from the local news channels. Finally, I barreled home – and found no information at all. Thirty-five long minutes later, another email from the school declared an all-clear. I don't know if it's possible to hold your breath for thirty-five minutes, but damned if I didn't try.

So Olivia came home.

When she climbed into Hemi, the first thing she asked was, "Did they take Starlight away today?" Yes, I said. She stared hard at her lap. I thought about loss.

My girl came home today.

And yes, that helps. Despite. Anyway.

## DECEMBER 5, 2017

And so today's moment of happiness despite the news.

I had coffee today with my high school creative writing teacher. I have to say right off the bat, I love being able to say that. I'm 57. But my high school creative writing teacher is still in my life.

Since we both work on a local book festival together and there was a meeting later in the afternoon, we had a bajillion things to talk about. But I knew, with him, the hook was coming. The hook as in "he never lets me off the hook".

"So how's the new book coming?"

Hooked.

I explained that I was back at it, after what I was afraid was a permanent exit during radiation. That working on it one day this week, I actually stopped and thought, You know, this book is pretty good (for non-writers, it's an amazing thing when something you thought was going into the trash ends up not being trash at all). And that I was doing something different this time, something I'd never done before.

I've always barreled through first drafts. I don't look backwards, not until I get to the end and then start Draft Two. I don't know what's going to happen in a book or a story until I get to the end and it doesn't make sense to me to start the rewrite before I know what fits. But this time is different. Radiation knocked me off my feet and out of my writing chair. I lost track of the book, pretty much the same way I lost track of myself there for a while.

"I'm uncomfortable with this," I said. "But I'm doing it this way. I had to go back to page 1. I had to go back to when the book was just the book, and not the book being written by someone with breast cancer."

Honestly, having to go back to the beginning made me feel a bit like a failure. Not a bit. Like a failure. I don't sew, but I imagine it was like making a mistake and having to rip everything all out and start over.

He saw it differently. "You've always done that," he said. "It's not new. You've always done whatever you have to do to get the story out." He nodded. "Good job."

Suddenly, I didn't feel like a failure anymore.

I told him I just had the first formal essay I wrote on the breast cancer experience accepted for publication. He asked me if it was difficult to write. I appreciated his word choice. He didn't say hard. He said difficult. He wasn't talking about the writing.

"Yes," I said, and felt my eyes well up.

He sat back in his chair and clapped. For me.

Having someone in my life who believes in me, has believed in me, and will always believe in me is a positive force I treasure. While he believes in me, there's one thing that takes it even further: he refuses to expect anything less than what he believes I can accomplish.

In high school, I joked with him from time to time, calling him "sir" when he made demands. Once, I had assignments in two separate classes to write a short story. I asked to be able to write the same story for both classes. My high school creative writing teacher was the one who made the decision, while my second teacher waited in deference. "No," my teacher said. "You're more than capable. Write two stories. And knock us both dead."

I didn't think I could do it. But "Yes, sir," I said. It was what he expected of me. And then I did it.

Today, he told me I could and would write this new book, even if I'm using a different process than ever before.

"Yes, sir," I said. It is what he expects of me. And I will.

And yes, that helps. Despite. Anyway.

## DECEMBER 6, 2017

And so today's moment of happiness despite the news.

Once upon a time, well, maybe not so very long ago, I watched as my daughter Olivia walked into her kindergarten classroom for the first time. It was also the very first time she walked into an "average" classroom, an "everyday" public school classroom, after three years of attending a special early childhood program offered through our school district. We knew, soon after Olivia's first birthday, that she didn't do things quite the way other people did. There was nothing "average" about her. There was nothing "everyday" about her. She didn't speak until she was past three years old, and when she did, the first word she uttered was, "Dumbass!" When she was three, we learned that the non-averageness and the non-everydayness placed her on the autism spectrum.

But to us, it just made her Olivia. Anything she did that was not so everyday, we placed in a category we named Livvyonian. And despite all the talk about spectrum, we expected great things. We placed her on the great expectrum.

When I returned that first kindergarten day to pick Olivia up, I stopped in the early childhood classroom to say hello to her teacher of the past three years. I told her, from what I could see, this first transition to kindergarten went well. I told her how, while Michael and I hovered that morning, Olivia looked up at us, waved her hand like a queen, and said, "You can go now." And then I said to this teacher, "We expect everything for Olivia. We expect that she will go on to college and she is going to lead a full and happy life."

This teacher, who worked with my daughter for three years, who saw (I thought) the tremendous leaps she made, pulled me into a hug. And then she said, "Well...we can always dream."

I wish I could tell her how utterly devastated I felt that day, as I walked out to my car with my little girl trotting beside me, her backpack bouncing. My little girl who was never supposed to talk who was now chattering nonstop about her first day, using words like "fabulous" and "extraordinary". I wish I could tell the teacher how both Michael and I spent the next little bit of time wondering if we were living in a state of denial. Of hallucination. If we just didn't want to face the truth.

But we shook ourselves out of it. We knew this child better than anybody. And we were more amazed by her with each passing day. She was high up on the great expectrum.

Today, I went in to Olivia's high school for a meeting with her guidance counselor. It was time for the junior conference, where the counselor would help us determine what Olivia wanted to do after graduation next year. The counselor turned to Olivia and asked her what she thought she might want to do.

My daughter calmly and confidently answered, "I want to attend a four-year college. I'd like to go to either Mount Mary or to the University of Wisconsin – Green Bay. And I want to be an art or music therapist. And a writer too."

And then the counselor told us about Olivia's GPA – just under 4.0 – and how she is in the top 13% of her class.

*Dear Early Childhood Teacher: In a way, you were right. We CAN dream. We DID dream. And our little girl dreams too. She dreams BIG and what she dreams, she does. She makes her dreams reality. There is nothing "average" about her. There is nothing "everyday" about her. And we wouldn't have her any other way.*

*But you know what, Early Childhood Teacher? You were also wrong. And I am ever so glad we didn't listen to you. We listened to HER. We listened to every syllable uttered in Livvyonian. We always will.*

Am I a proud mama? Oh, yeah.

And yes, that helps. Despite. Anyway.

### DECEMBER 7, 2017

And so today's moment of happiness despite the news.

When I started this blog, I committed to writing it every day for a year. In that time, I've only missed one day.

October 4, 2017. The day Michael came home from the job he loved, which he'd only had for six months, and told me he was let go. Two weeks of severance. 27 days of health insurance.

I couldn't post any moment of happiness that day. I could have posted about the reverberations of fear and shock that shook us both. We've experienced job losses before, and insurance losses as well. But not since my diagnosis of breast cancer.

It's been 65 days. Today, I was able to announce that Michael found another job. Insurance begins in 30 days.

Last Friday, I went in to see my doctors for the first time since treatment ended. It's pretty rattling to say "doctors", plural. It's still hard to accept that I need more than one. But cancer comes with a handful of medical personnel that clasp hands and form a circle around you. I came to really appreciate that circle. Last Friday, two of my doctors, the medical oncologist and the radiation oncologist, informed me that I am just fine. Bloodwork: clear. Radiation: out of my system. Healed.

Cancer: gone. New job: acquired. Relief: profound.

I'd like to say that maybe now, my family's lives can go back to the way they were. But I don't think that's possible. We're all different. We've all been affected. I know that I've learned a lot.

I always thought that people in the arts were more compassionate, more humane, more sensitive than the world at large. Yet Michael was working in the arts when he lost his job. It was a small professional theatre that let him go. They were aware of the breast cancer. And it was these artsy folks that flatly said no when I asked for mercy, to please at least let us have three months of insurance to help us out while Michael looked for a new job.

So maybe not all people in the arts are compassionate, humane and sensitive.

However, as news of what happened spread, I was amazed at the response. From friends and family, students, the writing community, the cancer support community, and from absolute strangers. People I hadn't heard from in years stepped forward. People I never would have expected to help did. And they came from all walks of life.

The end result? I didn't lose faith in all humanity. I gained it. And I gained faith in the individual, from the police officer who didn't ticket me for driving without a seatbelt when I told him I was receiving radiation and the belt irritated already hurting skin to the women who gazed at me through a window and gave me fist pumps when I completed a walk at a labyrinth outside a cancer center. I don't look for kindness only in the arts world now, but in the world at large and in the faces of everyone I meet. And I am well aware that in all facets of our world, with no exceptions, there is some darkness. No place is all light. But boy, do I ever appreciate the light there is.

I bask in it.

I am free of cancer. Michael has a job.

Whew. I think I can breathe now.

And yes, that helps. Despite. Anyway.

## DECEMBER 8, 2017

And so today's moment of happiness despite the news.

This morning, there was a message on the studio's voicemail. Someone wanted to talk to me about a class for her granddaughter. "She really likes this writing stuff," she said in her message, "and she just finished a class in school and her teacher said she's good."

So I called. We ended up talking about this girl and the studio for quite a while. "She writes all the time," the grandmother said. "All the time. Sad poetry. Stories."

I remember someone who used to write sad poetry. Stories. That person's creative writing teacher said, "You'll never write deer and flowers stories." He was right.

There's nothing wrong with sad poetry and stories. This grandmother recognized that.

I explained the AllWriters' Teen Writers Workshop. And then I asked the grandmother if she'd like to give the workshop to her granddaughter for Christmas. "I can have a gift certificate made for you and emailed this afternoon."

"Oh…" the grandmother breathed. "Oh, that would be nice."

She explained that money was tight. She was raising her granddaughter. And I said I would register the girl now and reserve her seat and she wouldn't have to pay until the class begins in January. "That gives you time to get it together. It's a ten-week class and it's $70. Will that work?"

She agreed. And I offered up my faith that the spot I reserved for this girl would indeed be filled. I usually require payment at the time of registration. But not this time. I needed to do whatever it took to get this girl into my door.

Because of what this girl needed. She needed to come in my door.

I remember somebody who needed a door, a door just like mine.

I asked the grandmother what high school her granddaughter attended. "Waukesha North," she said.

I felt myself light up. Have you ever felt that? Where you feel the glow on your face? "Really? I was just there a few weeks ago," I said. "I spent the whole morning, talking to kids about the writing life."

"She came home that day," the grandmother said. "Told me an author came to the school. She didn't say writer, she said author. The way she said it! Told me she listened and then she suddenly felt like she could do just what she wants to do. And she put this big note on the refrigerator, asking me to check out the place where this author works."

"That would be me," I whispered. "That would be me."

It was me, who stood in front of the groups of kids that day. But you know, it was also me who needed someone to tell me that I could do what I wanted to do, so many years ago. Who needed to know that it was okay to write sad poetry and stories. There wasn't an AllWriters' then. But I did have a teacher who lifted me up. Who offered me every door he had. Who made me feel that the life I wanted was possible.

I believe strongly in giving back. And I am so grateful to have the chance to do so.

And yes, that helps. Despite. Anyway.

### DECEMBER 9, 2017

And so today's moment of happiness despite the news.

Christmas shopping today. Ugh. Christmas shopping does not help me to feel any better about Christmas, really. Maybe if I had the benefit of the mall all to myself, it would help. I don't do well in crowds, especially noisy rowdy crowds. But I don't like to do all my shopping online either. I like to support local businesses. So I braced myself, girded my loins, and went out.

It took me a half an hour to find a parking spot. A half an hour. That really didn't start the afternoon well.

Much, much, much later, I stood in line at the Starbucks kiosk. I needed my grande cinnamon dolce latte, with only two pumps, and I needed it right that minute. There were already trips out to the car to drop things off. Things were scratched off on my lists. Michael and Olivia were off doing their own shopping. There was just a little more for me to do. I was tired. I was grumpy. My back hurt. And I was really, really, really sick of the Christmas music that was playing everywhere. If I heard "Rockin' Around The Christmas Tree" one more time, I was going to have to throw a rock at a Christmas tree. And maybe Santa.

And then, in the slow line at Starbucks, I heard a little voice.

The song playing at the time was Band Aid 30's "Do They Know It's Christmas?" The little voice singing along was very young and I turned to trace it. Behind me, there was a little girl, about four years old, hanging on to her mother's coat and swaying with the music. She wasn't paying attention to anyone, she was just singing. She wasn't singing to perform; she wasn't aware of being watched or listened to. She just SANG. And she knew the words! I wondered at a little one who knew this song from 2014.

Santa was in his throne just across the aisle, but she wasn't looking at Santa. She wasn't looking at all the lights and decorations. She didn't pay a bit of attention to the noise. It was just not there for her. She was blissed out on the music. It was a glorious bubble around her. She swayed and she sang.

So I joined her. Just as the song shifted into its lyric of Feed the world (let them know it's Christmas time again), Heal the world (let them know it's Christmas time again). She looked up at me and she beamed. She smiled like she sang. All heart.

So did I.

When we finished the song, she giggled and began to twirl. I nodded at her mother, who looked as tired as I felt before the song, and I said, "You have a beautiful daughter. Merry Christmas."

Then I covered the tab for her latte and the little singer's juice box.

Hope and joy can be found in the strangest places. In a Starbucks line, where an impossibly young little girl sings earnestly about feeding and healing the world.

And yes, that helps. Despite. Anyway.

### DECEMBER 10, 2017

And so today's moment of happiness despite the news.

Sometimes, the nicest moments of happiness come from nothing at all.

For the majority of my day today, I was home alone. Michael was at work at the grocery store (he's given his two weeks' notice). Olivia was out laser-tagging with the boyfriend.

The house…was quiet.

The television wasn't on.

No one was calling my name.

No one asked me to do anything.

Doors weren't being slammed.

No cat threw up.

No dog made a mess.

There was no ticky-ticky-tick of pacing toenails on our concrete floors (the pets' toenails, not ours).

The studio phone wasn't ringing. No one calls on a Sunday.

The home phone didn't ring either.

My cell phone didn't ring.

There weren't even any sirens or train whistles.

I sat at my desk in the silence and I worked. Not on my own stuff, admittedly, but on the work of my students. There were no interruptions. There were no distractions. It was just...quiet.

In a life that is chaotic, at the end of a year that took Chaos and gave it a capital C, this just doesn't happen very often.

Later, of course, Olivia and the boyfriend came home and doors started slamming again. The pets woke up and the dogs made messes, though as of this writing, the cats have not thrown up. My cell phone rang and I had to go pick Michael up from the store and then, ironically, since he also did the grocery shopping, I had to go fetch the dinner.

During supper, I told Michael that I didn't have anything to write for my Moment Of Happiness. "I didn't do anything today," I said. "I didn't go anywhere. I just worked. It was quiet."

"Who's to say quiet can't be your moment of happiness?" he said.

And I considered that. Really. Who's to say?

Shhhhhhhh.

And yes, that helps. Despite. Anyway.

## DECEMBER 11, 2017

I am a bit of a neat freak. I like things put away and tidy. My counters cleared. My bed made. Files filed, books on shelves in alphabetical order, things right where they belong.

In a sense, I'm like that with my writing too. Not with the writing process itself, as I'm very much a write-down-whatever-comes-into-my-head kind of writer. I don't outline. I don't plan. When I have a thought for what might happen further down the road in whatever I'm working on, I jot it down in a notebook next to my computer. Sometimes I return to it, sometimes I don't; it depends on what happens between now and then, which could be anything.

But...when I write, I like to finish a scene before I'm done for the day. It's kind of like having a real mess behind my cabinet doors and closet doors. On the outside: neat and tidy. On the inside: pandemonium. On my page: scene ended, complete with its little set of asterisks (****). In my head: oh, don't look there.

Which leads me to today, when I faced a horrible decision. I'm back at work, finally, on the novel-in-progress, which is tentatively titled *If You Tame Me*, based on a poem by Antoine de Saint-Exupery:

*But if you tame me, then we shall need each other.*
*To me, you will be unique in all the world.*
*To you, I will be unique in all the world...*
*You will become responsible forever for what you have tamed...*

I started in later than usual for me, something which got under my neat and tidy skin and itched. And then, when it was time for my daily chauffer-run, I wasn't at the end of a scene. But it was 3:05 and I had to:
*pick up Olivia from school and drop her off at home,
*do the studio's banking,
*pick up Michael from the grocery store,
*get my daily mega-dose of caffeine from Starbucks.

So I patted my computer, promised I would be back, and left. I thought I'd be back in plenty of time for what I planned for the afternoon/evening: meditate at 4:30, then shift into teaching mode, with clients at five and six, an online class from seven to eight, and then reading student manuscripts. It was 3:05 – I'd likely be home by 3:45 and have a full 45 minutes to finish the scene.

Yeah, right.

Just-turned-red stoplights. Longest line ever at the bank. A teller who had to run her finger over every string of coded numbers on every check, then do it again while whispering softly to herself and then setting each check down with a "Hmph." A not-so-long line in the drive-thru at Starbucks, but a woman in front of me who ordered drink after drink and one of every food item on the menu (okay, maybe not, but it seemed like it). Then, finally, home.

4:15. Not enough time to finish the scene if I meditated. Not enough time to meditate if I finished the scene.

As of today, I've meditated at least once a day for 636 days in a row. Usually, it's twice a day – once when I switch from writing back to teaching, and once before bed. It's important to me. I was the world's biggest skeptic about meditation for most of my life, and now I'm the world's biggest believer. But...but...not finishing a scene?

Sigh.

I stood by my desk, looking from my computer screen, where my character Audrey waited, and at my phone and headphones, where my – well, what? – my sense of peace and relaxation waited.

And then…I chose who I am, by my own intense definition, way down at my core. I wrote. I sat down and finished the scene. I will meditate an extra ten minutes before bed to put my world back straight on its unique axis.

Audrey cheered. And oh, it was one hell of a scene.

And yes, that helps. Despite. Anyway.

## DECEMBER 12, 2017

And so today's moment of happiness despite the news.

After yesterday's difficult decision over whether I should use the blip of time I had for writing or for meditation, I was relieved to find an easier time of it today. My writing time was spent over coffee with my publicist. By the time I got home, I had twenty minutes before my first evening client. So…I meditated.

I don't go for the sitting-in-the-lotus-position meditation. When I first started, the person who encouraged me said, "I meditate in my recliner. Meditation requires comfort." I applauded that, and since then, have always meditated in my recliner. Most of the time, I am under an electric throw blanket, turned on high. I've learned that warmth and comfort lead to bliss. At least in my world.

So. Headphones on, blanket on, feet up, I began to listen to the drone of one of my favorite guided meditations.

And then…I plunged asleep. No fall. This was a steep dive over a cliff. There one minute, gone the next.

The sleep was bone-deep. It was a sleep where I was aware of my own unconsciousness. I knew I was out. And I was okay with that.

And then I dreamed. The warmth became a living being. I watched as the blanket became two red-robed arms, majestic arms, and then they wrapped themselves tightly around me. My memory is thick now with the sensation of my head tilting, my cheek rubbing against the rich material, and oh, the heat. Not the burning-from-the-inside-out that I've been experiencing with the anti-cancer medication, but just the most profound warmth. The comfort. There is no other word for what I did: I snuggled.

And then I woke up. My heated throw was up to my chin and there was a purring cat on my chest. My guided meditation finished, the timer told me, fifteen minutes before. I was now five minutes late for my client. Which led to a frantic scramble as the cat was tossed to one side, the blanket to another, and I tried to climb back to clarity and my computer screen.

My client wasn't upset. And the class I taught tonight was superb. Through it all, I held onto that embrace. Warmth was in my veins.

Hold on to small graces.

And yes, that helps. Despite. Anyway.

## DECEMBER 13, 2017

And so today's moment of happiness despite the news.

Oh my goodness. Stephen King likes me.

Back on October 4th, when Michael lost his job, I didn't know I was being set on the path of finding out how many people care, and just how much kindness there is in this world. It's been a real eye-opener for me. I've certainly witnessed many examples of supreme cruelty in my life. But now…well, I've witnessed a wumpus amount of kindness and compassion.

When Michael lost his job, and with it, our insurance, I reluctantly started a Go Fund Me account, so we could afford Cobra insurance offered by his ex-employer at an astronomical rate, that was still less than the Affordable Care Act. I was astonished at the result of the Go Fund Me – people I knew donated, and so did strangers. They responded!

Then I had a random email that mentioned the Authors' League Fund, an offshoot of the Authors' Guild. The Authors' League Fund was developed way back in the 1800s specifically to help writers in medical crisis which then spawned a financial crisis. I applied. And they responded!

And I was nominated by a student for a Random Act Of Kindness from This Time Tomorrow, a foundation that supports individuals affected by cancer and financial difficulty. They responded!

The folks at the Authors' League Fund suggested I also apply at The Haven Foundation. The Haven Foundation was formed by Stephen King, after his major bout of medical issues when he was hit by a van. King, of course, supports himself on his writing. But this experience opened King's eyes to reality: most authors are self-employed and so we are often under-insured or not insured at all. King's Haven Foundation helps writers in that type of situation.

I applied. And today…they responded!

I am overwhelmed by the sheer number of people who are making sure I'm cared for. Making sure that I keep on receiving the quality healthcare that has allowed me to step away from surgery and radiation treatment cancer-free, and continue the medication treatment and close surveillance that will keep me that way.

But today, with the addition of the Haven Foundation, there's a new level. And I hope I can say this without sounding too obnoxious.

The Authors' League Fund and the Haven Foundation are hard-hitting, supportive, powerful writing organizations that support professional writers.

And they are supporting me.

I feel like they're sitting on either side of my classroom table from me, and they're saying, "We SEE you, Kathie Giorgio. We see your novels and short stories and poetry. We see AllWriters' Workplace & Workshop. And it all has merit. It has impact. And we want you to keep going."

Really, it's the weirdest form of validation ever. Because the only way I could receive this kind of validation is to go through just what I've been going through – facing breast cancer.

Since the publication of *Rise From The River* in 2015, I have struggled with my own validation, my own sense of having a purpose – no, more than that. Having a purpose beyond my own declaration of it. I have struggled with wondering if anyone else in the world agreed with me that I am doing good work, that I am doing something important, that I am doing what I'm supposed to do. And while I've definitely received answers since I fell into this struggle, they only stuck for a little while. Then something would happen and I'd be questioning myself all over again.

And now this. Will this stick?

I think so. Because these are two major writing organizations telling me that I'm worthwhile. That I'm a professional. I'm the real deal!

They SEE me. I feel SEEN today.

And if it took cancer and crisis to finally make me feel this way, well, then, thank you, breast cancer. Now stay the hell aDEway from me and let me get my work done.

And yes, that helps. Oh my God, that helps. Despite. Anyway.

## DECEMBER 14, 2017

And so today's moment of happiness despite the news.

A couple weeks ago, when it became apparent that my big shiny aluminum Christmas tree (maybe painted pink!) was not going to work in a house with beagles, I set up a teeny Walgreens Christmas tree on the island between my kitchen and living room. We decorated it with teeny ornaments. We draped it with teeny lights and topped it with a not-so-teeny star – teeny stars are hard to come by, I discovered. Its tree skirt is a fake Christmas wreath. And, while it's not my color-wheeled vision of yesteryear, it's been okay.

Yesterday, when I came downstairs for breakfast, I found Muse, the teenier of our cats, sitting on the island by the teeny tree. The tree was upright, but all around Muse were the teeny ornaments. One was broken. I couldn't figure out how this cat could knock down all the ornaments without knocking down the tree. But I didn't care. I was mad.

"Muse!" I said. "What did you do? Why did you do that? Bad kitty!" And I pushed her from the island. She gave me that "nothing you do affects me" look that cats have down pat and wandered off to give herself a bath. I put the ornaments back on the tree, threw away the broken one, and snarled. Stupid tree. Stupid Christmas. Stupid pets.

Throughout my day, Muse is usually there. Waiting on the bathroom rug while I take a shower. Sitting by my laptop, watching the screen. Sitting on my lap during meditation. Sitting next to me at lunch. My clients who Skype in actually ask for her if she's not there, her gray face joining mine on the screen.

But yesterday, she stayed within my vision, but not next to me. And that baleful look was constant. I ignored her, except for a few muttered, "Bad kitties."

Before we went to bed last night, Michael suddenly said, "Oh, I'm sorry I didn't have time to put the tree back together before I left for work this morning. Olivia asked me to do it when she had to catch the bus for school, but I had to get out too."

"What?" I said. "I saw the ornaments."

"Yeah, when Olivia swung her backpack on, she accidentally knocked the tree over. I only had time to stand it back up."

Oh, no.

Yes, I apologized to a cat. Yes, I kissed her nose and told her I loved her and I was so, so sorry for blaming her for the tree. Yes, I lifted her next to the tree and told her to go ahead, take a bite. She didn't. All I got was the baleful look. When I meditated before bed, she did not join me. When I woke up partway through the night, she was not there.

Oh, no.

But then I woke up this morning. There was a teeny cat sleeping on my shoulder, with her purr in my ear. I normally don't let this cat sleep on my shoulder. She is restricted to the foot of the bed. But this morning, I let her stay there. I listened to her purr.

I was forgiven.

The teeny tree was intact too.

And yes, that helps. Despite. Anyway.

## DECEMBER 15, 2017

And so today's moment of happiness despite the news.

So last night, while he was downstairs in the classroom, teaching the Thursday Night Teen Writers' Workshop, Michael texted me. In my office on the 3rd floor, I read that one of the girls, 16-year old Rachel, just had her first poem accepted, in a legitimate and lovely literary magazine.

We've been holding the teen class for about a year now. And yep, they're right on time. You can start expecting a lot more.

I announced the publication on Facebook this morning, and that set me off to thinking about a whole row of happenings, this week and earlier:

*a student had her first online book launch, hosted by her publisher, on Facebook. Going to the publisher's Facebook page, I watched while my student, with headphones on, fielded questions like a pro. This was a student (like many students) who believed that this would never ever happen. Right as it ended, she texted me: "That was amazing! It finally feels real!" I answered, "It IS real. YOU are real!", and she said, "I believe you. I did this. We did this. I feel amazing."

*Another student, whose book was just accepted and is now going through its publication process, emailed me this afternoon and said, "I'm starting to get (even more) excited!" This was another student who believed it would never ever happen.

*I thought of a student who passed away a couple years ago at the age of 89. She was 87 when she joined my Wednesday Night Workshop. She'd been writing most of her life and was frustrated because only a little had appeared in print. I don't think she knew what hit her. Before she passed on, she went on a publishing streak. Piece after piece after piece. At 87 and 88 years of age.

*And then today, the 16-year old.

Michael has been in the process of putting together a Powerpoint that talks about AllWriters' success with publications, and on the screen, one by one, book by book, they all come up. Bam. Bam. Bam. Bam. Right after that, there is a solid screen of teeny tiny words, which make up the names of all the magazines and anthologies that AllWriters' writers have been in. He showed it to me last night and it left me giddy. Then, as I started to walk upstairs to go to bed, he hit replay. I had to stop and lean over the bannister to watch it again. I think I would stop dead in front of an oncoming train to watch it.

Michael looked up at me and said, "Would you look at that grin all over your face!"

Oh, it's more than all over my face. It's all over my everything.

16 years old to 89 years old. And every genre there is. Amazing.

And yes, that helps. Despite. Anyway.

### DECEMBER 16, 2017

And so today's moment of happiness despite the news.

Sometimes, I think I'm the worst grandmother ever.

Grandbaby Maya Mae was over today. I was teaching a class when she arrived and she walked without hesitation into my classroom and waved at my students. Then I brought her upstairs to Olivia, who would keep her company until I was done teaching.

Maya flung off her jacket. "Gamma Kaffee, your house looks diffwent," she said.

Diffwent. I was already charmed. Michael has always complained about children on television shows, showcasing the typical speech slips of the very young. He thinks it's cloyingly cute and contrived. But when it comes from my grandbaby's mouth…oh, melt. And that's why I'm an awful grandmother. I don't correct her. I love it.

"Why diffwent?" I asked.

"No, Gamma, diffwent," she insisted, and I knew someone was correcting her, but she didn't hear the correction yet. So I agreed and asked her why my house was different.

She pointed at the teeny Walgreens tree and the stockings on my staircase from the Dollar Store. And then she rebuked me. "Gamma," she said. "It's not Kwismas yet."

"I know. It's not Kwismas –" Glare. I corrected myself. "-- Christmas day yet, but it's Christmas time." I returned to my class.

When I came back up and got us some lunch, Maya Mae regaled me with Maya Mae speech. She asked me if I knew why she had vaniwa icing on her face. Because, she said, she ate a vaniwa doughnut. She said she liked my Kwismas sree (I still don't know why t's are s's) and the wittle ownaments, and that she had no wittle ownaments at home, but big ownaments. "Do you know where to find my swocking in my house?" she asked. Stocking, I realized. "On my Kwismas swee!" she shrieked and laughed as if it was the most outrageous thing ever.

Oh, man. I loved every little mispronounced word.

A few weeks ago, Maya Mae, Olivia and I went to an event sponsored by my real estate agent, the one who sold Michael and me our first house, then sold it for us, and who sold my son, Maya Mae's daddy, their house. We saw the movie Coco, which was fabulous. Before we went in, families were invited to have their photo taken. When I received mine in the mail, there was an extra one for Maya Mae. I presented it to her.

'Oh, sank you, Gamma Kaffee! Sank you! I wuv it! Maybe Mama will buy a fwame and put it in my woom and I will wook at it evewy day!"

Okay, now really. Can you stand it? That little voice. Those funny words. Ohmygod.

After we picked up Maya Mae's mama and we were on our way to their house, my daughter-in-law told me they had Maya's first progress report from 4-K. She was excelling in most everything. "They even said she's doing well in punctuation," Amber said. "And I thought, imagine that, her grandmother is a writer and she's doing well in punctuation."

Gamma, I corrected silently. Gamma Kaffee is a witer.

Oh, I'm a tewwible gwandmosser, I am.

And yes, that helps. Despite. Anyway.

### DECEMBER 17, 2017

And so today's moment of happiness despite the news.

Today was our first normal Sunday since Michael lost his job on October 4 and then started working at the grocery store. The store tended to schedule him on Sundays. But yesterday was his last day there...tomorrow, he starts in his new job, once again returning to the world of accounting.

So the day started side by side on our reclining loveseat, while we had breakfast and I read the paper. I read out loud the columns we both like, and we went through the recipes in the food section. That section's theme today was "spirited desserts", holiday desserts with a splash of alcohol. Every single one looked phenomenal and I finally told Michael I was going to tear the whole page out, hand it over, and insist that he make them all for Christmas.

I can do that. Michael is the chef in this house. I'm the willing taste-tester.

Michael was already planning to bake today. He was making holiday treats for the classes he teaches at AllWriters'. I'm hoping my students get to share in these too, though my Wednesday Afternoon Women Writers' Workshop has already begun listing the treats they're bringing, so I've no doubt that everyone in the on-site classroom this week will go away happy. I've been at work up in my office all day, and except for a few excursions down to the busy kitchen, I've not tasted, but only experienced the delicious other senses associated with baking. The scent. And the sounds.

The sounds? Oh, yes. Michael talks while he bakes. The kitchen is always infiltrated by at least three of our four pets. Muse, the teeny cat, usually has nothing to do with it. But Edgar, the bowling ball cat, and the two all-nose beagles, Donnie and Blossom, are there. And there. And there. Wherever Michael's foot goes, that's where they are. The dialogue culminated at one point to this rant:

"Edgar, leave the dogs alone. Quit rubbing against them! You're going to knock them over!"

"Blossom, get the hell out of here!"

"Donnie, don't exist!"

Poor Donnie. However, he's the stickler. The other two quit to take naps. Donnie, nose in constant sniff, just never gave up. "Donnie! Donnie! Donnie!"

But Michael talks to the air too:

"Where the hell IS that?"

"What the hell is this DOING?"

"Oh, no. Oh, no, no, no."

"Well, that's not right."

The "that's not right" piqued my curiosity, so I ventured down. He was making little cake ornaments, all different colors and flavors. Red, green, orange. But when I arrived, he was staring morosely at a pile of little gray cakes. Gray.

"What're those?" I asked.

"They're supposed to be purple. They're made with rum."

Well, rum doesn't translate to purple, apparently. I really liked the red ones, made with Fireball Whiskey. I suggested he use the gray ones as lumps of coal. Not everyone at AllWriters' has been good this year.

But the aromas all day long…Oboy. Besides the cakes, there is a pear and cinnamon cheesecake cooling in the fridge. There is chili steaming on the stove, soon to go into the fridge to be crockpotted tomorrow. He made sloppy joes for dinner. Vanilla, cinnamon, rum, whiskey, peppermint, peppers, garlic, chili powder, all wafting up the stairs…to me. I'm full from just breathing.

The kitchen is a disaster. But Michael the chef also knows he'd better be Michael the cleaning crew.

Is there any better match than a husband who cooks and bakes and a wife who appreciates good food? I don't think so.

In a little while, I know there will be a piping hot cup of coffee and a plate filled with pear cinnamon cheesecake, just for me. Yum.

And yes, that helps. Despite. Anyway.

### DECEMBER 18, 2017

And so today's moment of happiness despite the news.

I'm starting to get little red flag milestones that I'm about to lose my last child to adulthood. A couple weeks ago, I went to school to speak with Olivia's guidance counselor for her junior year planning session in preparation for college and beyond. Today, I received my first notification about her taking the ACT. When we went Christmas shopping a couple weekends ago, she went into a non-gaming store to get her boyfriend something just lovely for his present (I can't say what, just in case he reads this – you'll have to wait until he gets it!). There are no toys on her own Christmas list, but she wants clothes from a store called Feminist Apparel.

Oh, man. Where did the little girl go?

Granted, she's always had what everyone calls an old soul. She's extremely intuitive. One of my most memorable moments with her comes from when she was five years old. I'd had a bad day. A really bad day. A bad day that just had me tied in knots and my knots were tied in knots. At the time, we had a hammock on the third floor deck and I went outside to lay/lie/stretch out in it (I am unapologetic about my absolute inability to understand the whole lay/lie thing). I had one arm over my eyes and those eyes were closed as well, to keep the tears inside.

Olivia came out and climbed into the hammock with me. Her head was at one end, mine was at the other. She put her arm over her eyes as well. And she wiggled just enough to set the hammock into a rock-a-bye swing. "Breathe in, breathe out, Mama," she said. "Breathe in, breathe out."

Oh, that little girl.

So this afternoon, while I was thinking of all this, I pulled up to her high school to pick her up. And there she was, snuggled up to her boyfriend, leaning in for a kiss…and wearing hot pink polka-dotted one-piece fuzzy pajamas. Brown fuzzy slippers. And she carried a stuffed panda bear.

It was pajama day at school. I have always protested pajama day. It seems to me that after a certain age, pajamas belong at home. Pajama day worries me, it makes me mad, but I've always let her participate. I'd forgotten that today was pajama day.

And so I was blissed by the surprise of my little girl, still there in polka-dotted one-piece fuzzy pajamas. Hot pink, her favorite color forever. The polka dots were black, tied for her favorite color since becoming a teenager.

There she was. Still there.

Now granted, when she got home, she disappeared in her teenage way into her bedroom, behind a closed door. But not entirely. She sent me two poems to look at. One was about Post Traumatic Stress Disorder. The other was about gun control.

That was my glimpse at the adult she's going to be. And that provided bliss as well.

But...hot pink polka-dotted one-piece fuzzy pajamas. And a stuffed panda.

Thanks to the school for pajama day.

And yes, that helps. Despite. Anyway.

## DECEMBER 19, 2017

And so today's moment of happiness despite the news.

I think we can all agree that the English language is pretty bizarre. For me, the obvious proof of this is that the word "phonetics" isn't spelled phonetically. If it was, we would pronounce it "puh-hone-et-icks". And well...we don't. Ph = F.

But when you combine our goofy language and then you put me with an Australian student in a chatroom...oh, we have a good time. I've known Eva since 2011. We meet in the AllWriters' private online classroom. So everything we say to each other is typed.

One of the stories we discussed today is an oldie, but a goodie – Eva showed it to me soon after we started working together. I was still learning "Aussie-isms" at that point. In it, Eva described a woman wearing "candy bathers with hibiscus on her places of dispatch." To which my response, naturally, was, "Huh?"

A pink swimming suit with a hibiscus on it, covering her, well...crotch and butt. Her places of dispatch. I laughed for weeks.

Today, as we talked, more differences came to the surface. Once again with the swimsuit, Eva's main character said she "had a pair" like the hibiscus-wearer. "A pair of what?" I asked. "Breasts?"

"No!" she said. "A pair of swimmers!"

I knew that swimmers meant a swimsuit. "Swimsuits come in pairs?"

"When they're bikinis."

"She's wearing two bikinis?"

"No! When you wear bikinis, you have on a two-piece."

In a way, I suppose, this makes sense. Two pieces. A bikini top. A bikini bottom. Bikinis. "Here," I said, "bikini is singular. You wear a bikini." Then I thought for a moment. "But we wear a pair of pants. I've never understood that one."

Apparently, they don't wear pairs of pants in Australia. "That's very funny," Eva said. "Why a pair of pants?"

"Two legs, I guess."

"So then if you only had one leg, would you wear a pant?"

"Maybe. Though we also say a pair of underwear. But we don't say a pair of bra. Which, when you think of it, does hold a pair."

Even though we're in a chatroom, even though I am at one end of the earth and Eva is on the other, even though my evening is her morning, my winter her summer, I could hear Eva laughing. And I know she could hear me laughing too.

Eva did look up "pair of pants" on Google, and supposedly, pair of pants came from the original pantaloons, which were in two pieces, so you wore a pair of pantaloons.

I have at times also tried to explain our way of dealing with health insurance here, and our higher educational system, and the lack of gun control. Eva and my other overseas clients are flabbergasted. When the Orange Asshat was elected, I fielded an outcry of "What is your country thinking?" Try explaining the electoral system that would allow the majority to lose.

I'd much rather explain a pair of pants. And a bikini. And I'd much rather howl over places of dispatch covered by a hibiscus on candy swimmers.

And yes, that helps. Despite. Anyway.

## DECEMBER 20, 2017

And so today's moment of happiness despite the news.

Tonight, I had to run over to Walgreens (which is literally right behind my home) to get a black Sharpie. My daughter uses mine to draw from time to time and, well, I pulled off the cap today and the poor pen was dead. I will likely be using it for gift tags when I wrap Christmas presents in a few days and so I decided to buy a new one right away, before I forgot.

I complain a lot about the cold here in Wisconsin. I've lived in either northern Minnesota or the Madison and Milwaukee areas of Wisconsin since I was six years old, so you would think I'd be acclimated. I'm not. I swear the cold just reaches through the seams of whatever I'm wearing and slices me open. Bone-chilling is not just a phrase. It's a reality.

But there is a benefit of the cold, and I took advantage of it tonight. I don't know the scientific explanation for it, but the night sky is drawn more sharply on a cold winter night. Even when there are city lights keeping the dark from being profound.

Halfway to Walgreens, I stopped and looked up. None of the clichéd descriptions did the sky justice. Pinpricks of silver on black velvet. Diamonds in the sky. Sparkles. Twinkles. All of those applied, but didn't quite make it. And then there was the moon.

The moon seemed brighter than the sun.

It was just breath-taking, and it did take my breath, visual puffs of my living self floating from me to the sky.

I know that some feel humbled when looking at a night sky. They feel smaller, tiny against the grandeur of the universe. They offer up wishes and hopes. Stars in the sky are like the white dandelions in our lawns. Wish-worthy. Maybe it says something about my personality that I don't feel that way. Not humbled. Not smaller. And I don't offer wishes, but thanks. I feel safe. I can't say what the stars signify to me, but that light in the darkness just does me good.

I like a daylight sky too, when it's blue. Puffy clouds or not, a blue sky makes me happy. Sunset skies make me introspective. Stormy skies scare the hell out of me. But a night sky...a night sky makes me feel safe. I feel watched over. Soothed.

From my poetry files:

*MOONGLOW my eyes see the moon but it's my soul that glows bright silver reflection.*

In the cold of this night, my soul glowed bright and I like to think that my exhaled breath, a soft bit of me, rose to the stars and shared my appreciation.

And yes, that helps. Despite. Anyway.

## DECEMBER 21, 2017

And so today's moment of happiness despite the news.

There were two books that I finished reading recently sitting out on the kitchen island. So I brought them down to the classroom and the bookshelves to be put in their permanent homes. The classroom, when there's not a class going on, takes on its own quiet personality. I tend to keep the overhead lights off when I'm in there alone and everything becomes muted and peaceful. That room is normally at a high buzz of creative energy, but with the lights down and the chairs empty, it just becomes home for me.

As I traced my fingers over the books' spines, looking for the proper places for these two new books to be, I couldn't help but think of the books that have affected me over the years. They're like friends. Some, I still have. Others have drifted away.

In the third grade, my teacher, Mrs. Campbell, took a little bit of time after every lunch recess to read us a chapter from a book. When the book was finished, we had the opportunity to bring it home and read it for ourselves. One book, named *Daddles*, by Ruth Sawyer, completely took me over. Other students zapped their hands up faster than I did, and I was fifth or sixth to finally get to bring it home. I must have read that book a hundred times. And somehow, despite reminders, it didn't make its way back to school. On a night months later, my mother made me accompany her to a PTA meeting and she insisted I bring the book to give it back to Mrs. Campbell. When I held it out to her, along with an apology for keeping it for so long, she must have seen something in my face. Probably the tears. "You keep that book, Kathie," she said and she hugged me. "It so belongs to you."

Somewhere along the way, past college and into my first marriage, that book was lost. But I can still see the cover. I can still feel the pages. I can still hear its voice.

A few years later, I checked out a book called *A Candle In Her Room* by Ruth M. Arthur from the public library. And then I checked it out again. And again. To be fair, I always returned the book, waited a week, then checked it out again if it was available. *Daddles* taught me to share with others. I don't know how many times I checked that book out. I do remember the librarian telling me they had to order a new copy because I'd worn the old one out. The old one was given to me by yet another kind woman. Several years ago, I lent the book to a student who never returned it. I bought another copy, finding it at a used book seller. I won't lend it out anymore.

All the way through my life, books have influenced me, lifted me up, taught me things, given me experiences I wouldn't otherwise have. Books keep me company when there is no other company. And they keep me company when I'm surrounded.

As I was putting the two new books away today, I heard a scuffle outside. Looking out the window, I saw a woman at our Little Free Library. Someone wiped us out of books the other day, something that happens far too often and that makes me wonder if the books are being sold somewhere. But there were still a few books left, including one that I placed in there yesterday. The book that was debuted yesterday at a student's book launch. I stayed in the shadow of the dim classroom, watching, and the woman lifted the book out, read the back, smiled, and took it away with her.

I talk a lot about the importance of community, both in general and how important it is specifically to me. Thanks to women like Mrs. Campbell and that librarian, and to books like *Daddles* and *A Candle In Her Room*, I have that community and I provide it too. I provide it to readers with my own books. To writers, with the studio. And to strangers who wander by, take a look in the Little Free Library, find a friend to keep them company, and move on.

It's a foggy night, cold, a mix of rain and sleet in the air. I like to imagine that woman, sitting in a chair wherever she lives, one light on in the room, like a little spotlight on her life. Reading the book that my student wrote and that I provided.

You can never be alone, in the company of a book.

And yes, that helps. Despite. Anyway.

## DECEMBER 22, 2017

And so today's moment of happiness despite the news.

Today, when I drove in to pick my daughter up at school, she was sitting and talking with another girl. They both came over to the car and Olivia introduced her. "She's in my psych class," she said, "and she's reading your books!" The girl nodded vigorously.

"Wow!" I said. "That's really cool!"

Then she told me that in her English class, she had to write a sestina (a sestina is a poem with six stanzas each with six lines and a final stanza with three lines. All of the stanzas have the same six words at the line-ends in six different sequences that follow a pattern, and all six words appear in the closing triplet) about a book she's reading.

"Do you know what a sestina is?" she asked me.

"Yes," I said.

"Well, of course you do," she said and laughed.

That "of course you do" made me smile.

She told me she wrote her sestina to *Enlarged Hearts*.

"Wow!" I said again. "Would you be willing to show me?"

She agreed.

Eventually, I ended up giving her a ride home. She called her mother for permission, and off we went.

Partway through the ride there, the girl said, "This is so weird!"

"What is?" I asked.

"Well, I was just reading you. And here you are!"

There I was. Grinning from one side of my face to the other. This wasn't weird at all. It was so, so cool.

Meanwhile, the girls chatted. Turns out they knew of each other, but they weren't friends, until today. Today, the girl was reading in class and Olivia saw my photo on the back of my book. "That's my mom," she said. "You're reading one of my mom's books."

"Kathie Giorgio is your MOM?" the girl squealed.

So my 17-year old daughter admitted to being related to me. Bonus!

Can you just imagine what this did for my day? My spirits went up like a sudden fever. I've always written, in my head, to adults. I never even considered what type of impact my books would have on high schoolers.

Apparently…there's impact.

High school was such a difficult time for me. The thought that maybe my books can help with the difficulty…that's a new idea. And a new level of satisfaction and excitement.

Wow.

And yes, that helps. Despite. Anyway.


### DECEMBER 23, 2017

And so today's moment of happiness despite the news.

A couple days ago, I posted a Moment that concerned books, favorite books, books that just grabbed me and stayed with me for years. One of these was a book called *Daddles*, read to my class when I was in the third grade.

When I brought the book home to read it for myself, it somehow didn't find its way back to school, and eventually, my teacher, Mrs. Campbell, allowed me to keep it as a gift. The book disappeared on one of my moves as a young adult.

When I posted the Moment, a couple people mentioned that *Daddles* was available on Amazon. I knew that already, as I went there, looking for the name of the author. When I was in third grade, authors didn't matter. Only the story did, and the characters. Before I looked, I couldn't have told you who wrote the book, but I could have told you the book is about a beagle named Daddles and two kids, a boy named Peterkins and a girl named Snoodie, who "owned" Daddles for two summers while they visited family on a farm. The dog was called Daddles by the kids because when they saw the dog walk, they said, "He doesn't dawdle and he doesn't waddle – he daddles." I've had three beagles, and two of them daddled. The one mixed with a coonhound was too long-legged.

Those telling me that the book was on Amazon urged me to buy it. I admit, I went back to that listing several times over the next several days. It seemed silly. This was a children's book, although a children's book that I loved above all others, and I was now 57 years old. But two days ago, I caved to silliness and I bought it.

Today, it arrived in my mailbox.

I knew what was in the package as soon as I saw it. When I brought it and the rest of the mail upstairs, I dealt with the other envelopes first and then set them aside. When I opened the padded envelope, it was with nothing else on the counter. Just me and what was inside.

When the book slid out and into my hands, it was like my memory was a picture puzzle with one missing piece, and this was it. Oh, it fit in my fingers just like it used to. I know my hands are larger now than the third-grade baby ones that first held this book, but I was likely in my teens the last time I hid in my walk-in closet to read it. All those years just flowed together, and if it wasn't for the fact I was due downstairs to teach a class, I would have sunk to the floor, sprawled on my belly, raised my feet up in the air and crossed them at the ankles, propped my cheeks in my fists, and I would have barreled into the story. Daddles, Peterkins, Snoodie and me.

It was probably a good thing I had a class. I would have needed help getting up from the floor.

I read this book everywhere. On the floor. In bed at night. Outside in the grass, under a tree. In a tree. In the car, headed toward a family vacation. Even when my other books were replaced with Beverly Cleary and Walter Farley, then Louisa May Alcott and Laura Lee Hope, Mary Stewart and Victoria Holt, Dickens, Melville, Twain, Hawthorne, then Tyler, Oates, Gilchrist, Irving and on and on…there was always a little blue book with a beagle and two kids on the cover.

Until it disappeared.

Today, it's back in my grasp and it fits like it never ever left. And I know the author's name now – Ruth Sawyer. *Daddles* was published in 1964, when I was four years old, but I wouldn't read it until 1968, when I was eight years old. Sawyer died two years later, in 1970, when I was ten. But her book sure didn't die. It's stayed with me all this long while. Even when I wasn't able to hold it in my hands anymore.

I can hold it now. I can breathe in its pages and its story and run barefoot through the fields alongside the two kids, even though I likely would need help getting up off the floor now.

Yes, I'm going to read it. Every single word. I can't wait.

And yes, that helps. Despite. Anyway.

### DECEMBER 24, 2017

And so today's moment of happiness despite the news.

Recently, one of my favorite baristas returned to Starbucks. He'd taken another job and after a while, found himself unhappy there. So he came back to where he was happy. When I drive through the drive-thru, he doesn't ask the usual, "Welcome to Starbucks, what can I get started for you?" Instead, he calls, "Your usual, Kathie?" He usually says hello to whatever car I'm driving. His dream car is a Dodge Charger, and once, when Hemi was in the shop, the rental place gave me exactly that. My barista nearly fell out of the window. "NO WAY!" he shouted before I explained it was a rental.

He's young. He's earnest. He's good-natured. He punctuates everything he says with, "For sure!" And he's found his way back to Starbucks. He's trying to find his path.

About a week ago, he told me he'd started reading. And he did, in a very impressive way, beginning with Albert Camus' *The Stranger*. We talked about it for as long as we dared with a line behind me in the drive-thru. I was delighted with his enthusiasm and ambition.

Yesterday, he leaned out the window and said, "Guess what? I'm reading more books! I got a library card!" He told me that now he was reading

Dickens' *Great Expectations.* "It's hard," he said and we talked about difficult language from past eras. I suggested Bradbury's *Fahrenheit 451.*

I swear I am watching this young man's mind unfold. The ability, the potential, has always been there. He just hasn't tapped into it. And now he's not tapping. He's drilling. Not only is he digging deep into literature, he's realizing the importance of community, of having supportive people around you, in the workplace and in your life. He's also learning the importance of loving what you do, what it does to your psyche and your soul.

I drove home and thought about him, about someone who would decide to start reading by grabbing some pretty high-falutin' stuff off the shelves. By the time I went to bed last night, I decided he needed to read someone who was still breathing. Not that there's anything wrong with reading the dead guys; there isn't. They're an important part of our literary history. But it was time to open another fold in my barista's brain. Let's move into our time and into the world around us.

So when I went to fetch my latte today, I didn't do the drive-thru. I went inside. After ordering, I went to the counter where the drinks are handed over. My barista was there, making one drink after another. "Hi, Kathie," he said. "Did you do a mobile order today?"

"No," I said. "I just gave my order. And I wanted to give you this." I handed him a signed copy of *The Home For Wayward Clocks.*

"NO WAY!" he yelled, just like at the Dodge Charger outside his window. "Ohmygod, ohmygod, ohmygod." He snatched the book out of my hands.

I was ohmygodding with him. Have you ever watched someone light up from the inside out, radiating warmth, brightening a face, lifting shoulders, zapping the air with electricity and amazement? I felt like I'd just given the best gift ever. "NO WAY!" he yelled again, clasping the book, and then tucking it in a safe spot on the counter.

I told him it was my first book and gave him a brief synopsis. I also told him how, before his time, there was a store copy at that Starbucks. Back then, I knew each and every barista. They counted down the days til the book was released. I gave the store a copy and it made the rounds. I don't know where it ended up. That store was also the first place I ran into a stranger reading one of my books – this book. One of the baristas leaned out the window that day and told me someone was reading it in the café. I had to park and go look.

Oh, the importance of community. The importance of loving what you do.

"I'm going to start reading it tonight," he declared.

So he's setting aside Dickens for me. I'm okay with that. For sure.

And yes, that helps. Despite. Anyway.

## DECEMBER 25, 2017

And so today's moment of happiness despite the news.

One would think that with it being Christmas Day, there would be a ton of moments to choose from. And there were. But really, those moments all spun together and blended into one wonderful thing.

For several hours there, my whole family was under one roof.

When the kids were little, I never really thought about a future where they would not be a part of my everyday life. My children from my first marriage were all born within four years. My first two are 26 months apart, and then numbers two and three are 13 months apart. For pretty much every moment of every day during those years, I had someone calling my title (Mom!) or yanking at my pants leg or arm, and usually, I had at least two someones vying for attention and the third wasn't far behind. While it was frazzling having children that close in age, I loved it. I was young as well, 24, 26 and 27 respectively when I had them, and in many ways, I feel like I grew up alongside them.

So I never pictured a future where they weren't a part of my daily life. But then I also didn't picture a future where I would leave their father after 17 years of marriage and reluctantly agree to joint custody and not get to be with them for half of every week. I didn't picture meeting someone else, getting remarried at 39 and having my fourth child at 40, 13 years after the birth of my third.

There's just so much that we don't picture. And now, having everyone under my roof is an event, not a routine. The family has grown as well. Together today were my two boys, my two girls, one son-in-law, one daughter-in-law, and one granddaughter. I watched them all as we ate lunch, opened presents, flung balled-up wrapping paper through the air, tripped over the dogs, and talked. My kids interacted as adults, but spiced those interactions with behavior left over from childhood; the teasing, the old stories, the poking, the laughter.

Last night, on Christmas Eve, when my big kids were at their father's, as has been the tradition since I left my first marriage in 1998, Michael, Olivia and I went to an outdoor Christmas light show. We've done this for years, to set up our own the-three-of-us tradition, but also to offset the sadness I feel when my big kids are missing. I very much remember that first Christmas Eve without my children. I've re-felt it every Christmas Eve since. As the years went by and the kids grew up, that sadness has been tempered with the anticipation of Christmas Day, when they would be with me. My oldest boy proposed to my daughter-in-law in my home on a Christmas Day. There was one hormonal Christmas where I was in menopause, my daughter-in-law was entering her ninth month of pregnancy, my oldest daughter was in full-blown young womanhood, and my youngest daughter was entering puberty. Holy cow. I've seen seasons pass with the growth of my children. I mark my life with their leaps and changes.

Last night, I posted on Facebook a photo of Michael, Olivia and me at the light show. Someone left a comment, saying that I am a "strong and talented matriarch."

And I suppose I am.

Mostly, though, I am Mommy (what my big kids called me), Mom (what they call me now) and Mama (what Olivia calls me and I hope she never ever stops). I'm a mother like so many other mothers who wait for their kids to come home.

They all did today, along with my oldest son's wife, my oldest daughter's husband, my oldest son's daughter.

It was an hours-long moment of happiness.

Merry Christmas.

And yes, that helps. Despite. Anyway.

## DECEMBER 26, 2017

And so today's moment of happiness despite the news.

My hair was cut and colored today, and for a change, I didn't read student manuscripts while I was under the dryer. I am on break this week and so I brought a book, a real actual book, and I sat in the heat and roasted and read. It was wonderful.

I'm currently reading Claire Messud's novel, *The Burning Girl*. As I read this afternoon, I came across this sentence: *"You don't hide if you don't need to."* Now, I think writers read differently than readers. We're readers too, don't get me wrong, but every now and then, when a writer reads, it's like a pinball machine. Someone else's words cause synapses to go off, bing, bing, bing, and your own mind starts flying and then ideas start coming. And that sentence did it to me.

I had to set the book aside for a while and let my mind go through its herky-jerky bouncy-jouncy motions – bing, bing, bing. What would make someone hide? Why would they hide? What would they do? Where would they go? What would happen? What if…what if…what if…

And then my mind bounced off a bumper and went backwards, as if the little pinball marble landed where it was supposed to, but then bounced its way back to the little spring where I shot it in the first place. I don't know how many writers experience this, but I do. It's taking a premise and turning it inside out. If no one hides unless they need to, then what would cause someone to hide without need? Why would a person live in the shadows? Why would they choose to, if there wasn't a reason? Who would make that choice? Who hides who isn't afraid? What other emotions could cause hiding?

Bing, bing, bing, bing.

Whenever I write, particularly the novels, I try to write a separate piece, usually a short story, from the antagonist's viewpoint. That's part of my mind moving backwards through the premise. I don't feel like it's fair for me to write a "bad guy" without knowing what made the bad guy bad. Consequently, I've written stories from a rapist's point of view, an abuser's point of view, a dumper's point of view (as opposed to the dumpee, donchaknow). And when I say I write these, it's with a sympathetic perspective. It's about the moment that makes a person become bad. No one is born bad. At least, I don't believe so.

These are hard stories to write. Writing from a rapist's pov, making it sympathetic? Just about killed me. But I did it. In the end, it does something for me. I'm not sure what that is, exactly, but my shoulders relax and my mind stops twisting. When I feel that I've seen a story from all sides, I just feel better about what I'm saying. And hopefully, that is for the reader's benefit too.

But back to the bing, bing, bing of today. It took just over five minutes for all the bings and buzzes and clicks and clacks to die down and the little marble to come to rest. Then I was able to pick up the book and continue to read and get great enjoyment out of doing so. I know that the bings are still going on, but internally. You know the place where the pinball marbles are stored? Out of sight, but then the next one pops into place when it's time to shoot it? That's where the binging is going on right now, in the secret marble storage in my brain. I know that eventually, the "You don't hide if you don't need to" inspiration will come out as a short story. Or maybe the Who hides if they don't need to? inspiration. Either way, it will come out. It might be next week. It might be months down the road, because right now, I'm shoulder-deep in a new novel. But it'll happen.

It's something that writers do for each other without ever intending to. We just can't help it. We bing bing bing off each other. And I love it. Words are the ultimate turn-on in my world.

Thank you, Claire Messud.

And yes, that helps. Despite. Anyway.

## DECEMBER 27, 2017

And so today's moment of happiness despite the news.

When you have a child, you delight in all of the milestones:

*the first step!

*the first day of school!

*the first concert!

*the first sleepover!

*the first date!

And…the ever-so-momentous…

*the first time trying to eat a bowl of fancy French onion soup in a restaurant!

Today was Michael's 53rd birthday, and to celebrate, we went to a very nice restaurant (his choice) for dinner. At my request, we were seated immediately in front of the fireplace – the lip of our table hung over the hearth. Oh, toasty after being outside in four below temps!

Olivia, at seventeen, is not a newcomer to nice restaurants. She still slips up every now and then, doing the not-so-mannerly stuff…singing out loud along with the piped-in music (especially Christmas music), using her straw to blow bubbles in her milk (which drives her dad crazy), belching and then going wide-eyed and exclaiming, "What?!" when I glare. She likes soup and usually veers toward chicken dumpling or cream of broccoli. But tonight, they didn't have either of those and so she went for the greatest soup challenge of all…cheese-covered French onion soup. Both Michael and I were surprised. It's not a typical Livvyonian choice.

When our soup arrived, Olivia stared at it. She poked it cautiously with her spoon. "Um…" she said. "How do I eat this?"

"Very carefully," was of course my answer. Then I told her that the cheese melted from rim to rim of the bowl was the difficult part and the soup was hiding underneath. "Use your spoon to chop at it, to try to get bite-size pieces. You can kind of trap the cheese against the side of the bowl and then scrape the edge of your spoon against it."

She looked dubious.

I told her that my first experience with French onion soup was in 1988, when I was 28 years old. I was in Rhinelander, Wisconsin, attending UW-Madison's School of the Arts week-long program as a scholarship student. On the last night, my mentor, Ellen Hunnicutt, invited me to come along with the faculty to dinner. She told me to order the French onion soup. When it arrived, I must have stared at it with the same expression Olivia did, because Ellen waved her fork and knife at me. "I'm not proud," she said. "I cut it with these before I take a bite." So while everyone around us somehow managed to eat the soup with delicate grace, Ellen and I chopped it like a steak and then ate it that way. I still think of Ellen every time I eat French onion soup. And every time, I am tempted to use my knife and fork.

Olivia looked doubtfully at her knife and fork. But then she picked up her spoon and had at it. She ATTACKED.

She sawed the cheese with her spoon.

She smacked it.

She scooped it up, flipped it over, flung it down.

She snarled.

And finally, finally, she stabbed the cheese with the end of her spoon, lifted it away from the soup, chewed off a piece with her head hanging over the bowl, then shoved the rest to the side and spooned in some soup. She smiled cheesily in triumph.

Hey, it worked. And I have to say…I've done the same.

Some milestones pop up by surprise when you least expect them. And then all you can do is watch and cheer as your child finds her own way, after you tell her all of yours.

And when those firsts come with a bright memory of your own, washing you with the warmth of soup and the love of a special friend, so much the better.

And yes, that helps. Despite. Anyway.

### DECEMBER 28, 2017

And so today's moment of happiness despite the news.

A couple weeks ago, I was contacted by a woman named Denise who works for an organization called Putting Abilities To Work. She helps those with disabilities figure out what they want to do and how to get there. She works with mostly adults, but she also sees high school kids, and that's why she was calling me.

"I have a seventeen-year old girl who is interested in learning about writing," she told me over the phone. "She's very high-functioning autistic. I was wondering if you'd be willing to sit down and talk with her."

I thought about what I do and where I've been. And I thought about my own seventeen-year old, who is high-functioning autistic and wants to be a writer, among other things. "Denise," I said, "you have no idea. Bring her to me. This is a match made in heaven."

Today, I met with the girl and with Denise. We talked first about how I got into writing, what this girl writes (poetry), and what she wants to do with her life (write). And then I asked for her first question.

"How do I get into writing as a career?" she said.

Oh boy.

I honestly do not remember a time when I didn't want to be a writer. It's been with me forever. Despite my teachers' praise, despite being published for the first time at fifteen, and despite being allowed as a freshman into UW – Madison's graduate level workshops, my parents told me I couldn't major in English and that I had to leave writing as a hobby. I wasn't good enough to succeed, they said, and it wouldn't pay the bills. They told me the only way they would help to pay for my education was if I majored in anything else.

I tried. First, I majored in Special Ed, with an interest in working with autistic children. There's some irony. But in my first semester, I flunked the first class I took that was specifically for my major. I begged my professor to raise the grade to a D, which he did, but I was horrified. I'd never gotten such a low grade. So then I switched my major to social work. I decided to take one semester (my fourth) without any literature or writing classes whatsoever. I wanted to see what that life would be like and if I could handle it.

I couldn't. Halfway through that semester, I trudged up Bascom Hill to South Hall (I think) where I officially changed my major to English, with an emphasis on creative writing (that's what they called it then). I did it without telling my parents. When I went home for Christmas break, I informed them of the change and said that if they decided to no longer support me, I would drop out of school and get a job until I could afford to come back. I quaked in my boots. But I meant it.

They supported me, financially, anyway. From that day on, when my father was asked what I majored in, he said, "Oh, she's getting married." I was. Years later, when I was an adult, married, with three children, my father told me that he considered my college education the biggest waste of his money in his lifetime.

I wish he could see me now. That money was not wasted. It was never ever wasted. My life continues to be enriched because of my education, because of the people I met and worked with, because of the teachers that believed in me.

So today, with this girl, that career question again. We talked honestly about how most writers don't make enough money to live on. And then we sat down and talked about work she could do that would feed her creativity and love of writing, that would empower her, that would make her excited to hit the computer screen every chance she had. We talked about working in the publishing industry. We talked about working for arts organizations. And we talked about teaching. We came up with a battle plan. When that girl left today, she was beaming. She would be able to write all of her lifetime. And she would be able to do what she loved as well. She also left as a new student in the AllWriters' On-Site Thursday Night Teen Writers Workshop.

Denise thanked me and said, "Do you know that you just light up when you talk about teaching?"

I do. Just like my teachers did.

Not a waste, Dad. Never ever a waste.

And yes, that helps. Despite. Anyway.

### DECEMBER 29, 2017

And so today's moment of happiness despite the news.

I'm pretty sure everyone has had that dream, THAT dream, where your spouse does something that leaves you aggravated. When you wake up, you are still aggravated, and so you yell at your spouse, even though he or she didn't really do anything. Except in your dream.

Well, I had a dream like that. But it wasn't my spouse that got to me. It was my car, Hemi.

For a couple of months now, I've had great difficulty sleeping. It's been a shock to have this issue come back —I was a lifelong insomniac until almost two years ago, when I began to meditate. But now – the sleep issues returneth. I blame the estrogen-suppressing drugs I'm taking to keep the banished breast cancer away. I either fall asleep immediately and then wake up around four to spend the next three hours up and wandering around, or, like last night, I don't sleep at all. I fell into a fitful sleep around seven this morning, and gave up at 10:45 when the dogs would simply not stop whining for their breakfast.

In that fitful sleep, though, I had a dream. I was selling Hemi, my Chrysler 300C with a Hemi engine. There was a slick new model and I was seduced. I barely watched as Hemi was driven away.

Now you have to understand…I am amazingly overly crazily in love with my car. He is my bodyguard. He has memory seats, so he waits until I sit down and then he automatically maneuvers my seat, my steering wheel, and the mirrors to the spot that is best for me. When I turn the car off, he slides my seat back and raises my wheel so that I can get out comfortably. When I'm cold, he heats my seat. He lets me choose the air temperature, which is always warm. He has a sun roof/moon roof combo that, even when it's closed, keeps me from feeling claustrophobic. His power is incredible; all I have to do is ask and he surges ahead of the other cars. And he and I jive to a sound system that just doesn't quit. He even appreciates my taste in music.

I love my car. I know I shouldn't – he's a material thing. But he's not. He's my Hemi. He has a voice and a personality and I believe that he would do anything to keep me safe. He would never betray me, never leave me, unless I told him to go. And in this dream, I brazenly told him to go. I replaced him with a younger, shinier, slicker new model. The years of Hemi's faithfulness and care no longer mattered.

So weird – I feel ashamed as I write this, and it was a freakin' dream!

As I climbed into the new car, I immediately felt the difference. This car didn't care for me at all. He was just a hunk of metal on wheels. I looked up then to see Hemi being pulled behind a cage corral, surrounded by cars that were beat-up, abandoned, abused, sad. I shrieked.

And I woke in mid-shriek. The first thing I did when I got out of bed was look out the window. Yep, he was still there. Faithful.

In the fog of fatigue from not near enough sleep, I got into my car and he eased me into place. It was 8 degrees outside. But I took Hemi for a bath anyway. A nice hot bath. With attendants that dried him with soft and fluffy towels.

As we floated through the carwash, in a sound tunnel of whirring jets and brushes and hot wax, I took advantage of the intimacy and told my car I loved him. A car is a car, but every day, this car brings me a bolt of joy. He takes care of me. He is a car that I never thought I would own. He fits himself to me and caters to me. Is it normal to feel loved by a car? I do.

And yes, I know that he's a car and not a living breathing thing. But he is. I told him I appreciated him. Which I do. I told him I was sorry I sold him to a place that stuck him behind a fence with cars that were on just this side of death. Which I didn't. But I felt like I did.

Some days, you just have to appreciate what you have. You have to, as the cliché says, stop and smell the roses. So today…I smelled my 2006 Chrysler 300C Hemi…named Hemi.

And yes, that helps. Despite. Anyway.

### DECEMBER 30, 2017

And so today's moment of happiness despite the news.

Things were fairly mellow in the Giorgio household today. From Olivia's bedroom, we first heard the sound of her practicing the violin, then the acoustic guitar, then her ukulele. When Olivia practices, it's a really gentle time in the condo. Because she has her door closed, the sound is muted and sometimes feels more imaginary than real.

And then…BAWANG!

Oh, dear.

Somewhere after Thanksgiving, Olivia came home from her guitar lesson (and her ukulele lesson too) babbling about this electric guitar in the store. It was pink and white, she said. It was sparkly, she said. It was so cool, she said. "Mom," she said, "can I have an electric guitar?"

I reminded her that she had her violin. That she'd received her pink acoustic guitar as a surprise on the last day of school this past spring, a special reward for making it through a particularly challenging year. That for her birthday, she found a pink ukulele waiting for her, because she'd begun to rave about the ukulele and I'd happened to see a pink one at the music store shortly after I was diagnosed with breast cancer in June. Feeling fatalistic at that time, I bought it and hid it away, even though her birthday wasn't until October.

"You have three instruments already," I said.

"I know, but I've always wanted an electric guitar!"

There are times I wish I had a child who was enthusiastic about bubble gum. Buying different packages of bubble gum and learning to chew gum from different countries likely wouldn't be that pricey. Or space-consuming. Maybe she could be into thumbtack-collecting. Star-gazing! All I'd have to do is find her some sky!

But no. Music. And music she could play, not just listen to.

I bought the electric guitar and hid it away for Christmas. The nice man at the music store was sympathetic. He made me a deal with the guitar, which was used, a used amp, a boogie bag, and a strap.

The guitar and amp were too big to wrap. We decided, after wrapping the other presents on Christmas Eve, to leave the guitar and amp in the classroom downstairs until Olivia went to sleep. Then we would sneak them up and she'd find them – surprise! – on Christmas morning. But then, we forgot and sent her downstairs to fetch something. She found them there.

But she was still delighted.

She didn't know how to plug the guitar into the amp. Today, a few days after Christmas, in the quiet of an afternoon that was gifted with the sounds of a classical violin, a softly strummed acoustic guitar, and the tinsel sound of a ukulele, the rock star was born.

BAWANG!

Oh, dear.

I wondered what I'd done.

But then I thought of my own musical tastes. I run the gamut, from classical to soft rock to alternative to, selectively, rap. Music matches my moods. It helps to dispel them, explore them, even them out. I don't know that I believe that "music soothes the savage beast". I suppose it does, but it also brings peace to the already peaceful, enthusiasm to the enthusiastic, joy to the joyful. It's reflective in the truest sense.

And today, my daughter found a new level of expression.

BAWANG!

It'll be okay.

And yes, that helps. Despite. Anyway.

## DECEMBER 31, 2017

And so today's moment of happiness despite the news.

Well, first off, I have to say that I am absolutely thrilled that today is the last day of 2017. This has been, without a doubt, one of the hardest years of my life. From my assault by the guy in the Make America Great hat, to Michael's losing his job, to Olivia's experiencing such horrific social media bullying that we had to pull her from her school, to my breast cancer diagnosis, to Michael's losing his job again…it's been tough. If what doesn't kill you makes you stronger, then I am a 57-year old version of Wonder Woman. I am not unhappy to see this year end. And I am amazed that the faith and hope that has a home in me somewhere, maybe my heart, maybe my head, is still looking ahead and I am looking forward to 2018.

I doubt that at midnight, you will find me cheering and yelling and blowing on a paper horn. You will likely find me weeping from pure relief.

But…that's not what today's moment is about. Today, I had to go do the grocery shopping, usually Michael's job. He is out for the count with an infected toe – he's supposed to walk as little as possible. He wasn't enchanted with the idea of riding in one of those little scooters, so he wrote me a list and off I went.

Since my partial mastectomy last July, I've experienced weakness in my right arm. I don't notice it much. It mostly comes into play when I have to reach over my head. When I flew to Denver in the middle of radiation to see my story being performed on stage, I had my first major realization when I tried to put my carry-on in the bin over my seat. I couldn't do it. My arm came up to shoulder-height, and then it just wouldn't go anymore. On the flight to Denver, a nice man helped me. On the way back, I flew first class and the attendant took my bag and heaved it overhead before I even began to try. Today, my undoing was the soda aisle.

Michael wanted me to get soda. 2-liter bottles were on sale. So I hit the aisle, admired all of the colorful boxes of canned soda that were within my reach, and then looked up. All of the 2-liter bottles were over my head, corralled behind a fence-like shelf. I could reach the bottles, but I had to lift them up and over the fence to get them to me. I could lift a bottle only so far…and then I got stuck.

I worked at it for a while, trying to shove my fingers through the fence rungs and under the bottle, and then push it up and over. I tried shoving the bottles backwards so that when the first bottle in line crashed back down, maybe it would tip over and fall into my arms. I tried willing them to just jump down into my cart by the force of my aggravated Wonder Woman glare. Nothing worked. And I felt horrible. I was no longer capable of grocery shopping?

One of the drawbacks of the medication I'm on to squash my estrogen is hot flashes. But another is rocketing emotions that make my previous years as an emotional roller coaster look like I was really just in the Tunnel of Love. Tears are never far away right now, much to my mortification. Sometimes I find myself crying and I don't even know what I'm crying about. Other times, I'm not even aware of the tears. This was one of the latter – as I jabbed my fingers, shoved bottles, and glared, I also had tears running down my cheeks.

And someone noticed.

"Ma'am," I heard a voice say. "Let me help you."

A young man, a teenager, in Pick'N'Save's uniform of green shirt and gray apron, reached over my head and pulled down the bottle of soda. He placed it in my cart, and then he asked, "Would you like any more?"

"Yes," I said and asked for two more (they were on sale for 3 for something). I realized the tears then and quickly swiped my face. "Thank you," I said. I didn't even care that he called me ma'am.

He smiled and put two more bottles in my cart. He told me he thought the store was making these shelves too high. Then he bent close to me and whispered, "I know who you are. My mom had breast cancer too. If we need soda in the house now, I get them for her." He gave me a fast pat on the shoulder.

He left me dumbfounded and grateful. Whoever his mom is, she's raising a wonderful man.

And yes, that helps. Despite. Anyway.

(And goodbye, 2017!)

# Chapter 13

## The New Year
## JANUARY 1, 2018!

And so today's moment of happiness despite the news.

For some, it's the putting up of the Christmas stuff that brings such great joy. The decorating. Flinging garland. Tossing tinsel. Admiring ornaments and hanging them carefully on tree limbs and light fixtures and window latches. Jingle bells dangling from doorknobs. A Santa here, a crèche there, a reindeer, a musical snowglobe. Wreaths made of Christmas cards, Christmas cookies in the oven, wrapping paper, bows, cunning little name stickers.

But for me? January 1st. And RIP IT ALL DOWN!

Maybe it's a sickness in me, a fault, a chromosomal mistake. But this morning, after showering and dressing, I grabbed my scissors and attacked the garland wrapped around the bannister leading downstairs. I hacked and hacked and pulled and pulled and then gathered it all up in a big armful of silver and sparkle and threw it in the trash. I tugged down all of the stockings, folded them and shoved them in a grocery bag. Then the tree. The teeny Walgreens tree. I plucked off the little teeny ornaments like miniature overripe fruit. The star came off like an especially delectable Christmas cookie. All into the paper bag temporary grave until next year when I will reluctantly haul it out again. The tree went into the bag too. Oh, especially the tree. And the wreath I used as a tree skirt. Gone! Gone! Gone!

And I sang:

*"Up in the condo, Kathie caws!*
*Down comes dumb ol' Santa Claus!*
*Into the bag with the tree and stuff,*
*She just can't dump it fast enough!*
*Ho, ho, ho!*
*Off it goes!*
*Ho, ho, ho!*
*Off it goes!*
*Up in the condo, cut, pluck, yay!*
*Christmas is gone 'til another day!"*

Sitting on the loveseat, nursing his sick toe, Michael muttered, "Don't overwhelm me with your Christmas joy."

No! No! No Christmas joy! AFTER-Christmas joy! I have that in abundance!

My island, which separates my kitchen and my living room, is clear again. I can see all the way through. I can eat my lunch at the center barstool with all this space around me, because the tree is no longer there. My bannister, modern, sleek, no longer glints with Dollar Store garland and 13 stockings.

It's my house again. Aaaaaaaaaaaah.

Tomorrow, Michael returns to work and Olivia returns to school. I resume teaching.

And there are no doctor's appointments until February.

Normal. Normal, normal, normal.

YES!

And yes, that helps. Despite. Anyway.

## JANUARY 2, 2017 – FINALE

And so today's moment of happiness despite the news.

Well, the Moment IS the Moment, really. I spent a lot of time today, both in meditation and just in general, considering the Moment. What started out as a desperate whim (I'm overwhelmed, so I'm going to post one moment a day that made me happy on Facebook) became something much bigger. From a few sentences at the beginning to what I would now call quiet, unedited essays, I kept at it, writing just what came to mind. I was determined to not make the Moment a professional endeavor. I wasn't writing for publication, I wasn't writing for an audience. I wanted to keep it as simply a Moment that made me happy and examine why. That was a struggle for me as I became aware that there was indeed an audience – an audience that caused my website to crash several times because of traffic! I'm a professional writer, I tend to even edit my thoughts and whatever I say before I say it, not to mention edit everything I read, from news articles to books to comic strips. But I wasn't going to edit, I wasn't going to improve the pieces – in a sense, Today's Moment is *Kathie Giorgio – Unplugged.*

I've learned so much from writing the Today's Moments. I learned, first of all, that there is at least one great Moment in almost every day. Even on dark days. I might have to look for it, but it's there. And that was a lesson unto itself

– happiness is an active endeavor. It isn't something that just comes along and happens to you. Sometimes you have to look for it.

So I've learned to look.

But alternatively, I've also learned to honor sadness and anger and fear. I couldn't chase these away by writing about a Moment of Happiness. I couldn't chase them away by becoming aware of a Moment either. A Moment isn't a pill I could take that would provide instant happiness. There is no pill, no prose, no prettiness that will keep a person happy one-hundred percent of the time. Today's Moment allowed me to release a very unrealistic expectation – that if I could just find One Big Thing to make me Happy, I would never ever be unhappy again.

But finding that One Moment helped me to navigate through some pretty dark times. It gave me the one good thing to hang onto. Some days, that was like holding onto a rope while dangling off a cliff.

One of my favorite Moments is the one where I was told I didn't have to be strong all the time while I was going through breast cancer. That I could be scared, that I could be sad, that I could be weak. That illustrates what I'm trying to say about the unrealistic expectation. I know now to look for the Moment of Happiness, but not to expect that finding it means I'm going to waltz down whatever path opens before me next.

But the Today's Moment does keep me looking ahead and looking up. As I've said in these posts, my favorite quote from literature, which is engraved into a ring I wear every day, is from John Irving's *The Hotel New Hampshire*: "Keep walking past the open windows." I've now edited it a bit, to "Keep looking for Today's Moment."

So what's going to happen to *Today's Moment Of Happiness Despite The News*, now that I've reached my goal of one solid year?

It's not going away, but it is changing. It's going to become *This Week's Moment Of Happiness Despite The News*. I will only post it one day a week, and I've chosen Thursdays, at least to start. There has been no small amount of pressure, trying to come up with something every day. I'm looking to relieve that pressure, but also to expand my vision and understanding. I think that by having to sort through many moments every week to pick out just one to share, I will become further aware of just how many Moments there are in this world and in every life. I'll give it a shot.

If you are worried that you might forget to check my Facebook page on a Thursday, then just go to my website and the blog and click on subscribe. Then you'll receive a notification when each new Moment appears.

⟨http://www.kathiegiorgio.org/blog/⟩

When I look back on this year, I could be focused on the many bad things that happened. I had to deal with an assault, my daughter's being bullied, my husband's job losses, and above all, breast cancer. But what I focus on instead is the amazing coincidence ⟨if you believe in coincidences⟩ of my starting Today's Moment at a time when it would turn out that I needed it most. It got me through. And everyone involved, by reading the Moments, by commenting on them and discussing them, got me through too.

Incredible.

And yes, that helps. That always helps. It will continue to help. Despite. Anyway.

*The End*

View other Black Rose Writing titles at www.blackrosewriting.com/books and use
promo code **PRINT** to receive a **20% discount** when purchasing.

# BLACK ROSE
## writing™

CPSIA information can be obtained
at www.ICGtesting.com
Printed in the USA
FFHW01n0653251018
48959345-53197FF